THE '27 YANKEES

THE '27 YANKEES

For Jane and Ralph,

With best wishes from

Fred Glueckstein

Fred Glueckstein

Library of Congress Number: 2005901559
ISBN: Hardcover 1-4134-8427-1
Softcover 1-4134-8426-3

This book was printed in the United States of America.

Picture Credits:
George Brace Collection

To order additional copies of this book, contact:
Xlibris Corporation
1-888-795-4274
www.Xlibris.com
Orders@Xlibris.com

27183

CONTENTS

Part 3: Clinching the Pennant

List of Illustrations

DEDICATION

In loving memory
of my father,
Joseph Glueckstein
1912-1999

Prologue

Heavy rain swept through New York City all night and into the early morning hours of Sunday, October 10, 1926. Water pummeled the heavy tarpaulins covering the infield and drenched the outfield grass and seats at Yankee Stadium in the Bronx. When dawn arrived, the weather was wet and cold and it seemed highly unlikely that the St. Louis Cardinals and New York Yankees would play the seventh and deciding game of the World Series that afternoon.

Expecting the game to be postponed, thousands of fans decided to stay home. However, by early afternoon the rain ended, and the Stadium workers began removing the tarpaulins, raking the grounds and laying the white chalk lines at home plate and down the foul lines. The fans, who had taken a chance hoping the game would be played, took their seats as the band entertained them.

With the day overcast, damp, and very cold, the spectators wore heavy coats and furs. Looking down from the radio booth, WLJ announcer Graham MacNamee noted amusingly the only fashion note on that dreary day was one purple parasol in the crowd. When the Yankees ran onto the field to take their positions, the crowd of 38,000, the smallest ever to see a series game at the stadium, cheered loudly.

The Cardinals led by a score of 3 to 2 in the seventh inning. In the home half of that frame, however, the Yankees loaded the bases against St. Louis starter, Jesse Haines. At 6-feet-tall, the 33-year-old Haines, whose 13-4 win-lost record helped the Cards capture their first franchise pennant, had already shut out the Yanks in game three of the World Series—a feat that would not happen again to the Yankees for sixteen years.

With Yankee centerfielder Earle Combs on third base, leftfielder Bob Meusel at second, and first baseman Lou Gehrig on first, Tony Lazzeri, the second baseman, came to bat with two outs. As a rookie, Lazzeri had batted a respectable .275 and drove in 114 runs—second only behind Babe Ruth in the American League. A single by Lazzeri would give the Yankees two runs and the lead, and with Herb Pennock, the Yanks' best pitcher hurling in relief, the Cardinals knew their prospects of winning would be bleak if the Yankees went ahead.

Rogers Hornsby, the Cardinals' manager and second baseman, walked to the mound and called his infielders over for a conference. The St. Louis players sported gray caps with a red bill and red piping at the seams. Sewn across the top of their gray jerseys was the word Cardinals with a motif of two red birds perched on an upwards sloping bat that crossed the large letter "C". With gray pants secured with a black belt, they wore white stockings with a wide red stripe bordered by a thin dark band.

Hornsby looked at Haines's bloody index finger, a result of a blister that had burst from throwing knuckleballs. The Cardinal manager talked the situation over with Haines, catcher Bob O'Farrell, first baseman Jim Bottomley, third baseman Les Bell, and shortstop Tommy Thevenow.

It was a long meeting.

George Hildebrand, the home plate umpire, finally walked to the mound. When the gathering broke up, Haines took off his glove and walked to the bench. Hornsby, meanwhile, signaled by hand for a relief pitcher to the visitor's bullpen in the far left field corner.

With fog and mist enveloping Yankee Stadium, a tall, lanky figure in a blazing red Cardinals' sweater and a gray cap perched slightly sideways on his head could be seen walking towards the bullpen gate. The crowd and players were very surprised to see 39-year-old Grover Cleveland Alexander, a veteran right-hander, pass through the gate and onto to the field and wet outfield grass.

Alexander, a former star of the Philadelphia Phillies and Chicago Cubs, had pitched nine brilliant innings the day before and helped the Cardinals to a 10 to 2 victory, which had tied the World Series at three games apiece. After celebrating late into the evening, Alexander was sleeping in the bullpen with a pint of whiskey in his pocket when Hornsby signaled. According to Flint Rhem, who was sitting in the bullpen, Alexander staggered a little, handed him the pint, hitched up his britches, and walked straight as he could toward the mound.

Lumbering slowly across the outfield grass, Alexander was met by Hornsby, who had walked out beyond the infield. Hornsby looked into

Alexander's eyes and filled him in on the situation—bases loaded, two outs, Lazzeri up.

"Do you feel all right? Hornsby asked.

"Sure, I feel fine," answered Alexander. "Three on, eh. Well, there's no place to put Lazzeri, is there. I'll just have to give him nothin' but a lot of hell, won't I?"

Alexander, who had already won two World Series games, was given a warm reception by the crowd when he reached the mound. Hornsby, O'Farrell, and Alexander agreed that Lazzeri should be pitched low and away and would not see a high pitch.

Meanwhile, in the Yankee dugout, Lazzeri, who knew that Alexander had not warmed up in the bullpen, turned to Yankee manager Miller Huggins.

"Should I smack the first one he pitches?" Lazzeri asked.

"No, wait him out," Huggins ordered, thinking Lazzeri might draw a base on balls and force in a run.

Lazzeri walked to the plate determined to hit the ball hard and clinch the World Series. Alexander, who had taken off his sweater and threw a few leisurely warm-up pitches to O'Farrell, was ready. Lazzeri stepped into the batter's box.

The crowd was unusually silent.

As Combs, Meusel and Gehrig moved off the bases, Alexander's arm came up and he threw his first pitch, a curve that was too far inside. Lazzeri held his swing in check. Hildebrand called ball one.

Knowing that Lazzeri would not swing at the next pitch, Alexander delivered a fast ball on the inside corner. Again Lazzeri did not swing. Hildebrand called strike one. On the third pitch, Lazzeri swung and hit a vicious drive deep toward the left field stands. As the crowd roared, the ball curved foul by maybe ten feet. Lazzeri had just missed a grand slam home run.

The pitch Lazzeri hit foul had been high. O'Farrell ran out to Alexander.

"I thought we were going to pitch him low and outside?" O'Farrell asked.

"He'll never get another one like that!" Alexander answered.

With a count of one and two, Alexander delivered a perfect low curve ball, which Lazzeri swung at and missed by at least eight inches for the third strike and final out of the inning. As Alexander walked off the mound to the bench, the entire Cardinals' club rushed over to congratulate him.

In the eighth, Alexander retired the Yanks in order. After setting down the first two men in the ninth, Alexander walked Babe Ruth. On the first pitch to Bob Meusel, Ruth, to everyone's surprise, took off for second base. O'Farrell caught the ball and rapidly fired it to second base, where Hornsby tagged out Ruth attempting to steal second, ending the game.

The St. Louis Cardinals won the '26 World Series.

PART 1

Opening the 1927 Season

Chapter 1

Edward Grant Barrow

In December 1917 at the annual meeting of the International League at the Hotel Imperial in New York City, Edward Grant Barrow was forced out as league president. Knowing that Barrow would be ousted, Harry Frazee, a well-known theatrical producer and owner of the Boston Red Sox, waited in the lobby. Frazee told Barrow that with the United States at war in Europe, Jack Barry, Boston's player-manager, had joined the Navy. Frazee needed a new manager, and he offered Barrow the job for the 1918 season; Barrow happily accepted the position.

It was in Boston that Ed Barrow first met a young ball player named George Herman (Babe) Ruth. A talented left-handed pitcher, Ruth had joined the Boston Red Sox in 1914 and was a member of the championship teams that won the World Series in 1915 and 1916. The club finished second in 1917. During that time, Ruth became one of the premier pitchers in the American League; he also showed prowess as a hitter.

With many of the Red Sox players at war, Barrow felt that Babe Ruth's bat was important in the line-up, and played him in the outfield when not pitching. Ruth ended the 1918 season with 11 home runs, a league high, and for the second straight season, he won 23 games as a pitcher, helping Barrow not only to guide the Red Sox to the American League pennant, but also to defeat the Chicago Cubs in the 1918 World Series.

As the 1919 season approached, Barrow had a plan that would subsequently transform Ruth's career and turn baseball into the exciting offensive game it became in the twentieth century. Knowing that the Babe was an excellent hitter, an accomplished fielder, a fine base runner, and possessed an accurate throwing arm, Barrow decided to go ahead and convert Ruth from a pitcher to an everyday player.

Through the first month of the 1918 season, Ruth took a regular turn in the Red Sox pitching rotation and, at other times, played the outfield. Later that season, Barrow told Ruth he would have a great future as a hitter and should consider becoming an everyday player. The Babe agreed, and he gave up a very successful career as a pitcher to become an everyday Red Sox outfielder.

One day Ruth complained of weariness. Attributing his tiredness to running around and carousing all night, Barrow chastised Ruth, telling him to take better care of himself. However, Ruth was twenty-four-years-old, trim, strong, and he liked having a good time. Needless to say, Ruth did not take Barrow's advice.

Later that season, Barrow and Ruth had their most serious disagreement; one that came close to a fistfight. As the club's manager, Barrow had the practice of staying up at night when the team was on the road until all the players were in the hotel. Sitting up one evening in the Raleigh Hotel in Washington, D.C., Barrow waited until 4:00 a.m. for Ruth before finally going to bed. Deciding not to wait up the next night again, Barrow gave the hotel porter a few dollars to let him know when Ruth came in. Next morning at 6:00 a.m., the porter knocked on Barrow's door and told him that Ruth had just returned to the hotel.

Putting on a dressing gown and slippers, Barrow went down the hall to the room that Ruth shared with Dan Howley, a coach who was assigned to watch over him. When Barrow reached Ruth's door, light showed through the transom and voices could be heard inside.

After knocking on the door, the light went out and the voices stopped. The door was unlocked and Barrow found Ruth in bed smoking a pipe. The covers were pulled up over his neck. Howley was nowhere in sight; he was hiding in the bathroom. When Barrow asked Ruth why he was smoking a pipe so early in the morning, the Babe told him that it relaxed him. Pulling the covers down, Barrow saw that Ruth was fully dressed, wearing even his socks and shoes. Barrow told Ruth and Howley to see him at the ballpark that afternoon and left.

When Barrow arrived in the clubhouse, the players were dressing. As he was tying his shoes, Ruth peeked at Barrow out of the corner of his eye. He watched as Barrow locked the door. The Red Sox manager warned the players that there would be no further violations of the rules. Most of his remarks were directed at Ruth and after listening for awhile, the Babe spoke back and threatened to punch Barrow in the nose.

A hush fell through the clubhouse.

"All you fellows finish dressing and get out of here," said Barrow, "all except Ruth. You stay here, Babe, and I'll give you a chance to punch me in the nose."

When the players finished dressing, they began to leave the room; Ruth was among those that left.

Before the game started, Barrow was filling out the starting line-up on the card that is given to the umpires. When asked by Ruth if he was playing, Barrow told him he was suspended and to go into the clubhouse and take off his uniform. On the train back to Boston, Ruth asked to see Barrow and they had a long talk. Touched by the story of Ruth's tough childhood, Barrow came to understand him better. He realized how much Ruth loved playing baseball and that a suspension was the worst thing that could happen to him.

Ruth told Barrow that he would follow the team's rules and offered to leave him a note in his box every night the team was on the road, telling him what time he got back to the hotel. Barrow couldn't say no. Afterwards, Ruth always left a note addressed to "Dear Eddie" or "Dear Manager." Barrow never knew whether the Babe ever lied to him or not and never checked up on him. He took Ruth at his word.

Playing the outfield regularly for the Boston Red Sox in 1919, Ruth led the major leagues with 29 home runs, a new record passing the mark of 25 by John Buck Freeman of Washington (National League, 1899), and 103 runs scored. However, even with Ruth's impressive numbers, Boston finished in sixth place.

That winter brought more disappointment.

Needing cash for his theatrical shows and notes due on the ball club, Harry Frazee, the Red Sox owner, sold Ruth to the New York Yankees for $100,000 and a personal loan of $350,000 from Colonel Ruppert, one of the Yankee co-owners. Ironically, Frazee put up Fenway Park, the home of the Red Sox as security for Ruppert's loan.

Without Ruth, Barrow's Red Sox team in 1920 finished in fifth place. Meanwhile, Babe Ruth batted .376 and hit an astonishing 54 home runs for the Yankees. After the season, Frazee recommended Barrow to the Yankees as the club's business manager [general manager] to replace Harry Sparrow, who died earlier that year. Frazee told Barrow to seriously consider the position and to talk with Yankee co-owner Cap Huston.

With the Red Sox in decline and Frazee planning to sell more players to raise money for his theatrical business, Barrow gave serious thought to leaving Boston. As he considered a job with the New York Yankees, the 52-year-old Barrow thought about the events and people that had shaped his life.

His reflections went back to another era.

On August 29, 1864 at Hillsboro, Ohio, a nineteen-year-old farmer named John William Barrow enlisted in the Union Army. A small man at five feet seven, Barrow had blue-eyes, light hair, and a fair complexion. Assigned to the 178th Ohio Infantry, he was later transferred to the 175th. Afflicted with dysentery and loss of hearing, Barrow was hospitalized in Nashville, Tennessee in late 1864 and early 1865. Discharged on June 27, 1865, John Barrow returned to his native Ohio, where he met Effie Ann Vinson-Heller in 1866. After a short romance, the couple married in July 1867.

As soldiers who fought for the Union, John and his brother Charles were eligible for a land grant of 160 acres each in Nebraska. Both men decided to head west and farm. With horses pulling the wagons and the cattle trailing behind, John Barrow, his wife, two brothers, two sisters, and mother set out from Ohio in four covered wagons.

The Barrow family traveled slowly across the country in the summer and stayed with farm families in the winter. On May 10, 1868, John and Effie-Ann Barrow's first child was born during the first winter stop at a relative's hemp farm in Springfield, Illinois. When John Barrow insisted that the newborn be named after his wartime hero, General

Ulysses Simpson Grant, his wife, who had other thoughts on the matter, finally agreed to name the boy Edward Grant Barrow.

The trip to Nebraska took almost two years. At the end of the journey, the Barrow family settled near Nebraska City, not far from the Iowa boundary. The land was desolate and life was hard. After six difficult years of facing hostile Indians, prairie fires, and grasshoppers which destroyed the crops, the family again moved by covered wagon, settling on a farm about ten miles outside Des Moines, Iowa.

In poor health, John Barrow finally gave up farming after three years, and he moved the family to Des Moines, where his son Ed grew into a young man. As a youngster, Ed Barrow went to the Third Ward School, where he learned the game of baseball. As he grew older, he played ball on the sandlots, for a YMCA team, and for the high school. While pitching for a local team on a cold rainy day at the age of seventeen or eighteen, Barrow hurt his arm and shoulder. After developing neuritis, he could no longer throw a ball hard and decided, instead, to manage local semi-pro baseball teams.

When his father's health broke down completely, Barrow quit school and went to work as a clerk on the newspaper, *The Des Moines Daily News,* later called the *Leader*. He soon joined another newspaper, *The Des Moines Blade.* After leaving the *Blade*, he returned to the *Leader*, becoming the paper's Advertising Manager.

Seeing few entrepreneurial opportunities in Des Moines, Ed and his brother Frank invested $500 of their savings and went to Chicago to open an advertising business. When that venture proved unsuccessful, the brothers then invested $3,500, which included a loan of $3,000 from their parents, in a new business selling cleaning soap in Pittsburgh, Pennsylvania. But when that enterprise also failed, Frank returned to Des Moines, and Ed stayed in Pittsburgh to earn enough money to repay his parents.

As a day clerk and assistant manager at the Staley Hotel in Pittsburgh, Ed Barrow met Harry M. Stevens, a businessman who sold programs in theaters and scorecards, sandwiches, and peanuts at Exposition Park, home of the Pittsburgh Pirates. The two men got along well, and in the winter of 1893 Barrow accepted a partnership in Harry M. Stevens's concession business. Barrow spent the summer of 1894 at Exposition

Park, where he became friendly with the players on the Pirates and began a lifelong friendship with the team's catcher Connie Mack.

While in Pittsburgh, Barrow built up a reputation as an amateur boxer. Tough and powerfully built, he often worked out in the police gymnasium against the best in the force. One day Billy Delaney, trainer of Jim Corbett, then the world heavyweight champion, came to the hotel and introduced himself to Barrow. He explained that Corbett was in town to box a three-round exhibition match. Needing an opponent, Delaney wanted him to fight Corbett. Although Barrow declined, he and Corbett became good friends.

With Harry M. Stevens's financial backing in the fall of 1894, Ed Barrow purchased the Wheeling, West Virginia baseball franchise in a newly formed minor league called the Inter-State League. He arranged to have a local businessman build a ballpark, and Barrow signed players from the Pittsburgh area. Zane Grey, who eventually became a famous writer of western stories, was one outfielder that Barrow signed.

Barrow ended up managing the team, commuting between Pittsburgh and Wheeling. However, the league folded half way through the season with Wheeling in first place. Barrow and Stevens then moved the team into the Iron and Oil League, where the club finished the season on top.

When the Atlantic League was formed in the fall of 1895, Barrow decided to seek a franchise. Unable to obtain the Hartford, Connecticut club, Barrow was given the Paterson, New Jersey franchise for $800. Although his friend and business partner Harry M. Stevens wanted him to stay in Pittsburgh and look after the concession business, Barrow, who had by now grown to love the business end of baseball, decided to go to Paterson. His partnership with Stevens was dissolved, but they remained life-long friends. Harry M. Stevens eventually went to New York and became a millionaire in the concession business.

Organizing a baseball club in Paterson was a risky affair. By 1896, the city had fallen on hard times: a big strike closed the silk mills, and a lack of orders had shut down the Rogers Locomotive Works. Despite no ballpark in Paterson for his new franchise and a lack of money, Barrow pressed ahead. Fortuitously, he met Garrett A. Hobart, who was Paterson's leading citizen and president of a streetcar company.

Hobart thought a ballpark would be good for the city and his trolley line, and he proceeded to build a ballpark between Paterson and Passaic for $4,000. Later that year, Garrett A. Hobart was elected Vice President of the United States on the same ticket with William McKinley. Meanwhile, needing players for his new Paterson baseball team, Barrow returned to the Pittsburgh area, where he signed a shortstop named Johannes Peter (Honus) Wagner.

An exceptional ball player, Honus Wagner batted .348 in his first year at Paterson (1896). National League managers visiting New York went to Paterson to see Wagner play. They were impressed. At mid-season of his second year, Wagner was hitting .379, and Barrow sold him for $2,100 to Louisville of the National League. After the 1899 season, the National League consolidated to eight clubs and dropped Louisville, Cleveland, Baltimore, and Washington from the circuit. Wagner, nicknamed the "The Flying Dutchman," moved on to Pittsburgh, where he played for eighteen years.

Besides Wagner, Barrow signed others that proved from the start that he could assess talent. On that 1896 Paterson club were Dick Cogan, who later pitched for the Cubs and Giants; Emmett Kid Heidrick, who played in the St. Louis Browns' outfield, and outfielder Bill Armour, who became manager at Cleveland and Detroit.

On July 4, 1896, Barrow experimented with night ball at Wilmington, Delaware, where Paterson played under the lights for the first time. The lights were old-fashioned arc types with two sticks of carbon between which the flame burned. The lighting was terrible. By night's end the crowd demanded their money back.

In 1897, Ed Barrow assumed his first executive position in baseball when he was elected president of the Atlantic League. When the league began to struggle financially, Barrow tried hard to come up with novel ideas to bring people to the ballparks. He found a girl pitcher named Lizzie Arlington and scheduled her for appearances in league cities. Heavyweight boxers John L. Sullivan and Jim Jeffries umpired games, and Jim Corbett played first base. By 1899, however, the war with Spain had captured the nation's attention and ballpark attendance suffered; soon the Atlantic League disbanded.

After a short venture in the vaudeville business in Richmond, Virginia, Barrow bought a quarter share of the Toronto Maple Leafs baseball club of the Eastern League, which had started in 1884 and was then known as the International League. By 1900, the Eastern League was the longest running and most successful minor league operation anywhere.

By 1902, Barrow also managed the Toronto club and raised enough capital to build a new ballpark, signed some good ball players, and won the Eastern League pennant. Barrow's successes brought him to the attention of many important people in baseball. Four major league teams asked him to manage; however, he turned down the offers, deciding to stay in Toronto.

In early 1903, Win Mercer, who was slated to be the Detroit Tigers' new manager, was losing his battle with tuberculosis and committed suicide in San Francisco. After his tragic death, the Tigers asked Barrow if he wanted the job. Intrigued with the new American League and admiring its founder Bancroft "Ban" Johnson, he agreed to take the job at Johnson's urging. Signing a two-year contract, Barrow was paid a salary of $5,000 with a bonus of $2,500 worth of club stock.

When Barrow became the Detroit Tigers' manager in 1903, the American League had eight teams. Disappointingly, Barrow and the Tigers finished fifth that season. Further difficulties arose when Frank Navin joined the club as the business manager in the winter of 1903 and 1904; the two men disagreed on personnel matters and did not get along. After finishing seventh in 1904, Barrow left Detroit. Frank Navin later became the President of the Tigers and one of the wealthiest men in baseball.

After leaving Detroit, Ed Barrow managed Montreal of the Eastern League in the final weeks of 1904; the Indianapolis club of the American Association in 1905, and Toronto again in 1906. His teams did poorly. Feeling he was a failure, Barrow left baseball and went into the hotel business in Toronto. But he missed the game and returned to Montreal as the club's manager in 1910. Subsequently, he was elected president of the Eastern League, where he demonstrated his executive skills through a number of significant actions.

Most notably as the league's chief executive, Barrow reduced rowdiness between the managers, players, and umpires by strengthening the authority of the umpires. Barrow also elevated the status of the league to AA, restored the name International League, and successfully fought the challenge of the new Federal League, which competed in many of the same cities as organized baseball and raided its players.

One of the teams in the International League that faced stiff competition by the Federal League was Jack Dunn's Baltimore Orioles. When Dunn's club could no longer stay in business, Barrow was forced to move the Baltimore club to Richmond, Virginia. When the war with the Federal League successfully ended after the 1915 season, Barrow made Dunn pay a fee of $15,000 to return to Baltimore, telling the Orioles' owner the payment was to help defray debts incurred by the International League.

Dunn resented this action bitterly and with some other owners forced Barrow from office in 1917. After Harry Frazee, the owner of the Boston Red Sox, offered him the job of manager, Barrow guided the Red Sox, to the World Championship in 1918. However, Barrow and the team finished sixth in 1919, and fifth in 1920 after the team's star, Babe Ruth was sold to the New York Yankees.

On Harry Frazee's recommendation, co-owners Jacob Ruppert and Cap Huston offered Barrow the position of business manager with the New York Yankees. Barrow accepted the job and moved into the club's front office on October 29, 1920. The first thing Barrow did was to send for the Yankee skipper Miller Huggins.

"You're the manager," said Barrow. "You'll get no second guessing from me. Your job is to win and my job is to see that you have the players to win with. You tell me what you need and I'll make the deals. And I'll take full responsibility for every deal I make."

Barrow was a tireless worker, spending long hours at work. When he went out to lunch, it was to grab a sandwich and a cup of coffee downstairs in the building. Often he would eat in. Everyday a barber came in and shaved him between telephone calls. When the Yankees were at the Stadium, Barrow spent mornings in the office and afternoons at the ballpark. Spending all day in the office when the club was on the road, he was the last person out of the office when darkness fell.

Feeling that the spotlight was for the players and the players alone, Barrow never visited the clubhouse, the manager's office, or went onto the field. Nicknamed Cousin Egbert and Cousin Ed by the press in New York, he was involved in every aspect of the Yankees' operations. Sportswriters followed his dealings closely. His round face and glasses, sweeping forehead and black bushy eyebrows were often seen in the sports pages of the city's newspapers.

After taking over as business manager of the Yankees in 1920, Barrow found Ruppert and Huston, the two Yankee owners, constantly feuding and interfering with the team. When Barrow gave explicit orders for both men to stay out of the clubhouse, they were surprised at his boldness but agreed.

Working to improve the club immediately, Barrow made a trade with his former employer, the Boston Red Sox, for pitcher Waite Hoyt and catcher Wally Schang. In 1921, Hoyt won 19 games and Schang batted .316 for the Yankees. With their contributions, the club finished in first place, winning the first pennant in the franchise's history. Facing the New York Giants in the '21 World Series, the Yankees lost the series 5 games to 3. [In 1903 and 1919-21, the World Series was best of eight.]

Looking to further improve the club in 1922, Barrow bought Lawton (Whitey) Witt, a centerfielder, from the Philadelphia Athletics, and in mid-season he obtained third baseman Jumpin' Joe Dugan from the Boston Red Sox. Both moves paid off: Witt played in 140 games and batted .297, while Dugan played in 60 games and hit .286. With Bullet Joe Bush winning 26 games and Waite Hoyt 19, the Yankees won the pennant for the second straight year in 1922. And for the second straight year, the club lost the World Series to the New York Giants—4 games to 0 and a tie.

After the Yankees' second World Series loss to the Giants, Huston wanted Huggins fired, but Ruppert disagreed and when they couldn't resolve their differences, Huston agreed to sell his interest to Ruppert for $1,500,000. Ruppert asked Barrow to raise part of the money—a sum of $350,000.

Barrow went to his old friend Harry M. Stevens for a loan. Stevens hated Huston because the Yankee co-owner tried to break the Stevens's family concession in the Polo Grounds and put his own son in their place. [The Yankees and New York Giants had been co-tenants in the Polo Grounds since 1913.] Stevens loaned the $350,000 to Barrow, who then endorsed Steven's check over to Ruppert. In return for the money, Barrow received a ten per cent interest in the club, repaying the loan to Stevens out of the dividends.

With Ruppert now the sole owner of the Yankees, Miller Huggins was given absolute authority over the players. Firmly believing his role was finding the best players for the club and spending Jacob Ruppert's money judiciously, Barrow worked hard behind the scenes.

The 1923 season was momentous for Ruppert, Barrow, and Huggins. In April, the new Yankee Stadium opened in the Bronx. By September the club had clinched their third straight pennant, finishing the season sixteen games ahead of the Detroit Tigers. Pitcher Herb Pennock was one reason for the club's success.

Obtained from the Boston Red Sox at the start of the season, Pennock won 19 games, and for the third consecutive time, the Yankees met the New York Giants in the World Series. This third time was the charm. The Yankees defeated the Giants 4 games to 2 in the '23 World Series.

It was the Yankees' first world championship.

Before Clark Griffith, President of the Washington Senators, named Bucky Harris manager of the club in 1924, he asked Barrow if he wanted the job. Barrow declined the post, preferring to remain with Ruppert. As it turned out, the next couple of years turned out less successful for the Yankees and Barrow: the club finished second in 1924, two games behind the Senators, and the 1925 season was far worse as the Yankees finished seventh, 28 ½ games behind the Senators, who won their second straight pennant.

Losing and playing poorly during 1925, Barrow and Huggins felt the Yankees had lost their will to win. Even before that season, both men knew that the franchise had to be rebuilt. Barrow told Paul Krichell, chief scout for the Yankees, and the others on the staff, Joe Kelly, Ed Holly, and Bob Gilks, to find new talented players. Their efforts were successful.

In 1923, Paul Krichell saw a young ball player named Lou Gehrig play for Columbia University in New York City and enthusiastically recommended the young man to Barrow, who signed the slugger. Based on recommendations from the scouting staff, Barrow bought the contract of Earle Combs, an outfielder from Louisville of the American Association in 1924.

The hunt for new players went on.

In 1925, Yankee scout Ed Holly went to Salt Lake City in the Pacific Coast League to look at a second baseman named Tony Lazzeri. When Holly reported that Lazzeri was sensational, Barrow bought him from Salt Lake City for $50,000 and five players, a very high price in those days.

That same year when Krichell and Huggins saw an infielder named Mark Koenig play, they recommended that the Yankees obtain him. Barrow agreed and bought Koenig's contract from St. Paul of the American Association for $35,000. Meanwhile, during the winter Barrow got rid of Wally Schang, Deacon Scott, Wally Pipp, and other veterans of the1925 club.

When Spring Training opened in 1926, the Yankees were almost a new team. The center fielder was Earle Combs, who played between Babe Ruth and Bob Meusel in the outfield. Lou Gehrig was the first baseman. Two rookies were in the infield; Tony Lazzeri at second base and Mark Koenig at short stop. Rounding out the infield was veteran third baseman Joe Dugan, and Benny Bengough, who caught behind the plate.

Unexpectedly, the Yankees won the pennant in 1926, but lost to the St. Louis Cardinals in the World Series, which was remembered for Grover Cleveland Alexander's crucial strikeout of Lazzeri in the seventh game with the bases filled.

While the season ended in disappointment for the Yankees, there was much to take pride in. Ruth bounced back from a poor season to hit 47 home runs and to drive in 146 runs, which were both league highs. Gehrig, in his first full season as a regular, hit 16 home runs and batted in 107 runs, and Lazzeri and Koenig played well in their rookie seasons. On the mound, Pennock was outstanding, winning 23 games.

Following the '26 World Series, Ed Barrow made a number of moves to improve the Yankees: catcher Johnny Grabowski and infielder Ray Morehart were picked up from the Chicago White Sox; outfielder Cedric Durst and pitcher Joe Giard were obtained in a trade with the St. Louis Browns, and pitcher George Pipgras and infielder Julie Wera were signed from St. Paul of the American Association.

Barrow's most important acquisition, however, was an unknown journeyman minor leaguer named Wilcy Moore, who was obtained from Greenville of the South Atlantic League.

Chapter 2

Spring Training

Under sunny skies at Crescent Lake Park in St. Petersburg, Florida on Monday, February 28, 1927, Yankee manager Miller Huggins stood on the dirt infield with arms folded across his chest. As he watched the players on the practice field during the Yanks' first morning workout of Spring Training, Huggins saw a mix of rookies, newly acquired players, and a few of the team's regulars. The club's star, Babe Ruth, and the other veterans were expected to report on Sunday and begin workouts the next day.

Practicing that day were pitchers Bob Shawkey, Dutch Ruether, Myles Thomas, Joe Giard, Henry Johnson, Roy Chesterfield, James Wiltse, George Pipgras and Shep Cannon; catchers Johnny Grabowski, Ed Phillips, Virgil Davis and Baxter Williams; infielders Lou Gehrig, Mike Gazella, Spencer Adams, Julie Wera, Don Flickinger, Hugh Ferrell, and Earl Blair, and outfielders George Davis and Elias Funk. Coaches Charley O'Leary and Arthur Fletcher were also on the field.

The opening of Spring Training was overshadowed by news surrounding Babe Ruth, who was in Hollywood having just completed a movie titled "Babe Comes Home." Ruth's contract with the Yankees ended with the 1926 season without him signing a new one for 1927. Five years earlier in 1922, the Yankee slugger had signed a three-year contract calling for $52,000 a year with an option for two additional years. The Yankees exercised that option, which expired at the close of the 1926 season.

Before leaving California for New York, Ruth sent Yankee owner Colonel Jacob Ruppert a letter with his salary demands: a new two-year contract at $100,000 a season and a refund of $7,700 in fines and the costs of a hospital bill incurred in 1925.

Ruppert was interviewed at his upper Fifth Avenue home in Manhattan after Ruth left California. Although he had not yet received the letter, Ruppert was familiar with its contents, telling reporters:

"I guess Babe did not want to take any chance on the letter missing me," said the Colonel. "Just to make certain of this he gave it out to the newspapers before leaving California."

When asked about Ruth's salary demands, an amount far exceeding the highest ever paid a baseball player, Ruppert only smiled.

As the Twentieth Century Limited came slowly to a stop on Wednesday, March 2, a hundred or so fans were on the train platform at Grand Central Station waiting to greet Babe Ruth. Outside the entrance to the train station another 2,000 admirers also awaited his appearance.

After departing the train, he walked in the midst of the crowd. A smiling Ruth waved and hurriedly walked a half block to the gymnasium of his private trainer, Artie McGovern. While at McGovern's, Ruth called his wife Helen, who was ill at St. Vincent's Hospital and then telephoned Colonel Ruppert, arranging a meeting for later that day. When asked by reporters afterwards about his willingness to back down from his demands, Ruth replied that he would not report to camp unless signed.

Ruth visited his wife at St. Vincent's Hospital before the meeting with Ruppert at the owner's brewery at Ninety-first Street and Third Avenue in Manhattan. Ruth arrived at 12:20 p.m. to meet with the Yankee owner and Ed Barrow. While the Babe talked with reporters and posed for photographers, Ruppert and Barrow waited impatiently.

The conference finally started at 1 o'clock in Ruppert's spacious private offices. After fifty-five minutes behind closed doors, Barrow invited the twenty sports writers into the conference room.

"Babe has accepted a three-year contract calling for $200,000," announced Colonel Ruppert.

"I sure have," said Ruth, "and I'm glad that's off my mind."

"Babe Ruth (he always pronounced his name "Root') now is the highest paid man in baseball," announced Ruppert proudly. "We came to terms without any trouble. Babe will go to camp on Saturday and everything is fine."

Babe Ruth's contract of $70,000 a year was a compromise by Ruppert to extend the length of the contract for Ruth's agreement to cut his salary demand. Ruth's new annual salary was the highest in baseball history, surpassing even Commissioner Kenesaw Mountain Landis's salary of $65,000, Ty Cobb's $60,000 and Tris Speaker's $40,000.

One had to assume that Ruth's teammates were a little envious of the new contract: Joe Dugan had signed for $12,000, Waite Hoyt—$11,000, Dutch Ruether—$11,000, Bob Shawkey—$10,500, Lou Gehrig—$8,000, Tony Lazzeri—$8,000, Benny Bengough—$8,000, Mark Koenig—$7,000 and Pat Collins—$7,000. Wilcy Moore, the journeyman minor leaguer, signed for $2,500 and an additional $500 if he played for the club the entire season. Herb Pennock, Bob Meusel, Earle Combs, and Urban Shocker were unsigned.

When Miller Huggins heard the news in Florida from reporters that Ruth had signed his new contract, he told them that he was glad to hear that it was completed quickly. Huggins told reporters he hoped Ruth was satisfied and ready to play.

With the sun shining and a cool breeze blowing in from Tampa Bay, the players went through routine workouts in the morning and afternoon on Thursday, March 3. The workout saw Moore, Shawkey, and Beall pitch batting practice. Infield practice followed with Gehrig at first, Adams at second, Gazella at third, and Flickinger at short. Later another foursome made up of Gehrig, Morehart, Wera, and Ferrell took up positions in the infield.

Generally, a crowd of tourists sat behind the wire screen and watched the players. Occasionally, an old timer would come by. The Reverend Billy Sunday, a famous evangelist and former baseball player for the Cubs, Pirates, and Phillies in the 1880's, was one notable visitor. The Reverend Sunday posed with Huggins for photographers and took a turn at bat.

Huggins later talked to reporters about the Yanks' pitching staff.

"If any of the young pitchers shows me anything," said Huggins, "they will get a chance. I'll start any youngster who has the stuff. I'll admit that in the past I've been cautious about using rookies, but that was in the past. The whole thing is that the Yankee pitching staff has reached the stage where I must gamble. These old fellows aren't going on forever."

Bob Shawkey was 37 years old, Urban Shocker 34, Dutch Ruether 33, and Herb Pennock 32.

Huggins felt youngsters like George Pipgras, Roy Chesterfield, and Myles Thomas were on the verge of blossoming into starting pitchers. One 'old' youngster that attracted the manager's attention was a 30-old right-handed pitcher wearing uniform number 46.

His name was Wilcy Moore.

Smiling, calm and reserved, Moore had broad shoulders and powerful arms. A farmer from Oklahoma, he had been in the minor leagues since 1921. Ed Barrow had signed him sight unseen from Greenville of the South Atlantic League based on his record of 30 wins and 4 defeats in 1926; a season where Moore had pitched 305 innings and walked only 70 men.

Moore was a fast ball pitcher, who kept his ball low. He delivered the ball with a side arm motion that broke down much like a spitball; the players called it a 'sinker.'

"He seems to have pretty good stuff, but it's too early to get an accurate line on a pitcher," said Huggins. "After I have seen him work in some real ball games I will have a better idea of his worth."

Recognizing that thirty was old for a pitcher to break into the majors, Huggins added: "Despite Moore's remarkable record last year, I figured it is more sensible to take a pessimistic view of his chances to make the grade."

Each day in St. Petersburg, Miller Huggins worked hard and taught his players how to play the game properly. For instance, one afternoon, he watched Don Flickinger, a short stop, throw the ball without stepping out with his right foot and went over to correct him. Gehrig was weak going to his left, and Huggins instructed him to play further off the bag toward second. He had him stop balls hit to his left. Huggins also wanted Gehrig to work on fielding bunts, telling an observer on the bench that the first baseman needed to know when to come in and when to stay back and let the pitcher field the bunt.

Always watching his players closely, Huggins saw a problem with pitcher Walter Beall's motion and talked to him about it. He also planned on working with Mark Koenig, the club's regular shortstop, when he reported. Huggins felt that Koenig was weak going to his left, and a great shortstop had to go to his left.

And so it went each day late into the afternoon.

Everyone was impressed with Babe Ruth's condition when he appeared at Crescent Lake Park on Monday, March 7. The Babe reported to camp at 223 pounds and looked more lean and muscular than any time in recent years. Ruth and Huggins were in good spirits when they met with reporters.

"If Ruth wants to work with us every day, I think he could easily make the team his first year," Huggins told reporters jokingly.

"The movies were beginning to pall on me, anyway," Ruth remarked.

Afterwards, the Babe took batting practice, ran the bases, and threw the ball hard to Benny Bengough, one of the team's catchers. Other regulars—second baseman Tony Lazzeri, shortstop Mark Koenig, third baseman Joe Dugan and pitcher Waite Hoyt—were also on the field for the first time.

Holdouts not in camp included outfielders Earle Combs and Bob Meusel and pitcher Herb Pennock. Working out with the club but unsigned was another veteran pitcher, Urban Shocker.

The Yannigan games began on Tuesday, March 8. In baseball slang a Yannigan was a rookie—a player not on the regular team. In Spring Training, the Regulars played on the first team in practice games and the Yannigans were on the second team. The word 'Yannigan' was believed to come out of the American lumber camps and had been used in baseball as early as 1899. By 1927, the term was common in baseball.

In the first practice game of the spring at St. Petersburg, Elias Funk led the Yannigans over the Regulars 7 to 2. Funk had two hits, scored two runs, and threw out Lou Gehrig at third base with a beautiful throw from centerfield. Babe Ruth played first base for the rookies, his sacrifice fly in the first inning scoring a run. Shep Cannon and Joe

Giard pitched for the Regulars, and Henry Johnson and Jim Wiltse hurled for the Yannigans.

On Thursday, March 10, 18 Yankee players, the manager, and coaches took a four-hour bus ride to Orlando, Florida to play the Cincinnati Reds. The game with the Reds opened the Yanks' exhibition season, which was only against National League teams. Accompanying the team and umpiring the Yankee games was American League Umpire Clarence Rowland.

On Babe Ruth Day, Reds' President Garry Hermann invited all the school children of Orlando to be his guests at the game. A record crowd of 4,000 people saw the Yankees win 8 to 5. However, the Babe was forced to leave the game in the fourth inning after he pulled a charley horse in his left leg while running the bases. With Ruth in pain, Yankee trainer Doc Woods massaged the leg and then taped it.

On the field, George Davis, a rookie center fielder from New York University, had two singles and a double. Yankee hurlers George Pipgras, Wilcy Moore, and Walter Beall held the Reds to three hits and one earned run.

During Spring Training at St. Petersburg, the Boston Braves and the New York Yankees shared Waterfront Park. When playing each other the two teams alternated as the home team. That day, Saturday, March 12, the Braves hosted the game, which the Yankees won by a score of 8 to 4.

Because of the charley horse suffered while playing the Reds, Babe Ruth rested on the bench in civilian clothes. He was expected to be out a week. Yankee center fielder George Davis had three of the club's fourteen hits and two runs driven in. On the mound, Yankee pitchers Joe Giard, Henry Johnson, and Jim Wiltse limited the Braves to six hits.

Off the field, Urban Shocker and Earle Combs signed their contracts for $13,500 and $10,500, respectively. Meanwhile, Yankee outfielder Bob Meusel, who was unsigned, arrived in camp from California the next day. Meusel planned to talk to Huggins the following day about a contract. Herb Pennock remained the only holdout.

Lou Gehrig and Mark Koenig, two of the Yankee's young stars, joined a team of rookies and traveled by bus to Auburndale, Florida on

Sunday, March 13, to play the Baltimore Orioles, a minor league team of the International League. Due to the absence of Ruth, less than 500 people attended the game.

The Yankees had eighteen hits and won 11 to 2, scoring seven runs on seven hits in the eighth inning. Second baseman Ray Morehart and right fielder Cedric Durst each had four hits. Limiting the Orioles to five hits that day were pitchers Walter Beall, Shep Cannon, and George Pipgras.

Back at St. Petersburg, Bob Meusel was in uniform and practiced with the regulars. That afternoon Meusel met with Huggins in the Yankee clubhouse and discussed his contract. However, before deciding on any financial terms Meusel wanted to wait and to discuss the matter with Colonel Ruppert, who was to arrive in St. Petersburg on Wednesday.

The Yankees hosted the Boston Braves at Waterfront Park in St. Petersburg on Tuesday, March 15, and won 6 to 5, even though the Braves out hit the Yanks twelve to eight. Cedric Durst hit a bases loaded home run in the fifth inning. Playing for the first time since his injury in Orlando, Babe Ruth pinch-hit without success in the sixth. Yankee hurlers Waite Hoyt, Dutch Ruether, and Wilcy Moore pitched against the Braves.

That day Colonel Jacob Ruppert arrived in St. Petersburg. After checking into the Yankees' headquarters at the Princess Martha Hotel, he met with Bob Meusel to discuss the outfielder's salary. Surprisingly, Ruppert agreed to Meusel's request for a two-year contract rather than the one-year offered, and the outfielder signed for $13,000 a year for 1927 and 1928.

The only player still unsigned was Herb Pennock, the Yankees' best pitcher in 1926. That season Pennock won 23 and lost 11, with 2 saves, and a 3.62 era. Ruppert offered Pennock approximately $18,000 for the upcoming season, but the Yankee left-hander demanded $20,000.

"Pennock wants a salary greater than was ever paid to any pitcher in the American League, and, I am certain in the National League. This goes for Walter Johnson, [George] Uhle, [Dazzy] Vance and others," said Ruppert. "Now, Pennock is a great pitcher and pitched wonderful ball last year, but I don't think he deserves the highest salary paid to any pitcher in the history of baseball. He is covering a lot of ground there."

Yankee centerfielder Earle Combs, who recently signed his contract, joined the team in St. Petersburg on Wednesday, March 16. He looked thin and underweight, which was attributed by some to a recent operation to remove his tonsils.

In the heat at Crescent Lake, Combs and the others took hitting and fielding drills. Returning from his recent injury, Babe Ruth played first base for the Yannigans and hit into two double plays as the Regulars won 13 to 1. Bob Shawkey and Jim Wiltse pitched for the Regulars; Urban Shocker and Joe Giard were on the mound for the Yannigans. Shocker gave up eleven runs and twelve hits in three innings.

Off the field, Colonel Ruppert put pressure on Herb Pennock to end his holdout.

"If Pennock hasn't signed by early next week," said the Colonel, "I intend to send him formal notice either to sign the contract or return it. If he fails to sign, he will be put on the ineligible list, and then he will have to make his peace with [Commissioner] Landis before he can return to the game."

With a crowd of 2,500 at Waterfront Park in St. Petersburg, the Boston Braves hosted the Yankees on Saturday, March 19. Although the club came into the game with four straight wins, the Braves won by a score of 6 to 4. Tony Lazzeri, the Yankees' second baseman, had four of the team's nine hits, including a triple; Mark Koenig, the short stop, had three hits. Apparently still affected by his recent charley horse, Babe Ruth had a disappointing day. He dropped a ball in right field that allowed two Braves' runs. Ruth's three turns at bat were no better having grounded out twice and struck out.

On the mound, Walter Beall was wild and gave up five runs in four innings; however, George Pipgras pitched well after coming on in the fifth, giving up only one run on two hits in four innings. The first cut of the spring took place the next day when pitcher Jim Wiltse was released to Buffalo of the International League.

With Bob Meusel playing in his first game of the spring on Monday, March 21, and hitting a home run over the left field fence in the sixth to break a scoreless tie, the Yankees edged the Cincinnati Reds at St. Petersburg, 2 to 1. After the Reds tied the score, Cedric Durst's sacrifice fly with the bases loaded in the ninth won the game. Babe Ruth walked, singled, bounced out with a man on, and struck out. Dutch Ruether and Waite Hoyt held the Reds to nine hits.

The Yankees played the Cincinnati Reds again the next day, but a sudden rainstorm after five innings ended the game in a 0 to 0 tie. Urban Shocker pitched four innings and Joe Giard one.

Babe Ruth hit two home runs and a double as the Yankees hosted the Boston Braves at Waterfront Park on Wednesday, March 23, and won 16 to 7. Yankee outfielder Bob Meusel also had a home run and a double; Lou Gehrig a triple, and Tony Lazzeri and Mark Koenig a double each as the Yanks pounded out a total of sixteen hits.

Wilcy Moore followed Bob Shawkey and Myles Thomas on the mound and gave up only one run on an error and two hits over the last four innings. Meanwhile, Herb Pennock sent word to Huggins that he would be in St. Petersburg later in the week to talk things over. Later that evening, the Yankees announced outfielder Elias Funk had been released on option to St. Paul of the American Association.

In the last exhibition game against each other, the Boston Braves hosted the Yankees on Thursday, March 24 at Waterfront Park.

The game was a wild affair.

The Braves won 10 to 9 as National League Umpire Frank Wilson ejected eighteen Yankee players, or more precisely, he tossed out the same nine Yankees twice!

In the first inning, after catcalls were hurled at Wilson by some of the players, the umpire walked to the dugout and nine Yankees came out. Wilson ejected the players and they left the bench for the clubhouse. Wilson soon got embroiled in an argument with Eddie Moore of the Braves, who also was ejected. While Wilson was busy with the Braves' bench, the nine ejected players returned to the Yankee bench unnoticed and quietly got back into the game.

In the fifth, Wilson noticed that the Yankees had too many players on the bench and on the field. Realizing what happened, Wilson ejected the nine players for the second time in the game! On the playing field, Bob Meusel hit a home run in the fourth to give the Yankees a 5 to 2 lead, but the Braves scored four in the fifth off Henry Johnson and four more in the seventh off Walter Beall.

Herb Pennock, the Yanks' last holdout, arrived and worked out that day at Crescent Lake Park. Afterwards, Pennock had a long meeting with Huggins and then held a separate conference with Ruppert at the Princess Martha Hotel. At 3 o'clock, Pennock and Ruppert came into the lobby and talked with newspaper reporters. Ruppert announced Pennock had agreed to sign a new contract for $17,500 for each of the next three seasons—1927, 1928 and 1929—and an additional bonus of $1,000 for any season he won 25 games.

Further player cuts took place: Virgil Davis, a catcher, and Hugh Ferrell, an infielder, were sent on option to Reading of the International League, and infielder Spencer Adams was sold to the St. Louis Browns. Looking ahead, the Yankees prepared to play the defending world champion St. Louis Cardinals in the first of a series of eight exhibition games.

Under bright blue skies at Avon Park, Florida, the 'little World Series' between the New York Yankees and St. Louis Cardinals began on Sunday, March 27. The Cardinals won 13 to 2 as Bill "Wee Willie" Sherdel and Al Smith held the Yankees to nine hits. Huggins was not happy watching George Pipgras and Walter Beall give up twelve runs in six innings. Myles Thomas yielded one run over the final two. On the bright side, Babe Ruth tripled in three at bats.

Grover Cleveland Alexander, who last appeared against the Yankees in the World Series in October, pitched for the Cardinals as the Yankees hosted St. Louis at Waterfront Park in St. Petersburg on Monday, March 28. After giving up four runs in the first capped by Joe Dugan's double, Alexander pitched scoreless ball over the next six innings.

The Cardinals fought back and cut the lead to one run in the fourth and then scored two runs in the ninth and won, 5 to 4. Babe

Ruth singled, walked, and struck out against Alexander and singled off Jimmy Ring. Waite Hoyt gave up three runs on nine hits in five innings. Dutch Ruether took the loss, giving up two runs on four hits in four.

The Yankees began preparations to break camp and head north on a nine-day trip before opening the season with the Philadelphia Athletics at Yankee Stadium on April 12. Miller Huggins decided to leave some players in St. Petersburg to work out as the club traveled north. Remaining in Florida were Herb Pennock, who had just joined the team; pitcher Roy Chesterfield, and catcher Benny Bengough. Tony Lazzeri also stayed behind because of a boil on his knee.

Further player cuts took place: outfielder George Davis was assigned to Reading of the International League, and infielder Don Flickinger was sent to Binghamton of the New York-Pennsylvania State League. Down to twenty-nine players, the Yankees would need to cut four more players to be at the twenty-five-man limit by June 15.

On the trip north, the Yankees stopped in West Palm Beach, Florida on Thursday, March 31, to play the Cincinnati Reds. Pitchers Wilcy Moore and Myles Thomas held the Reds scoreless for eight innings, but the Reds' hurlers, Eppa Rixey and Art Nehf, pitched just as well, and there was no score until the top half of the ninth when the Yankees scored three runs.

Opening the last half of the ninth, Chuck Dressen fouled out to Babe Ruth in right field; however, four straight singles by Curt Walker, Rube Bressler, Wally Pipp, and George Kelly made the score 3 to 2. With two runners on base, Red Lucas pinch-hit for Horace (Hod) Ford and singled home two runs. The Reds won 4 to 3.

An overflow crowd of 10,000 fans at Durkee Field in Jacksonville, Florida, saw the Yankees and Cardinals play under the ground rules on Friday, April 1. With the score tied at two after seven, Babe Ruth, who went hitless against Grover Cleveland Alexander faced the new Cardinals' pitcher Art Reinhart.

Ruth drove Reinhart's pitch into the excess crowd in the right field for a ground's rule double. When Lou Gehrig attempted a sacrifice, Reinhart threw to third base wildly to catch Ruth, who scored on the bad throw. The pitching was better. Bob Shawkey gave up only four hits and one run in five innings, and Urban Shocker yielded three hits and one run over the final four. The Yankees won by a score of 3 to 2.

As Miller Huggins walked on the field before the game on a hot sultry afternoon on Saturday, April 2 at Municipal Stadium in Savannah, Georgia, a high wind swept dust all around. With 15,000 spectators looking on, the Cardinals hammered the Yankees, 20 to 10. Pitchers Dutch Ruether, Henry Johnson, Joe Giard, and Walter Beall gave up a total of twenty-two hits. Frank Snyder hit a home run off Ruether with the bases loaded.

For the Yanks, Babe Ruth singled to center and tripled to left. After the three-bagger, a large group of children poured onto the field from the bleachers and field boxes and mobbed Ruth. The Babe grinned and good-naturedly waded his way through them and returned to the bench.

On Sunday, April 3 the Yankees and the Cardinals resumed their series in Montgomery, Alabama, where Babe Ruth drove in two runs with a pair of doubles and also scored a run on a hit by Lou Gehrig. The Yankees won 4 to 2 on twelve hits off Jesse Haines and Eddie Dyer. Yankee outfielder Earle Combs had three hits, including a long double that scored the last run.

That day Waite Hoyt and Wilcy Moore pitched particularly well: Hoyt held the Cardinals to eight hits and two runs in seven innings, and Moore gave up only two hits in the final two frames. On the field, Ray Morehart ended the game with forty-eight errorless chances in the field since filling in for Tony Lazzeri at second base.

In Atlanta, Georgia the next day, the Yanks pounded out fourteen hits against Grover Cleveland Alexander, Wee Willie Sherdel, Hal Smith, and Vic Keen, defeating the Cardinals, 15 to 8. Huggins was pleased to see Babe Ruth have an excellent day belting two doubles and throwing out two runners at the plate. Earle Combs, Ray Morehart, Joe Dugan, and Pat Collins also each had two hits. However, the club's pitching was again erratic as George Pipgras went six innings and was hit hard.

When the game the next day was called off because of rain, the Yankees and Cardinals shared a special train to Chattanooga, Tennessee, where Miller Huggins started rookie Wilcy Moore on Wednesday, April

6. The Yanks scored four runs in the fourth on Joe Dugan's home run with the bases loaded. With the score tied in the seventh, Waite Hoyt came in and pitched scoreless ball. In the tenth inning, the Yankees won 5 to 4 as Earle Combs led off with a base hit, went to third on Babe Ruth's single to right, and scored on Lou Gehrig's sacrifice fly.

With the Yankees leading the series over the Cardinals, 4 games to 3, the two teams played for the final time in Knoxville, Tennessee on Thursday, April 7. Frankie Frisch, the Cardinals' second baseman, accounted for six runs with two home runs and two doubles as St. Louis won that day, 10 to 8.

Pitchers Bob Shawkey and Myles Thomas gave up a total of ten hits. Babe Ruth hit a home run. Tony Lazzeri played second base for the first time since rejoining the team. Before his return, Ray Morehart had fielded fifty-six chances without an error.

After the game in Knoxville, the Yankees traveled by train to New York City for the last two exhibition games of Spring Training with Manager Wilbert Robinson's Brooklyn Robins, also known as the Dodgers.

On Saturday, April 9, a cold spring day in New York City, a crowd of 15,000 people gathered at Ebbets Field in Brooklyn and watched the Yankees beat the Robins, 6 to 5. With the score tied at five in the eighth, Bob Meusel doubled to right field and scored on Mark Koenig's single. Earlier, Babe Ruth singled home two runs, and in the seventh inning, the Babe also hit a home run with two men on off the Robins' ace Jesse Petty. Waite Hoyt, Dutch Ruether, and Urban Shocker pitched for the Yanks.

The spring exhibition series ended for the Yankees and Robins as a record pre-season crowd of 25,000 packed Ebbets Field in Brooklyn on Sunday, April 10. On another very cold afternoon, the Yankees won 4 to 3 as Babe Ruth continued to hit well: in four plate appearances he singled three times and walked once.

Huggins liked the effort of the pitching staff that afternoon. Herb Pennock went three innings and gave up no runs and only one hit. Wilcy Moore pitched the next six, giving up three runs on six hits and striking out seven batters.

With Spring Training completed, the Yankees were eager to start the new season on Tuesday at the Stadium. Miller Huggins was asked by *The New York Times* to predict the outcome of the American League pennant race.

"I look for a closer race this time. Six clubs, with almost equal chances, must be considered as contenders," said Huggins. "The Yankees, Senators and Tigers have everything but pitching, while the Athletics, Indians and White Sox are well-equipped in the [pitching] box. If the Yankees can develop just two dependable young pitchers we'll be a hard team to beat."

Chapter 3

Opening Day

With a light wind stirring the flags and bunting at Yankee Stadium in New York City, the sun shined brightly on Opening Day, Tuesday, April 12, 1927. By noon the temperature was a warm 59 degrees. Preceding the game at 3:30 p.m., fans arrived by crowded subways, busses, and hundreds of taxicabs.

The gates opened promptly at noon.

Although all of the Stadium's field boxes and reserved seats had been sold out days in advance, forty thousand unreserved seats were on sale. Those were sold quickly, and the ballpark filled rapidly. The seating below the scoreboard had been kept closed but was soon ordered opened, and thousands rushed and filled the section within moments.

Outside Yankee Stadium, another 25,000 fans pushed against the barricades and closed gates looking to buy tickets. The police turned them away. Inside the ballpark, the seats, rafters, aisles, and runways were filled with fans. Ushers in scarlet jackets tried hard to get the people in the seating areas to sit down.

By game time, every available foot of seating and standing room was taken. People were standing three feet deep behind the rear rows of the two lower tiers. The large crowd was noisy and excited. There was a circus atmosphere in the ballpark.

It was the largest crowd ever. The attendance was 72,000 and included 62,000 paid admissions, 9,000 invited guests, and 1,000 who had passes. The record attendance broke the mark of 63,600 at the second game of the 1926 World Series in New York.

The great interest in opening day was the fans' desire to see the New York Yankees and the Philadelphia Athletics and their stars Babe

Ruth, Lou Gehrig, Ty Cobb, Eddie Collins, and Zach Wheat. Both clubs were expected to contend for the American League championship.

There were many notable people at Yankee Stadium. British tea merchant and yachtsman Sir Thomas Lipton was a guest in the box of Yankee owner Col. Jacob Ruppert. Others at the Stadium were Dr. Wilhelm Cuno, former Chancellor of the German Republic; Mayor Jimmy Walker of New York City; Patrick Cardinal Hayes; Alderman Joseph McKee, and entertainer George M. Cohan.

With pre-game ceremonies taking place, Miller Huggins walked to the visitors' dug out on the first base side. Connie Mack, the Athletics' manager, came out of the visitor's dug out and met Huggins.

Photographers rushed back and forth on the sun-drenched field. Huggins and Mack posed together for photographs. Babe Ruth and Ty Cobb, the former Detroit Tigers' star, also had their photographs taken.

In the traditional opening day march to the centerfield bleachers the players and dignitaries paraded in disarray. When they arrived at the bleachers, the Seventh Regiment Band, dressed in smart gray uniforms, began playing the national anthem. The crowd rose and took off their hats. On the field, workers dropped their rakes and tampers.

With everyone looking towards the flagpole in centerfield, the American flag and the 1926 Championship pennant were raised. The pennant had a white field with red and blue letters and read 'Champions American League, 1926'. With the ceremonies over, the teams returned to their dugouts.

Fifteen minutes before the game, Yankee announcer Jack Lenz, a small stout man, walked over to Mack and Huggins. He was given two copies of each line-up card. Lenz then gave a set to the home plate umpire Will Evans and kept a set. He then quickly called the press box and gave the reporters the names of the starters.

With his over-sized megaphone, Lenz then embarked on his ten-minute ritual of journeying around the field, bellowing out to the crowd the starting pitcher and catcher of each team. Customarily, he directed the megaphone toward the bleachers and then to the upper and lower decks. With the large crowd expected, the Yankees asked George Levy, the announcer at the Polo Grounds, to join Lenz on the field.

Wearing a black derby and dark blue overcoat, Mayor Walker threw out the first ceremonial pitch to Yankee catcher Johnny Grabowski at 3:25 p.m. With the opening day ceremonies ended, umpire Evans had a long conference at home plate over the ground rules of Yankee Stadium with the teams' captains.

With its unique copper frieze hanging from the roof of the upper grandstands and its manicured grass outfield, the Stadium looked splendid. Its dimensions were 296 feet down the right field foul line; 281 down the left field line and almost 500 feet to the barrier in center.

Waite Hoyt was the starting pitcher for the Yankees. Traded to New York from the Boston Red Sox after the 1920 season, Hoyt became one of the stars of the pitching staff. From 1920-1925, the affable and good-looking right-handed pitcher averaged 18 victories a season. In 1926, Hoyt won 16, lost 12, posted 4 saves, and had a 3.84 earned run average (era).

Lefty Grove opened the season for the Athletics. Robert Moses Grove, a smart and crafty left-hander from Lonaconing, Maryland, began his major league career with Philadelphia in 1925, winning ten. In 1926, he won 13, lost 13 and posted 6 saves. Grove's 2.51 era and 194 strikeouts were best among all pitchers in the major leagues.

The Line-Ups

Athletics	Yankees
Eddie Collins 2b	Earle Combs cf
Bill Lamar lf	Mark Koenig ss
Ty Cobb rf	Babe Ruth rf
Al Simmons cf	Lou Gehrig 1b
Sammy Hale 3b	Bob Meusel lf
Dudley Branom 1b	Tony Lazzeri 2b
Mickey Cochrane c	Joe Dugan 3b
Joe Boley ss	John Grabowski c
Lefty Grove p	Waite Hoyt p

Eddie Collins, a left-handed batter, stepped up to the plate. Collins wore a dark cap with white piping up the seams and a plain gray flannel road uniform with a black belt. On Collins's jersey was a symbol of a white elephant. He had on black shoes with a dark stripe at the top of his white stockings and dark stirrups. Collins spat on his hands, rapped each shoe with his bat, and faced Hoyt.

The game began.

With no score in the Yanks' half of the first, Babe Ruth came up to bat. The Babe wore a navy blue cap with a white interlocking "NY" on the front. His flannel uniform was white with navy blue vertical pinstripes. Ruth's jersey had a "V" neck collar style with a brief tapered extension around the neck. He wore a black belt and black cleats with navy blue stirrups.

With Ruth at the plate, home plate umpire Evans stopped the game. Mayor Jimmy Walker came on the field and presented the Babe with a silver loving cup given by newspaper publisher William Randolph Hearst. Ruth had won the trophy in a player popularity contest.

In the first and second innings, Grove struck out Ruth, Gehrig, Meusel, and Lazzeri. There was no score after four and one-half. Dugan opened the Yankees' fifth with a single to right field. After Grabowski walked, Hoyt bunted. Branom, the Athletics' first baseman, dropped the ball attempting to throw to third base to get Dugan.

With the bases loaded, Combs then doubled over the head of Lamar in left field, scoring Dugan and Grabowski. On the play, Hoyt raced to third base and Lazzeri reached second safely. Grove then retired Koenig and struck out Ruth. When Gehrig's grounder took a bad hop past Collins into right field for a double scoring Hoyt and Combs, the Yankees led 4 to 0.

After Ruth complained of dizziness at the top of the sixth, Huggins replaced him in right field with Ben Paschal. With the score 4 to 2 in the bottom of that inning, Lazzeri doubled over the heads of Cobb and Simmons. Dugan's bunt single moved Lazzeri to third. When Dugan ran on what he believed was a wild pitch, Cochrane, the Athletics' catcher, threw him out at second base.

Grabowski then singled to left, scoring Lazzeri. When Hoyt sacrificed, Grabowski crossed the plate. Combs then reached first on an error by Boley, the shortstop. The rally went on when Koenig tripled to deep center field, scoring Combs. Paschal's single to right sent Koenig home. The Yankees led 8 to 2.

With one out in the Athletics' eighth, Simmons doubled inside third base and scored on Hale's single. Former Yankee right-hander Jack Quinn, 43, who replaced Grove an inning earlier held the Yankees to one hit in the seventh and eighth.

Zach Wheat, the former Brooklyn Robin who began his career across town in 1909, was given a friendly reception by the fans when he batted for Quinn in the ninth. Wheat, whose nickname was "Buck", singled to center and stole second base uncontested. Wheat was stranded there after Hoyt retired Collins and Lamar.

Final score: Yankees 8, Athletics 3.

Yankee Notebook for Tuesday, April 12, 1927: Yanks' starter Waite Hoyt (1-0) gave up eight hits, three walks, and struck out three on Opening Day . . . Hoyt held Eddie Collins hitless in four plate appearances . . . Cobb managed only a bunt single . . . The Yanks opened the season with a total of ten hits, including three singles by Dugan; a triple and single from Koenig, and doubles by Combs, Gehrig, and Lazzeri.

Miller Huggins met with reporters after the game.

"Beating Grove is bound to give the entire team a lot of confidence. I was pleased because it proved the fallacy that our team can be stopped by good left-handers," said Huggins. "They figure that if they have Combs, Ruth and Gehrig stopped they can keep us from scoring. However, we have some husky right-handed hitters on the club, and they did break through just as they did against Grove. They better get over the idea that we are suckers for left-handers."

On Opening Day 1927, there were sixteen professional baseball teams in the major leagues, eight each in the American and National Leagues. The National League clubs and their ballparks included the Boston Braves (Braves Field); Brooklyn Robins (Ebbets Field); Chicago Cubs (Wrigley Field); Cincinnati Reds (Redland Field); New York Giants (Polo Grounds); Philadelphia Phillies (Baker Bowl); Pittsburgh Pirates (Forbes Field), and St. Louis Cardinals (Sportsman's Park).

The American League was comprised of the Boston Red Sox (Fenway Park); Chicago White Sox (Comiskey Park); Cleveland Indians

(Dunn Field); Detroit Tigers (Navin Field); St. Louis Browns (Sportsman's Park); Washington Senators (Griffith Stadium); Philadelphia Athletics (Shibe Park), and New York Yankees (Yankee Stadium).

President and Mrs. Calvin Coolidge watched the American League's Washington Senators get off to a good start in the nation's capital on Opening Day with a win over the Boston Red Sox, 6 to 2. Stan Coveleski replaced an injured Walter Johnson as Washington's starting pitcher. At Dunn Field at Cleveland, George Uhle, who topped all American League pitchers with 27 victories in 1926, led the Cleveland Indians to a win over the Chicago White Sox, 3 to 2. Uhle won his own game with his second hit, a double in the ninth that brought home the winning run. Rain postponed Opening Day at Sportsman's Park in St. Louis between the Detroit Tigers and St. Louis Browns.

In the National League, a record-breaking crowd of 45,000 at Wrigley Field in Chicago saw the Chicago Cubs defeat the 1926 World Champion St. Louis Cardinals 10 to 1. The Cubs hit three home runs, two by Earl Webb and one by Charlie Grimm. At Baker Bowl in Philadelphia, 22,000 fans watched the visiting New York Giants beat the Philadelphia Phillies, 15 to 7. Bill Terry, Rogers Hornsby—who had been traded from the Cardinals to the Giants after the '26 season—and George Harper hit home runs for the Giants.

With 15,000 people at Braves Field in Boston, the Brooklyn Robins defeated the Boston Braves, 6 to 2. The Robins last lost on Opening Day in 1918. A record-breaking crowd of 35,000 saw the Pittsburgh Pirates beat the Cincinnati Reds, 2 to 1 at Redland Field in Cincinnati. Pirate hurler Ray Kremer, a 20 game winner in 1926, gave up only six hits.

The attendance for the seven major league opening day games was 241,000; 18,000 more than attended opening day games in 1926. The American League had an attendance of 124,000 (Detroit-St. Louis was rained out). The National League total was 117,000. The total attendance of 241,000 topped the previous record of 233,000 in 1925.

With 10,000 fans at Yankee Stadium in New York under cloudy skies on Wednesday, April 13, Walter Henry "Dutch" Ruether, a 33-year-old left-hander started for the Yanks against the Philadelphia Athletics. Born in Alameda, California on September 13, 1893, Ruether began his career with the Chicago Cubs in April 1917. He also played for the Reds from 1917-1920 and the Brooklyn Robins from 1921-1924.

Ruether won 19 games in 1919 and 21 in 1922. Traded to the Washington Senators in 1925, he won 18. The left-hander started the 1926 season with the Senators, but he was then traded to New York, where he started five games, winning two critical games in the pennant stretch.

Ruether's mound opponent that afternoon was Samuel David Gray, a right-hander, who broke into the majors with the Athletics in 1924. Gray won eight games that season; sixteen in 1925, and eleven in 1926. Nicknamed "Sad Sam," Gray, 29, hailed from Van Alstyne, Texas.

The Yanks were ahead 2 to 1 when Simmons, the Athletics' centerfielder, came up in the third and hit the ball deep off Ruether to right field. It sailed over Ruth's head and landed in the stands for a home run, tying the game at two. In the fourth the Yankees went ahead when P. Collins hit a fly ball off Gray that fell for a double between Boley, the shortstop, and left fielder Lamar. Ruether's single scored Collins, and base hits by Combs and Koenig and a wild pitch led to two more runs. With none out, Connie Mack brought in Charley (Lefty) Willis.

Ruth was Willis's first batter.

On a two-strike pitch, the Babe singled sending Koenig to third base. Gehrig then hit a long triple to the outfield, and as Simmons and Cobb chased the ball to the fence, Koenig and Ruth scored making the score, 7 to 2. The Athletics' added a run in the fifth, but the Yankees scored three more in the sixth off Willis and another off Joe Pate, a left-hander.

The last run of the day was scored in the seventh. Athletics' infielder Jimmy Dykes, a right-handed batter, pinch-hit for Pate and doubled to left. Dykes later scored on Lamar's single over Koenig's head at short. Howard Ehmke, a right-hander, pitched the seventh and eighth and held the Yankees to one hit. Ruether pitched a scoreless eighth and ninth.

Final score: Yankees 10, Athletics 4.

Yankee Notebook for Wednesday, April 13, 1927: In the second game of the series, the Yanks collected sixteen hits off four Athletics' pitchers . . . Koenig, the Yankees' shortstop, became the first player that season to have five hits—all singles—in five at bats . . . Koenig also drove in two and scored twice . . . Combs, Ruth, Gehrig and Lazzeri each had two hits.

In going the distance, Ruether (1-0) gave up fourteen hits, walked three, and struck out six . . . For the Athletics, Eddie Collins, who seldom strikes out, was fanned on three pitches . . . Simmons gave Ruether trouble all afternoon; he had a home run, a double, and two singles. Ruether finally walked Simmons in his last at bat.

In the field, Koenig and Meusel helped Ruether with their gloves: Koenig speared a high throw from Collins and made a quick tag on Perkins in the fourth, and Meusel threw home from left in the seventh, just catching Cobb at the plate.

That day in other American League action, Bill Hunnefield, batting for shortstop Roger Peckinpaugh, started a six run rally in the ninth by reaching first base on an error as the White Sox defeated the Indians, 7 to 2, at Dunn Field. Rain postponed the scheduled games between the Red Sox and Senators at Washington, D.C. and the Tigers and Browns at St Louis.

In the National League, Jesse Haines of the Cardinals shutout the Cubs, 5 to 0, on two hits at Wrigley Field. Tommy Thevenow, the Cards' shortstop, singled three times. With less than 1,500 people at Braves Field, the Braves behind the pitching of Larry Benton defeated the Robins, 4 to 2. Rain postponed the Giants and Phillies at Philadelphia and Pirates and Reds at Cincinnati.

Bob Shawkey started against the Athletics in the third game of the series in New York on Thursday, April 14. James Robert (Bob) Shawkey was born December 4, 1890 in Sigel, Pennsylvania. Signed by Connie Mack, the 5' 11" right-hander debuted with the Philadelphia Athletics on July 16, 1913. In his first full season with the Athletics in 1914, Shawkey won 16 games.

Shawkey came to the New York Yankees in July 1915 and was the ace of the staff the first three years the franchise won American League championships—1921 through 1923. During that span, he averaged eighteen victories a season. Overall, Shawkey won twenty or more games in four seasons—1916 (24-14); 1919 (20-11); 1920 (20-13), and 1922 (20-12). In 1926, he won 8 and lost 7, posted 3 saves, and had a 3.63 era.

The Athletics' starter was a 29-year-old right-hander named Edwin Americus Rommel from Baltimore, Maryland. After beginning his career with the Athletics in 1920, Rommel won 27 games in 1922, the most in the major leagues. He won 18 games in 1923 and 1924 and 21 in 1925. In 1926, Rommel won 11 and lost 11 with a 3.08 era.

Down 3 to 0 in the first inning, Miller Huggins signaled to the bullpen. On that sunny and clear afternoon, Wilcy Moore, a tall, thin right-hander, walked through the bullpen gate and crossed the outfield grass. After toiling in the minor leagues for six years, Moore, who was going to be 30-years-old in May, was making his major league debut.

The fans gave him a warm reception.

Earlier the Athletics had taken the lead after Shawkey loaded the bases on a walk to Lamar and singles to Cobb and Simmons. When Hale followed with a triple, the base runners scored. To make matters worse, Dugan didn't jump fast enough as Hale slid into third base and was spiked above the right knee. Mike Gazella replaced him.

With the warm-ups done, Moore went on to retire the side.

With Combs, Ruth, and Meusel on the bases in the home half of the first, Lazzeri tripled off Rommel, tying the game at three. The Athletics' went ahead 4 to 3 in the second, and Moore gave up three more runs in the fifth; Hale's second triple of the game the big hit.

Down by four runs, the Yankees fought back a second time to tie the game at seven in the home half of the fifth. After Moore gave up two runs in the sixth to give the Athletics a 9 to 7 lead, Huggins brought Urban Shocker, a right-hander, into the game with no one out. Shocker retired the side.

The Yankees tied the game again in the eighth off Rube Walberg, a left-hander, who had started that inning. Mack then brought in southpaw Joe Pate, who retired Koenig but walked Ruth. Gehrig came to the plate with a chance to give the team the lead.

With Yankee Stadium engulfed in darkness and cold, Gehrig hit Pate's pitch on a line drive towards third base. Hale threw up his arm and made a one-handed catch to end the inning and save the game. Waite Hoyt, a right-hander, pitched the ninth and tenth, giving up no runs and two hits. Lefty Grove pitched the tenth and did not allow a hit.

The game was called a draw at 9 to 9 after the tenth because of darkness.

Yankee Notebook for Thursday, April 14, 1927: A change to baseball's playing rules in 1920 called for a draw to have individual and team averages incorporated in the official playing records . . . The Yankees had fourteen hits; Combs, Gazella, and Grabowski each had two . . . Meusel drove in four runs with a triple and two singles.

For the first time, one of the club's starters was knocked out of the game. Shawkey (0-0) gave up three runs in one-third of an inning and walked one batter . . . The Yankees shipped a couple of right-handed pitchers back to the minor leagues that day: Henry Johnson was released on option to the Milwaukee club of the American Association, and Shep Cannon was returned to the Waco team in Texas.

At Griffith Stadium, Hollis "Sloppy" Thurston, pitching his first game for Washington, held the Red Sox to four hits as the Senators took the second game of the series from Boston, 5 to 2. Thurston had pitched for the White Sox the last four years. At Dunn Field, sensational relief pitching by southpaw Sherrod Smith in the ninth allowed the Indians to defeat the White Sox, 3 to 2. Smith relieved starter Benn Karr with two on and one run across the plate; he retired the next three batters. Rain postponed the game between the Tigers and Browns at St. Louis.

In Philadelphia, veteran pitcher Jack Scott led the Phillies to a win over the Giants, 9 to 6. Scott also had a perfect day at bat with two singles, a double, and home run. With less than 500 fans at Braves Field on a bitter cold day, Foster Edwards pitched a complete game and led the Braves to a win over the Robins, 7 to 3. At Redland Field,

Lee Meadows scattered eight hits as the Pirates handed the Reds their second straight loss, 6 to 2. Pirate teammates Pie Traynor, Paul Waner, and Kiki Cuyler each doubled. Cold postponed the game between the Cardinals and Cubs at Chicago.

Thirty-three-year-old Herb Pennock, a left-hander, was the Yanks' starter at the Stadium in the Bronx on Good Friday, April 15, 1927. Born February 19, 1894 in Kennett Square, Pennsylvania, Pennock began his career with the Philadelphia Athletics in 1912 before going to the Boston Red Sox in 1915. He was traded to the Yankees in 1923.

From 1923-1925, Pennock won a total of 56 games, averaging almost 19 victories a season. In 1926, the Yankee left-hander won 23 and lost 11, with 2 saves, and a 3.62 era; only George Uhle of the Cleveland Indians had more victories with 27.

Howard Ehmke, a 32-year old from Silver Creek, New York, pitched for the Athletics. The right-hander was with Buffalo of the Federal League in 1915 and played for the Detroit Tigers from 1916 through 1922. He went on to pitch for the Boston Red Sox in 1923 and 1924 and won 20 and 19 games, respectively. Ehmke started the 1926 season with the Red Sox and won 3 and lost 10 before coming to the Philadelphia Athletics, where he had a record of 12 wins and 4 losses and a 2.82 era.

Ruth came to the plate with two outs in the bottom of the first.

The Babe hit Ehmke's pitch deep into the right field stands for his first home run. The crowd of 20,000 went wild with excitement. As Ruth circled the bases, the fans were on their feet cheering. As he crossed the plate, Gehrig congratulated him. The Babe tipped his cap to the spectators.

Going to top of the seventh, the Yankees led 4 to 0, but the Athletics stormed back to make the score 4 to 3. Joe Pate, a left-hander, was on the mound in the bottom of the seventh when he quickly ran into trouble. Pate walked Ruth, fumbled a bunt by Gehrig, and then walked Meusel.

With the bases loaded, Pate then threw two wild pitches to Lazzeri. At that point, Connie Mack brought Rube Walberg, a left-hander, into the game. Lazzeri greeted Walberg with a single to right, scoring Ruth and Gehrig. Pennock pitched a scoreless eighth and ninth.

Final score: Yankees 6, Athletics 3.

Yankee Notebook for Friday, April 15, 1927: That day Babe Ruth's home run ended his poor-hitting streak. Having batted ten times, the Babe had only three singles, no extra base hits and no runs batted in. He had also struck out three times . . . Contributing to the scoring was Gazella, who had two triples . . . Gehrig ended the day with one official at bat, having walked and sacrificed twice.

Pennock (1-0) gave up seven hits, walked two, and struck out none . . . Eddie Collins, Philadelphia's star second baseman, went hitless for the fourth straight game . . . The attendance at Yankee Stadium for the four game series with the Philadelphia Athletics was almost 125,000 . . . The Boston Red Sox were in New York next to play the Yankees.

At Griffith Stadium in Washington, D.C., Alvin Floyd (General) Crowder held the Red Sox to five hits as the Senators swept the opening series winning, 7 to 1. Washington's Goose Goslin had three hits and Tris Speaker two. Meanwhile in Cleveland, Ted Lyons, an 18-game-winner in 1926, pitched a six-hit complete game as the White Sox defeated the Indians, 6 to 1, and tied the series. After rain prevented the opening of the season for the Tigers and Browns, the teams finally played at St. Louis. But rain fell again after the fifth and the game was stopped with the score tied at two.

In Chicago, Cardinals' pitcher Bill Sherdel held the Cubs to two hits, but one was Hack Wilson's second-inning home run that gave Chicago a victory over St. Louis, 1 to 0, at Wrigley Field. Cub southpaw Percy Jones gave up six hits. At Baker Bowl, Freddie Fitzsimmons went the distance giving up eleven hits and walking five as the Giants beat the Phillies, 6 to 3.

Reds' pitchers Eppa Rixey and Art Nehf were hammered as the Pirates won, 10 to 6, at Redland Field. The Robins lost their third game in a row to the Braves, 3 to 1, at Braves Field. Boston's starter Charley Robertson, who pitched a perfect no-hit game in 1922 as a member of the White Sox, gave up only five hits.

Major League Baseball Standings
April 15, 1927
American League

	Won	Lost	Percentage
New York	3	0	1.000
Washington	3	0	1.000
Cleveland	2	2	.500
Chicago	2	2	.500
Detroit	0	0	.000
St. Louis	0	0	.000
Boston	0	3	.000
Philadelphia	0	3	.000

National League

	Won	Lost	P.C.
Pittsburgh	3	0	1.000
Boston	3	1	.750
New York	2	1	.667
Chicago	2	1	.667
Philadelphia	1	2	.333
St. Louis	1	2	.333
Brooklyn	1	3	.250
Cincinnati	0	3	.000

Chapter 4

Boston Red Sox

On Saturday, April 16, 1927 at Yankee Stadium, Urban Shocker, a 36-year-old right-hander, started for the Yankees against the Boston Red Sox. Born Urbain Jacques Shockcor on August 22, 1890 in Cleveland, Ohio, Urban Shocker began his career with the Yankees in 1916 but was later traded to the St. Louis Browns. Shocker was spectacular with the Browns from 1918 through 1924, winning twenty or more games four seasons in a row. He re-joined the Yankees in 1925, winning twelve. In 1926, Shocker won 19 and lost 11, with 2 saves, and a 3.38 era.

On the mound for the Red Sox was Charles "Red" Ruffing, a 20-year-old right-hander from Granville, Illinois, who broke in with Boston in 1924. He had no wins or losses in 1924 and won nine in 1925. For the last place Red Sox in 1926—the club finished 44.5 games behind the Yankees—Ruffing won 6 and lost 15, posted 2 saves, and compiled a 4.39 era.

The Line-Ups

Red Sox	Yankees
Pee Wee Wanninger ss	Earle Combs cf
Topper Rigney 3b	Mark Koenig ss
Jack Tobin rf	Babe Ruth rf
Ira Flagstead cf	Lou Gehrig 1b
Baby Doll Jacobson lf	Bob Meusel lf
Phil Todt 1b	Tony Lazzeri 2b
Bill Regan 2b	Mike Gazella 3b
Fred Hofmann c	John Grabowski c
Charles Ruffing p	Urban Shocker p

With the Red Sox leading 1 to 0, Combs led off the first inning. On the mound, Ruffing wore a plain gray cap with a red bill. The words "Red Sox" in red block letters were etched on the jersey of his gray flannel road uniform. He wore gray pants with a black belt and black shoes. The top half of his white stockings was red.

Ruffing opened the bottom of the first with a walk to Combs. Koenig then singled to left but was out on an attempt to reach second base. On the play, Combs went to third. Ruffing then walked Ruth. With Combs on third and Ruth at first, Gehrig came to bat and singled, scoring Combs and tying the game. On the hit, Ruth reached third base, later scoring on Meusel's fly to Tobin in right field.

The Yankees loaded the bases in the fifth on Combs's single and walks to Koenig and Ruth. When Ruffing walked Meusel, Combs was forced home, making the score 3 to 1. The Red Sox cut the lead to 3 to 2 in the sixth on three consecutive singles and a ground out.

Tony Welzer, a right-hander, was on the mound for the Red Sox in the seventh. Welzer walked Koenig, who was forced at second base by Ruth. The Babe then advanced to second on Gehrig's out and scored on Meusel's single. Lazzeri then doubled to left field. When Jacobson fumbled the ball, Lazzeri tried for third base but was called out; however, Meusel scored giving the Yankees a three run lead. Shocker pitched a scoreless eighth and ninth.

Final score: Yankees 5, Red Sox 2.

Yankee Notebook for Saturday, April 16, 1927: The victory was the Yankees' fourth straight without a loss . . . Shocker (1-0) gave up ten hits, walked two, and struck out two. He also picked off Wanninger at second base in the third . . . Koenig, the Yankee shortstop, received a big cheer every time he came up to bat. He had two hits in two official at bats and played errorless in the field with four assists . . . The Yankees had only six hits, but the Red Sox pitchers walked nine batters . . . Lazzeri had a double; the team's only extra base hit . . . The Red Sox's loss was their fourth in a row.

In Washington, D.C., Ty Cobb singled in the ninth and scored the deciding run on a double by Al Simmons and a sacrifice fly by Sammy Hale as the Athletics handed the Senators their first defeat of the season, 8 to 7. At Sportsman's Park, Sam "Sad Sam" Jones, making his pitching debut with the Browns, held the Athletics to four hits as St. Louis won, 3 to 1. Jones spent the last five seasons with the Yankees. Rain postponed the game between the Tigers and Indians at Cleveland.

By beating the Cardinals, 5 to 4, the Reds won their first game of the season at home. Red Lucas relieved Reds' starter Adolfo Luque in the ninth and saved the game after St. Louis threatened with two men on base and only one out. At Wrigley Field, the Pirates suffered their first loss when the Cubs bunched hits in the seventh and won, 5 to 2. Cub pitcher Guy Bush scattered six hits.

At Braves Field, Rogers Hornsby's home run with a man on in the seventh gave the Giants what proved to be the winning run over the Braves, 7 to 6. In Philadelphia, a capacity crowd of 17,000 at Baker Bowl saw manager Stuffy McInnis' Phillies narrowly defeat the Robins, 3 to 2. Philadelphia's Alex Ferguson gave up eight hits and one walk.

More than 35,000 fans came out to Yankee Stadium on Easter Sunday, April 17, 1927. Yanks' skipper Miller Huggins started Waite Hoyt, who opposed the Red Sox's Jack Russell. Both were right-handers.

At the age of twenty-one, Jack Erwin Russell from Paris, Texas broke into the major leagues with the Red Sox in 1926. Pitching mainly in relief, the slim 6'1.5" hurler won 0 and lost 5 and had a 3.58 era.

After giving up a single to Combs to open the home half of the first, Russell walked Ruth. Gehrig came to the plate and hit Russell's pitch deep to right field. The ball landed just inside the right field foul line for a home run.

With the fans on their feet cheering, Combs, Ruth, and Gehrig circled the bases.

The Yankees added two runs in the second and led 5 to 0. In the fourth, Koenig went over to his right and fielded Rigney's hard hit grounder and made a beautiful throw to first base to get him. Tobin then hit a home run off Hoyt into the right field seats. When Gazella made a great throw from third base to get Flagstead at first, the Red Sox ended the fourth trailing by four.

The Yankees scored in the fourth, fifth, and sixth and went ahead 9 to 1. Right-hander Danny MacFayden pitched the eighth for the Red Sox. After he walked Ruth, Gehrig hit his second home run of the game into the pavilion in right field. MacFayden then gave up singles to Meusel and Lazzeri, a double to Gazella, and a base hit to Collins. Boston scored one more run in the ninth before Hoyt retired the side.

Final score: Yankees 14, Red Sox 2.

Yankee Notebook for Sunday, April 17, 1927: The win was the Yankees' fifth straight . . . The club was hitting close to .400 . . . Gehrig's home runs were his first and second; he also singled, scored three runs, and drove in six . . . In tallying fourteen, every Yankee scored a run.

Hoyt (2-0) pitched his second complete game. He gave up eight hits—four in the last two innings—struck out five, and walked none . . . Filling in again at third base for Dugan, Gazella had two hits and four assists . . . When Meusel threw his bat at a pitch-out with Gehrig going on a hit-and-run, his aim was perfect. The ball went for a Texas leaguer over the shortstop's head.

In Cleveland, Sam Gibson held the Indians to eight hits as the Tigers played their first game of the season after six weather postponements and won, 5 to 1. At Griffith Stadium, Ty Cobb had four hits and a stolen base and Al Simmons homered as the Athletics battered the Senators, 13 to 3. With a spectacular nine run rally in the ninth, the White Sox evened the series with the Browns, 12 to 5, at Sportsman's Park.

At Ebbets Field, a near capacity crowd of 23,000 saw the Braves defeat the Robins, 7 to 2. Official Opening Day ceremonies at Ebbets Field were to be held Wednesday. Behind Grover Cleveland Alexander, the Cardinals edged the Reds, 2 to 1, in Cincinnati. Reds' star second baseman Hughie Critz, who had been a hold out signed a one-year contract for $12,000. Before a crowd of more than 45,000 at Wrigley Field, the Pirates defeated the Cubs, 8 to 3. At Providence, Rhode Island, 12,000 people came out to see the New York Giants beat the Grays of the Eastern League in an exhibition game, 6 to 5.

The late customers arriving at Yankee Stadium at 5 o'clock to see the last five innings of the game on Monday, April 18, 1927 were surprised to find the game over. The Yankees and Boston Red Sox had played the first five and a half innings in an hour; the entire game was played in only one hour and twenty-nine minutes.

Dutch Ruether, a left-hander, pitched for the Yankees. His opponent was right-hander William Jennings Bryan "Slim" Harriss, 30, from Brownwood, Texas. After having spent six full seasons with the Philadelphia Athletics, the 6' 6", 180 pound Harriss joined the Boston Red Sox during the 1926 season and won 6 and lost 10 with a 4.46 era.

In the first inning, Combs singled and moved to second when Harriss walked Ruth. Both runners advanced on Gehrig's infield out. With Combs on third and Ruth on second base, Meusel singled off the glove of Rigney, the Red Sox's third baseman. As Combs scored, the ball rolled toward second base. In a daring move, Ruth suddenly dashed home safely making a beautiful slide over a corner of the plate.

The Yankees took a 3 to 0 lead in the sixth after Gehrig singled to center and scored on Lazzeri's double past Flagstead. Over the final three innings, Ruether pitched scoreless ball, finishing with a three-hit shutout.

Final score: Yankees 3, Red Sox 0.

Yankee Notebook for Monday, April 18, 1927: It was the Yank's sixth straight win without a defeat . . . Ruether (2-0) used a combination of curves, fast balls, and a change of pace to shutout Boston. He struck out three and walked two . . . Ruether also hit Wanninger and Jacobson . . . Only one Red Sox runner reached third base and another to second . . . Harriss gave up ten hits . . . Meusel singled twice and Gehrig had two hits . . . Gehrig also batted in two runs giving him twelve, most by any Yankee.

Harriss had a very deceptive delivery; the ball appeared to drop down on the players . . . The Yankees hit into double plays in the third, fourth, and fifth . . . Gehrig made an admirable effort at a backhand catch of a foul ball over the roof of the Boston dug out before it hit the concrete . . . Over 75,000 fans attended the three games played so far with the Red Sox . . . In the seven games since the start of the season, 190,000 people had visited Yankee Stadium.

At Sportsman's Park in St. Louis, Browns' shortstop Walter Gerber singled in the eighth and drove in the winning run to defeat the White Sox, 5 to 4, in the third game of the series. In Cleveland, Dutch Levsen pitched a strong 8 2/3 innings over the Tigers as the Indians won, 3 to 2, and tied the series. Garland Buckeye relieved Levsen after a run scored and there were two runners on with two outs. With good support in the field at Griffith Stadium, Hollis Thurston shutout the Athletics, 4 to 0, on eight hits as the Senators took the third game of the series. Ossie Bluege, the Senators' third baseman, drove in two runs with the bases loaded.

Doubles by Rogers Hornsby and Eddie Farrell in the eleventh inning broke a tied game as the Giants beat the Braves in Boston, 11 to 10; Virgil Barnes won in relief. At Wrigley Field, Pirate hurler Lee Meadows scattered four hits and the Pirates defeated the Cubs, 9 to 1. Cub pitcher Tony Kaufmann hit Paul Waner twice. With 20,000 fans filling Baker Bowl, the Phillies sent the Robins to their sixth straight defeat, 7 to 3. Hal Carlson pitched scoreless ball into the ninth before Irish Meusel cracked a home run into the left field bleachers with two on. Rain postponed the game between the Cardinals and Reds at Cincinnati.

On Tuesday, April 19, 1927 veteran right-hander Bob Shawkey took the mound for the Yankees in the final game of the series with the Boston Red Sox at Yankee Stadium. Opposing Shawkey was Harold (Hal) James Wiltse, a 23-year-old left-hander from Clay City, Illinois, who broke into the major leagues with the Red Sox in 1926. That season he appeared in 36 games and pitched 196 innings; Wiltse won 8 and lost 15 with one shutout and a 4.22 era.

With Rothrock on third base and Tobin at second with two outs in the first, William Chester "Baby Doll" Jacobson came to bat for the Red Sox. Jacobson singled, scoring Rothrock and Tobin. The Yankees tied the game at two in the home half of the first. Combs singled. Koenig forced him at second base and scored on Gehrig's double. When Meusel singled to left field, Gehrig crossed the plate.

Leading 4 to 2 in the top of the sixth, Hartley doubled for the visitors. When Wiltse singled, Hartley headed for home plate and scored on an error by Collins. After Wanninger singled, Huggins brought in Wilcy Moore, a right-hander, who retired the side. Right-hander George Pipgras pitched the eighth and walked Todt, who moved to second on Haney's sacrifice and scored on a single by Hartley, giving the Red Sox a 6 to 2 lead.

In the bottom half of the ninth, Wiltse gave up singles to Gehrig and Meusel. With none out, Gehrig scored the final run when Lazzeri hit into a double play.

Final score: Red Sox 6, Yankees 3.

Yankee Notebook for Tuesday, April 19, 1927: The victory was the Red Sox's first of the season . . . Shawkey (0-1) was ineffective in his second start giving up five runs and eight hits in 5 2/3 innings . . . Moore did not allow a hit over the next 1 1/3 . . . Pipgras gave up one run and one hit over the final two.

The Yankees had nine hits . . . Ruth had a bad day at the plate; he struck out and hit into two double plays . . . Collins should have caught Wanninger stealing in the third as the Red Sox went on to score two runs . . . Meusel made a very good catch in the fifth to take away a bid for a triple by Haney . . . The Yanks left for Philadelphia the next morning for Opening Day at Shibe Park.

At Griffith Stadium in Washington, D.C., Ty Cobb stole home on a triple steal ahead of a pitch by General Crowder as the Athletics beat the Senators, 3 to 1. In St. Louis, the Browns pounded White Sox pitching for twelve hits and won the final game of the series, 7 to 5, at Sportsman's Park. Frank O'Rourke, the Browns' second baseman, had two singles, a double, and a triple in five times at bat. Poor relief pitching by Indian hurler Jake Miller and three costly errors by teammates gave the Tigers the final game of the series over the Indians, 8 to 5, at Dunn Field. Lil Stoner yielded ten hits for Detroit.

By scores of 9 to 5 and 5 to 4, the Braves defeated the Giants in morning and afternoon games at Braves Field. A crowd of 37,000 attended the afternoon contest. At Redland Field, Jesse Haines gave up only five hits and led the Cardinals to a win over the Reds, 9 to 1. Jim Bottomley and Chick Hafey each hit a home run for St. Louis.

It was the seventh straight loss for Manager Wilbert Robinson's Robins as the Phillies' Jack Scott gave up four hits and threw a shutout, 4-0, at Baker Bowl. Cy Williams hit a home run, his second in two days. Rain postponed the game between the Pirates and Cubs at Chicago.

Major League Baseball Standings
April 19, 1927
American League

	Won	Lost	P.C.
New York	6	1	.857
St. Louis	3	1	.750
Detroit	2	1	.667
Washington	4	3	.571
Philadelphia	3	4	.429
Cleveland	3	4	.429
Chicago	3	5	.375
Boston	1	6	.143

National League

	Won	Lost	P.C.
Pittsburgh	5	1	.833
Boston	6	3	.667
Philadelphia	4	2	.667
New York	4	3	.571
Chicago	3	3	.500
St. Louis	3	3	.500
Cincinnati	1	5	.167
Brooklyn	1	7	.125

Chapter 5

Miller Huggins

Miller James Huggins was born March 27, 1879 in Cincinnati, Ohio. He was the third child of four and youngest son of Sara (Reid) and James Thomas Huggins. Even as a youngster Miller Huggins loved the game of baseball and dreamt of becoming a professional player someday. Growing up in Cincinnati, he attended public school and became a very good shortstop at Walnut Hills High School.

His father did not, however, approve of him playing baseball. Many people such as the elder Huggins held baseball players in low repute because of poor behavior on and off the field. He wanted Miller to enter a profession that was solid and reputable like his own. James Huggins, who had emigrated from London, England, had been in the retail grocery business for over forty years.

To please his father, Huggins enrolled at the University of Cincinnati in 1898 and studied law. One of his instructors was William Howard Taft, who was elected President of the United States ten years later. While at the University of Cincinnati, Huggins played baseball with local and semi-pro teams and used the fictitious name William Proctor (taken from Cincinnati's soap company Proctor & Gamble), because his father disapproved of him playing ball on Sundays.

Huggins later toured in New York with the Fleischmann Catskill Mountain Team, owned by Julius (Max) Fleischmann, a one-time mayor of Cincinnati and part owner of the Cincinnati Reds. In 1900, Huggins switched to the second base position from shortstop. Off the field, he received a law degree and passed the Ohio bar exams in 1902, but he decided not to pursue a law career; instead, Huggins chose professional baseball.

Performing well with the Fleischmann team, Miller Huggins won a chance to play second base for St. Paul of the American Association. As a switch-hitter he batted over .300 from 1901-03. Huggins was also considered an excellent fielder and a very good base stealer. When the Cincinnati Reds purchased Huggins from St. Paul in 1904, he happily returned to his hometown as the club's second baseman. In his first major league game on April 15, 1904 against the Chicago Cubs, Huggins played against the famous Cubs' infield of Ever-to-Tinker-to-Chance.

Because of his small stature of 5' 6" and 140 pounds, Huggins was nicknamed "Little Mr. Everywhere," "Rabbit," "Mity Mite" and "Hug." His small size and crouching-style at the plate also made him a perfect lead off man, leading the National League with walks four seasons.

Huggins only hit nine home runs in his career, but one was very special. On June 19, 1907, he led off against Christy Mathewson of the New York Giants and hit a home run in the Reds' home park, the Palace of the Fans. The home run so astonished the fans that in appreciation they presented Huggins with a pair of shoes, a gold watch, a 5-pound box of chocolates, a scarf pin, and a Morris chair.

While with the Cincinnati Reds, Huggins studied the game under the legendary manager Ned Hanlon, who had won five pennants with the Baltimore Orioles and Brooklyn Superbas in the 1890's. For most of the 1909 season, however, he was sidelined with a sore arm and was traded in February 1910 to the St. Louis Cardinals, where Huggins became the club's regular second baseman.

Three years later, Helene Britton, owner of the Cardinals, named him player-manager to replace Roger Bresnahan. Huggins was elated. Given a contract to manage the Cardinals for one-year—1913—his salary for playing and managing was $8,000. Miller Huggins saved his money and made profitable investments.

Miller Huggins's first season as a manager was a major disappointment as the Cardinals finished the season in last place, 49 games behind the New York Giants. He convinced Mrs. Britton to retain him as manager for another season. Some newspaper accounts reported him pleading for one more chance. In order to improve the club, Mrs. Britton gave

Huggins greater freedom to make player deals. Partly because of a three-for-five player deal he made with the Pittsburgh Pirates, the Cardinals of the 1914 season were much better.

The St. Louis Cardinals played well in 1914. As late as August 26, the club was only half a game out of first place, but George Stalling's Miracle Boston Braves finished first after being in last place in early July. While the New York Giants finished second and the Cardinals third, it was St. Louis's best finish since 1876 when the club and the National League came into being.

Following the Cardinals' success, Mrs. Britton rewarded Huggins with a three-year contract for 1915, 1916, and 1917. He was paid $25,000 for all three years. Huggins made a number of good investments with his money and with financial backing by Max Fleischmann of Cincinnati, he almost bought the Cardinals in 1916, but a St. Louis syndicate headed by James C. Jones eventually purchased the club in early 1917. Wesley Branch Rickey, a former catcher and manager of the St. Louis Browns, was made president of the club.

After Jones and Rickey took over the franchise, Huggins turned over second base to Rogers Hornsby and became the team's full-time manager. He piloted the Cardinals to third place in 1917, but Rickey did not care for Huggins's personality or managing style, and he was fired after the season, ending his stay in St. Louis with a managerial record of 346 wins and 415 losses.

Following the 1917 season, the New York Yankees were looking for a new manager after Wild Bill Donovan, the Yankees' skipper since 1915, had been fired. Piloting the club in 1917 to a sixth place finish, Donovan and the Yankees finished 28.5 games behind the Chicago White Sox. When Jacob Ruppert, co-owner of the Yankees, asked American League President Ban Johnson to help him find a new manager, Johnson asked his friend Ed Barrow, President of the International League, for his recommendation.

Surprising Johnson by recommending a National League candidate, Barrow suggested Huggins. Having watched him closely with the Cardinals, Barrow liked how he worked with the players to achieve success with little financial assistance. Ban Johnson told Ruppert that Huggins was his choice. However, Huggins was not interested. In his opinion the Yankee managerial position was a step down because the franchise was mediocre.

Huggins knew the Yankees' history. Ban Johnson, the founder of the American League in 1901, wanted a presence in New York City to battle the National League and John McGraw's New York Giants. To that end, Johnson moved the Baltimore Orioles, an original franchise of the American League, to Manhattan in 1903. Frank Farrell and Bill Devery paid $18,000 for the franchise, then known as the New York Highlanders.

In January 1915, Colonel Jacob Ruppert, a brewery owner, and Colonel Tillinghast L'Hommedieu (Cap) Hutson, an engineer, purchased the franchise from Farrell and Devery for $460,000; each owned fifty percent of the club.

Huggins also knew the Yankees had never won a pennant—the best the franchise ever finished was second in 1904 and 1906. At Ban Johnson's request, a friend of Huggins, J.G. Taylor, publisher of the national publication *The Sporting News*, urged him to take the managerial position.

Huggins finally agreed.

On October 26, 1917, Ruppert signed Huggins to a two-year contract. Cap Hutson was in Europe with the United States Army and was not informed of the signing. When he learned of Ruppert's action, the Yankee co-owner was very upset. Hutson had wanted his friend, Wilbert Robinson, manager of the Brooklyn Robins, to pilot the club. Always resenting Ruppert's decision to act alone, Hutson took the opportunity to undermine and criticize Huggins whenever possible.

By trading five players and cash for Del Pratt, a second baseman with the St. Louis Browns, Huggins began to improve the Yankees. The press criticized the trade. However, Pratt greatly improved the infield and the club finished 1918 in fourth place (60-63 record) thirteen and one-half games behind the Boston Red Sox. The Yankees improved further in 1919, ending the season third (80-59), seven and one-half games behind the Chicago White Sox.

Late in 1919, Miller Huggins recommended that the club acquire Babe Ruth from the Boston Red Sox. When the Yankees inquired about Ruth, Red Sox owner Harry Frazee told them he was available. Before completing the deal, however, Ruppert and Hutson sent Huggins to Los Angeles to talk to Ruth, who was on the West Coast playing exhibition games for additional income.

Ruth later wrote about that meeting with him: "I didn't know Huggins very well at the time . . . . I'd heard Miller had been a pretty good second baseman and leadoff man and wondered how such a small guy could ever have been a good ballplayer. He didn't seem strong enough to swing a bat, or live through a spiking."

Huggins asked Ruth how he would like to play for the Yankees. Ruth told him that he liked Boston, but if Frazee sent him to the Yankees, he would try to play as hard there as he ever had in Boston.

"We haven't put through the deal yet, but I want to know," asked Huggins, "whether you will behave yourself if we do obtain your services for the New York Yankees? I know you've been a pretty wild boy in Boston, Babe, and if you come to New York it's got to be strictly business."

Wagging his finger at Ruth, Huggins went on: "There are many temptations in the big city for an outstanding baseball hero, and I am asking whether you think you can measure up to it."

Getting fed up with Huggins's "sermon," as he later called it, Ruth replied: "I've already told you I'll play the best I can, for the Yankees or anybody else. But listen, if I go to New York I'll want a lot more dough than the $10,000 Frazee paid me last year."

"I am coming to that," said Huggins. "We know you've built yourself to the top. Colonel Ruppert is a generous man and if you promise to behave yourself when you come to us the Yankees will tear up your old Red Sox contract and make it $20,000."

A few days later the newspapers broke the story that Frazee had sold Ruth to the Yankees.

Babe Ruth hit 54 home runs in his first season with the Yankees in 1920, but the club again finished third (95-59), three games behind the Cleveland Indians. In October, Ed Barrow was signed as the business manager of the Yankees, and he and Huggins worked well together. For the first time in the franchise's history, the New York Yankees won the American League Championship (98-55) in 1921 but lost to the New York Giants in the World Series.

In 1922, Huggins again guided the Yankees (94-60) to the American League championship; unfortunately, they again lost the World Series to the New York Giants. In 1923, the Yankees (98-54) won their third straight American League pennant, but this time went on to defeat their rivals, the New York Giants, in the World Series, winning the franchise's first world championship.

Miller Huggins' success as a manager did not come without adversity. The Yankees of the early '20s were unruly, and he had problems keeping discipline. Some said his quiet, shy, and unobtrusive manner coupled with his small size and frailty did not command the respect of those hard living men. There was probably some truth to that, but he persisted.

There was the Waite Hoyt incident during the 1921 season. Huggins had ordered Hoyt to walk a hitter. When he got back to the bench, Hoyt had words with his manager and got into an argument. The hot-headed Hoyt tried to throw a punch at Huggins before another player grabbed his arm.

There was also the Carl Mays episode in the 1921 World Series. With the Giants ahead, 2 games to 1, the Yankees needed to even the series. The club went ahead 1 to 0 in the fifth on Ruth's home run. Mays had only given up two singles up to the eighth, when all of a sudden he gave up four hits and three runs. The big blows were a triple by Irish Meusel and a double by George Burns.

Before Meusel's triple, Huggins signaled from the bench for a fastball. Mays disregarded the instruction and threw a slow-breaking curve. Meusel drove the ball to the wall and the Giants soon had three runs. The Yankees lost that game, 4 to 2, and went down 3 games to 1, ultimately losing the 1921 World Series. Huggins never forgot Mays' insubordination, and he played less and less over the next two seasons. Clearing waivers in the American League, Mays was sold to the Cincinnati Reds after the 1923 season.

Then there was the incident with Joe Bush in the 1922 World Series. In the fifth game of that series with the Giants, Bush carried a small lead into the eighth. Huggins ordered the right-handed Bush to walk the left-handed Ross Youngs, and take a chance on the right-handed George Kelly.

Bush turned to Huggins and yelled: "What for, you stupid . . . (obscenity)."

Bush's voice carried to the press box and was heard by hundreds of box holders. Bush walked Youngs as ordered, but then he put one "right down the pike" to Kelly, who hit if for a single that turned the game around. Bush was traded to the St. Louis Browns after the 1924 season.

Babe Ruth, however, was Huggins's biggest problem. Ruth paid no attention to curfew, never took the room assigned to him, and often showed up in the club house just before game time. Ruth's life style and refusal to stay in shape irked his manager. Confrontation between the two men was inevitable.

Following the championship season of 1923, the Yankees fortunes changed. By 1924, Ruth partied a great deal and defied the team's rules. Ruth and Huggins argued in July of that year and Huggins berated him during a train trip. Contrary to legend, however, Ruth did not respond by hanging him over the rear platform of the train. On the field, the club finished the 1924 season in second place (89-63).

Babe Ruth's wild lifestyle and contempt for the team's rules continued in 1925. The confrontation came in St. Louis in late August. The team had been playing poorly and was in seventh place. Ruth was hitting .250. A few days earlier in Chicago, he again defied Huggins's authority on the field. Ruth had bunted with two runners on base in the first inning instead of swinging away. Then in the ninth with the club trailing by one run with two on, he swung away rather than bunting and lined into a double play.

Finally, Huggins had enough.

In late August 1925, Ruth did not show up for a couple of nights in his room at the Chase Hotel in St. Louis. After his second night out, Ruth appeared at Sportsman's Park the next day—August 29—after the team was already in uniform and taking batting practice on the field. As Ruth was starting to change into his uniform, Huggins went over to him and asked him to explain his conduct. Ruth responded by telling him that he had been taking care of personal business.

"Well you've had too much personal business lately," said Huggins. "Don't bother to dress. You're suspended. And I am fining you $5,000."

Huggins told Ruth to go back to New York on the 5:00 o'clock train. Ruth was outraged."

Five thousand dollars?" said Ruth incredulously. "Five thousand dollars? Fuck you, you little son of a bitch. Who do the hell do you think you are?"

After more obscenities, Ruth shouted; "If you were even half my size, I would punch the shit out of you." Huggins was six inches shorter, weighed a hundreds pounds less and was fifteen years older than Ruth at the time.

"If I were half your size, I'd have punched you," responded Huggins. "And I'll tell you something else, mister. Before you get back in uniform, you're going to apologize for what you've said, and apologize plenty. Now go on. Get out of here."

Ruth did not go to New York, but went to Chicago instead to see Commissioner Landis, who was out of town. While in Chicago, Ruth told the press that Huggins was the reason the Yankees lost the pennant to Washington the year before.

When asked about the Yankees, he replied: "I'm through with them. I won't be playing with them next year if Huggins is still there. Either he quits or I quit, because I'll never play for him again."

Before taking the action against Ruth, Huggins had gotten Barrow's and Ruppert's approval and support.

"I'm behind Huggins to the limit," Ruppert said from New York. "There will be no remission of the fine, and the suspension will last as long as Huggins wants it to last. I understand Ruth says he will not play for the Yankees as long as Huggins is manager. Well, the situation is this: Huggins will be manager as long as he wants to be manager. So you can see where we stand and where Ruth stands."

Ruth went to New York and met with Ruppert.

After the meeting at the owner's brewery both men met with the press. When asked if Ruth was reinstated, Ruppert answered: "No, he is not reinstated. The fine and suspension stand. I told Ruth, as I tell you now in front of him, that he went too far. I told him Miller Huggins is in absolute command of the ball club, and that I stand behind Huggins to the very limit. I told him it is up to him to see Huggins, admit his errors and apologize for his hotheadedness. It is up to him to reinstate himself."

Ruth spent nine days out of the lineup, eventually paying the fine and apologizing in front of the team. After eight difficult years, Miller Huggins had firmly established control of the ball club; however, the turmoil and Ruth's poor year (.290 batting average, 25 home runs and 66 runs batted in) had dramatic consequences—the Yankees finished seventh (69-85) in 1925. Huggins's health was also affected. He suffered at various times from chronic neuritis, bad nerves, dental problems, sinus headaches, and indigestion.

To the surprise of many, the Yankees won the American League Championship (91-63) in 1926, but lost to the Cardinals in the seventh game of the World Series. However, in a preseason poll of 42 baseball experts in 1927, only nine picked the Yankees to repeat as American League champions.

Chapter 6

Shibe Park

Under partly cloudy skies on Wednesday, April 20, 1927, a crowd of 40,000 came out to Shibe Park on Opening Day to watch Connie Mack's Mackmen host the New York Yankees. The prices for seats were the same as the year before—fifty cents for the bleachers, $1.10 for grandstand, and $2.20 for box seats.

Twenty-five hundred box seats, the only reserved seats in the ballpark, were sold days before. All the bleacher seats were gone within one hour and soon every seat inside the ballpark was filled. Hundreds of fans were clustered in the aisles and in the rear of the upper and lower pavilions. Others sat or stood along steel girders and on the roof of the stands in left field.

At 2:20 p.m., an hour before the game was scheduled to begin, Philadelphia's Mayor W. Freeland Kendrick escorted by Police Inspector William McFadden walked along the field into his box. Following the mayor were members of his Cabinet and other city officials. As Club President Tom Shibe led them to their boxes, the photographers took pictures of the notables. J. Franklin "Home Run" Baker on the Athletics' bench was photographed with Eddie Collins. As expected, both Ty Cobb and Babe Ruth were the object of much interest by reporters and photographers.

There was a festive mood at Shibe Park. Maurer's Band entertained the crowd, playing everything from Beethoven to Berlin. Usherettes in the stands wore new navy blue belted smocks with oversea caps to match. The Athletics dispensed with the regular opening day rituals and there was no parade to centerfield.

Joe Dugan took batting practice, but his injured leg kept him out of the line-up. When Herb Pennock, who was scheduled to start, hurt his foot in batting practice, Yankee manager Miller Huggins had to make a last minute pitching replacement and called on Urban Shocker, a right-hander.

With batting and fielding practice ended, the crowd and players came to attention for the national anthem. Unfurling in the breeze, a new American flag was raised slowly by an employee of the Athletics standing in the extreme corner of the grandstand roof. Afterwards, Ty Cobb, Eddie Collins, and coach Kid Gleason of the Athletics were presented with three big floral horseshoe wreaths from the Penn Athletic Club and other donors. Teammates Jimmy Dykes and Ed Rommel were given traveling bags from the Strawbridge & Clothier Athletic Association.

Wearing new blue coats and gray flannel trousers, the umpires took their positions. With the Athletics in the field, Lefty Grove, the Athletics' pitcher, was ready. Wearing the home uniform of the Athletics, Grove's flannel jersey and pants were white and he wore a black belt. The familiar symbol of the white elephant was sewn on the left side of Grove's jersey with sleeves that ran just below the elbow. His cap was white with a dark bill and dark piping along the seams. He wore black cleats and white stockings with a blue stripe.

After Mayor Kendrick rose in his box and threw the ceremonial first pitch to Mickey Cochrane, the Athletics' catcher, Earle Combs, the Yankees' lead off hitter, stepped to home plate swinging three bats and discarding two. Combs wore a gray flannel uniform with the word "YANKEES" in navy blue block letters across the chest. He wore two colored stirrups, navy blue on top and rust on the bottom.

The Line-Ups

Yankees	Athletics
Earle Combs cf	Eddie Collins 2b
Mark Koenig ss	Bill Lamar lf
Babe Ruth lf	Ty Cobb rf

Lou Gehrig 1b
Bob Meusel rf
Tony Lazzeri 2b
Mike Gazella 3b
John Grabowski c
Urban Shocker p

Al Simmons cf
Sammy Hale 3b
Dudley Branom 1b
Mickey Cochrane c
Joe Boley ss
Lefty Grove p

With the game scoreless in the top of the fourth, Combs singled to left field. With Koenig at bat, Grove unleashed a wild pitch and Combs went to second base. When Koenig doubled to left field, Combs scored. However, the Athletics jumped ahead 3 to 1 in the bottom of the inning on triples by Simmons and Cochrane, singles by Branom and Boley, and a sacrifice by Hale.

Opening the fifth, Grove walked Meusel. After retiring Lazzeri and Gazella, Grabowski singled to left. When the ball got passed Lamar in left field, Meusel scored. Grabowski advanced to third. Grove then walked Shocker. With runners on the corners, Combs singled to left. Grabowski scored, tying the game at three.

With the game tied at four after six, the Athletics took a three-run lead in the seventh when Shocker gave up singles to Collins and Lamar and a walk to Cobb. With the bases loaded, Huggins brought in Wilcy Moore, a right-hander. On a three and two count, Simmons singled over second base, scoring Collins and Lamar. Cobb raced to third. When Hale forced Simmons at second base, Cobb came home. The Athletics led 7 to 4.

In the eighth, Gehrig's wild return throw to third base to double up Branom gave the Athletics' another run. In the final frame, Gehrig doubled to left and scored when Meusel singled past Hale at third base; however, Jack Quinn, a right-hander, went on to retire the Yanks.

Final score: Athletics 8, Yankees 5.

Yankee Notebook for Wednesday, April 20, 1927: The loss was the Yankees second in a row . . . On the mound, Shocker (1-1) gave up ten hits in 6 1/3 innings, and Moore yielded two hits in 1 2/3 . . . For the Athletics, Grove went five innings and Quinn four . . . Combs and Gehrig each had three hits . . . Koenig had two doubles . . . Ruth went hitless in four official plate appearances . . . The Yanks also hit into four double plays; infielders Collins, Boley, and Branom figured in three of them. Simmons doubled Koenig at the plate in the fourth after catching Gehrig's fly . . . Gehrig, Gazella, and Meusel made errors.

On Opening Day at Comiskey Park in Chicago, a crowd of 30,000 watched the White Sox lose to the Indians, 5 to 4. At Detroit's Navin Field, Tiger southpaw Earl Whitehill went the distance and shutout the Browns, 7 to 0, with more than 35,000 on hand. Detroit's Bob Fothergill hit a home run over the left field fence and drove in two runs in the fifth.

For the first time in thirty-eight years, the St. Louis Cardinals unfurled the league championship pennant in St. Louis. With 12,000 people at Sportsman's Park, Wee Willie Sherdel held the Cubs to five hits as the Cardinals won 4 to 2. At the Polo Grounds in New York on Opening Day, 50,000 people saw the Giants defeat the Phillies, 5 to 1. On the official Opening Day at Ebbets Field in Brooklyn, 20,000 fans and National League President John A. Heydler watched the Robins beat the Braves, 4 to 3. The win ended Brooklyn's seven-game losing streak.

The fans that came early to Shibe Park on Thursday, April 21, 1927 witnessed some long ball hitting in batting practice. Babe Ruth hit three balls over the right field wall in succession, and Al Simmons socked one over the roof of the left field stands.

Named after the Athletics' principal owner, Ben Shibe, Shibe Park opened on April 12, 1909. The ballpark was in North Philadelphia, located between Lehigh Avenue, North 20th Street, Somerset Street, and North 21st Street. Shibe Park was the first ballpark built totally of concrete and steel.

Alterations to the ballpark occurred over the years. By 1927 it was double-decked, roofed, and enclosed with the exception of the playing field in right. There was a 12-foot high concrete wall in right field and a 12-foot fence in left field, constructed of a concrete base and wire screen. Down the foul line it was 334 feet from home plate to left field; 468 feet to center field, and 331 down the foul line to right field.

With a crowd of 25,000 in the stands, Waite Hoyt, a right-hander, started for the Yankees. Right-hander Samuel Gray opened for the Athletics. Leading off the game, Combs singled to center field. After Koenig lined to Cobb in right, Ruth walked. Gehrig became the base runner when he forced Ruth at second base. Meusel then tripled, scoring Combs and Gehrig.

After the Athletics went ahead 3 to 2 in the third, the Yankees tied the game in the fourth and took a 6 to 3 lead in the fifth. After the Athletics' fought back to tie the game at six in the fifth on timely singles by Branom and Cochrane, Huggins brought Wilcy Moore, a right-hander, into the game. With one out, Zach Wheat, who batted for Boley, fouled out to Collins, the Yankee catcher, and Moore tossed out Rommel to end the rally.

The Yankees broke open the game in the sixth. Combs singled to left, but he was forced by Koenig at second base on a throw from Rommel to Chick Galloway, who had replaced Boley at short. On the attempted double play, Galloway threw wild to Branom at first. Koenig moved to second. Rommel walked Ruth. Gehrig came up to bat with runners at first and second. The young slugger hit a ball against the base of the upper deck in left field for a home run. As Koenig, Ruth, and Gehrig circled the bases, the Yankees led 9 to 6.

With Gehrig and Meusel on base in the eighth and one run in, Lazzeri belted a home run into the left field balcony. Moore retired the Athletics in the eighth and ninth.

Final score: Yankees 13, Athletics 6.

Yankee Notebook for Thursday, April 21, 1927: Waite Hoyt pitched 4 1/3 innings and gave up nine hits and six runs . . . Moore (1-0) gave up one hit in 4 2/3 innings and walked one . . . It was Moore's first major league victory . . . At the plate, the Yankees had fifteen hits; three each by Combs, Lazzeri, and Meusel . . . Meusel had a single, double, and triple . . . Gehrig's home run was his third . . . Ruth was walked four times and had his first hit of the series—a bunt single.

Gehrig and Lazzeri each had a total of five runs driven in . . . So far that season, Gehrig had driven in 19 runs, Meusel 14, Lazzeri 13, and Ruth 1 . . . After an argument the previous day, Lazzeri and Simmons exchanged words again.

Miller Huggins was informed after the game that an X-ray of Pennock's left foot showed an old fracture that had healed over; Pennock never knew about it. The present injury, which happened during batting practice the day before, was diagnosed as only a bad bruise. On crutches, Pennock was not expected to pitch for a week.

At Fenway Park in Boston, the Red Sox opened their home season with a loss to the Senators, 7 to 4. Five runs off Red Sox hurler Ted Wingfield were enough to give the Senators the victory. Jack Tobin hit a home run with the bases loaded in Boston's half of the sixth. Meanwhile, rain postponed the game between the Browns and Tigers at Detroit, and wet grounds in Chicago cancelled the contest between the Indians and White Sox.

In front of 10,000 shivering fans in Brooklyn, Braves' right-hander Bob Smith pitched a two-hit shutout over the Robins at Ebbets Field, 3 to 0. The loss was the Robins' eighth in ten starts. At the Polo Grounds, the Phillies defeated the Giants 4 to 2 behind the strong pitching of Alex Ferguson. Russ Wrightstone and Cy Williams hit home runs for the Phillies. Freddie Lindstrom homered for the Giants.

Rain delayed the beginning of the game as a crowd of 30,000 came out to Forbes Field in Pittsburgh on Opening Day and saw the Pirates defeat the Reds, 3 to 2. Pirate hurler Ray Kremer homered to tie the score.

The attendance figures for the last two opening day games of the 1927 season—30,000 at Pittsburgh and 10,000 at Boston (AL)—raised the total for the 16 openers to 478,500, exceeding the 1926 mark of 440,000 by 38,500.

Rain postponed the game on Friday, April 22 between the Yankees and Athletics in Philadelphia. The weather actually helped Miller Huggins with his pitching plans. With the injury to Pennock, he would have had to start either Joe Giard or George Pipgras that day. With the game rained out, however, Ruether was then scheduled to be the starter the next day, Shocker at Washington on Sunday, Hoyt at New York on Monday, and possibly Pennock on Tuesday.

In Boston, Stan Coveleski and Firpo Marberry held Boston to six hits as the Senators beat the Red Sox in the second game of the series,

7 to 3, at Fenway Park. Rain postponed the scheduled game between the Browns and Tigers at Detroit. The game between the Indians and White Sox at Chicago was canceled because of cold weather.

Reports circulated in the New York newspapers that Mayor James J. Walker of New York City had received an offer to be President of the American League at a salary of $100,000. Ban Johnson, the President of the American League, was expected to relinquish his position due to age and recent illness.

In near freezing weather 4,000 fans at Forbes Field in Pittsburgh saw the Pirates, behind the fine pitching of Lee Meadows, continue their winning streak by defeating the Reds, 3 to 1. Wet grounds postponed the scheduled games in New York City between the Phillies and Giants and Braves and Robins. Cold weather forced the rescheduling of the game between the Cubs and Cardinals at St. Louis.

With clear weather in Philadelphia on Saturday, April 23, 1927, 35,000 fans came out to Shibe Park to see the Yankees and Athletics. Miller Huggins started left-hander Dutch Ruether. Connie Mack sent Rube Walberg, also a left-hander, to the mound. Thirty-year-old George Elvin Walberg from Pine City, Minnesota stood six feet and one and half inches tall. The slender southpaw was in his fifth season with Philadelphia, winning twelve and losing ten (2.80 era) in 1926.

Coming to bat against Walberg in the first inning, Ruth and Gehrig hit back-to-back home runs for the first time that season. Trailing 2 to 1 in the third, the Athletics' came back and took a 3 to 2 lead on walks to Collins and Cobb and singles by Simmons, Hale, and Branom. In the fourth, the Yankees tied the game on a walk to Lazzeri, a single by Gazella, and sacrifice fly by Grabowski.

Huggins ran out from the bench in the fifth to complain over a decision by umpire Brick Owens. He had called Combs out for interfering with Eddie Collins, who had fielded a grounder hit by Koenig. On the play, Combs was running at top speed and tried to jump over the ball and made contact with Collins. In the bottom half of the inning, Huggins complained when Simmons made no attempt to dodge a slow pitch by Ruether and was awarded first base.

Huggins lost both arguments.

With the game tied at three, right-hander Wilcy Moore, who came into the game in the eighth, pitched the bottom of the ninth. Batting for Perkins, Zach Wheat hit a line drive toward center field. Koenig rushed over, fielded the ball, and threw out Wheat from a twisting position. After singles by Boley and Walberg, Mickey Cochrane batted for Dykes. Cochrane hit a grounder to Lazzeri, who tossed to Koenig at second, forcing Collins. When Koenig threw to first base on the attempted double play, his throw was high. Gehrig did not leave his feet. The ball sailed away. With the ball rolling to the stands, Boley scored the winning run.

Final score: Athletics 4, Yankees 3.

Yankee Notebook for Saturday, April 23, 1927: The Yankee pitching staff turned in another fine effort that afternoon despite the loss . . . Ruether pitched seven innings and gave up eleven hits and three runs . . . Moore (1-1) pitched 1 2/3, yielding two hits in the ninth . . . The Babe hit Walberg's first pitch over the right field wall for his second home run of the season . . . Gehrig hit his fourth . . . Before the late inning error, Koenig had a fine day handling nine chances perfectly in the field . . . The time of the game was 1:57.

At Comiskey Park in Chicago, the White Sox defeated the Indians, 8 to 2, tying the series. Winning their first home game of the season at Fenway Park, the Red Sox defeated the Senators, 5 to 4. Boston hurler Slim Harriss pitched a complete game. In Detroit, a total of 21 Tigers players, including six pitchers, was used as the Browns triumphed 15 to 10. George Sisler had four hits for St. Louis.

In St. Louis, Flint Rhem held the Cubs to two hits in his first start of the season as the Cardinals won 7 to 0. Ten thousand fans came out to Ebbets Field in the cold to see Wilbert Robinson's Robins play Dave Bancroft's Braves as Boston beat Brooklyn, 4 to 2. Meanwhile, John McGraw's pitching staff turned in a third straight day of good pitching as Hugh McQuillan and the Giants turned back the Phillies, 5 to 1. While at Pittsburgh, snow fell for several minutes during the game at Forbes Field as the Reds won their second game by defeating the Pirates, 6 to 4.

Major League Baseball Standings
April 23, 1927
American League

	Won	Lost	P.C.
New York	7	3	.750
St. Louis	4	2	.667
Washington	6	4	.600
Detroit	3	2	.600
Philadelphia	5	5	.500
Cleveland	4	5	.444
Chicago	4	6	.400
Boston	2	8	.200

National League

	Won	Lost	P.C.
Pittsburgh	7	2	.778
Boston	8	4	.667
St. Louis	5	3	.625
New York	6	4	.600
Philadelphia	5	4	.556
Chicago	3	5	.375
Cincinnati	2	7	.222
Brooklyn	2	9	.182

Chapter 7

Griffith Stadium and Fenway Park

The Yankees traveled by train from Philadelphia to Washington, D.C. for one game with the Senators on Sunday, April 24, 1927. Under partly cloudy skies, 20,000 fans came out to Griffith Stadium to see the two teams play each other for the first time that season. Located in Northwest Washington, D.C., Griffith Stadium was about two miles north of the White House, located between Georgia Avenue, U Street, Fifth Street, and W Street NW.

In 1920, the old League Park was rebuilt and renamed after Clark Griffith, the owner and president of the Senators. It was 407 feet from home plate down the foul line to left field; 421 to center field, and 320 down the foul line to right field. There was a 30-foot concrete wall in right field. A ball hit off the wall was in play. That afternoon right-hander Urban Shocker of the Yankees faced the Senators' Hollis "Sloppy" Thurston.

John Hollis Thurston, 27, from Fremont, Nebraska was obtained by the White Sox from the Browns in 1923. In his rookie season that year, Thurston, who was nicknamed "Sloppy," won seven for the White Sox. In his second season, 1924, he won 23; but in 1925 and 1926 he was less effective winning 10 and 6, respectively. The Senators signed Thurston for the 1927 season.

The Line-Ups

Yankees	Senators
Earle Combs, cf	Sam Rice rf
Mark Koenig ss	Bucky Harris 2b
Babe Ruth rf	Tris Speaker cf

Lou Gehrig 1b	Goose Goslin lf
Bob Meusel lf	Joe Judge 1b
Tony Lazzeri 2b	Buddy Myer ss
Mike Gazella 3b	Ossie Bluege 3b
Pat Collins c	Muddy Ruel c
Urban Shocker p	Hollis Thurston p

The Senators took their positions in the field. They wore plain white uniforms with piping on the sleeve ends and collar. A red, white, and blue patriotic shield patch was sewn on the left sleeve. The caps were white with a red bill and there was a dark blue "W" on the front. The players' stockings were solid white with a narrow blue stripe bordered by red stripes at the calf.

Meusel swung at Thurston's pitch and hit the ball well. It landed in the left-field bleachers for a home run. It was Meusel's first of the season. The Senators threatened in the fourth after Shocker walked Harris, but Speaker hit into a lightning fast double play—Lazzeri to Koenig to Gehrig. With the bases empty, Judge then doubled, but he was stranded there. With the score tied at one in the sixth, Ruth hit a home run off Thurston that sailed over the right field fence. Meusel then singled and Lazzeri and Gazella walked. With the bases loaded, Huggins sent Cedric Durst up to bat for Collins. When Durst tripled, Meusel, Lazzeri, and Gazella scored. Harris then brought Firpo Marberry, a right-hander, into the game. On a squeeze play by Shocker, Durst scored from third. The Yankees went ahead 6 to 1.

In the home half of the seventh, Gazella made a bad throw from third base after making a good one-handed stop of Rice's slow grounder. After Rice moved to second on the throwing error, he scored on Harris's double. Shocker retired the Senators in the eighth and ninth.

Final score: Yankees 6, Senators 2.

Yankee Notebook for Sunday, April 24, 1927: Ruth's home run was his third. The ball cleared a forty-five foot wall, some 328 feet from the plate and traveled more than 400 feet before it disappeared . . . That afternoon the Babe had a total of three hits; Meusel and Gazella each had two . . . On the hill, Shocker (2-1) pitched a complete game, scattering eight hits, walking two, and striking out four . . . Lazzeri handled eight chances in the field without a miscue . . . Gazella made an error.

When Marberry hit Meusel on the right elbow, Trainer Doc Woods and Huggins came onto the field. Fortunately, Meusel was not injured . . . After the game, the Yankees and Senators traveled in a special train to New York arriving about midnight . . . The teams were scheduled to begin a three game series the next day at Yankee Stadium.

Scoring five runs in the second inning at Dunn Field, the Browns knocked Indians' starter Dutch Levsen out of the box and went on to win, 9 to 4. In the first game of the series at Comiskey Park, a double steal by Bob Fothergill and Lu Blue and some bunched hits gave the Tigers a win over the White Sox, 4 to 3. At New Haven, Connecticut, the Athletics lost to an Eastern League all-star team, 3 to 2. Joe Wood, a former American Leaguer and the baseball coach at Yale University, was at the game and visited with Ty Cobb and other friends.

Cardinals' star Grover Cleveland Alexander bested former Chicago Cub teammate Vic Aldridge of the Pirates in a pitching duel, 2 to 1. Pie Traynor homered for Pittsburgh. At Redland Field, Charlie Root scattered seven hits over nine innings as the Cubs defeated the Reds, 5 to 3. In New York, the Braves came into the Polo Grounds for one game and were battered by the Giants, 12 to 8. Meanwhile, on a bitter cold day at Ebbets Field, 15,000 fans saw the Phillies send the Robins to their tenth loss out of twelve starts since the start of the season, 5 to 1.

Babe Ruth was talking to reporters in the Yankee clubhouse on Monday, April 25, 1927. The subject turned to home runs.

"I don't suppose I'll ever break that 1921 record [59 home runs,]" said Ruth. "To do that you've got to start early, and the pitchers have got to pitch to you. I don't start early, and the pitchers haven't really pitched to me in four seasons. I get more bad balls to hit than any other six men—and fewer good ones."

With 5,000 fans braving the cold at Yankee Stadium in New York, Miller Huggins gave the pitching assignment to right-hander Waite Hoyt. Senators' manager Bucky Harris sent George Murray, a right-hander, to the mound. The twenty-eight year old native of Charlotte,

North Carolina, nicknamed "Smiler," began his career with the Yankees in 1922 (4-2, 3.95 era). He played with the Red Sox in 1923 and 1924, winning 7 and 2, respectively. After spending 1925 in the minors, the six foot two inch Murray joined the Senators in 1926, winning six and losing three, posting a 5.67 era.

The Line-Ups

Senators	Yankees
Sam Rice rf	Earle Combs cf
Bucky Harris 2b	Mark Koenig ss
Tris Speaker cf	Babe Ruth rf
Goose Goslin lf	Lou Gehrig 1b
Joe Judge 1b	Bob Meusel lf
Buddy Myer ss	Tony Lazzeri 2b
Ossie Bluege 3b	Mike Gazella 3b
Mickey O'Neil c	John Grabowski c
George Murray p	Waite Hoyt p

Sam Rice came to the plate to open the game. Rice wore a plain gray uniform, with a red, white, and blue patriotic patch on the sleeve and a black belt and black cleats. He wore a gray cap and red bill. On the front of the cap was a dark "W". Rice's stockings were white with a narrow blue stripe bordered by a red stripe.

With the Senators leading 1 to 0 in the second inning, Murray was at bat with two strikes. He seemed to have swung at a ball that should have been the third strike. When Umpire Brick Owens said no, Huggins and Hoyt complained. After Owens called in the other umpires, Red Ormsby and George Hildebrand, he reversed himself and called Murray out.

The Senators complained vociferously.

Insults were directed at Owens. He warned the bench twice. When the taunts continued and Owens could not tell who said them, he sent the 20 reserve players from the Senators' dugout to the clubhouse. The march there looked like the parade to the flagpole on opening day.

When the game resumed in the home half of the second, Gazella doubled past Bluege. After stealing third base, Gazella scored when Grabowski's sharp grounder got past Myer at short.

Garland Braxton, a left-hander, pitched the fourth for the Senators. After Gazella walked, Hoyt doubled him home. The Yankees led 2 to 1. In the fifth, Braxton walked Gehrig, who went to second on Meusel's sacrifice and scored on Grabowski's single. Horace Lisenbee, a rookie right-hander, pitched the seventh for Washington. Lisenbee walked Combs. When Gehrig tripled, Combs scored.

Trailing 4 to 1 in the seventh, Rice singled off Hoyt. When Harris singled, Rice raced to third and scored on Speaker's sacrifice fly. Down by two runs, Goslin hit Hoyt's first pitch into the right-field seats. The game was tied at four.

In the top of the eighth, the Senators went ahead, 5 to 4. Hoyt walked Bluege with one out. After he stole second, Ruel hit a grounder to Koenig, who threw to Gehrig for the out. Bluege moved to third on the play. Sam West, who had replaced Rice in right field, then hit a slow grounder to Lazzeri. When West beat the throw for an infield hit, Bluege scored.

The Yankees threatened in the eighth. After Koenig singled, Lisenbee struck out Ruth swinging for the second out. Gehrig then doubled to left. Koenig raced to third base. Meusel ended the threat, however, when he flied out to Goslin. Lisenbee retired the Yankees in the ninth.

Final score: Senators 5, Yankees 4.

Yankee Notebook for Monday, April 25, 1927: Hoyt (2-1) pitched a complete game and took the loss. He gave up five runs and nine hits, walking five, and striking out five . . . For Washington, Murray went two innings, Braxton four, and Lisenbee three . . . Lisenbee was the winning pitcher . . . Offensively, the Yankees had nine hits and left thirteen men on the bases . . . Koenig had three singles . . . Gehrig smashed two doubles . . . Gazella and Hoyt also doubled.

The fans saw a pretty play when Judge stroked a grounder off Gehrig's foot and the ball bounded to Lazzeri, who tossed the ball to Hoyt covering first base before Judge touched the bag . . . Sending the

Senator reserves to the clubhouse delayed the game. Whenever a pinch hitter or a substitute runner was needed, a messenger was sent. That took from five to eight minutes.

In Chicago, White Sox reliever George Connally replaced Red Faber in the sixth and stopped a Tiger rally as Chicago defeated Detroit in ten innings, 7 to 6. At Dunn Field, Benn Karr held the Browns to four hits, and his teammates pounded out fourteen as the Indians won 9 to 1. Cold weather postponed the game between the Athletics and Red Sox at Boston.

At Sportsman's Park, Jesse Haines won his third straight in as many starts as he outpitched Ray Kremer and the Cardinals defeated the Pirates, 1 to 0. In Cincinnati, a seven-run Reds' rally in the eighth featured five consecutive singles and gave the hometown team a victory over the Cubs, 11 to 9. At Baker Bowl, the Phillies took the first game of the series from the Braves, 12 to 4.

Cold weather cancelled the scheduled game with the Senators at Yankee Stadium in the Bronx on Tuesday, April 26, 1927. Huggins almost smiled when the game was called off. The postponement gave his pitchers more time to recuperate and rest. The strong start by the club has surprised many, even Huggins. The team's performance prior to the season did not give him the expectation of a fast start.

Huggins felt Koenig's play had been exceptional. He was batting .429 and had played well in the field. During spring training, Koenig did not look very good and his game was off. There had even been some discussion about benching him in favor of Ray Morehart.

At Fenway Park in Boston, Ty Cobb stole home, had three hits, and ended the game with an unassisted double play as the Athletics overcame a six run lead by the Red Sox to win, 9 to 8. In Cleveland, Willis Hudlin held the Browns to five hits as the Indians won, 6 to 2. Meanwhile at Comiskey Park, Ted Lyons gave up only six hits as the White Sox hammered four Tiger pitchers and won, 9 to 3.

Under a cold, gray sky at Ebbets Field, the Giants defeated their metropolitan rivals Robins, 7 to 2. At Sportsman's Park, Lee Meadows won his fourth straight as the Pirates regained first place after triumphing over the Cardinals, 9 to 5. In the third game of the series at Redland

Field, the Reds scored six runs in the sixth and beat the Cubs, 8 to 5. Threatening weather postponed the game between the Braves and Phillies at Philadelphia.

The Yankees had another day off as rain cancelled the game at the Stadium in New York with the Senators on Wednesday, April 27, 1927. That night the Yankee players, club officials, and some film critics went to the Friars Club in New York City as guests of Babe Ruth. They watched a pre-release of Ruth's Hollywood film, "Babe Comes Home," which would be soon on Broadway.

The "Babe Comes Home" was about a ball player named Babe Dugan played by Ruth. Dugan was filthy and careless about his tobacco chewing. His laundry girl, played by Anna Q. Nilsson, finally rebelled about his habit and the condition of his clothes. There was some note exchanging and a meeting. They fell in love and planned on marrying. However, just before the wedding, she became angry over a wedding gift of hand-painted cuspidors and a huge box of plug tobacco; she cancelled the wedding and returned to the laundry.

Babe's film portrayed familiar events of the time. There was a big game for the pennant. Dugan was in a slump because he has sworn off tobacco chewing. The girl leaned over the box and handed Dugan a plug of chewing tobacco. Dugan hit a home run and the team won the pennant. Dugan and the girl were together again. Although critics thought Ruth was better than expected, none of the critics felt John Barrymore or any other actor had to be worried about the Babe as a competitor.

In Boston, the Athletics won their second in a row behind the strong pitching of Lefty Grove and defeated the Red Sox, 4 to 1. In extra innings at Dunn Field, the Browns defeated the Indians, 4 to 2, and evened its series. At Comiskey Park, the White Sox made it three out of four as they defeated the Tigers, 7 to 2, in the final game of the series.

At Redland Field, Pete Donohue lost his third game by a score of 2 to 1 as the Cubs defeated the Reds behind Sheriff Blake. The scheduled games between the Giants and Robins at Brooklyn and Braves and Phillies at Philadelphia were postponed because of rain.

ii

The Yankees were idle for the third straight day as cold weather cancelled the game with the Boston Red Sox at Fenway Park on Thursday, April 28, 1927. Despite the sunshine, chilling winds swept over Boston from early morning. The postponement was announced at noon. Many Red Sox fans, however, made the trip to Fenway Park unaware the game had been called off. Fans always came out in large numbers to watch the Babe, for whom they still had a warm affection. They remembered when he played in Boston years ago.

Miller Huggins decided that several of the players were in need of work and sent a squad out to Fenway Park early that afternoon. The players got into uniform and worked out for about an hour. Huggins included Herb Pennock and Joe Dugan, both recovering from injuries. Urban Shocker and one or two other veterans made the trip voluntarily. All the young pitchers and second string players also worked out.

The Yankees were told that the afternoon's postponed game would be played when the team returned to Boston June 20 for a four game series.

At Shibe Park in Philadelphia, Connie Mack's Athletics pounded six Senator hurlers and moved into second place with a win, 15 to 7. Meanwhile, the Tigers scored five runs in a seventh inning rally and beat the Indians, 6 to 5, at Navin Field. In a pitching duel between Chicago's Tommy Thomas and St. Louis's Tom Zachary, the White Sox defeated the Browns, 2 to 1 in eleven innings, at Comiskey Park.

Flint Rhem won his second start in a row as the Cardinals defeated the Reds, 3 to 1, at Sportsman's Park. At Forbes Field, the Cubs pounded four Pirate pitchers for seventeen hits and won, 16 to 4. Zeke Barnes turned in a strong pitching performance at the Polo Grounds as the Giants beat the Braves, 4 to 3. Rogers Hornsby of the Giants led the league in batting with a .438 mark. At Ebbets Field, with the score tied in the ninth, Russ Wrightstone hit a grand slam home run as the Phillies beat the Robins, 8 to 4.

The weather finally cleared in Boston on Friday, April 29, 1927. Before the game with the Red Sox at Fenway Park, Babe Ruth and Will A. "Babe" Philbrick clowned for the photographers. Philbrick was a well-known comedian appearing in the "The Vagabond King" in town. There was the natural exchange of roles; Ruth was clowning and Philbrick was slugging. That day Dutch Ruether, a left-hander, and right-hander Slim Harriss opposed each other.

The Line-Ups

Yankees	Red Sox
Earle Combs cf	Pee Wee Wanninger ss
Mark Koenig ss	Fred Haney 3b
Babe Ruth lf	Jack Tobin rf
Lou Gehrig 1b	Ira Flagstead cf
Bob Meusel rf	Baby Doll Jacobson lf
Tony Lazzeri 2b	Phil Todt 1b
Joe Dugan 3b	Bill Regan 2b
Pat Collins c	Fred Hofmann c
Dutch Ruether p	Slim Harriss p

The Red Sox players wore plain white uniforms with pinstripes. The caps were white with a red bill. There was no lettering on the caps. The upper half of the white stockings was red, and they wore black belts and black cleats. Combs opened the game with a walk. When Koenig singled to right, Combs raced to third base. Ruth then hit a hot grounder toward right field. Todt, the first baseman, fielded the ball and turned it into a double play—Todt to Wanninger to Todt—as Combs scored.

In the third, Combs was safe on Regan's error and scored on Koenig's triple to right center. When Ruth singled to right, Koenig scored. After Gehrig tripled to center, Ruth scored. Meusel then struck out, but Lazzeri singled, scoring Gehrig. The Yankees led 5 to 0.

With Harriss on the mound in the fifth, Ruth hit a home run that landed in the bleachers in right field. Lazzeri then doubled to right. Dugan singled to center. Both runners scored when Collins tripled to the right field bleachers making the score 8 to 0. Ruth doubled off the high fence in deep left center off right-hander Del Lundgren, who pitched the sixth for the Red Sox. When the ball bounded back to center fielder Flagstead, Ruth held at second. After Meusel tripled to right, Ruth scored.

Lundgren pitched a scoreless seventh, and Rudy Sommers, a left-hander, hurled the final two innings. Ruether held the Red Sox scoreless in their final turn at bat.

Final score: Yankees 9, Red Sox 0.

Yankee Notebook for Friday, April 29, 1927: Ruether (3-0) pitched a complete game, giving up no runs, allowing six hits, striking out one, hitting a batter, and walking four . . . Ruether was strong when the Red Sox threatened. In eight of the nine innings, Boston had one or more runners on base but reached second in only two innings.

The Babe had three hits: a home run, double, and single, and he drove in two runs and scored three times . . . Ruth and Gehrig led the American League with four home runs a piece . . . For the Red Sox, Harriss, Lundgren, and Sommers gave up twelve hits for twenty-five bases . . . Koenig, Gehrig, Meusel and Collins tripled.

Ruth walked that day, his 17th in 14 games, and was on a pace to set a new record for base on balls . . . By actual count, the Babe was handed 15 notes on the bench sent from friends at the game . . . The Yankees led the American League in batting at .342 . . . Individual Yankee batting averages after thirteen games played: Gehrig .447; Koenig .429; Meusel .415; Combs .357; Ruth .273 and Lazzeri .250.

Scoring seven runs in the sixth, the Athletics overcame the Senators' lead and won their fifth straight game by a score of 8 to 7 at Shibe Park. At Detroit's Navin Field, Rip Collins started his first game and led the Tigers to a victory over the Indians, 5 to 2. Rain postponed the game between the Browns and the White Sox at Chicago.

Home runs by Freddie Lindstrom, Ty Tyson, and Bill Terry paced the Giants over the Braves, 10 to 3, at the Polo Grounds. In Brooklyn, southpaw Jim Jumbo Elliott pitched a four-hit shutout as the last place Robins defeated the Phillies, 7 to 0. Rain postponed the games between the Cubs and Pirates at Pittsburgh and Reds and Cardinals at St. Louis.

On Saturday, April 30, 1927, 17,000 fans, the largest crowd of the season at Fenway Park, came out to see the Red Sox and Yankees. Mayor Jimmy Walker of New York City was at the ballpark and sat in a box seat behind the Yankee dugout. Urban Shocker, a right-hander, faced left-hander Hal Wiltse.

The Yankees led 1 to 0 after eight innings.

In the ninth, Meusel singled to left and Lazzeri sacrificed him to second. After Grabowski was intentionally walked, Shocker singled to right, scoring Meusel.

Down by two runs in the Red Sox ninth, Flagstead led off and singled to left. When Jacobson beat out a grounder behind third, Red Rollings came in as a pinch runner. Todt bunted. Shocker threw to third to get Flagstead, but Umpire Will Evans called him safe. Jack Rothrock then pinch-hit for Regan. With the bases loaded, Rothrock doubled down the right field line. Flagstead and Rollings scored, tying the game at two.

Huggins then brought Wilcy Moore, a right-hander, into the game. Hartley was intentionally walked. With the bases filled, Moore struck out Wiltse. Then Wanninger hit to Lazzeri, who threw home and forced Todt. With two outs, Moore got two strikes on Haney. The count ran to three and two. With the runners in motion, Moore threw the ball high and inside. Rothrock was forced home with the winning run.

Final score: Red Sox 3, Yankees 2.

Yankee Notebook for Saturday, April 30, 1927: The Yankees had kept the Red Sox scoreless in the series through seventeen innings before the ninth inning rally . . . Shocker (2-2) took the loss, pitching eight innings and giving up eight hits . . . For the Red Sox, Wiltse pitched a complete game, his second against the Yanks . . . The Yankees out hit the Red Sox ten hits to eight . . . Meusel's double was the team's only extra base hit . . . Combs had a stolen base.

The Yankees were scheduled to play the Athletics the next day at the Stadium in the Bronx . . . A crowd of 65,000 to 70,000 fans was expected . . . Afterwards, the Yankees would go on the road until May 24, when they would return and host the Athletics again.

At Comiskey Park in Chicago, Ted Blankenship pitched a four-hit shutout over the Browns as the White Sox won their fifth straight game, 2 to 0. In Detroit, the Indians beat the Tigers to take the third game of the series, 6 to 2. The Indians' Willis Hudlin pitched the entire game, yielding ten hits, walking two, and striking out three. Rain postponed the game between the Senators and Athletics at Philadelphia.

The Reds and Cardinals split the season's first double header with St. Louis winning the first game, 8 to 4, and losing the second, 9 to 8, at Sportsman's Park. At Forbes Field, home runs by Earl Webb and Hack Wilson led the Cubs over the Pirates, 5 to 4. Going into the ninth one run behind at the Polo Grounds, the Giants rallied and defeated the Braves, 8 to 7. The Braves' Jack Fournier homered. For the second day in a row the Robins beat the Phillies, 2 to 1. Ten thousand fans were at Ebbets Field that afternoon.

Major League Baseball Standings
April 30, 1927
American League

	Won	Lost	P.C.
New York	9	5	.643
Philadelphia	9	5	.643
Chicago	9	7	.563
Washington	7	7	.500
Detroit	6	6	.500
St. Louis	6	6	.500
Cleveland	7	9	.437
Boston	3	11	.214

National League

	Won	Lost	P.C.
New York	11	4	.733
St. Louis	9	5	.643
Philadelphia	8	6	.571
Pittsburgh	8	6	.571
Chicago	7	7	.500
Boston	8	9	.471
Cincinnati	5	11	.313
Brooklyn	4	12	.250

Chapter 8

Heading West

Before the club began an extended road trip, 70,000 fans watched the Yankees play the Philadelphia Athletics at Yankee Stadium on Sunday, May 1, 1927. Both teams were tied for first place, and the Athletics came into the game with five straight wins. The game was in New York that afternoon because blue laws in effect in Philadelphia did not permit professional baseball to be played on Sundays. Athletics' fans came by train to New York City to see the game.

With the gates at the stadium closing before 3 o'clock, some 20,000 looking for general admission tickets were turned away. Ed Barrow, the Yankees' business manager, announced that 65,000 people had paid to attend the game; it was a new major league record for paid admissions.

Returning from his foot injury, Yankee southpaw Herb Pennock, who last pitched on April 15 against the Athletics at Yankee Stadium, was on the mound. Veteran right-hander John Quinn pitched for the Athletics.

The Line-Ups

Athletics	Yankees
Eddie Collins 2b	Earle Combs cf
Bill Lamar lf	Mark Koenig ss
Ty Cobb rf	Babe Ruth rf
Al Simmons cf	Lou Gehrig 1b
Sammy Hale 3b	Bob Meusel lf
Dudley Branom 1b	Tony Lazzeri 2b
Cy Perkins c	Joe Dugan 3b

Joe Boley ss	Pat Collins c
John Quinn p	Herb Pennock p

Ruth's ball sailed over his Cobb's head in right field. The Athletics' outfielder never even turned around; he just looked skyward and shrugged his shoulders. The ball landed at the exit gap in the right field bleacher section. Ruth's home run off Quinn with Koenig on first base gave the Yankees an early 2 to 0 lead.

With the Athletics leading 3 to 2 in the bottom of the sixth, Quinn walked Koenig. Gehrig then blasted a home run, making the score 4 to 3 in favor of the Yanks. When Quinn walked Meusel, manager Connie Mack brought in Charles William (Lefty) Willis, who retired the side.

In the eighth, the Yankees pulled ahead 7 to 3. Ruth got the scoring started when he hit his second home run of the game, this time off lefty Rube Walberg, who came into the game in the seventh. Gehrig then singled and scored after Meusel doubled down the right field line. On the throw to the plate, Meusel advanced to third, and Lazzeri's sacrifice fly brought him home. Pennock retired the Athletics in the ninth.

Final score: Yankees 7, Athletics 3.

Yankee Notebook for Sunday, May 1, 1927. That day Ruth hit two home runs and Gehrig one . . . The Babe had six home runs for the season and Gehrig five . . . Ruth's two home runs put him ahead of his 1921 pace when he hit a season high 59 home runs; the Babe hit his sixth that year on May 2.

The Yankees had only five hits, but they were good for fifteen bases . . . Pennock (2-0) pitched a complete game and gave up twelve hits . . . Quinn had the only extra base hit for the Athletics—a double . . . Pennock struck out one and did not walk a batter . . . In the field, Meusel and Dugan made errors . . . The Yanks left for Washington, D.C. that night and would visit the West—Chicago, St. Louis, Detroit, and Cleveland—before returning home on May 24.

At Navin Field in Detroit, Earl Whitehill blanked the Indians as the Tigers took the final game of the series, 7 to 0. At Griffith Stadium, Horace Lisenbee, in his first major league start, hurled a seven-hit shutout as the Senators defeated the Red Sox, 6 to 0. In Chicago, the

White Sox won their sixth straight game defeating the Browns, 7 to 6, at Comiskey Park.

In St. Louis, Frankie Frisch's third home run in two days paced the Cardinals to a victory over the Reds, 12 to 4. At Wrigley Field, a crowd of 35,000 watched the Pirates score two runs in the ninth and defeat Chicago, 7 to 6. Cubs' pitcher Charlie Root walked three men and gave up a hit in the ninth. In Brooklyn, 30,000 fans packed Ebbets Field and watched the Robins rally for two runs in the ninth to defeat the Giants, 4 to 3.

The Yankees began a long road trip at Griffith Stadium in Washington, D.C on Monday, May 2, 1927. Before the game with the Senators, Babe Ruth gave out new baseball gloves and balls to a group of boys. Walter Johnson, Washington's star pitcher, was presented with a silver loving cup at home plate by Nicholas F. Longworth, the Speaker of the U.S. House of Representatives. The trophy was first prize in a local newspaper contest.

Bucky Harris, the Senators' player-manager, took himself out of the starting line-up after he was hit in the leg and suffered a muscle bruise in morning batting practice. Meanwhile, in an effort to bolster their defense the Senators traded Charles "Buddy" Myer to the Red Sox for Emory "Topper" Rigney that morning. Both were shortstops. In 1926, Rigney led all American League shortstops with a .967 fielding mark. Rigney rushed over from Philadelphia in time to play in the game.

For the Yankees, Tony Lazzeri went into that game having played errorless ball. In sixteen games, the Yankee infielder had seventy-nine chances in the field. Right-hander Waite Hoyt pitched for New York.

Stan Coveleski, a right-hander, started for Washington. Stanley Anthony Covesleski—born Stanislaus Kowaslewski—was born July 13, 1889 in Shamokin, Pennsylvania. Signed by the Athletics in 1912, he won two and lost one; Coveleski did not pitch again in the major leagues until four years later. In 1916, he began a very successful career with the Cleveland Indians, winning more than twenty games from

1919-1923. He joined Washington in 1925 and won 20 and lost 5, for a .800 winning percentage. Coveleski won 14 the next season—1926.

The Line-Ups

Yankees	Senators
Earle Combs cf	Stuffy Stewart 2b
Mark Koenig ss	Sam Rice rf
Babe Ruth rf	Tris Speaker cf
Lou Gehrig 1b	Goose Goslin lf
Bob Meusel lf	Joe Judge 1b
Tony Lazzeri 2b	Topper Rigney ss
Joe Dugan 3b	Ossie Bluege 3b
John Grabowski c	Muddy Ruel c
Waite Hoyt p	Stan Coveleski p

Combs opened the game with a bunt. He reached first base on an error by Coveleski and raced to third on a single by Ruth. When Gehrig hit a sacrifice fly to Goslin in left field, Combs scored. Goslin was charged with an error on the throw in. Ruth went to second and later scored on Meusel's single to left field.

In the third, Garland Braxton, a left-hander, replaced Coveleski and the Yankees took a 4 to 1 lead. Braxton gave up a double to Gehrig on a ball that bounced against the right field signboard. Gehrig then scored on Meusel's single. In the home half of the third, the Senators picked up a run on a single by Speaker and a triple by Judge.

In the sixth, Lazzeri singled and scored after Dugan tripled to centerfield, making the score 6 to 2. After the Senators cut the lead to 6 to 4 in the seventh, General Crowder, a right-hander, replaced Braxton in the eighth. In that inning, Lazzeri hit a long drive for a home run into the centerfield bleachers.

The Yankees added two more runs in the ninth. When the Senators batted in the bottom of the inning, Bluege and Ruel singled off Hoyt. After Nick Cullop, hitting for Burke, singled, Bluege scored. Huggins then brought in Wilcy Moore, a right-hander, who forced the next three batters to ground out. Ruel scored on one of the groundouts.

Final score: Yankees 9, Senators 6.

Yankee Notebook for Monday, May 2, 1927: That afternoon the Yankees had seventeen hits . . . Meusel, Lazzeri and Dugan each had three, and included a home run by Lazzeri; triples by Dugan and Grabowski, and doubles by Gehrig and Meusel . . . Lazzeri's home run was his second . . . On the mound, Hoyt (3-1) weakened in the ninth after gave up two runs. Overall, he gave up nine hits, walked one and struck out one . . . In relief, Moore retired all three batters he faced in the ninth on ground balls.

Defensively, Dugan had two errors and Koenig one . . . Lazzeri had four chances in the field and played them cleanly, handling 83 chances in the Yankees' first 17 games without an error . . . Combs had a stolen base.

At Shibe Park in Philadelphia, the Athletics won the opener of a four game series over the Red Sox, 6 to 5 in ten innings. Scoring five runs in the ninth at Sportsman's Park, the Browns defeated the Indians, 7 to 6. In Detroit, the White Sox won their seventh straight game behind Ted Lyons and defeated the Tigers, 3 to 1, in the opening game of the series.

In New York, the Robins visited the Polo Grounds and beat the Giants, 10 to 7. Two clubs played exhibition games: the St. Louis Cardinals played the Springfield Eagles in Springfield, Ohio and won 14 to 0, and the Pittsburgh Pirates defeated Jeanerette, Louisiana of the Middle Atlantic League, 5 to 3. Rain postponed the games between the Phillies and Braves at Boston and Reds and Cubs at Chicago.

That night Babe Ruth attended a benefit concert for St. Mary's Industrial School of Baltimore at Catholic University in Washington D.C. After being placed in St. Mary's as a youngster by his parents, St. Mary's was the Babe's home off and on until the age of twenty.

Ruth enjoyed the concert. He wielded a baton for 150 musicians from St. Mary's Industrial School Band and *The Evening Star* Newsboys' Band. The Babe also made a heartfelt speech in appreciation of St. Mary's and what it had done for him. A new song titled "Batterin' Babe" was given out as a souvenir. The song was sung by the Catholic University Glee Club as Ruth left the benefit concert.

Also that evening, the Senators' Goose Goslin collapsed in the Wardman Park hotel lobby and had to be carried to his room. A physician was called and found Goslin's temperature at 103 degrees. Goslin was diagnosed with dry pleurisy. Sam Rice, meanwhile, came down with sinus trouble, an aftermath of his recent grippe attack. Both men missed the game the next day at Griffith Stadium.

On Tuesday, May 3, 1927, George Pipgras, 27, started for New York. For the 6' 1½" right-hander from Ida Grove, Iowa, it was his first start after spending 1925 and 1926 in the minor leagues. Last appearing with the Yankees in 1924, Pipgras won 0 and lost 1, with one save, and a 10.20 era.

At 6' 1", right-hander Firpo Marberry, 28, pitched for Washington. In 1926, Fred "Firpo" Marberry from Streetman, Texas, nicknamed for the Argentine fighter Luis Firpo, won 12 and lost 7 with a 3.00 era for the Senators. Marberry also had 22 saves, most in the major leagues. Hooks Dauss of the Tigers finished second in saves with 9 in the American League. Chick Davies of the Giants led the National League with 6.

The Senators led 1 to 0 when Combs and Koenig singled off Marberry in the third. Ruth followed with a single, scoring Combs. Gehrig then had a base hit and Koenig crossed the plate, giving the Yankees a 2 to 1 lead.

With the game tied at two, Combs tripled to center field in the seventh and scored on Koenig's triple to left center. After Ruth fanned, Meusel hit a sacrifice fly to Speaker, scoring Koenig.

The Senators fought back to tie the game at four in the bottom of the seventh. Opening the top of the eighth, Marberry struck out Grabowski, who had replaced Collins, and Wilcy Moore, who had relieved Pipgras. Combs then singled past Rigney at short stop. When Koenig singled to right, Harris brought Stan Coveleski, a right-hander, into the game. Coveleski walked Ruth. With the bases loaded, Gehrig grounded behind second. Stewart made a backhand toss to Rigney to force Ruth, but the Babe beat the throw and Combs scored. With the bases filled again with Yanks, Coveleski walked Meusel, forcing Koenig home. The Yankees led 6 to 4.

General Crowder, a right-hander, pitched the ninth and retired the Yanks. The Senators threatened in the bottom of that inning. Stewart led off with a single and reached third base, but he was stranded there when Moore forced West to hit a grounder to Lazzeri, Speaker to fly to Meusel, and McNeely to strike out.

Final score: Yankees 6, Senators 4.

Yankee Notebook for Tuesday, May 3, 1927: The Yanks had thirteen hits off three Senator hurlers . . . Combs, Koenig and Gehrig had three hits each . . . Gehrig's three hits raised his batting average to .421, third best in the American League . . . Detroit's Fothergill led the league at .509 and Meusel was second at .431 . . . Combs and Koenig had consecutive triples.

Pipgras pitched six innings before Moore relieved him . . . Pipgras gave up only four hits, but he walked seven and struck out none . . . Moore (2-1) went the final three innings. He gave up a single in the eighth to Ruel with one out and Bennie Tate, who batted for Coveleski, hit into an inning-ending double play—Lazzeri to Koenig to Gehrig . . . For the Senators, Marberry went seven and two-thirds and had seven strikeouts. He struck out Ruth on three pitches in the first.

At Shibe Park in Philadelphia, the Athletics won their second straight game from the Red Sox, 7 to 2. In Detroit, the White Sox's seven-game winning-streak ended when the Tigers won the second game of the series, 5 to 1. In St. Louis, Garland Buckeye hurled a complete game as the Indians evened the series at Sportsman's Park by defeating the Browns, 5 to 3.

The Braves bunched hits off three Phillies' pitchers in three different innings at Braves Field and won, 7 to 4, in the opening game of the series. At Wrigley Field, Charlie Grimm's timely hitting led the Cubs to a victory over the Reds, 4 to 3. In Pittsburgh, the Pirates scored two runs in the ninth inning to defeat the Cardinals, 11 to 10, at Forbes Field. At the Polo Grounds, the Robins won their fifth straight by overcoming a five-run lead and edged the Giants, 7 to 6.

The Washington Senators faced the Yankees at Griffith Stadium on Wednesday, May 4, 1927 with a number of their veterans ailing. Out due to illness or injury were Goose Goslin, Sam Rice, Ossie Bluege, and player-manager Bucky Harris. The Senators fielded a team that included four rookies. Miller Huggins started Dutch Ruether, a left-hander and winner of his last three games. The Senators' sent right-hander Hollis Thurston to the mound.

Combs tripled to open the game. The fleet-footed outfielder scored on Koenig's single, who was later out at second base when he over ran the bag on Ruth's grounder to Thurston. With the Babe on first base, Gehrig slugged a home run over the right field fence, giving the Yankees a 3 to 0 lead.

The lead did not last long.

Ruether was pounded in the bottom half of the first. Stewart, the Senators' leadoff hitter, began the scoring when he tripled over left fielder Meusel's head. McNeely singled, scoring Stewart. Speaker then singled to right and McNeely advanced to second. When Grabowski threw wildly to first base attempting to catch Speaker off the base, McNeely went to third. After Speaker was out trying to steal, Ruether's fast curve hit Cullop in the head.

Cullop was on the ground for several minutes. Huggins offered to let someone run for Cullop without forcing him from the game, but Manager Harris declined. Cullop stayed in the game. Judge then doubled and McNeely scored. Rigney beat out a hit down the third base line, scoring Cullop. Reeves, filling in for Ossie Bluege, singled and Judge scored. Rigney moved to third.

Bob Shawkey, a right-hander, relieved Ruether with one out. Ruel greeted Shawkey with a triple to center field, scoring Rigney and Reeves. When Thurston singled to left, Ruel came home, making the score 7 to 3.

The Yankees picked up a run in the second. Myles Thomas, a right-hander, followed Shawkey and pitched scoreless ball over the next seven innings. Thurston also pitched well after the second, but weakened in the ninth. With one out, Combs singled. After Koenig flied to McNeely for the second out, Ruth walked. With two balls on Gehrig, Harris called in left-hander Garland Braxton, who walked the batter.

With Combs on third, Ruth on second and Gehrig on first, Meusel faced Braxton. The Yankees needed three runs to tie. After Braxton threw three balls, Meusel swung at the next ball thrown and flied out to West in right field to end the game.

Final score: Senators 7, Yankees 4.

Yankee Notebook for Wednesday, May 4, 1927: Gehrig's home run was his sixth, tying Ruth for the home run lead in the American

League . . . The Yanks' had a total of twelve hits; Combs and Koenig had three hits each . . . Ruether (3-1) was hit very hard. Six of the first seven batters hit the ball sharply off the southpaw; he also hit a batter. The left-hander yielded seven hits, walked two, and struck out one in 1/3 inning . . . Yankee catcher Grabowski threw out three base stealers.

After hit in the head, Cullop stayed in the game; however, he left in the next inning. Ruether was not charged with a hit batsman. The scoring rules gave the batter a base on balls when the pitch that hits him was the fourth ball . . . In the field, Lazzeri fielded seven more chances without an error; he had handled ninety-seven without a miscue.

The Yankees were scheduled to play the final game of the series with the Senators the next day. The club then traveled to Fort Wayne, Indiana for an exhibition game before opening in Chicago on Saturday.

Taking advantage of wildness by Tiger hurler Sam Gibson, the White Sox grouped their hits and took the third game of the series from the Tigers at Navin Field, 11 to 5. In other news, Ty Cobb was to be given a 'welcome home' celebration on Tuesday at Detroit. Cobb was returning to the city for the first time in the uniform of a rival: the Philadelphia Athletics. Cobb had been with the Tigers since 1905. At Sportsman's Park, the Browns scored six runs in the sixth and went onto to defeat the Indians, 13 to 3. Rain stopped the game between the Red Sox and Athletics at Philadelphia after three innings.

At Wrigley Field, the Cubs pounded Reds' pitching in the third inning and scored eight runs on eight hits and went on to win, 13 to 9. In New York, the Robins lost to the Giants at the Polo Grounds, 4 to 3, in ten innings. At Forbes Field, Jesse Haines won his fifth straight game as the Cardinals defeated the Pirates, 8 to 3. Pittsburgh celebrated "Bill McKechnie Day" by honoring the former Pirates' manager. Cold weather postponed the game between the Phillies and Braves at Boston.

Ten thousand fans came out to Griffith Stadium in the nation's capital on Thursday, May 5, 1927 to see the Senators play the Yankees in the final game of the series. Miller Huggins started Urban Shocker, a right-hander. Bucky Harris also went with a right-hander, Horace Lisenbee.

Born September 23, 1898 in Clarksville, Tennessee, Horace Milton Lisenbee was a rookie. At 5' 11", the slender 28-year-old was to have a memorable 1927. That day Bucky Harris, Goose Goslin, Sam Rice, and Ossie Bluege were not in the line-up due to injury or illness.

Combs opened the game with a single. Ruth also singled, moving Combs to second base. When Gehrig forced Ruth at second, Combs advanced to third. When Stewart dropped Ruel's throw to catch Gehrig at second on an attempted double steal, Combs scored.

In the third, with the score tied at one, Shocker led off with a single. After Combs walked and Koenig flied to West, Lisenbee walked Ruth to load the bases. When the right-hander forced Gehrig to pop up to Judge and struck Meusel out for the second time in a row, the Yankees did not score.

In the home half of the third, Ruel singled off Shocker. Lisenbee was given a great hand when he came to bat. He surprised everyone when he bunted with two strikes and was safe on Collins' bad throw. Stewart then forced Ruel and McNeely popped up; however, Speaker singled to right, scoring Lisenbee. The Senators led 2 to 1. The Senators added runs in the fifth, sixth and eighth, and the Yankees came up in the ninth trailing by five runs, 6 to 1.

Lazzeri opened the inning with a single to right; however, Lisenbee fanned Dugan and Collins. With two outs, Huggins then sent Cedric Durst up to bat for pitcher Joe Giard, who replaced Shocker in the eighth. When Durst popped up to Senators' third baseman Reeves, the game ended.

Final score: Senators 6, Yankees 1.

Yankee Notebook for May 5, 1927: Horace Lisenbee's teammates called him Liz. It seemed that someone on the Senators thought the name Horace was too classical for baseball and gave him the nickname . . . Lisenbee was good that day, allowing only six hits and striking out eight. The one run he gave up was unearned. His curve ball was excellent, and the heart of the order—Ruth, Gehrig, Meusel and Lazzeri—managed only three hits . . . Lisenbee fanned Meusel and Collins three times each and Lazzeri and Dugan once . . . After the first inning, the Yankees only got two men beyond first base.

Shocker (2-3) pitched six innings and gave up five runs . . . Giard pitched the final two innings, giving up one run . . . The fielding was poor . . . Collins made two errors and Koenig, Ruth, Meusel and Shocker one each.

Speaker, the Senators' centerfielder, went back to the flagpole for Ruth's fly in the fifth . . . Cullop, who was hit in the head the day before by Ruether, reported he was fine . . . The Yankees left Washington, D.C. for an exhibition game at Fort Wayne, Indiana.

In Philadelphia, Ty Cobb and Al Simmons of the Athletics were ejected in a dispute over a ball hit by Cobb that was ruled foul in a game won by the Red Sox, 3 to 2, at Shibe Park. At Navin Field, second baseman Marty McManus broke a tie in the ninth when he singled home the winning run with the bases loaded and gave the Tigers a win over the White Sox, 3 to 2. Rain postponed the game between the Indians and Browns at St. Louis.

At Forbes Field, Grover Cleveland Alexander scattered seven hits as the Cardinals made it two out of three games by defeating the Pirates, 4 to 2. In other action, Rogers Hornsby's fourth home run of the season with two men on in the seventh at the Polo Grounds gave the Giants a victory over the Robins, 4 to 1. Rain postponed the game between the Phillies and Braves at Boston.

Major League Baseball Standings
May 5, 1927
American League

	Won	Lost	P.C.
New York	12	7	.632
Philadelphia	11	7	.611
Chicago	12	9	.571
Detroit	9	8	.529
Washington	10	9	.526
St. Louis	8	8	.500
Cleveland	8	12	.400
Boston	4	14	.222

National League

	Won	Lost	P.C.
St. Louis	12	6	.667
New York	13	7	.650
Pittsburgh	10	8	.556
Philadelphia	8	7	.533
Chicago	9	8	.529
Boston	9	9	.500
Brooklyn	7	14	.333
Cincinnati	5	14	.263

Chapter 9

Babe Ruth

After Harry Frazee, the owner of the Boston Red Sox, agreed to sell Babe Ruth to Jacob Ruppert and Cap Hutson and the financial terms were worked out, Miller Huggins was sent to California to meet with Ruth. The men talked about Ruth's past behavior in Boston and whether he would be strictly business if he came to the Yankees.

Ruth assured Huggins that he would play the best he could and changed the subject to money. Huggins and Ruth met a couple of times and haggled over salary and soon agreed on the financial terms: $20,000 a year for 1920 and 1921 and a bonus of $1,000. When Huggins wired Ruppert that the deal was done, the Yankee co-owner called in the press on January 5, 1920 and announced that the Yankees had bought Babe Ruth from the Boston Red Sox.

The news generated a great deal of excitement in the baseball world and changed the fortunes of both the Yankee and Red Sox franchises.

George Herman Ruth, Jr. was born to Katherine (Schamberger) and George Ruth on February 6, 1895. To escape the noisy and distracting surroundings of the family's saloon and home a few blocks west, Katherine, known as Kate, delivered the baby at her father's house at 216 Emory Street in Baltimore, Maryland. After she delivered her son, the Ruth family returned to their home.

Young George spent most of his first seven years living over his parent's saloon in Baltimore's rugged waterfront neighborhood. As a youngster, he came into contact with the tough characters frequenting the barroom. They had a poor influence on him. His parents worked long hours and Ruth's behavior must have been too much to deal with.

"Looking back on my early boyhood, I honestly don't remember being aware of the difference between right and wrong," Ruth wrote years later. He admitted stealing from his parents and chewing tobacco at the age of seven.

Unable to deal with the boy, the Ruths' decided to send him away. On June 13, 1902, George Herman Ruth, Sr. placed his 7-year-old son in St. Mary's Industrial School for Boys in Baltimore. Both a reformatory and orphanage, St. Mary's held eight hundred children. George Herman Ruth, Jr. was listed as "incorrigible" in St. Mary's records.

In the years 1902 through 1911, Ruth would be released and then returned by his family to St. Mary's no less than on seven occasions. In 1912, he returned and stayed until 1914. While there, Ruth was taught to be a tailor and shirt maker. He also learned baseball from Brother Matthias, a member of the Xaverian Catholic Order that ran St. Mary's. Brother Matthias saw early that Ruth had a talent for catching and throwing. He worked with the youngster and made him a catcher.

Over the years, Ruth became a very good ball player and always played with the older boys and on the best teams at the school. But Ruth was left-handed and catchers were normally right-handed, so at the age of 14 or 15, Brother Matthias moved him from catcher to pitcher. The new position felt natural to Ruth, and he pitched his last two years at St. Mary's. Ruth became so accomplished that he came to the attention of Jack Dunn, owner of the Baltimore Orioles of the International League. Ruth signed a contract with Dunn at the age of nineteen for $600 a year—a large amount of money for a poor boy.

On February 27, 1914, Ruth left St. Mary's. The last item in Ruth's school record said simply, "He is going to join the Balt. Baseball Team." Traveling for the first time by train, Ruth left Baltimore for the Orioles' spring training camp at Fayetteville, N.C. While there, young Ruth was nicknamed 'Babe' by the Orioles' players. During the exhibition season, Ruth pitched against Connie Mack's Philadelphia Athletics and beat them. He also faced the New York Giants and Philadelphia Phillies and defeated both teams.

Ruth played his first game in the International League in Baltimore on April 22, 1914. He shutout Buffalo with six hits and the Orioles won the game, 6 to 0; Ruth also had two of the team's ten hits, both singles. In mid-season, Dunn sold Ruth, pitcher Ernie Shore, and catcher Ben Egan to Joe Lannin, owner of the Boston Red Sox. The reported price for the three players was $8,500.

Lannin gave Ruth a new contract at $2,500. The Babe joined a Red Sox team that had been world champions in 1912 and still had one of the greatest outfields of all time: Duffy Lewis, Tris Speaker, and Harry Hooper.

Hooper remembered when the 19-year-old Ruth joined the Red Sox in the middle of 1914.

"He was a left-handed pitcher then, and a good one. He had never been anywhere, didn't know anything about manners or how to behave among people—just a big overgrown green pea . . . ." recalled Hooper. "George was six foot two and weighed 198 pounds, all of it muscle. He had a slim waist, huge biceps, no self-discipline, and not much education—not so very different from a lot of other nineteen-year old would-be ball players. Except for two things: he could eat more than anyone else, and he could hit a baseball further."

Babe Ruth's major league debut came against the Cleveland Indians on July 11, 1914. Ruth pitched seven innings, giving up eight hits, all singles; Shoeless Joe Jackson had two of the hits. Dutch Leonard finished that game and the Red Sox won, 4 to 3. Ruth spent about a month with the Red Sox and won two games and lost one.

When it became clear that the Red Sox could not catch the Athletics in the American League pennant race, Lannin sent Ruth to Providence of the International League, where he helped that club clinch the pennant. Overall, with Boston and Providence in 1914, Ruth won 22 games and lost 9 for a winning percentage of .709.

Ruth's first full season with the Red Sox was 1915. He won 18 and lost 8 and pitched in 32 games, hurled 218 innings, struck out 112, and posted a 2.44 era. Ruth also appeared as a pinch hitter and played in 42 games, batting .315, with 10 doubles, one triple, and four home runs. The four home runs were significant when one considered that in 1915 Braggo Roth, with both the Chicago White Sox and Cleveland Indians, led the American League with seven.

The Red Sox won the pennant in 1915, defeating the Philadelphia Phillies in the World Series in five games. When Manager Bill Carrigan went with his more experienced pitchers in the series, Ruth did not pitch; however, he appeared as a pinch hitter, grounding out.

By 1916, Ruth became the premier left-handed pitcher in the American League. The Babe won 23 and lost 12, with a league best 1.75 era, and he led the league with nine shutouts. Pitching 324 innings, he struck out 170 batters. He played 67 games and batted .272, with three home runs. The Red Sox won the pennant that year and played the Brooklyn Robins in the 1916 World Series.

Ruth got his first start in the second game of the World Series on October 9, 1916. In one of the most memorable World Series games ever played, Ruth pitched 14 innings in a game the Red Sox won, 2 to 1. The Red Sox went on to win the World Series in five games.

The Babe had another great year in 1917, when he won 24 and lost 13 with a 2.02 era and six shutouts. Leading the league with 35 complete games in 38 starts, Ruth pitched 326 innings and struck out 128. He played in 52 games and batted .325, with two home runs.

In February 1918, Ed Barrow became manager of the Boston Red Sox. With many of the regulars in the armed services, Barrow told Ruth during the season that he needed his bat in the line-up. He asked Ruth to play the outfield on the days when he was not pitching.

Ruth agreed to give it a try and was in the line-up everyday a right-hander pitched against the Red Sox, playing mostly left field, and sometimes first base. When a left-hander faced the Red Sox, Barrow usually worked it out so Ruth would pitch against him. On the occasion when he did not play, Ruth was available in the bullpen to pinch-hit or come into the game as a relief pitcher.

The Red Sox won the pennant in 1918. Ruth appeared in 20 games as a pitcher and won 13 and lost 7 with a 2.22 era. As a batter, he played in 95 games and came to the plate 317 times, the most so far in his career. Batting .300 with 26 doubles, 11 triples and 11 home runs; Ruth's home run total tied Tilly Walker of the Philadelphia Athletics for the American League lead.

The Boston Red Sox faced the Chicago Cubs in the 1918 World Series. Barrow surprised the Cubs by starting Ruth in Game One in Chicago. Ruth pitched nine innings and the Red Sox won 1 to 0. Counting his final 13 scoreless innings going back to the 1916 World

Series, Ruth had pitched 22 consecutive innings without giving up a run.

With the Red Sox leading two games to one in the Series, Ruth started Game Four and went seven innings leading 2 to 0 before giving up two runs in the eighth. When the Red Sox regained the lead in the home half of the eighth, 3 to 2, Ruth went back to the mound in the ninth. After he walked the first two Cubs, Barrow called in Joe Bush and sent Ruth to left field. Bush retired the Cubs and the Red Sox won, 3 to 2, and went on to win the 1918 World Series.

With his seven scoreless innings in Game Four, Ruth had pitched 29 consecutive innings without giving up a run in the World Series, surpassing the 28 consecutive innings mark achieved in 1905 and 1911 by Christy Mathewson of the New York Giants.

As it turned out, 1919 was Ruth's last year with the Red Sox. Playing in 130 games, he batted 432 times (.322 average) and led the league in runs scored (103), home runs (29), and runs driven in (114). On the mound, he appeared in only 17 games, winning 9 and losing 5, with a 2.98 era. The Red Sox finished sixth that year.

In early January 1920, the Yankees announced that the franchise had bought Ruth from the Red Sox. On February 28, 1920, Ruth traveled from Boston and met the Yankee players at Pennsylvania Station in New York for the train trip to Jacksonville, Florida for Spring Training. More than a dozen newspapers sent reporters to cover Ruth and the Yankees.

"There was something in the air and it was exciting," Ruth wrote later. "The club had finished third in 1919, but we all felt we were headed upward."

Ruth joined a club that already had some good hitters. A season earlier, in 1919, Bob Ripley drew a cartoon of Roger Peckinpaugh, Wally Pipp, Frank Baker, Del Pratt, and Ping Bodie swinging their bats. He captioned it: "Murderers Row."

Off the field, Ruth had a good time in Florida, occasionally playing golf, and often in the company of a woman. His wanderings were legendary. On the road, Ruth would go from the train station directly to a girl friend's home or went looking for new female companionship. When the luggage was delivered to the hotel, his roommate Ping Bodie picked up his suitcase and Ruth's and took them to the room. When the team left the hotel, Bodie brought his suitcase and Ruth's downstairs to the lobby.

One day a reporter asked Bodie what Ruth was like since the two men roomed together.

"I don't room with him," said Bodie. "I room with his suitcase."

By midseason of 1920, Ruth matched his record of 29 home runs. When the season ended, he had hit 54 and finished his first year as a Yankee with a batting average of .376, with 36 doubles and 9 triples. He also scored 156 runs and drove in 137. Ruth's slugging percentage was .847.

The Yankees came close to winning the pennant in that 1920 season, fighting the Indians and White Sox down to the last week of the season, but they lost the flag on the last Western trip. The Indians finished first and the White Sox second. The Yankees ended in third place, three games out.

Ruth's performance in 1921 was the best of his career. Batting .378, he hit 59 home runs, 16 triples and 44 doubles, while scoring 177 runs and driving in 170. After battling the Indians into late September, the club won the pennant; the first in the franchise's history but lost to the Giants in the World Series.

Following the series, Ruth, Meusel and others went barnstorming in violation of baseball's rules and warnings by Commissioner Kenesaw Landis. The Commissioner fined Ruth and Meusel their World Series share ($3,362) and both were suspended for the first six weeks of the 1922 season.

Before Spring Training opened in New Orleans, Louisiana, Ruth and Huston discussed a new contract. Ruth wanted more than the $20,000 he was paid for his first two seasons. After much haggling, Huston finally offered him a deal for $50,000 a year over five years; a contract worth $250,000.

"Make it fifty-two thousand and it's a deal," Ruth told Huston.

"Fifty-two thousand? All right, agreed. But why fifty-two thousand?" asked Huston surprised.

"Well, said Ruth, "there are fifty-two weeks in the year, and I've always wanted to make a grand a week."

With the salary issue resolved, the club named Ruth captain, a special honor. Ruth and Meusel were reinstated from their suspensions on May 20, 1922. Ruth got off to a terrible start and the fans were booing him. Five days later on May 25, 1922, he tried to stretch a single into a double, but umpire George Hildebrand called him out at second. Frustrated with the call, he threw dirt into the umpire's face. Hildebrand threw him out of the game; the first time he was ejected as a Yankee.

On the way to the dug out, he was heckled badly by a fan and Ruth climbed into the stands to fight the spectator. The heckler fled. Ban Johnson fined Ruth $200 and suspended him one game. Johnson also told the Yankees to strip him of his position of captain; Everett Scott succeeded him.

In June 1922, while in Cleveland, the Yanks were in the midst of a seven-game losing streak. On a close play on a throw to second base by Meusel, Huggins got embroiled in an argument with the umpire Bill Dineen. Ruth came in from left field and also had words with Dineen, who threw him out of the game. Dineen filed a report with Johnson, who suspended Ruth for three days. When he was given the news, Ruth was so angry he approached Dineen and came close to a fight. Johnson suspended him two more days—the fourth suspension for Ruth that season.

After that Ruth vowed not to get suspended ever again because of an argument with an umpire. However, on August 1, 1922 Ruth was called out on strikes and had words with umpire Tom Connolly. Johnson notified him that he was suspended for a fifth time; this time three days for abusing Connolly.

After battling the Browns late that season, the Yankees won the pennant for the second straight year but lost to the Giants again. Playing in 110 games, Ruth batted .315 with 35 home runs, 8 triples, and 24 doubles. He scored 94 runs and drove in 99. After the season, Ruth vowed to work harder, no longer drink, and become a better model for the young people of the country.

In 1923, the Yankees won their first World Series. The Babe had a superb year and was named the Most Valuable Player in the American

League. He batted .393 with 41 home runs, 13 triples, and 45 doubles. Ruth also drove in 131 runs and scored 151. His 205 hits were the most since joining the Yankees. 1923 was also the year that Yankee Stadium opened in the Bronx, and the Babe hit the first home run at the stadium into the right field bleachers, which was afterwards called Ruthville.

Although the club did not win the pennant in 1924, Ruth had another good season, batting .378 with 46 home runs, 7 triples, and 39 doubles. He scored 143 runs and drove in 121.

If 1921 was the best season of his career, 1925 was the worst. Ruth's problems began during Spring Training. While in Atlanta playing an exhibition game, Ruth came down with a severe pain in his stomach. Feeling better he played over the next few days but was ill again in Asheville, North Carolina.

Accompanied back to New York by Yankee scout Paul Krichell, Ruth collapsed upon arriving and was hospitalized at St. Vincent's Hospital. Diagnosed with an intestinal abscess, Ruth underwent surgery on April 17, 1925. His doctor informed the press that Ruth's medical problems were caused by his carelessness in what he ate and drank. Writer W.O. McGeehan termed Ruth's illness "the bellyache heard around the world." Ruth did not return to the club until May 26, 1925.

The club was terrible that year. Ruth helped little. Playing better by August, he had once again returned to his wild life style and was openly defying the club's rules and Huggins. The men had a confrontation on August 25, 1925 in St. Louis. Huggins suspended him, fined him $5,000 and told him to return to New York. With Ruppert and Barrow's backing, Ruth was out of the line-up nine days before he apologized and returned to the line-up. Batting only .290 and playing in 98 games, Ruth hit only 25 home runs, drove in 66 runs and scored 61. The Yankees finished in seventh place.

The Babe rebounded in 1926; his 47 home runs, .372 batting average, and 145 runs driven in helped the Yankees win the pennant.

Chapter 10

Comiskey Park

Before going to Chicago to play the White Sox, Miller Huggins sent the club's regular infielders and outfielders, with the exception of Joe Dugan, to Fort Wayne, Indiana. The Yankees played an exhibition game there on Friday May 6, 1927 against a local semi-pro team named the Lincoln Lifes. Meanwhile, the regular pitchers and catchers, Dugan, and Huggins went onto Chicago. Coach Arthur Fletcher was in charge of the club at Fort Wayne.

That day Ruth played first base and Gehrig played right field. The Fort Wayne team gave the Yankees a hard fight and even took the lead in the eighth, 3 to 2. The Yankees, however, tied it at three in the eighth, and batting last that day tried hard but failed to win it in the ninth.

The game went to the tenth.

Just before Ruth came to the plate in the bottom of that inning, he greeted several hundred boys on the field in front of the New York bench. When the Babe stepped to the plate, he waved to the crowd of 35,000 signaling that they could start for home. Ruth then hit a home run far over the right field fence. Mike Gazella, who was on first base, trotted home ahead of Ruth and the game was over. After hitting the home run, the boys, who had greeted him earlier at the bench, swarmed around the Babe after he crossed the plate.

In upstate New York, the Philadelphia Athletics defeated Buffalo of the International League in an exhibition game 5 to 3. Ty Cobb injured himself sliding into second base. Rain postponed the game between the Indians and Browns at Sportsman's Park. Off the field, Washington's Goslin was resting comfortably after complaining of intense pain in the morning. Doctors advised Goslin to remain in the hospital for three or four days.

At Braves Field, Carl Mays won his first game of the season as the Reds began their tour of the East by defeating the Braves, 5 to 3. Reds' outfielders George Kelly and Ethan Allen hit home runs. The games between the Cubs and Giants and Cardinals and Robins at New York and Pirates and Phillies at Philadelphia were postponed because of rain.

On a very cold afternoon at Comiskey Park in Chicago, 35,000 fans came out to see the White Sox and Yankees on Saturday, May 7, 1927. The crowd was the largest of the season. Among the spectators was the Vice President of the United States: Charles G. Dawes. Mr. Dawes arrived just before the start of the game and the crowd greeted him warmly. The Vice President acknowledged them with a bow. After he made his way to a flag-draped box near the Chicago dugout, White Sox manager Ray Schalk went over to visit with him.

Schalk wore a plain white uniform with blue-collar trim and white cap and blue visor. On his left breast in solid blue was the emblem S-O-X in serif lettering. Schalk wore white stockings and black cleats

During batting practice, the crowd cheered as Ruth socked a ball that cleared the second tier of bleachers in right field. Also prior to game time, local admirers gave catcher Johnny Grabowski, who played for the White Sox in 1926, a traveling bag as a gift.

That afternoon Miller Huggins started southpaw Herb Pennock. Pitching for the White Sox was Ted Lyons, 26, a 5'11", 200 pound right-hander from Lake Charles, Louisiana. Theodore Amar (Ted) Lyons debuted with the White Sox on July 2, 1923. Two years later, Lyons and Ed Rommel of the Athletics led the American Leagues in victories with twenty-one. Lyons also led the major leagues that season with five shutouts. In 1926, he won 18 and lost 16, saved three, and posted a 3.01 era.

The Line-Ups

Yankees	White Sox
Earle Combs cf	Willie Kamm 3b
Mark Koenig ss	Bill Hunnefield ss
Babe Ruth lf	Bill Barrett rf
Lou Gehrig 1b	Bibb Falk lf
Bob Meusel rf	Earl Sheely 1b
Tony Lazzeri 2b	Alex Metzler cf
Joe Dugan 3b	Aaron Ward 2b
John Grabowski c	Harry McCurdy c
Herb Pennock p	Ted Lyons p

In the second, Grabowski singled to center field and raced to third on Pennock's base hit to right. When Combs singled to center, Grabowski scored. With runners on second and third and none out in the third, the White Sox threatened, but Pennock held them from scoring. Again in the fifth, the White Sox had men on first and second with none out, but they did not score.

Both Pennock and Lyons battled through the seventh. In the eighth, the Yankees went ahead 2 to 0 after Ruth singled to right, moved to third when Meusel singled to right and scored on Lazzeri's base hit to right. With Lyons still on the mound in the ninth, the Yankees erupted for six runs and took a commanding 8 to 0 lead. The rally began when Grabowski singled to left. When Pennock bunted, Grabowski was safe at second after Hunnefield dropped the ball. Combs also bunted. Sheely fielded the ball and threw to first, but the ball hit Combs as he neared the bag.

With the bases loaded and none out, Koenig singled to right, scoring Grabowski. With the bases filled again with Yankees, Ruth hit to Sheely at first base, who threw low to the plate as Pennock scored. With Combs, Koenig, and Ruth on the bases, Gehrig then blasted a grand slam home run into the new right field pavilion. Pennock retired the White Sox in the ninth.

Final score: Yankees 8, White Sox 0.

Yankee Notebook for Saturday May 7, 1927: Yank's hurler Pennock (3-0) gave up only five hits and pitched a complete game shutout, walking three, and striking out three . . . For the White Sox, Lyons gave up thirteen hits and struck out eight . . . Gehrig's home run in the ninth was his seventh and the second grand slam of his career. His first was on July 23, 1925 . . . Gehrig hit the ball hard each time at bat and was one of three players that did not strike out . . . Ruth singled, walked, struck out, flied to Ward, and grounded to Sheely.

Lazzeri had four more chances without an error. His best play was in the third when he grabbed Kamm's squeeze play bunt and threw out Ward at the plate . . . Meusel made the catch of the day off Lyons in the seventh as he caught the ball off the grass tops.

In the series opener at Dunn Field in Cleveland, the Indians beat the Athletics, 11 to 10 in ten innings. Opening their Western trip, the Red Sox defeated the Tigers, 5 to 3, at Navin Field. At Sportsman's Park, Sad Sam Jones went down to his first defeat after three straight victories as the Senators defeated the Browns, 16 to 9.

A crowd of 26,000 at the Polo Grounds in New York watched Charlie Root pitch a complete game as the Cubs beat the Giants, 6 to 4. At Philadelphia, Cy Williams hit a home run in the ninth inning with one man on to give the Phillies a 6 to 5 win over the Pirates at Baker Bowl. In Boston, the Braves rallied for four runs in the ninth at Braves Field, but fell short as the Reds won, 9 to 8. Visiting the Robins at Ebbets Field for the first time, the Cardinals lost, 3 to 0.

The largest crowd in Chicago's baseball history, an estimated 52,000 fans, came out to Comiskey Park on Sunday, May 8, 1927. The turnout was the greatest in the mid-west and second only to the records set back east in New York. The newly remodeled Comiskey Park seated 55,000. The stands were filled as were the center field bleachers. The only empty seats were in one section of the upper deck in right field and a section in the left field pavilion.

Yankee hurler Waite Hoyt, a right-hander, opposed White Sox right-hander Ted Blankenship. Born May 10, 1901 in Bonham, Texas, Theodore Blankenship debuted with the White Sox on July 2, 1922.

From 1923-1924, he averaged 8 victories a season; however, Blankenship came into his own in 1925 winning seventeen and losing eight. The next year 1926, he won 13 and lost 10 with a 3.62 era.

In the first inning, the Yankees loaded the bases on Koenig's single to right, Ruth's single off Clancy's glove, and Ward's error at second base on a grounder by Gehrig. Meusel then bounced a hit past Kamm at third base, scoring Koenig. In the third, Gehrig tripled and scored on Meusel's single. Lazzeri and Dugan singled. When Meusel scored on Dugan's hit, the Yanks took a 3 to 0 lead. Sarge Connally, a right-hander, relieved Blankenship. With Collins at the plate, the runners tried a double steal, but Lazzeri was tagged out as he slid into third base.

The Yankees went ahead 5 to 0 in the fifth after Connally walked Gehrig and Meusel reached first when Hunnefield could not pick up his grounder. Lazzeri then singled to right, scoring Gehrig. As the ball rolled between Barrett's feet in the outfield, Meusel also scored. In the seventh, the Yankees picked up another run on Collins's round-tripper off a fast ball thrown by Connally that landed in the left field stands.

Bert Cole, a left-hander, pitched the ninth for the White Sox. Gehrig hit a hard line drive to centerfield that rolled to the bleachers for a triple. Meusel walked. Lazzeri then hit a grounder to Kamm at third base, who threw low to first base after deciding he could not get Gehrig at the plate. Dugan then sacrificed Meusel to third, scoring Lazzeri.

While Cole was winding up to deliver the pitch to Collins, Meusel stole home and Lazzeri took third on the double steal. Collins walked. On a squeeze play bunt by Hoyt, Lazzeri scored. The Yankees led 9 to 0. Hoyt pitched a scoreless ninth.

Final score: Yankees 9, White Sox 0.

Yankee Notebook for Sunday, May 8, 1927: Commissioner Kenesaw Mountain Landis was among the spectators that afternoon . . . Hoyt (4-1) yielded nine hits and pitched a complete game shutout, walking only one batter . . . The shutout was the fourth for the Yankee pitching staff and the second in a row . . . The club had thirteen hits . . . Gehrig had two triples and scored three runs . . . Ruth had two hits, a double, and a scratch single . . . Lazzeri handled nine chances in the field perfectly, while White Sox fielders committed four errors. The official scorers were generous; they could have given them two more.

Meusel enjoyed the stealing of home off Cole. He and Cole were in the middle of a brawl on June 13, 1924 when Cole, who was then with the Tigers, hit Meusel with a pitch. Meusel thought Cole hit him deliberately and charged the mound. Both benches rushed onto the field. A fight took place. Cole and Meusel were given ten-day suspensions.

In Cleveland, the Indians took the second game of the series from the Athletics, 4 to 2, at Dunn Field. Ty Cobb and Al Simmons did not play. Before the game, American League President Ban Johnson suspended both men indefinitely. On May 5, umpire Emmett Ormsby ejected Cobb and Simmons in the Athletics-Red Sox game in Philadelphia, setting off a melee by fans that required police protection for Ormsby.

Combining eight hits and six bases on balls, the Browns defeated the Senators, 8 to 3, at Sportsman's Park. In Detroit, with the score tied in the ninth at Navin Field, Marty McManus singled with the bases loaded, giving the Tigers a win over the Red Sox, 3 to 2.

Before a capacity crowd of 30,000 at Ebbets Field in Brooklyn, Flint Rhem gave up only two hits as the Cardinals trounced the Robins, 5 to 1. At the Polo Grounds, Bill Terry's hit in the ninth, with the score tied, sent home the deciding run as the Giants edged the Cubs, 5 to 4.

After yesterday's record crowd of 52,000 people at Comiskey Park in Chicago, only 7,000 fans were at the ballpark on Monday, May 9, 1927. For the final game of the series, Miller Huggins sent southpaw Dutch Ruether to the mound. Ruether last pitched Wednesday in Washington, D.C and lasted only a third of an inning in a loss to the Senators.

The White Sox started veteran right-hander Urban Charles (Red) Faber from Cascade, Iowa. The slim 6'2" hurler began his major league career with Chicago in 1914. Faber won 20 games or more four times: 1915 (24-14); 1920 (23-13); 1921 (25-15) and 1922 (21-17). In 1926, he won 15 and lost 9, and posted a 3.55 era.

In the White Sox's half of the first, leadoff hitter Alex Metzler hit a ground ball to Lazzeri, who made an error after having gone through twenty-two games without one. The error, however, did not hurt as the White Sox did not score.

Faber and Ruether pitched scoreless ball over the first four innings. In the fifth, Gehrig tripled deep into right center field and scored on Meusel's long sacrifice fly. The White Sox tied the game in the eighth. When they threatened in the ninth, Huggins brought in Wilcy Moore, a right-hander. The rookie stopped the rally.

The game went into extra innings.

Faber retired the side in the tenth. In the White Sox's half of the tenth, Metzler hit a liner into centerfield. Combs fumbled the ball momentarily but made an accurate throw to second base. Koenig was ready to take the throw and it looked like Metzler would be out. Instead of letting the ball go through to Koenig, Lazzeri took the throw and relayed it to Koenig. Metzler beat the throw and slid safely into second.

With Kamm at bat, Gehrig moved to the plate to cover the expected bunt. Kamm dropped a bunt. With Lazzeri covering first base, Moore's throw was wild. Metzler, who was off and running with the pitch, came home and scored the winning run.

Final score: White Sox 2, Yankees 1 (Ten innings).

Yankee Notebook for Monday, May 9, 1927: Ruether pitched a strong game. With a one run lead, he breezed through the fifth, sixth, and seventh innings . . . Before tying the game in the eighth, the White Sox had only six hits off the Yankee left-hander, who gave up a total of ten hits, struck out one, and walked none . . . The winning run came in the tenth off Moore (2-2) with none out . . . At the plate, the Yanks had only had seven hits off Faber; Combs and Grabowski each had two . . . Gehrig had his third triple in two days . . . After the game, the Yankees traveled by train to St. Louis, Missouri for four games with the Browns.

At Dunn Field in Cleveland, Southpaw Joe Shaute won his first game as the Indians defeated the Athletics 6 to 1. Pounding five Red Sox pitchers for twenty-two hits at Navin Field, the Tigers took the closing game of that series, 17 to 11. Rain postponed the game between the Senators and Browns at St. Louis.

In other news, President Ban Johnson of the American League had been flooded by telegrams urging him to reinstate Ty Cobb in time for Detroit's 'welcome home' celebration the next day. Johnson announced that he would make a ruling on Cobb's indefinite suspension the next morning.

All the scheduled games in the National League were rained out.

Major League Baseball Standings
May 9, 1927
American League

	Won	Lost	P.C.
New York	14	8	.636
Detroit	11	9	.550
Chicago	13	11	.542
Philadelphia	11	10	.524
Washington	11	10	.524
St. Louis	9	9	.500
Cleveland	11	12	.478
Boston	5	16	.238

National League

	Won	Lost	P.C.
St. Louis	13	7	.650
New York	14	8	.636
Philadelphia	9	7	.563
Chicago	10	9	.526
Pittsburgh	10	9	.526
Boston	9	11	.450
Brooklyn	8	15	.348
Cincinnati	7	14	.333

Chapter 11

Sportsman's Park and Navin Field

For the first time that season, the Yankees visited the St. Louis Browns at Sportsman's Park on Tuesday, May 10, 1927. Located in northwest St. Louis, Sportsman's Park had been the home of the Browns since 1902. The St. Louis Cardinals became tenants of the Browns in 1920 and both clubs shared the ballpark since. The Yankees last visited St. Louis on October 5 through 7, 1926 to play the Cardinals in the World Series. The Yanks won two of the three games played, but lost the seventh game and World Series back in New York on October 10.

George Pipgras, a right-hander, started for the Yankees. Milt Gaston opened for the Browns. Nathaniel Milton Gaston was born January 27, 1896 in Ridgefield Park, New Jersey. The 6'1" right-hander began his career with the Yankees in 1924, winning five and losing three. Obtained by the Browns in 1925, Gaston won fifteen and lost ten in 1926.

The Line-Ups

Yankees	Browns
Earle Combs cf	Frank O'Rourke 3b
Mark Koenig ss	Spencer Adams 2b
Babe Ruth lf	George Sisler 1b
Lou Gehrig 1b	Ken Williams lf
Bob Meusel rf	Harry Rice rf
Tony Lazzeri 2b	Fred Schulte cf
Joe Dugan 3b	Wally Gerber ss
Pat Collins c	Wally Schang c
George Pipgras p	Milt Gaston p

Gaston wore a plain white uniform with a "V" neck collar and buttoned pullover style jersey that went below the elbows. His cap was white with a brown visor. On his left sleeve was a brown ST-L monogram. Two brown stripes adorned his white stockings. Gaston wore a black belt and black cleats.

Combs opened the game with a ground ball that bounded away from O'Rourke, the Browns' third baseman. Koenig then grounded to Adams at second, who also misplayed the ball. With Combs and Koenig on base, Ruth blasted a home run off Gaston into the right-field pavilion.

Pipgras gave up a run in the third and two in the fourth, which tied the game at three. After Pipgras walked Sisler in the fifth inning, his sixth bases on balls, Huggins brought in Joe Giard, a left-hander; however, a walk, triple and sacrifice fly led to three runs; the Browns led 6 to 3.

The Yankees battled back.

After Gehrig singled in the sixth, Meusel smacked a home run into the right-field stands and the Browns' lead was cut to 6 to 5. Wilcy Moore, a right-hander, followed Giard in the seventh, and he retired the side. In the eighth, the Browns scored a run on singles by Schang and O'Rourke and took a 7 to 5 lead.

With Gaston still on the mound in the ninth, Cedric Durst batted for Dugan and walked. Grabowski then singled to left, and Huggins sent Mike Gazella in to run for him. After Ben Paschal, batting for Moore, lined to Miller, Combs walked. With the bases loaded, Koenig hit a sacrifice fly to center, scoring Durst; the Yankees trailed by one run. Ruth walked and the bases were filled again. Then Gehrig singled over second base into center, scoring Gazella and Combs. The Yankees led 8 to 7.

In an unusual relief appearance, Herb Pennock, a left-hander, came into the game in the ninth. Meanwhile, Benny Bengough replaced Grabowski as the catcher. Pennock walked the first batter he faced: Sisler. When Miller singled to center, Howley, the Browns' manager, had Rice sacrifice the runners. With Sisler on third and Miller at second with one out, Huggins ordered Pennock to walk Schulte to fill the bases.

Huggins also moved the infield back, improving the team's chances for a double play. With the bases loaded, Gerber grounded to Koenig at short, who tossed to Lazzeri at second base to force Schulte. Lazzeri's throw to Gehrig beat Gerber to first base for a game-ending double play.

Final score: Yankees 8, Browns 7.

Yankee Notebook for Tuesday, May 10, 1927: Ruth's home run was his seventh . . . The Babe and Gehrig were tied for the American League lead . . . The home run was Ruth's only hit; he was thrown out twice by Adams, hit a ball deep to Schulte in centerfield and walked . . . Ruth also made a spectacular one-handed catch while running at top speed . . . Gehrig hit a foul over the top of the double-deck right-field stand just before the ninth inning single that decided the game.

George Pipgras was not hit hard, but he was wild . . . Moore (3-2) followed Giard and his sinker gave the Browns trouble . . . Eleven batters faced Moore in three innings, and he gave up only a scratch hit and a walk . . . Pennock gave up one hit in the ninth and was credited with a save.

Playing in his first game of the season, Benny Bengough caught Pennock in the ninth. He had been disabled by neuritis since early in spring training. While he was not yet fit for regular duty, Bengough was much improved. The year before, he appeared in 36 games for the Yanks and batted .381.

At Comiskey Park in Chicago, Tommy Thomas pitched a strong game and drove in three runs as the White Sox defeated the Senators in the first game of the series, 4 to 3. In Cleveland, the Red Sox scored five runs in the fifth and went on to beat the Indians, 6 to 5, at Dunn Field.

Ty Cobb and Al Simmons had their suspensions lifted in time for the game between the Athletics and Tigers at Detroit, where more than 30,000 fans came out to Navin Field on Ty Cobb Day. Before the game at home plate, Cobb was presented with an automobile, a sombrero, silverware, and a floral piece. Cobb's double helped the Athletics defeat the Tigers, 6 to 3.

At Baker Bowl in Philadelphia, Hack Wilson, Gabby Hartnett, and Riggs Stephenson each hit for the circuit as the Cubs won the opening game of the series from the Phillies 6 to 3. Wet grounds postponed the games between the Cardinals and Giants, Pirates and Braves, and Reds and Robins.

In the third game of last October's World Series in St. Louis, Babe Ruth was the first batter in the history of Sportsman's Park to hit a home run into the centerfield bleachers. Ruth duplicated the feat on Wednesday, May 11, 1927.

On a very cold afternoon, Urban Shocker, a right-hander, was on the mound for the Yankees. Ernie Nevers, the former star halfback at Stanford, pitched for the Browns. Ernest Alonzo Nevers, 23, was from Willow River, Minnesota. As a rookie in 1926, Nevers appeared in eleven games, winning two and losing four with a 4.44 era.

Combs walked to open the game.

After Koenig forced him at second base, the Babe came up to bat. With Koenig on base, Ruth hit a long home run off Nevers into the center field bleachers. In the second, the Yankees added a run as Lazzeri singled past Adams at second base, stole second base, went to third on Dugan's sacrifice, and scored on Grabowski's single to left field.

In the home half of the second, Shocker gave up three straight singles to right field by Rice, Schulte, and Gerber. With the bases loaded with Browns and none out, Rice scored when Gehrig tagged out Schang. Nevers grounded to Dugan, but the throw home to catch Schulte at the plate was high. Schulte's run made the score 3 to 2.

After Ruth doubled to the wall in right center field in the third, Gehrig doubled to the same spot. Ruth scored and the Yanks led 4 to 2. Shocker, meanwhile, pitched well over the next six innings. He had the Browns backing away from the plate and swinging wildly. From that point on, St. Louis got only two men past first base and did not score again.

Final score: Yankees 4, Browns 2.

Yankee Notebook for Wednesday, May 11, 1927: Ruth's home run was his eighth . . . The Babe also had a double as did Shocker and Gehrig . . . Shocker (3-3) limited his old club to eight scattered hits, walking two and striking out four . . . For the Browns, O'Rourke had three hits, two doubles, and a single . . . Nevers, the Browns' starter, settled down after the third and kept the Yankees scoreless. He gave up a total of seven hits . . . Lazzeri had a stolen base and an error . . . The game was played in 1:49 . . . The Yankees had won four out of five in the West.

American League President Ban Johnson sent Connie Mack, the manager of the Philadelphia Athletics, a letter notifying him that Ty Cobb and Al Simmons were each fined $200 for their actions on May 5 that led to a near riot and the ejection of both players. At Navin Field, Jack Quinn out pitched Detroit starter Ken Holloway as the Athletics defeated the Tigers, 3 to 1, for the second straight time. Cobb hit safely in his fifteenth straight game.

The Senators' Horace Lisenbee was defeated by the White Sox, 4 to 1. Before that day's loss, Lisenbee had won three games in a row. Rain postponed the game between the Red Sox and Indians at Cleveland.

At the Polo Grounds, Rogers Hornsby faced his former club and hit a double and home run to lead the Giants over the Cardinals by a score of 10 to 1. Ed Farrell, the Giants' shortstop, also homered. In Philadelphia, a three-run rally in the seventh inning off Bob Osborn gave the Phillies a win over the Cubs, 5 to 2. Hack Wilson hit a home run for the Cubs. With 8,000 fans at Ebbets Field, the Robins routed the Reds, 7 to 5. Reds' left fielder Rube Bressler had three hits, including a home run.

Rain cancelled the game between the Pirates and Braves at Boston after eight innings with the score tied at four.

Former Yankee teammates Herb Pennock, a left-hander, and "Sad Sam" Jones, a right-hander, opposed each other at Sportsman's Park in St. Louis on Thursday, May 12, 1927. Samuel Pond Jones, 34, from Woodsfield, Ohio began his major league career with the Cleveland Indians. After spending two seasons with the Indians (1914 and 1915), the six foot Jones played for the Boston Red Sox (1916 through 1921). For the Red Sox in 1921, Jones won 23 and lost 16, with 1 save, and a 3.22 era, leading the American League with five shutouts.

In December of 1921, the Yankees obtained Jones from the Red Sox along with Joe Bush and Everett Scott for Roger Peckinpaugh, Jack Quinn, Rip Collins and a minor leaguer. Sam Jones was the ace of the pitching staff in 1921, the first year the club won a World Championship. That season he won 21 and lost 8, posted 4 saves, with a 3.63 era. In February 1927, Jones was traded to the Browns for outfielder Cedric Durst and pitcher Joe Giard.

Jones opened the game by striking out Combs, Koenig, and Ruth.

Pennock and Jones pitched scoreless ball over the first three innings. In the fourth, Jones walked Koenig and Ruth singled. Meusel hit a sacrifice fly and Koenig and Ruth advanced. When Lazzeri singled to right, both runners scored.

The Yankees took a 4 to 0 lead in the fifth. Collins singled to left and was sacrificed to second by Pennock. When Combs singled, Collins moved to third, and he scored after Koenig hit a sacrifice fly to Miller in left field. Ruth then doubled against the right field barricade, scoring Combs.

The Browns scored two runs in the seventh off Pennock, who found himself in trouble again in the eighth when Sisler doubled and scored on Miller's two-base hit. With the Browns trailing by one run, Pennock fanned Rice for the third out. After Jones held the Yankees scoreless in the ninth, the Browns came up in the bottom of the inning. Pennock retired Schulte, Otto Miller, who had replaced Gerber at short, and Schang.

Final score: Yankees 4, Browns 3.

Yankee Notebook for Thursday, May 12, 1927: Pennock (4-0) was in complete control except for the seventh and eighth. The southpaw gave up nine hits, struck out three, and walked one . . . Jones, the Browns' starter, gave up nine hits and struck out eight . . . Ruth had two hits, a single and double . . . Meusel and Collins also had two singles a piece . . . Meusel, Pennock, and Koenig sacrificed . . . The series with St. Louis concluded the next day.

At Navin Field in Detroit, Rip Collins won his fourth start as the Tigers took the third game of the series from the Athletics, 9 to 7. In Chicago, the White Sox won their fourth straight defeating the Senators, 5 to 4. Rain postponed the game between the Red Sox and Indians at Cleveland.

In Brooklyn, Dazzy Vance won his third straight game by holding the Reds to four hits as the Robins won, 6 to 3. Max Carey stole home in the eighth for the Robins' final run. At Baker Bowl, the Cubs scored in the second and fifth innings off Jack Scott to defeat the Phillies, 4 to 1. In New York, the Giants tied the Cardinals in the seventh inning and went onto to win in the eleventh, 3 to 2. Taylor Douthit hit a home run for St. Louis. At Braves Field, the Pirates scored two runs in the eighth to overcome the Braves' one run lead and went on to win, 8 to 7.

The Yankees played the final game of the series with the Browns at Sportsman's Park in St. Louis on Friday, May 13, 1927. Waite Hoyt, a right-hander, opposed left-hander Ernie Wingard. Born in Prattville, Alabama on October 17, 1900, Ernest James Wingard signed with the Browns, and in his rookie year 1924 the left-hander won thirteen. During the next two seasons—1925 and 1926—Wingard won nine and five, respectively.

Wingard retired Combs to open the game, but then Koenig tripled to the bleachers in left field. Ruth walked. With Koenig on third and Ruth at first, Gehrig hit a sacrifice fly, scoring the runner at third. Over the next five innings Hoyt and Wingard pitched scoreless ball.

In the sixth, Wingard walked Ruth again. When Meusel tripled, Ruth scored and the Yankees led 2 to 0. The Browns reached Hoyt for a run in the home half of the sixth, but in the seventh the Yanks took a 3 to 1 lead after Grabowski singled, went to third on Hoyt's double, and scored on Combs's sacrifice fly to Rice.

O'Rourke opened the Browns' seventh with a single, but Mellilo hit into a double play; Gehrig to Koenig and back to Gehrig. After Sisler and Williams followed with singles, Hoyt retired Rice to end the inning. Elam Vangilder, a right-hander who replaced Wingard, retired the Yanks in the top of the ninth. Hoyt set down the Browns in the bottom half of the ninth.

Final score: Yankees 3, Browns 1.

Yankee Notebook for Friday, May 13, 1927: Hoyt (5-1) needed to constantly work out of trouble, but he completed the game, giving up ten hits, walking four, and striking out none . . . The Browns outhit the Yankees ten to nine . . . Wingard walked Ruth three times . . . Koenig and Dugan came out of their batting slumps with a hit each . . . Combs had two sacrifices and Gehrig and Koenig one each . . . The Yanks turned three double plays.

With the victory that afternoon, the Yankees won six of seven in the West . . . After the game the team left for Detroit to open a series the next day . . . Ruether was scheduled to open at Navin Field.

In Detroit, Al Simmons had a home run, double, and single as the Athletics won the final game of the series from the Tigers, 10 to 3. With a bunt single in the fourth, Ty Cobb had hit safely in seventeen successive games. Cobb also had a stolen base. At Dunn Field, Del Lundgren's three-hit shutout led the Red Sox to victory over the Indians, 7 to 0. Lundgren also tripled. Ira Flagstead's spectacular play in centerfield helped Lundgren. Rain postponed the game between the Senators and White Sox at Chicago.

At the Polo Grounds, Bill Sherdel allowed seven hits and his teammates pounded four opposing pitchers as the Cardinals took the final game of the series from the Giants, 11 to 1. The Cardinals drove Freddie Fitzsimmons from the game in the first inning as everyone on the team batted as the visitors scored seven runs. At Philadelphia, home runs by Cy Williams, Freddie Leach, and Jimmy Wilson led the Phillies to a win over the Cubs, 4 to 1.

Cubs' hurler Tony Kaufmann's clout tied a major league record for consecutive game home runs hit by a major league team; fourteen home runs in eleven straight games. At Ebbets Field, the Robins made it three in a row over the Reds, 5 to 4. Cold and rain postponed the game between the Pirates and Braves at Boston.

ii

Officials tried to play the game between the Tigers and Yankees at Navin Field in Detroit on Saturday, May 14, 1927, but it had to be cancelled because of rain. Several thousand fans had been admitted before it was called off. All reserved seats had been sold for that game as well as the next day. Those admitted were given rain checks, and they were expected to return tomorrow. A great deal of confusion was expected with more fans than seats for the game. The delay may not have been so long if Frank Navin, the Tiger's President, had been in town, but he was at Louisville watching the Kentucky Derby.

Concerned about the Yankees' pitching, Miller Huggins had a dilemma. Huggins wanted to win as many games as we could, but he also wanted try out Myles Thomas, George Pipgras, and Wilcy Moore as starters. To start any one of them risked a victory; however, Huggins knew he would need to pitch them soon.

That day Tris Speaker, the former manager of the Indians, returned to Cleveland, where his old team beat his present club the Senators, 5 to 2. George Uhle, who came back after nearly two weeks away with a lame arm, limited Washington to seven hits. In a ceremony before the game, Speaker was presented with a $1,500 chest of silver and other gifts. At Sportsman's Park, Bing Miller had four hits, including a home run, as the Browns pounded out sixteen hits against three Athletics pitchers and won 12 to 2. Rain postponed the game between the Red Sox and White Sox at Chicago.

With the Cardinals at bat with one out in the top of the seventh and the Phillies leading 12 to 3, there was a thundering roar as ten rows of the lower grandstand tier collapsed at Baker Bowl in Philadelphia. Fans rushed onto the field in the confusion; one man died and fifty people were injured with cuts and bruises. Umpire-in-chief Frank Wilson called the game immediately.

He gave his reason as "panic."

It was the second time in the history of baseball that a game was called for that reason. The first time was August 8, 1903, in the second game of a doubleheader with the Boston Braves at the same ballpark when the third base stands collapsed onto 15th Street. Twelve people died and several hundred people were injured that day.

At Braves Field, Guy Bush pitched the Cubs to an eighteen-inning victory over the Braves, 7 to 2. Bush's teammates scored five runs in the eighteenth and knocked out Boston's starter, Charley Robertson. The game was the longest of the season. In New York, Eddie Farrell's single to left in the sixth inning sent Bill Terry home with the deciding run as the Giants defeated the Reds, 2 to 1. Visiting Ebbets Field for the first time, the Pirates sent the 20,000 fans home disappointed after hammering the Robins, 6 to 1.

Heavy rain and light snow on Sunday, May 15, 1927 cancelled the game for the second day in a row at Detroit between the Yankees and Tigers.

"Can you beat it?" Miller Huggins remarked late that afternoon to reporters. "Honestly, they ought to play the first quarter of the season in Florida. Here my team is going along great and likely to clean up in the West and what does the weatherman do but throw us for a two day loss."

The bad weather helped Detroit. Their two best pitchers, Earl Whitehill and Rip Collins, were expected to be ready to face the Yankees.

Meanwhile, with time on his hands, Huggins figured out mathematically how the club could win the pennant. If they were to win ten more than half of the remaining 128 games to be played, or seventy-four, the Yankees would finish with ninety-two victories, enough in Huggins's opinion to win the flag.

On a cold, windy day in St. Louis, Wally Schang's home run with the bases loaded led the Browns to a victory over the Athletics, 8 to 6. Mickey Cochrane and Eddie Collins each hit solo home runs for the Athletics. At Comiskey Park, the Red Sox bunched three of their four hits with a sacrifice and a wild throw to score two runs in the first inning and went on to defeat the White Sox, 2 to 1. Rain postponed the game between the Senators and Indians at Cleveland.

In New York, Hugh McQuillan allowed seven hits as the Giants defeated the Reds, 6 to 3, at the Polo Grounds. Bill Terry had a four-bagger with Rogers Hornsby on base. That day, the Pirates moved into second place with a win over the Robins at Ebbets Field, 9 to 6. Joe Harris homered for Pittsburgh. The St. Louis Cardinals played an exhibition game against York of the New York-Penn League at York, Pennsylvania. St. Louis won, 4 to 1.

After a section of the right field grandstand at Baker Bowl collapsed, the game the next day between the St. Louis Cardinals and the Philadelphia Phillies was moved to Shibe Park, home of the Philadelphia Athletics. Engineers of Philadelphia's Bureau of Building Inspection and officials of the Department of Public Safety inspected the pavilion at Baker Bowl. Greatly concerned over their findings, the engineers determined that the collapse of the right field stand may have weakened the entire pavilion.

With several thousand fans at Navin Field in Detroit on a very cold afternoon, the Yankees finally played the Tigers after two cancellations due to bad weather on Monday, May 16, 1927. The ballpark's history began in the fall of 1911, when Bennett Field, the Tigers' home at the corner of Michigan and Trumbull, was torn down after sixteen seasons. Fearful of a fire in the wooden structure, a new ballpark of steel and concrete was constructed at the site. The new ballpark was named Navin Field after the Tigers' owner—Frank Navin

Navin Field opened on April 20, 1912, and it held 23,000 spectators. A covered grandstand stretched down the first and third base lines. There were bleachers in right field. The first major additions to the ballpark occurred in 1923 when a second deck was built between first and third base, and a press box was added at the top of the roof. The seating capacity rose to 30,000. The dimensions of Navin Field were 365 feet down the right field line, 340 down the left field line, and 400 feet to center field.

Dutch Ruether, a left-hander, pitched for the Yankees. Right-hander Ken Holloway started for the Tigers. Kenneth Eugene Holloway, 29, hailed from Thomas County, Georgia. The six foot, 180 pound hurler debuted with the Tigers in 1922; he pitched one inning. Holloway won eleven in 1924, fourteen in 1925. In 1926, he won 4 and lost 6, with 2 saves and a 5.12 era.

The Line-Ups

Yankees	Tigers
Earle Combs cf	Lu Blue 1b
Mark Koenig ss	Jack Warner 3b
Babe Ruth lf	Harry Heilmann rf
Lou Gehrig 1b	Bob Fothergill lf
Bob Meusel rf	Heinie Manush cf
Tony Lazzeri 2b	Marty McManus 2b
Joe Dugan 3b	Jackie Tavener ss
Pat Collins c	Merv Shea c
Dutch Ruether p	Ken Holloway p

Holloway wore a white pinstriped uniform with an orange and black tiger's head on the shirtfront. His cap was a solid navy blue with an orange colored old English style "D" on the front. On his solid blue stockings were two orange stripes. He wore a black belt and black cleats.

Holloway retired the Yankees in the first. The Tigers scored two runs in the bottom of the inning. With two outs in the third, Gehrig hit a home run off Holloway that landed in the right field bleachers. Meusel then singled and stole second. Lazzeri walked. With Dugan at bat, Lazzeri was trapped off first. As Lazzeri was caught in a rundown, Meusel headed for third. He made it and then raced for the plate as Lazzeri escaped the rundown. Blue threw home to Shea to catch the runner, but Meusel hooked the plate with his slide and was safe.

The game was tied at two.

Holloway and Ruether pitched scoreless ball in the fourth, fifth, and sixth innings. In the seventh, Holloway walked Combs. Koenig then singled, moving Combs to third. When Ruth hit a sacrifice fly, Combs scored. Next up was Gehrig, who doubled and scored Koenig. The Yankees led 4 to 2.

Ruether retired the Tigers in the seventh and eighth.

After Holloway was lifted for a pinch hitter, George Smith, a right-hander, pitched the ninth. Smith walked Collins, Combs and Koenig. With the bases loaded, Ruth came up to bat. George Moriarty, the Tigers' manager, brought in left-hander James Walkup to face Ruth. On a three and two count, Ruth singled down the right field line. Collins and Combs scored, making the score 6 to 2.

With one man on base in the Tigers' ninth, Huggins brought in Wilcy Moore, a right-hander, to replace Ruether. He walked Blue, putting men on first and second with none out. Moore then retired Warner, Heilmann, and struck out Fothergill to end the game.

Final score: Yankees 6, Tigers 2.

Yankee Notebook for Monday, May 16, 1927: Ruether (4-1) pitched a strong game. The southpaw gave up nine hits, walked four, and struck out two . . . Moore retired the Tigers in the ninth without a hit . . . Tiger hurlers Holloway, Smith and Walkup gave up ten hits . . . Gehrig had a home run, two doubles and drove in three runs . . . Gehrig's homer was his eighth, tying him with Ruth for most home runs in the American League.

On the bases, Meusel stole second, third, and home in the third inning. The only other Yankee to steal the same bases in one game was Fritz Maisel on August 17, 1915 . . . In the field, Koenig and Combs made errors in the second, and Lazzeri had one in the third . . . Ruth was limping and did not cover much ground. The slugger's big toe on his right foot bothered him.

At Sportsman's Park in St. Louis, the Athletics and Browns combined for twenty-four hits, but Philadelphia hit four home runs to defeat St. Louis, 10 to 8. Al Simmons clobbered two home runs and Mickey Cochrane and Ty Cobb one each for the Athletics. Browns' center fielder Harry Rice also homered. In Chicago, Ted Lyons won his fifth and led the White Sox to a victory over the Red Sox, 5 to 2. Rain postponed the game between the Senators and Indians at Cleveland.

The game between the Phillies and Cardinals was played at Shibe Park because of the collapse of a portion of the grandstand at Baker Bowl on Saturday. Jesse Haines outpitched Alex Ferguson as St. Louis defeated Philadelphia, 2 to 1. That evening George Elliott, Philadelphia's Director of Public Safety, announced that Baker Bowl would be closed until it was made "absolutely safe."

In Brooklyn, former Pirate Max Carey had four hits as the Robins defeated the Pirates, 9 to 5, at Ebbets Field. The loss dropped Pittsburgh out of second place. Rain postponed the games between the Reds and Giants at New York and Cubs and Braves at Boston.

The Yankees played the final game of the weather-shortened series with the Detroit Tigers at Navin Field on Tuesday, May 17, 1927. Coming into the game, the Yankees had won five straight. The club announced that outfielder Bob Meusel had broke a blood vessel in his right leg while stealing a base the day before. The doctor told Meusel to rest the leg for a day or two. Cedric Durst replaced Meusel in the outfield. Left-hander Herb Pennock pitched for the Yankees.

Rip Collins, 31, started for the Tigers. From Weatherton, Texas, Harry Warren "Rip" Collins was a 6'1", 205 pound right-hander. Collins broke into the major leagues with the Yankees in 1920 and won 14 and lost 11 in 1921. Traded to the Red Sox in 1922, Collins then joined the Tigers in 1923. His best year with Detroit was 1924 when he won fourteen. In 1926, Collins won 8 and lost 8, posted 1 save, and compiled a 2.73 era.

With the Tigers leading 2 to 0 in the third, Combs and Koenig singled and Gehrig walked. With the bases loaded, Durst hit a fly to Fothergill, scoring Combs. When Lazzeri hit a fly to centerfield, Manush fumbled the ball and was charged with a three-base error as Koenig and Gehrig crossed the plate. The Yankees led 3 to 2.

New York added one run in the fifth after Gehrig singled off Collins and moved to third on a base hit by Durst. On a squeeze play with Dugan at bat, Gehrig scored. In the sixth, Collins walked Combs and Ruth and gave up a single to Koenig. With the bases filled, Gehrig singled, scoring Combs. Koenig then scored on an infield out, making the score 6 to 2.

In the bottom of the fifth, Combs helped Pennock with a spectacular catch off Fothergill. With his back to the flagpole, Combs reached above his head and caught the ball with one hand in front of him.

With rain falling in the eighth, Ruth homered over the left centerfield fence. Gehrig followed with a double. After Durst singled, Gehrig scored. Lazzeri singled. When Dugan and Grabowski sacrificed, Durst scored. Ownie Carroll, a right-hander, pitched a scoreless ninth. Pennock retired the Tigers in the home half of the ninth.

Final score: Yankees 9, Tigers 2.

Yankee Notebook for Tuesday, May 17, 1927: Pennock (5-0) was in trouble all afternoon. The left-hander gave up twelve hits and his control was off, walking five; he struck out two . . . The Tigers left two men on base in the second, two in the third, three in the fourth, two in the fifth, and two in the sixth . . . At the plate, the Yankees pounded out fifteen hits . . . With the exception of Dugan, every player had at least one hit . . . Gehrig and Koenig each had three hits . . . Gehrig, Grabowski and Pennock doubled.

In the final game of the series at Comiskey Park in Chicago, the Red Sox defeated the White Sox, 6 to 3. Boston's Slim Harriss gave up twelve hits and pitched out of trouble when needed. At Sportsman's Park, Tom Zachary pitched a complete game for the Browns as his teammates pounded out sixteen hits off the Athletics' pitchers and won 11 to 4. Meanwhile, at Dunn Field, Horace Lisenbee hurled a four-hit shutout as his teammates knocked three opposing pitchers out of the game as the Senators defeated the Indians, 12 to 0. Washington's scoring was highlighted with a six run rally in the seventh.

With Philadelphia's Baker Bowl closed, the Phillies played the Cardinals at Shibe Park. Jack Scott and Grover Cleveland Alexander hooked in a pitching duel as the Phillies defeated the Cardinals, 4 to 3. In Boston, the Cubs beat the Braves in twenty-two innings at Braves

Field, 4 to 3. After giving up a total of three runs in the fourth and fifth, Boston starter Bob Smith pitched scoreless ball until Chicago scored in the top half of the twenty-second.

At the Polo Grounds, Burleigh Grimes of the Giants shutout the Reds for the first time that season, 2 to 0. In Brooklyn, Pirate pitchers Carmen Hill and Johnny Morrison allowed only three hits, but the Robins scored two runs to win, 2 to 1.

Major League Baseball Standings
May 17, 1927
American League

	Won	Lost	P.C.
New York	20	8	.714
Chicago	17	13	.567
Philadelphia	15	14	.517
Washington	12	14	.462
Detroit	12	14	.462
St. Louis	12	14	.462
Cleveland	12	15	.444
Boston	9	17	.346

National League

	Won	Lost	P.C.
New York	19	9	.679
St. Louis	15	11	.577
Philadelphia	13	10	.565
Chicago	14	11	.560
Pittsburgh	13	11	.542
Brooklyn	13	17	.433
Boston	9	14	.391
Cincinnati	7	20	.259

Chapter 12

Heading Home

After morning showers and threatening skies in Cleveland, the game between the Yankees and Indians at Dunn Field was postponed on Wednesday, May 18, 1927. The game was to be made up on Friday, which was originally an off day for both clubs. The Yankees were to have played an exhibition game at Massillon, Ohio, but it was arranged with the understanding that a postponement in Cleveland would mean a cancellation.

Urban Shocker and George Uhle, both right-handers, were expected to start the next day. Bob Meusel, who did not play in the last game in Detroit because of a leg injury, was scheduled to return. Hopeful of taking three of four games, the Yanks were taking nothing for granted and remembered the finish in 1926, when only their spring victories saved them from losing the pennant race. Following the series in Cleveland, the team was to visit Washington for one game before returning to New York for an extended stay at Yankee Stadium.

At Navin Field that day, Earl Whitehill struck out ten, fanning six in the first four innings, and allowed six hits as the Tigers defeated the Senators, 5 to 3, in the first game of the series. In St. Louis, Bing Miller had a home run and three singles and Ken Williams homered as the Browns defeated the Red Sox, 8 to 6, at Sportsman's Park. Boston's Fred Haney, Phil Todt, and Buddy Myer hit for the circuit.

Rain ended the game between the Athletics and White Sox at Chicago after the first inning. The White Sox took a 2 to 0 lead before the rain. The game marked Eddie Collins's first appearance in the windy city that season. Collins had played second base for the White Sox from 1915 through 1926. He also managed the club to fifth place finishes in 1925 and 1926. Collins's former teammates presented him with a wristwatch and a diamond stickpin.

At Braves Field, Larry Benton pitched a complete game as Boston took the first game of the series from St. Louis, 8 to 1. That afternoon, the Cubs visited Ebbets Field for the first time beating the Robins behind Charlie Root, 7 to 4. At the Polo Grounds, Glenn Wright and Pie Traynor hit home runs as the Pirates trounced the Giants, 13 to 6. Pittsburgh pounded out eighteen hits off Dutch Henry, Fred Fitzsimmons, and Bill Clarkson. Threatening weather postponed the game between the Reds and Phillies at Philadelphia.

Preliminary results from the investigation by engineers of the Bureau of Building Inspection in Philadelphia indicated that the collapse of the stands in Baker Bowl last Saturday was due to wet rot that weakened a main girder on the center of the right field pavilion.

On Thursday, May 19, 1927, the Yankees faced the Indians at Dunn Field in Cleveland for the first time that season. Originally named League Park, Dunn Field was located at the intersection of East 66th Street and Lexington Avenue. Cy Young, pitching for the Cleveland Spiders, inaugurated League Park on May 1, 1891. The ballpark was re-named Dunn Field in 1916 after Jim Dunn, a railroad contractor, who bought the club.

The distance from home plate to the left field foul pole was 375 feet; to center field 420 feet and to right field 290 feet. Extending down right field to the center field scoreboard was a 40-foot fence that had a 20-foot high concrete wall. On top of the wall was a 20-foot high wire screen and balls off the screen were in play. The capacity crowd in Dunn Field was 22,000.

The Yankees came into Cleveland having won eight of nine games on the Western tour. Bob Meusel was in uniform but did not play. Ben Paschal substituted for Meusel. Urban Shocker, a right-hander, started for the Yankees.

Opposing the Yanks was Garland Maiers "Gob" Buckeye, 29, a 260-pound left-hander from Heron Lake, Minnesota. At the age of twenty, Buckeye debuted for the Senators; he pitched two innings of one game, yielding three hits. He spent the next six years in the minor leagues, joining the Indians in 1925, winning thirteen. In 1926, Buckeye won 6 and lost 9 with a 3.09 era.

Line-Ups

Yankees	Indians
Earle Combs cf	Homer Summa rf
Mark Koenig ss	Lew Fonseca 2b
Babe Ruth rf	George Burns 1b
Lou Gehrig 1b	Joe Sewell ss
Ben Paschal lf	Luke Sewell c
Tony Lazzeri 2b	Charlie Jamieson lf
Joe Dugan 3b	Ike Eichrodt cf
Pat Collins c	Rube Lutzke 3b
Urban Shocker p	Garland Buckeye p

The Indians took the field wearing their home white uniforms with a large capital "C" in dark on the left front jersey, a dark cap with a white "C" above the bill and similar colored stockings. Combs opened the game with a single. After Koenig and Ruth were retired, Gehrig hit a long drive to centerfield that bounced against the scoreboard, scoring Combs. While Eichrodt played the ball and threw to J. Sewell, the short stop, Gehrig rounded the bases safely with an inside-the-park home run.

After tying the game in the home half of the first, Buckeye walked Lazzeri in the second. When Dugan singled, Lazzeri raced to third and came home on Collins's sacrifice fly. The Yankees led 3 to 2.

Shocker gave up singles to Eichrodt and Buckeye in the second. When Fonseca singled, Eichrodt scored, tying the game at three. Huggins then brought in Wilcy Moore, a right-hander, to face Burns, who batted right-handed. With two runners on and two outs, Moore retired Burns on one pitch.

Moore and Buckeye pitched scoreless ball over the next six innings. Moore's sinker and curve gave the Indians trouble. Between the fourth and ninth innings, the infielders threw out the Indians one after the other. At one point, Moore retired fifteen in a row.

In the ninth with the score tied at three, Dugan singled with one out. Collins then singled to right field. Dugan raced to third. When Moore laid a perfect bunt down the first base line, Dugan scored standing up and the Yankees took a 4 to 3 lead. Moore pitched the ninth. With two outs, Glenn Myatt pinch-hit for Buckeye and hit a fly to right. Luckily, the ball hit the wire screen and bounced back for only a double. Summa then hit the first ball thrown by Moore and popped up to Gehrig to end the game.

Final score: Yankees 4, Indians 3.

Yankee Notebook for Thursday, May 19, 1927: Gehrig had two singles and a home run, his ninth of the season, which tied Ruth for the club lead in home runs . . . Gehrig's three hits raised his batting average to .425, best in the American League . . . On the mound, Shocker lasted 1 2/3 innings before Moore relieved him . . . Moore (3-3) pitched seven and one-third innings and halted the Indian's attack, giving up only four hits and walking none . . . Five Indians reached first base against Moore, one of them on a force out. Only two Indians reached second base . . . With his appearance, Moore had faced every rival club in the league in his rookie season.

In American League action at St. Louis, Ken Williams's home run in the tenth inning gave the Browns a win over the Red Sox, 6 to 5, at Sportsman's Park. The victory was St. Louis's fifth in six games. At Navin Field, Hollis Thurston pitched a six-hit shutout as the Senators defeated the Tigers, 3 to 0, in the second game of the series. Thurston was the first pitcher to shutout Detroit that season.

In Chicago, Tommy Thomas won his sixth game in a pitching duel with Connie Mack's star southpaw Lefty Grove as the White Sox defeated the Athletics, 3 to 0. Ty Cobb singled in his first plate appearance for the Athletics and had at least one hit in nineteen consecutive games.

All the scheduled games in the National League were postponed because of rain. Meanwhile, in Philadelphia, workmen under the supervision of the Bureau of Building Inspection continued the task of "taking apart" Baker Bowl to determine its condition. Almost every piece of flooring, both lower and upper tiers, was ripped up so that the girders underneath could be inspected from all angles. Many of the girders were simply two wooden beams held together by steel bolts. The collapse of a section of the grandstand was traced to a defectiveness in one of these bolted beams. Inspectors found water had seeped between joists and produced wet rot.

At Dunn Field in Cleveland, Waite Hoyt pitched for the Yankees on the afternoon of Friday, May 20, 1927. George Uhle, who beat New York six times in seven decisions the year before, took the mound for the Indians.

A hometown boy from Cleveland, George Ernest "The Bull" Uhle, a right-hander, was born September 18, 1898. At six feet, 190 pounds, Uhle debuted with the Indians in 1919. Going into the 1927 season, Uhle had won 20 games or more three times: 1922 (22-16); 1923 (26-16) and 1926 (27-11). Uhle's record of 27 victories and 32 complete games in 1926 was best among American League pitchers.

Hoyt retired Summa and Jamieson in the Indians' half of the first. When Fonseca hit a little fly ball foul off third base, Dugan dropped the ball for an error. With another chance to bat, Fonseca singled. With Burns at bat, Fonseca tried to steal second. Grabowski, the Yanks' catcher, fired the ball to Koenig covering second. Koenig had the ball on the runner, but he dropped it and was charged with an error. With Fonseca safe on second base, Burns singled to center, scoring the runner. The Indians led 1 to 0.

Over the next six innings Uhle and Hoyt pitched well. Neither team scored. With the Indians still leading 1 to 0 in the eighth, Uhle walked Ruth. When Gehrig singled, Ruth advanced to third and came home on Durst's sacrifice fly to Eichrodt in center. With the game tied at one and two men out, Summa doubled to center. Jamieson's double past Dugan at third scored Summa. With the Indians leading 2 to 1, Uhle retired the Yankees in the ninth.

Final score: Indians 2, Yankees 1.

Yankee Notebook for Friday, May 20, 1927: Hoyt (5-2) pitched well, but took the loss . . . For Cleveland, Uhle hurled an excellent game and his teammates played well . . . Uhle struck out five; Gehrig fanned twice, once with the bases loaded . . . The Yankees had seven hits and six walks, leaving ten men on the bases . . . The infield played poorly—Koenig, Dugan, and Grabowski made errors.

Durst, who filled in for Meusel, hit a hard line drive to Lutzke in the second that the third baseman knocked down. Lutzke made a nice play to recover and threw Durst out at first . . . Jamieson walked in the third and was in a hurry to steal second; he took off without waiting for Hoyt to commit. Hoyt turned leisurely and threw him out . . . The Yankees' seven game winning streak ended that day.

At Comiskey Park in Chicago, the Athletics pounded three White Sox pitchers and won, 12 to 5. Philadelphia scored seven runs in the first. Ty Cobb singled and ran his consecutive hitting streak to twenty straight games.

At Ebbets Field, Babe Herman of the Robins hit two home runs, but the Cubs triumphed, 7 to 5. Chicago pounded Jumbo Jim Elliott for six hits and five runs in the fourth. In New York, Pie Traynor hit a grandslam home run in the top half of the twelfth inning at the Polo Grounds capping a five run rally, as the Pirates went on to defeat the Giants, 8 to 3. Lee Meadows pitched for Pittsburgh.

In Philadelphia, the Reds and Phillies split a doubleheader with Cincinnati winning the first game, 6 to 3, and the home team winning the second, 15 to 2. Cy Williams had a big day at bat with three home runs and a triple for the Phillies. Wet grounds postponed the game between the Cardinals and Braves at Boston.

With Dunn Field in Cleveland decorated in red, white, and blue bunting on a warm and sunny Saturday afternoon, May 21, 1927, pre-game ceremonies were held honoring the Indians' George Burns as the most valuable player in the American League for 1926. Henry P. Edwards, chairman of the Cleveland Chapter of the Baseball Writers, presented the Indians' first baseman with the American League diploma given annually to the most valuable player. A local automobile agency presented Burns with a sedan. He was also given a big silver hollowed bat filled with about $1,200 in paper bills and gold and silver coins.

Eight baseball writers, one from each American League City, voted for the most valuable player. The baseball writer selected one player from each team and points were given as follows: eight for first place going down to one for eighth place. The rules excluded player-managers and players that had previously won the award. Recent league award winners included George Sisler (1922); Babe Ruth (1923); Walter Johnson (1924) and Roger Peckinpaugh (1925).

That afternoon Dutch Ruether, a left-hander, pitched for the Yankees. Dutch Levsen, a six-foot right-hander, started for the Indians. From Wyoming, Iowa, Emil Henry "Dutch" Levsen, 29, began his major league career with the Indians in September 1923. In 1924 and 1925, he saw limited action, appearing in only four games each season. In 1926, Levsen played in thirty-three games and pitched 237 innings. He won 16 and lost 13, with a 3.42 era.

The crowd's interest was divided between the ball game and the progress of Captain Charles A. Lindbergh's first non-stop solo crossing of the Atlantic Ocean. Lindbergh had taken took off from Roosevelt Field, Long Island, New York at 7:52 a.m. on May 20th in his monoplane, *The Spirit of St. Louis.*

Combs opened the game with a single.

After Koenig was retired, Ruth singled. Gehrig doubled, scoring Combs. Durst, replacing the injured Bob Meusel, had a base hit, scoring Ruth. After Lazzeri made out, Dugan singled, sending Gehrig home. Willis Hudlin a right-hander, relieved Levsen and retired the side. It was announced during the inning that Lindbergh was approaching France.

The Yankees went ahead 4 to 0 in the third after Ruth doubled to left field off Hudlin. The Babe moved to third base on Gehrig's groundout and scored when Durst hit a long sacrifice fly to Eichrodt in center. The Indians scored one run in the third; two more in the sixth, and trailed 4 to 3. After Ruether walked Burns in the eighth, Huggins brought in Wilcy Moore, a right-hander. When Burns moved to second on J. Sewell's out, he scored on L. Sewell's single. The game was tied at four.

News of Lindbergh's landing outside Paris came over the wires in the last half of the seventh inning. Lindbergh had covered the more than 3600-mile flight across the Atlantic Ocean in thirty-three hours and thirty minutes. Word spread quickly through the crowd. The game was stopped and thousands stood in silence while the band played the "Star Spangled Banner."

Moore and Hudlin battled in the ninth, tenth, and eleventh innings. With the score tied in the Indians' home half of the twelfth inning, L. Sewell singled to left. McNulty reached first on a bunt after Moore's throw to Gehrig was late. Lutzke then forced Sewell at third. When Dugan made a bad throw of Hudlin's grounder, the bases were loaded. Lazzeri then fielded Summa's grounder, forcing McNulty at the plate for the second out.

With the bases filled again and the count two and two on Jamieson, Moore threw a pitch that he thought cut the center of the plate. Umpire Brick Owens called it a ball. Moore protested to no avail. With the count three and two, Moore walked Jamieson to force Lutzke home with the winning run.

Final score: Indians 5, Yankees 4 (Twelve innings).

Yankee Notebook for Saturday, May 21, 1927: Ruether had a rough first inning: Jamieson hit him in the mouth on a grounder, and Fonseca knocked him over with a line drive . . . The Yankee southpaw retired the Indians in the fourth on five pitched balls . . . Moore (3-4) worked five before weakening in the twelfth . . . The Indians had a number of chances to score against Moore—Burns doubled in the ninth but Moore held the Indians, and McNulty tried to steal home in the tenth . . . The Indians also had two on board in the eleventh . . . Dugan made one of his celebrated one-handed pick-ups to throw out Luke Sewell in the second. Dugan had two more tough chances in the third; one to his right and one to his left.

At the plate, Ruth, Combs, Dugan, and Durst each had two hits . . . Ruth drove a ball out of the Dunn Field two feet foul in the twelfth . . . For the Indians, Hudlin pitched eleven and two-thirds innings of beautiful baseball, striking out five and walking three.

Knocking Hal Wiltse out of the box in the third, the Browns went on to defeat the Red Sox, 7 to 4, at Sportsman's Park. The victory was the sixth in seven games and moved St. Louis into third place. At Navin Field, the Senators scored five runs on Tigers' errors and took the third game of the series, 6 to 5. Detroit hurler Ken Holloway pitched well but lacked support. The Senators won the game with two runs in the ninth.

In Chicago, Alex Metzler singled two runs home in the eighth inning and gave the White Sox a 7 to 5 win over the Athletics at

Comiskey Park. White Sox hurler Ted Lyons won his sixth. Ty Cobb extended his hitting streak to twenty-one consecutive games.

At Ebbets Field, the Cubs swept the series from the Robins, 6 to 4 and 11 to 6. The second game ended with thousands of fans swarming on the field attempting to attack the umpire Frank Wilson. The cause of the crowd's hostility was Wilson's failure to call the second game at 5:45 p.m. to permit the Cubs to catch a train as agreed upon by both teams. Only six minutes remained when the Cubs took their last turn at bat. The Robins were leading 6 to 2 at the time. The Cubs went on to score nine runs and win, 11 to 6. The Robins filed a protest.

In New York, the Pirates pounded Hugh McQuillan and beat the Giants, 6 to 3. The victory was the third straight game that Pittsburgh took from New York. The Reds swept a doubleheader from the Phillies, 5 to 2 and 6 to 5, at Shibe Park. At Braves Field, the Cardinals took both games of a doubleheader from the Braves, 5 to 3 and 6 to 2.

An overflow crowd of 23,000 came out to Dunn Field in Cleveland on Sunday, May 22, 1927. Fans stood along the foul lines and in fair territory in left field. Before the game, a group of Oklahoma Indians presented Cleveland manager Jack McCallister with a blanket. After Babe Ruth flied out during the game, he took everyone's attention by sitting with the Oklahoma Indians in the stands; he even wore one of their feathered headdresses. Ruth enjoyed himself in Cleveland. He appeared in person at the showing of his movie in a local theater and played a cowboy at a rodeo performance.

With two successive losses, Miller Huggins sent Urban Shocker, a right-hander, to the mound. Six foot left-hander Joe Shaute, 27, started for the Indians. Joseph Benjamin "Lefty" Shaute from Peckville, Pennsylvania began his career with Cleveland in 1922. Shaute's best year was 1924 when he won 20 games. In 1926, the southpaw won 14 and lost 10, with a 3.52 era.

In the third, Combs grounded to Sewell at short, but his throw went over Burns's head at first base for an error. When Koenig singled to right, Combs went to second. Ruth walked. With the bases loaded, Gehrig had a base hit to right field, scoring Combs and Koenig. Ruth raced to third. Paschal then doubled to left field, scoring Ruth and advancing Gehrig to third. Benn Karr, a right-hander, relieved Shaute. Karr retired the side. The Yankees led 3 to 0.

Dugan beat out an infield hit in the sixth and moved to second base on Shocker's sacrifice. Combs then singled, scoring Dugan. When Koenig bounced a double off the right field fence, Combs scored. With Koenig on second, Ruth hit a home run off Karr that sailed over the right field screen making the score 7 to 0.

Shocker weakened in the eighth. The Indians picked up two runs when Jamieson walked and Burns and J. Sewell doubled. Cleveland's Walter Miller, a left-hander, pitched a scoreless ninth. Opening the Indians' half of the ninth, McNulty and Lutzke singled. Indian pitcher George Uhle, a right-handed batter, then batted for Miller and hit into a double play—Dugan to Lazzeri to Gehrig. The game ended after Summa fouled out to Grabowski.

Final score: Yankees 7, Indians 2.

Yankee Notebook for Sunday, May 22, 1927: The Babe's home run was his tenth . . . Gehrig doubled and singled . . . On the hill, Shocker (4-3) pitched scoreless ball until the eighth. The Yankee right-hander gave up eleven hits, walked one, and struck out two . . . For the Indians, Shaute lasted 2 1/3 and the Yanks had eleven hits off him, Karr, and Miller . . . Combs, Koenig, Gehrig, and Paschal each had two hits . . . Only Grabowski and Shocker went hitless . . . The Yankees caught a train for Washington D.C. after the game to play one game against the Senators.

At Comiskey Park in Chicago, Howard Ehmke scattered five hits to lead the Athletics over the White Sox, 6 to 1. Ty Cobb, who had hit in twenty-one consecutive games, went hitless in four plate appearances. In St. Louis, the Browns rallied for two runs in the ninth at Sportsman's Park to come from behind and defeat the Red Sox, 6 to 5. The victory gave the Browns a four game series sweep.

Heinie Manush's home run in the ninth with two men on gave the Tigers a 6 to 6 tie with the Senators in the final game of the series at Detroit. The game was called in the ninth by agreement to allow the Senators to catch a train.

In Philadelphia, the Robins pounded three Phillies pitchers for twenty-two hits and won, 20 to 4, at Shibe Park. Dazzy Vance pitched for the Robins and won his fifth straight game. At the Polo Grounds, the Pirates took over first place after defeating the Giants, 9 to 4. The win gave Pittsburgh a four-game sweep. Meanwhile, the Reds pounded four Cubs' pitchers for a total of fifteen hits at Redland Field and won, 8 to 4. Cincinnati's victory ended Chicago's winning streak of six games. At Kingston, New York, the St. Louis Cardinals defeated the Kingston Colonials, 8 to 4 in an exhibition game.

Major League Baseball Standings
May 22, 1927
American League

	Won	Lost	P.C.
New York	22	10	.688
Chicago	19	15	.559
St. Louis	16	14	.533
Philadelphia	17	16	.515
Washington	14	15	.483
Cleveland	14	17	.452
Detroit	13	16	.448
Boston	9	21	.300

National League

	Won	Lost	P.C.
Pittsburgh	17	11	.607
Chicago	18	12	.600
New York	19	13	.594
St. Louis	17	12	.586
Philadelphia	14	14	.500
Brooklyn	14	21	.400
Boston	10	16	.385
Cincinnati	11	21	.344

PART 2

Facing the League

Chapter 13

Lou Gehrig

On April 26, 1923, Columbia University played Rutgers at New Brunswick, New Jersey. That day Lou Gehrig played right field and hit two home runs for the Columbia Lions. Paul Krichell, the Yankees' chief scout, was at the game and afterwards he was almost speechless when he told Ed Barrow, the Yankees' business manager, about Gehrig.

"I've got another Babe Ruth," Krichell said.

A bit skeptical of Krichell's report, Barrow went to see Gehrig himself and agreed the young man had the makings of an outstanding player. Gehrig eventually signed with the Yankees on June 12, 1923 and immediately reported to Yankee Stadium.

Both immigrants from Germany, Lou Gehrig's parents, Christina Fack and Heinrich Gehrig, were married in New York City in 1900. The only child of four that lived past infancy, he was born Heinrich Ludwig (Henry Louis) Gehrig in the Yorkville section of Manhattan on June 19, 1903. Henry Louis, known as Lou, lived in a very poor household. His father, who suffered from epileptic attacks, was a copper worker and worked irregularly.

For the family to survive, Christina Gehrig worked very hard as a maid—washing, cleaning, and cooking. As a youngster, Lou was very close to his mother. Although not close to his father, he often went with him to the German gymnasium, where he developed a powerful physique at a young age. In 1908, the Gehrig family moved from Yorkville to the Washington Heights section of Manhattan.

After graduating from elementary school, Lou at his mother's urging, enrolled in Manhattan's High School of Commerce, where he played baseball and football. In June 1920, the Commerce High School baseball team traveled to Chicago to play in an inner-city high school baseball game sponsored by a New York City newspaper.

The game was played at Wrigley Field, the home of the Chicago Cubs, and was attended by 10,000 people. With Commerce ahead 8 to 6, the left-handed Gehrig came up in the ninth inning and hit a long home run with the bases loaded. The ball sailed over the right field fence onto Sheffield Avenue. The Chicago and New York newspapers that covered the game lauded Gehrig's home run.

After graduating Commerce in 1921, Gehrig accepted a football scholarship to Columbia University in New York City, where he also planned to play baseball. John J. McGraw, the New York Giants' manager, saw Gehrig's baseball potential and wanted to sign him. After graduation, Gehrig went to see McGraw, who told him how well he had done in high school. However, McGraw told Gehrig that he wanted to see him hit professional pitching.

When McGraw offered him a contract with Hartford in the Eastern League, Gehrig told him that he had accepted a scholarship from Columbia and was expected to play football and baseball there.

"Oh, you can do both," said McGraw. "You'll play in Hartford under the name of Henry Lewis. Nobody will know that Lewis of Hartford is the same guy as Lou Gehrig of Columbia. A lot of ball players do that and have still kept their college eligibility."

Believing that the practice was common, the Gehrig family agreed. Lou played twelve games for Hartford, appearing at bat forty-six times and batting .261 with two triples, one double, and no home runs. After being visited by a very angry Andy Coakley, Columbia's baseball coach, Gehrig's stay with Hartford ended abruptly.

As a result of playing professional baseball, Columbia University disciplined Gehrig by barring him from all athletics in his freshman year. As it turned out, 1923 was the only season that Gehrig played baseball for the Columbia Lions. Playing first base and the outfield, Gehrig appeared in nineteen games and batted .444, with six doubles, two triples, and seven home runs.

Some of the home runs he hit at South Field went tremendous distances, including one, which cleared the center field fence and landed against the School of Journalism Building at 116th Street and Broadway. "Columbia Lou" scored twenty-four runs and had a .937 slugging percentage. Gehrig also pitched for the Lions and won 6 and lost 4.

Ed Barrow instructed his chief scout to meet with the family and sign Gehrig. Kritchell met with Mr. and Mrs. Gehrig and 20-year-old Lou in their apartment. Kritchell first had the family make a decision that when Lou was ready to turn professional it would be with the Yankees. Then the discussion centered on whether Lou should report immediately to the Yankees or continue his studies at Columbia for two more years and report after graduation in 1925.

Mrs. Gehrig, who wanted Lou to become an architect, voted for Columbia. Mr. Gehrig was neutral. Kritchell argued for Lou to immediately sign and report.

Lou Gehrig decided to sign, telling sportswriter Fred Lieb, "No matter what I do now, ultimately, I am going to be a ballplayer. I've now had two years of college, thanks to my scholarship and the sacrifices of my parents. But we are a poor family; we need money, and now it's my turn to earn money, real money, and make everything easier all around."

Gehrig reported to Miller Huggins at Yankee Stadium. On June 15, 1923, he got into his first game when he replaced Wally Pipp at first base in the ninth against the St. Louis Browns. Ruth often watched him at batting practice and saw him hit a couple of long balls into the bleachers.

He turned to someone there and said, "That kid sure can bust 'em."

The reporters apparently heard him and started calling him "Buster." It didn't last as long as his later nicknames of "The Iron Horse" and "Larrupin' Lou", but the reporters referred to him as "Buster" Gehrig for many years.

With Gehrig spending most of the time on the bench, watching and learning, Huggins knew that he needed more action and sent him back to Hartford of the Eastern League (Class AA), where he played in

1921. (By 1923, Hartford had a working arrangement with the Yankees.) While at Hartford, Gehrig batted .304 in 59 games, with 69 hits, 24 home runs, 8 triples, and 13 doubles.

After the Yankees clinched the American League pennant in 1923, Huggins brought Gehrig back to the club. When Pipp injured his ankle, Gehrig had an opportunity to play. On September 27, 1923, Gehrig had his first home run off Bill Piercy at Fenway Park in Boston, finishing the season with a .423 batting average.

Ineligible to play in the World Series because he joined the club after the September 1 deadline, the Yankees asked Commissioner Landis for permission to have Gehrig replace Pipp, who was injured. Landis told the club that John McGraw, whose New York Giants were to face them in the World Series, would have to give his approval. McGraw denied the request, and Gehrig did not play in the '23 World Series.

In 1924, Gehrig went with the Yanks to Spring Training in New Orleans. With Wally Pipp the club's regular first baseman playing every day, Gehrig saw action in only a few games at the start of the season. He was again sent to Hartford, where he was sensational. In 134 games, he hit 37 home runs, 13 triples, 40 doubles, and scored 111 runs. Returning to the Yankees in September 1924, Gehrig again saw limited action, playing in only ten games, batting .500, with six hits in twelve at bats.

Gehrig opened the 1925 season with the Yankees. On June 1, 1925, he pinch-hit for shortstop Pee Wee Wanninger. The next day, June 2, 1925, Wally Pipp reported he had a severe headache, and Gehrig replaced him, becoming the team's regular first baseman. Beginning with the pinch-hitting appearance the day earlier, Gehrig began a historic playing streak of 2,130 consecutive games that lasted until early 1939.

Gehrig played in 126 games in 1925 and batted .295, with 20 home runs; 10 triples; 23 doubles; 73 runs scored, and 68 runs driven in. He came into his own, however, in 1926. That season, Lou batted .313, with 16 home runs, had 47 doubles, led the league with 20 triples, and scored 135 runs—second behind Ruth's 139. Gehrig also drove in 107 runs. In the '26 World Series, the Yankees' first baseman batted .348, with two doubles and six singles.

By 1927, the 23-year-old Gehrig was a big, muscular man at 6'0", 200 pounds. Shy, quiet, and hard working, he was known by his teammates for his frugality. He lived with his parents at that time and was devoted to his mother, who watched every game at the Stadium seated near the Yankee dugout.

Chapter 14

Griffith Stadium

On Monday, May 23, 1927, the Yankees ended their road trip with a series against the Washington Senators at Griffith Stadium. On the mound for the Senators that afternoon was Hollis Thurston. Miller Huggins started Myles Thomas. Both pitchers were right-handers.

Born October 22, 1897 in State College, Pennsylvania, Myles Lewis Thomas debuted with the Yankees on April 18, 1926 and appeared in 33 games, starting 13. The five foot nine-and-a half foot hurler won 6 and lost 6, posting a 4.24 era.

Before the game, the Senators announced that Walter Johnson would pitch an exhibition game the next day against the Baltimore Orioles of the International League. It would be Johnson's first appearance of the season. He had injured his leg in Florida on March 9 and had been in a plaster cast most of that time. Walter Johnson began his major league career with Washington in 1907.

The Line-Ups

Yankees	Senators
Earle Combs cf	Sam Rice rf
Mark Koenig ss	Bucky Harris 2b
Babe Ruth rf	Tris Speaker cf
Lou Gehrig 1b	Goose Goslin lf
Cedric Durst lf	Joe Judge 1b
Tony Lazzeri 2b	Muddy Ruel c
Joe Dugan 3b	Topper Rigney ss

Pat Collins c	Ossie Bluege 3b
Myles Thomas p	Hollis Thurston p

Miller Huggins coached third base for the first time that year replacing Art Fletcher, who was the regular coach. Charlie O'Leary coached at first. After Thurston retired Combs and Koenig to open the game, Ruth hit a home run into the centerfield bleachers. Gehrig then clouted a home run that sailed over the high right field fence. In the third, Rigney tripled inside third base. Bluege hit a long ball to left field. After Durst made a spectacular catch against the wall, Rigney scored making the score 2 to 1.

Collins singled in the seventh. When Thomas bunted, Thurston fielded the ball and threw to second. It appeared Collins beat the throw, but umpire Bill Dineen called Collins out. Huggins was very upset and argued with Dineen.

In the home half of the seventh, Goslin tripled to left field when Ruth could not pick the fly ball off the grass. Judge's sacrifice fly to Ruth scored Goslin, tying the game at two. Ruel then reached first on a grounder to Koenig, who misplayed the ball. When Bluege walked, the bases were loaded. After Tucker walked, Stuffy Stewart, who ran for Ruel, was forced home, and the Senators took a 3 to 2 lead. Huggins then brought Bob Shawkey, a right-hander, into the game.

Shawkey retired the side.

Garland Braxton, a left-hander, replaced Thurston in the eighth. After Ruth doubled off the right field wall with two outs, Huggins sent Ben Paschal, a right-handed batter, up to bat for Durst against Braxton. Manager Bucky Harris replaced Braxton with Firpo Marberry, a right-hander. Huggins then recalled Paschal and sent left-handed batter Ray Morehart up to the plate. When Marberry struck out Morehart, the Yankees did not score.

The Yankees tried to tie the game in the ninth.

With one out, Dugan doubled and Mike Gazella came into the game to run for him. When Collins walked, Julie Wera replaced him on first base. With runners on first and second, Huggins sent

John Grabowski to the plate to bat for Shawkey, but Marberry struck him out. The game ended when Combs forced Wera at second base.

Final score: Senators 3, Yankees 2.

Yankee Notebook for Monday, May 23, 1927: Ruth's home run was his eleventh and Gehrig's tenth . . . One year before, Ruth had fifteen and Gehrig two . . . Before weakening in the seventh, Thomas (0-1) had only given up four hits . . . Shawkey relieved Thomas in the seventh and pitched the final 1 2/3 innings, allowing only one hit.

The Yankees had seven hits . . . Ruth and Dugan had doubles . . . Meusel appeared in the ninth inning for the first time in a week . . . After Gehrig walked to load the bases in the third, Speaker made a great catch in centerfield off Durst to end the inning. Later Durst made a perfect throw from deep left field to catch Thurston at the plate in the third.

The Yankees had three doubleheaders coming up . . . The next day the club was to open at Yankee Stadium with a twin bill against the Philadelphia Athletics. The first game was scheduled at 1:30 p.m . . . . On Friday, the Yankees would play two with the Washington Senators and two again the next day, which were make-up games due to rainouts in late April.

In St. Louis, White Sox hurler Tommy Thomas won for the seventh time in nine starts, 4 to 1, as he held the Browns to three hits at Sportsman's Park. At Dunn Field, the Indians and Tigers split a doubleheader with Cleveland taking the first game, 9 to 4, and Detroit the second, 7 to 5. Garland Buckeye pitched a complete game for the Indians in the opener.

At Shibe Park, Clarence Mitchell faced his former team and scattered seven hits as the Phillies beat the Robins, 7 to 1. Philadelphia broke open the game in the seventh with five runs. Meanwhile, Philadelphia's Director of Public Safety George Elliott gave the owners of the Phillies permission to restore the grandstand and bleachers in Baker Bowl. The cost of the project was estimated at $40,000.

The Reds' relief pitching was unable to hold off the Pirate batters as Pittsburgh defeated Cincinnati, 8 to 5, at Redland Field. Pirate third baseman Pie Traynor had four hits, a double, and three singles. The St. Louis Cardinals played New Castle, Pa. of the Ohio and Pennsylvania League in an exhibition game and defeated them, 6 to 1. Rain postponed the game between the Giants and Braves at Boston.

The doubleheader between the Philadelphia Athletics and Yankees at New York was called off because of rain on Tuesday, May 24, 1927. There would be two games the next day. The Yankees were to play an exhibition game at West Point on Thursday, and then doubleheaders with Washington on Friday and Saturday; a single game against the Red Sox on Sunday, and a doubleheader at Philadelphia on Memorial Day.

The Yankees had a tough game in Washington the day before and traveled all night to New York in a crowded, smoky Pullman. The day off helped the club, particularly Herb Pennock, who would have worked one of the two games; the left-hander was usually ineffective after long train rides.

Ruth changed his batting style in an effort to break his batting slump. His feet were farther apart, his right foot was planted well forward and he did not pivot so much. The Babe also appeared to have shortened his swing.

In the eighteen games the Yankees played since the road trip started on May 2, the club averaged ten hits a game. The club won twelve and lost six; four of the six losses were by one run.

At Dunn Field in Cleveland, the Tigers knocked George Uhle out of the box in the fourth inning and defeated the Indians, 6 to 3. Lil Stoner pitched a strong game for the Tigers until the eighth, when the Indians scored two runs on a triple by Charlie Jamieson and an error.

Walter Johnson of the Washington Senators made his first start of the season in an exhibition game in Baltimore against the Orioles of the International League. The right hander worked five innings and allowed five hits, one of which was a home run. Johnson fanned the first man he faced and two more later. He walked one. Meanwhile, the White Sox and Browns were rained out at St. Louis.

For the second day in a row, rain cancelled the scheduled doubleheader with the Athletics at Yankee Stadium on Wednesday, May 25, 1927.

"We have hopes of playing a ball game one of these days," said the Yankees' business manager Ed Barrow. "The weather man is making it very tough for us, but we are going to wait him out, and his control is bound to go bad one of these days. We've got the count up to three and two now, and he shows signs of cracking."

Barrow was looking at the schedule to reschedule that day's rainouts. Philadelphia would be in New York next on June 25, 26 and 27, with the 28th open. A doubleheader was already scheduled for the 25th, which falls on a Saturday. The next open dates were September 26, 27 and 29, and one of the games was expected to be scheduled then.

"If they would only let us play three games in one day, it would be easy," Barrow remarked.

The club had recently asked for waivers on Bob Shawkey, Walter Beall, Roy Chesterfield and Mike Gazella. Shawkey and Beall had been waived before. Chesterfield was considered questionable as a pitcher; he hurt his arm in the winter falling out of a tree. Asking waivers on Gazella was a surprise for some in the press; however, it was the club's purpose to see if other teams had an interest in a trade. Teams were interested in taking them for the waiver price, but declined to trade.

The Yankees were scheduled to travel to West Point to play the Cadets in an exhibition game the next day.

Ending their long home stand, the Indians defeated the Tigers, 9 to 6, as 21-year-old Willis Hudlin started and won. George Burns, Lew Fonseca, and Charlie Jamieson each tripled for Cleveland. At Sportsman's Park, the White Sox won both games of a doubleheader from the Browns, 14 to 8 and 1 to 0. The victories tightened Chicago's hold on second place. The losses dropped St. Louis from third to fifth place.

With almost 30,000 people at Wrigley Field, the Cubs and Cardinals split a doubleheader as St. Louis won the first game, 8 to 5, and Chicago took the second, 8 to 4. At Redland Field, the Pirates swept the Reds in the three game series by winning the final game, 2 to 0. Carmen Hill pitched a six-hit complete game shutout over the Reds. The games between the Giants and Braves at Boston and Robins and Phillies at Philadelphia were postponed because of rain.

Bob O'Farrell, Manager of the St. Louis Cardinals, was to be honored on June 4 as the National League's Most Valuable Player in 1926. Besides being known as "O'Farrell Day," the occasion was also to be celebrated as "Knothole Day," in honor of the St. Louis boys who usually were on the outside of Sportsman's Park looking in.

On Thursday, May 26, 1927, the Yankees visited the United States Military Academy at West Point, New York. The players arrived in buses at noon and went to the mess hall, where they received a tremendous ovation from the 1,200 cadets. The Yankees joined the cadets for lunch and put away half a dozen platters of steak, a couple of soup tureens of green peas, French fried potatoes, and tutti-fruit ice cream with a strawberry dressing.

"This," said Tony Lazzeri, as he loosened the lower button of his vest, "is what I call a good place to eat. I wish we had four games here. They ought to put this place in the American League."

Babe Ruth arrived after lunch in his automobile.

A beautiful dark green forest, a lake, and blue skies surrounded the west stadium at West Point. During batting practice before the exhibition game with the cadets, Ruth and Gehrig hit many balls into the lake.

The Yanks soon ran out of baseballs and stopped.

The Army team did not show up until just before game time as they had classes until 3:00 p.m. With the cadets excused from their duties and hundreds of people coming from surrounding towns, there was a big crowd at the stadium. Before the game, the Babe presented an autographed baseball to the top ball player of each of the twelve companies of cadets.

Combs walked to start the game. Koenig followed with a single. Each stole a base. Ruth faced Cadet Tim Timberlake in the first and struck out. The Babe went after bad balls in his eagerness to hit a home run. Gehrig then singled both runners home. Timberlake then struck out Meusel and Wera. The sun soon vanished and black clouds rolled in. It began to rain. The game was called after an inning and a half. One sports columnist remarked that there was so much water on the field he thought the Yankees were playing the Navy.

When the game was stopped Ruth was playing first base, Gehrig was in right, Wera at third, and Meusel in left field. Meusel seemed fully recovered from his leg injury and was expected to start against the Senators in the doubleheader at the Stadium the next day. Herb Pennock and Waite Hoyt were to oppose Walter Johnson and Hollis Thurston.

At Fenway Park in Boston, the Athletics and Red Sox split a doubleheader with Philadelphia, winning the first game behind Lefty Grove, 3 to 1. Boston took the second, 4 to 3, when Buddy Meyer singled off Samuel Gray and sent Fred Haney home with the winning run.

In St. Louis, the Browns and the Indians split a doubleheader as Frank O'Rourke hit a home run with two outs in the tenth inning as St. Louis won the first game, 2 to 1. Cleveland scored three runs in the ninth to come from behind and won the second, 9 to 7. At Navin Field, Chicago's Red Faber pitched scoreless ball over the last nine innings of a twelve-inning game against Detroit as the White Sox defeated the Tigers, 4 to 3. Faber pitched the entire game.

In Chicago, Charlie Root gave up a run in the first and the sixth as the Cubs hammered the Reds, 11 to 2. Chicago batters had seventeen hits in the game, fifteen off the Reds' starter Eppa Rixey. In Pittsburgh, Vic Aldridge gave up only three hits to the Cardinals as the Pirates won, 2 to 1, at Forbes Field for the club's eighth straight victory and longest winning streak in the league. The Pirates scored two runs in the first off Jesse Haines on a double by Glenn Wright that scored Kiki Cuyler and Paul Waner. Rain postponed the game between the Braves and Phillies at Philadelphia.

Major League Baseball Standings
May 26, 1927
American League

	Won	Lost	P.C.
New York	22	11	.667
Chicago	23	15	.605
Philadelphia	18	17	.514
Washington	15	15	.500
St. Louis	17	18	.486
Cleveland	17	20	.459
Detroit	15	19	.441
Boston	10	22	.313

National League

	Won	Lost	P.C.
Pittsburgh	21	11	.656
Chicago	20	13	.606
New York	19	13	.594
St. Louis	18	14	.563
Philadelphia	15	15	.500
Brooklyn	15	22	.405
Boston	10	16	.385
Cincinnati	11	25	.306

Chapter 15

Memorial Day at Shibe Park

Returning home after a long and successful road trip, the Yankees played the Washington Senators in a doubleheader in New York on Friday, May 27, 1927. The 25,000 fans at Yankee Stadium gave the team a friendly and noisy greeting. Out the last two weeks with a broken blood vessel in his leg, Yankee outfielder Bob Meusel was back in the line-up. For the Senators, outfielder Sam Rice and pitcher Stan Coveleski were not with the team; Rice had all his lower teeth extracted and Coveleski also had dental work.

The first game saw Horace Lisenbee, a right-hander, face left-hander Herb Pennock. In the second game, right-handers Irving (Bump) Hadley and Waite Hoyt opposed each other.

First Game
The Line-Ups

Senators	Yankees
Nick Cullop rf	Earle Combs cf
Bucky Harris 2b	Mark Koenig ss
Tris Speaker cf	Babe Ruth rf
Goose Goslin lf	Lou Gehrig 1b
Joe Judge 1b	Bob Meusel lf
Muddy Ruel c	Tony Lazzeri 2b
Topper Rigney ss	Joe Dugan 3b
Ossie Bluege 3b	John Grabowski c
Horace Lisenbee p	Herb Pennock p

In the home half of the first, Combs reached first on a hit, stole second base, and scored on a single by Gehrig. The Senators tied the game in the second and went ahead 4 to 1 in the third on singles by Speaker, Goslin, and Judge, a double by Ruel, a walk to Rigney, and a sacrifice by Bluege. After the Senators scored three more runs in the fourth, Huggins brought in right-hander George Pipgras, who retired the side. The Yankees picked up one run off Lisenbee in the fourth.

Over the next four innings Lisenbee and Pipgras pitched well; neither team scored. Joe Giard, a left-hander, pitched the ninth and the Senators did not score. The Yankees threatened in the bottom half of the ninth. With one out Ruth singled and Gehrig walked; however, Lisenbee forced Meusel to ground out to Judge, and he struck out Lazzeri to end the game.

Final score: Senators 7, Yankees 2 (First game)

In the second game, Waite Hoyt retired the Senators over the first three innings. In the bottom of the third, Combs doubled to center field off Hadley. Then Koenig singled, scoring Combs. When Ruth reached first on Rigney's error, Koenig moved to second. After Gehrig's out moved the runner to third, Meusel's scratch hit past Rigney scored Koenig and Ruth. The Yankees led 3 to 0.

After Garland Braxton, a left-hander, came into the game in the fifth, Gehrig hit a home run off him into the right field bleachers. In the eighth, Braxton walked Dugan. When Collins doubled to left, scoring the runner, the Yankees took a 5 to 0 lead. Meanwhile, Hoyt pitched very well, giving up only three hits in the first five innings; one to Goslin in the first, Tucker in the fourth, and Bluege in the fifth. Hoyt did not allow a hit over the last four frames.

Final score: Yankees 5, Senators 0. (Second game)

Yankee Notebook for Friday, May 27, 1927: Lisenbee continued his mastery over the Yankees in the first game. He gave up only four hits, two of which were in the first inning . . . The win was Lisenbee's third over New York . . . Pennock (5-1) lasted 3 2/3 and took his first loss . . . Pipgras allowed only one hit in 4 1/3 innings . . . Giard pitched a hitless ninth . . . On the bases, Speaker stole home in the fourth . . .

The Yankees made three errors in the fourth . . . Wera looked good playing third base for Dugan.

Hoyt (6-2) pitched a three-hit shutout in the second game. It was the first time the Senators were blanked that season . . . Only Tate reached second base after he walked and advanced on Bluege's hit in the fifth . . . Hoyt retired opposing players in order in seven of the nine innings . . . Gehrig hit his eleventh home run . . . Returning from his injury, Meusel had one hit in seven appearances at the plate and a stolen base in the doubleheader.

For the Senators, Bluege made several fine-fielding plays; many consider him the premier third baseman in the league . . . Ruether and Shocker were scheduled to oppose Thurston and Crowder in the twin bill the next day.

That afternoon, the Indians benefited from weak pitching and poor defense by the Browns and won, 7 to 3, at Sportsman's Park. Garland Buckeye pitched for the Indians. Browns' outfielder Bing Miller had three hits, two singles and a double, and scored two runs. In Detroit, Tommy Thomas held the Tigers to five hits as the White Sox won at Navin Field, 3 to 1. The victory was Chicago's fifth straight and Thomas's eighth win. Thomas had allowed only one earned run in his last 35 innings. Rain postponed the game between the Athletics and Red Sox at Boston.

At Forbes Field, Joe Bush, who relieved Johnny Morrison in the eighth, singled home the winning run in the tenth as the Pirates edged the Cardinals, 8 to 7. In Chicago, the Cubs defeated the Reds in the eleventh, 3 to 2, when Charlie Root won his own game in relief with a double. At Brooklyn's Ebbets Field, the Robins took two games from the Giants, 5 to 3 and 5 to 1. Dazzy Vance won the opener and Jesse Petty the finale. With 5,000 fans watching in the cold at Shibe Park, the Braves won a doubleheader from the Phillies by scores of 8 to 1 and 13 to 5.

On Saturday, May 28, 1927, the Fifth Royal Highlanders of Canada, more commonly known as the Black Watch, were guests of the Yankees at the Stadium before the first game of the doubleheader with the Senators. Led by a band, the Canadians, who numbered about 100, marched on to the field. The famous regiment was in New York City from Montreal for a three-day visit to participate in the Memorial Day parade.

Before a crowd of 45,000, right-handers Urban Shocker and Hollis Thurston pitched the first game. The second game had two of that season's best relievers—right-handers Wilcy Moore and Firpo Marberry—face each other. It was Moore's first start in the major leagues.

First Game
The Line-Ups

Senators	Yankees
Earl McNeely rf	Earle Combs cf
Bucky Harris 2b	Mark Koenig ss
Tris Speaker cf	Babe Ruth rf
Goose Goslin lf	Lou Gehrig 1b
Joe Judge 1b	Bob Meusel lf
Muddy Ruel c	Tony Lazzeri 2b
Topper Rigney ss	Joe Dugan 3b
Ossie Bluege 3b	John Grabowski c
Hollis Thurston p	Urban Shocker p

Harris, the Senators' player-manager, hit a ball to right field in the first inning that looked like a home run, but Ruth went back to the wire screen and caught the fly ball with his gloved right hand thrust across his left shoulder. The fans gave him a big hand.

With the Senators leading 2 to 0, Thurston gave up a single to Koenig in the sixth. After Gehrig walked, Meusel doubled against the left field stands, scoring Koenig. Down by one run, Lazzeri lined a double to left field with two strikes. Goslin fell after fielding a difficult chance and wrenched his shoulder. As teammates ran over to help him, both Gehrig and Meusel scored. The Yankees led 3 to 2. Goslin was uninjured and remained in the game.

The Yankees exploded for five runs in the seventh.

The rally began after Grabowski singled and was sacrificed to second by Shocker. When Combs singled, Grabowski scored. Koenig then singled. With Combs and Koenig on base, Ruth hit a long blast off Thurston into the centerfield bleachers. After Thurston retired Gehrig, Meusel homered into the left field stands. Meanwhile, Shocker went on to retire the Senators in the eighth and ninth.

Final score: Yankees 8, Senators 2 (First game)

In the second game, Wilcy Moore and Firpo Marberry pitched scoreless ball over the first three innings. In the Senators' fourth, Moore gave up his first hit when Goslin singled with two outs. Judge followed with a base hit as Goslin raced to third. On an attempted double steal, Lazzeri took a short throw from Collins, the catcher, and returned the throw to him as Goslin attempted to score. However, Lazzeri's throw sailed over Collins's head and Goslin scored.

In the sixth, Koenig doubled inside first base. West's throw from right field looked like it had the runner sliding into second base, but the umpire called Koenig safe. Harris unsuccessfully argued the call. Marberry then fanned Ruth. On a count of three balls and no strikes, Gehrig singled to centerfield, scoring Koenig and tying the game at one. A double play ended the inning.

The Yankees trailed the Senators 3 to 1 in the ninth. Lazzeri walked and raced to third when Cedric Durst, pinch-hitting for Dugan, singled. Marberry then struck out pinch-hitters Ray Morehart and Ben Paschal, who batted for Collins and Moore, respectively. With two outs, Combs singled, scoring Lazzeri. The Yankees were down by one run. The game ended, however, when Marberry retired Koenig on a fly to right.

Final score: Senators 3, Yankees 2 (Second game)

Yankee Notebook for Saturday, May 28, 1927: Shocker (5-3) pitched the entire first game and gave up eight hits and walked one. The Yankee right-hander got better as the game went on . . . Ruth had a home run, triple, and single. The Babe's home run was his twelfth, giving him one more than Gehrig . . . Ruth crossed up the Senators by hitting the ball into left field for a triple; his first of the season . . . Meusel's home run was his third . . . Dugan made a fine play in the third on McNeely's bunt . . . There wasn't a single strikeout in the game.

Moore (3-4) had the Senators shutout in the second game until the fourth when Goslin and Judge singled . . . Half the Senators' infield tried to catch Ruth's high fly in the first; Ruel caught it.

In Boston, the Athletics took both games of a doubleheader from the Red Sox, 8 to 6 and 4 to 3, at Fenway Park. Lefty Grove finished both games for manager Connie Mack. In the first game, Grove gave up two hits and no runs over the final four. In the second game, with Philadelphia leading 4 to 3 in the ninth, Grove pitched a scoreless ninth.

At Navin Field, Lil Stoner scattered eleven hits and outpitched Ted Blankenship as the Tigers took the third game of the series from the White Sox, 7 to 1. The victory ended Chicago's winning streak at five. Rain postponed the game between the Indians and Browns at St. Louis.

Glenn Wright's home run in the fifth inning ended a tie between the Pirates and Cardinals as Pittsburgh beat St. Louis, 6 to 4, at Forbes Field. The win was the Pirates' tenth in a row; it also was Lee Meadow's seventh victory. With 20,000 fans at Ebbets Field, the Giants ended a six-game losing streak as they defeated the Robins, 7 to 3. At Shibe Park, the Phillies and Braves split a doubleheader with Boston taking the first game 1 to 0; Philadelphia won the second, 8 to 3. In Chicago, Pete Donohue scattered six hits at Wrigley Field, as the Reds white-washed the Cubs, 8 to 0. The victory broke Cincinnati's five-game losing streak.

On Sunday, May 29, 1927, 35,000 fans were at Yankee Stadium and saw the Yankees play the Boston Red Sox. The game was played in New York because blue laws in Boston did not permit professional baseball to be played on Sundays. Miller Huggins started southpaw Dutch Ruether, and the Red Sox sent Hal Wiltse, also a left-hander, to the mound. Wiltse already had two victories against the Yankees.

The Line-Ups

Red Sox	Yankees
Jack Tobin rf	Earle Combs cf
Fred Haney 3b	Mark Koenig ss
Phil Todt 1b	Babe Ruth rf
Ira Flagstead cf	Lou Gehrig 1b

Baby Doll Jacobson lf	Bob Meusel lf
Buddy Myers ss	Tony Lazzeri 2b
Jack Rothrock 2b	Joe Dugan 3b
Grover Hartley c	John Grabowski c
Hal Wiltse p	Dutch Ruether p

Tobin opened the game with a bunt. When Dugan over ran it, Tobin was safe at first base. Singles by Flagstead and Jacobson gave the Red Sox an early 2 to 0 lead. The Red Sox added a run in the second on Hartley's home run to left. The Yanks picked up one run in the second after a walk to Dugan and singles by Grabowski and Ruether.

After Haney opened the third with a home run to left field giving the Red Sox a 4 to 1 lead, Huggins brought Myles Thomas, a right-hander, into the game. Thomas gave up two more runs on a double, a walk, and a single. In the bottom of the third, the Yankees scored two runs, cutting the Red Sox lead to 6 to 3. In the fourth, the Yanks came from behind and took a 7 to 6 lead against Wiltse, Fred Wingfield, and Danny MacFayden, benefiting from two errors, three bases on balls, and hits by Koenig and Meusel.

The Yankees added another run in the fifth after Grabowski singled, reached second on Thomas's sacrifice, and scored on Koenig's single. Thomas retired the Red Sox in the fourth, fifth, and sixth innings.

In the seventh, Boston scored a run and trailed 8 to 7; however, the Yankees erupted for seven runs in the eighth. With MacFayden on the mound, Ruth led off the inning with a home run into the left field stands. After Meusel and Lazzeri doubled, Herbert Bradley, a right-hander, replaced MacFayden. Bradley hit Dugan with a pitch. Grabowski and Thomas singled. Combs walked.

With the bases loaded, Koenig walked and forced in a run. With the bases filled again, Ruth came to bat for the second time in the inning and singled, driving in two more runs. Jack Russell, a right-hander, finished the inning. Thomas pitched a scoreless ninth.

Final score: Yankees 15, Red Sox 7.

Yankee Notebook for Sunday, May 29, 1927: The Babe's home run was his thirteenth . . . Gehrig's fly to Jacobson in left center in the first would have been a home run had it been hit to right . . . On the mound, Thomas (1-0) relieved Ruether in the third and pitched well over the last seven innings. From the fourth to the ninth, Thomas allowed one hit, a double by Tobin; he walked three and struck out four.

Eleven men batted in the eighth as the Yankees scored seven runs before three Red Sox pitchers could end the rally . . . The club had a total of seventeen hits . . . Grabowski had four singles and a walk . . . Gehrig singled in five appearances at the plate and was batting .399, second best in the American League. Bing Miller of the Browns led with a .405 mark . . . The Yankees left that night for Philadelphia to play a four game series at Shibe Park. Morning and afternoon games were scheduled the next day.

At Griffith Stadium in Washington, D.C., Al Simmons's two doubles and a triple and Rube Walberg's strong pitching paced the Athletics to a victory over the Senators, 6 to 1. Simmons drove in three of Philadelphia's runs and scored one himself. Ty Cobb had a double and scored three times. In St. Louis, the Indians and Browns split a double-header with St. Louis winning the first game, 7 to 4, and Cleveland the second, 10 to 2. The Indians won three out of the five games at Sportsman's Park. After the game, St. Louis left for Chicago on a month's road trip.

In Detroit, Ted Lyons won his eighth game as the White Sox defeated the Tigers at Navin Field in the final game of the series, 8 to 6. Lyons was hit hard in the last two innings, but pitched brilliantly over the first seven.

At Redland Field, the Cardinals hit Carl Mays hard and walloped the Reds, 11 to 3; Grover Cleveland Alexander gave up nine hits, four of which were doubles, but held the Reds to three runs. Cardinal second baseman Frank Frisch had three hits in five times at bat. In Pittsburgh, the Pirates defeated the Cubs, 8 to 5 behind Carmen Hill. Joe Harris homered for Pittsburgh. At Ebbets Field, the Robins closed out their home stand in front of 25,000 fans and beat the Giants, 5 to 2. Jumbo Jim Elliott allowed the Giants only four hits; he fanned nine. The Robins took three out of four games.

Major League Baseball Standings
May 29, 1927
American League

	Won	Lost	P.C.
New York	25	13	.658
Chicago	25	16	.610
Philadelphia	21	17	.553
Washington	17	18	.486
Cleveland	19	21	.475
St. Louis	18	20	.474
Detroit	16	21	.432
Boston	10	25	.286

National League

	Won	Lost	P.C.
Pittsburgh	24	11	.686
Chicago	21	15	.583
New York	20	16	.556
St. Louis	19	16	.543
Philadelphia	16	18	.471
Brooklyn	18	23	.439
Boston	13	17	.433
Cincinnati	12	27	.308

On Memorial Day, Monday, May 30, 1927, the Yankees and Athletics played morning and afternoon games at Shibe Park in Philadelphia. Two crowds of 40,000 packed the ballpark. An estimated 20,000 people were turned away after the police ordered the gates closed. The morning game started at 10 o'clock. Right-hander George Pipgras and Lefty Grove faced each other. After a two-hour break for ham sandwiches and apple pie, the afternoon game started at 3 o'clock. Herb Pennock, a left-hander, and right-hander Samuel Gray pitched.

Morning Game
The Line-Ups

Yankees	Athletics
Earle Combs cf	Eddie Collins 2b
Mark Koenig ss	Bill Lamar lf
Babe Ruth lf	Ty Cobb rf
Lou Gehrig 1b	Al Simmons cf
Bob Meusel rf	Jimmy Dykes 3b
Tony Lazzeri 2b	Mickey Cochrane c
Joe Dugan 3b	Jim Poole 1b
Pat Collins c	Chick Galloway ss
George Pipgras p	Lefty Grove p

During batting practice, Ruth did something that no one could remember ever happening before. The Babe hit the baseball so hard that it broke in two.

Combs opened the game with a single. Then Ruth and Gehrig doubled against the right-center field fence, Lazzeri singled, and Dugan doubled giving the Yankees a 3 to 0 lead. The Athletics scored a run in the bottom of the first. The Yankees added a run in the second to make the score 4 to 1.

After the Athletics scored twice in the third, Huggins brought in Bob Shawkey, a right-hander, with two outs. Shawkey retired the side. Trailing 4 to 3 the Athletics fought back, scoring four runs in the fifth and one in the sixth off left-hander Joe Giard. The Yankees cut the Athletics' lead to two after Meusel walked, Lazzeri and Dugan singled, and Collins doubled.

Yankee right-hander Walter Beall was on the mound in the eighth. With one out, Simmons doubled past Dugan at third. When he attempted to steal third, Dugan dropped Beall's throw; however, third base umpire Roy Van Graflan called Simmons out. When the Athletics argued, Van Graflan consulted plate umpire Clarence Rowland and reversed himself, calling Simmons safe. Huggins argued that Dugan held on to the ball long enough, but the decision stood.

When Simmons scored on Dykes's sacrifice fly, the Athletics led 9 to 6. The Yankees scored two in the ninth off Grove, before he retired the Yankees to end the game.

Final score: Athletics 9, Yankees 8 (Morning game).

Herb Pennock and Samuel Gray pitched scoreless ball over the first two innings in the afternoon game. The Yankees took an early 2 to 0 lead in the third. However, in the Athletics' fourth, E. Collins singled to right field and went to third on Cobb's single to right. The next batter was Al Simmons, who lifted a foul ball near the Athletics' dug out.

Grabowski caught it and went headfirst over a low iron railing and down a flight of stone steps into the dugout. The players on the Athletics' bench sprang to 'help' Grabowski and hindered him from getting up as Collins and Cobb scored. The entire Yankee team rushed onto the field. Huggins argued the Athletics stopped Grabowski from making a play and the runners should not be allowed to score.

The game was stopped for fifteen minutes.

After a long argument, the umpires finally allowed Collins to score and sent Cobb back to third. With the Athletics and fans in an uproar, Mack sent Collins to the umpire-in-chief Roy Van Graflan. Collins told him the game would be played under protest. Pennock closed out the inning. The Yankees led 2 to 1.

The Athletics went ahead 4 to 2 in the sixth, the big blow a home run against the upper left field stands by Cy Perkins, who batted for Cochrane. The Yankees took a 5 to 4 lead in the sixth. Gray walked Pennock, Combs singled, and Ruth was intentionally walked, while offering to hit with one hand. When Gehrig hit a hard single into center, Pennock and Combs scored. Gehrig took second base while the Athletics tried to get Ruth advancing to third. However, the Babe was safe and later scored on Meusel's sacrifice fly. Lazzeri ended the inning with a long fly that Lamar caught at the foot of the left field stands.

Pennock gave up three singles in a row in the bottom of the seventh to Jimmy Foxx, batting for Gray, Collins and Lamar and the score was tied at five. Huggins then brought in right-hander Wilcy Moore, who retired the side.

Left-hander Rube Walberg pitched a scoreless eighth for the Athletics. The Yankees took the field in the home half of the inning with changes in the infield—Lazzeri replaced Koenig, who injured his leg, at short stop. Ray Morehart was at second for Lazzeri. Mike Gazella at third base had earlier replaced Dugan, who hurt his knee and had left the game in the fifth. Moore retired the Athletics in the eighth and ninth.

The game went into extra innings.

In the Yankees' eleventh, Ruth hit a home run, his third in three days, into the left centerfield stands. Moore retired the Athletics in the bottom of the eleventh.

Final score: Yankees 6, Athletics 5 (Afternoon game in eleven innings).

Yankee Notebook for Memorial Day, Monday, May 30, 1927: In the morning game, George Pipgras went 2 2/3 before Shawkey relieved him . . . Shawkey (0-2) pitched 1 2/3 and took the loss . . . Giard and Beall pitched the final 3 2/3 . . . Grove pitched a complete game for Philadelphia and struck out eleven, fanning Combs, Koenig, and Ruth twice, and Gehrig, Lazzeri, Dugan, Giard, and Grabowski once . . . The Yanks out hit the Athletics fifteen to eight . . . Lazzeri, Dugan, and Collins each had three hits . . . Ruth singled and doubled. Gehrig also doubled.

In the afternoon game, Pennock pitched 6 1/3, striking out four and walking two . . . Moore (5-4) pitched 4 2/3 of scoreless baseball. He gave up four hits, struck out one, and did not walk a batter . . . Perkins's home run was the only extra base hit by the Athletics . . . Lamar had three singles . . . Gray and Walberg gave up thirteen hits . . . Ruth's home run was his fourteenth. The Babe also singled . . . Gehrig had four hits, three singles and a double . . . Combs doubled and singled twice . . . The Yankees left thirteen men on bases . . . The Yankees were scheduled to play two again the next day.

The Senators won both games of the holiday doubleheader from the Red Sox, 3 to 0 and 13 to 5, at Griffith Stadium. In the opener, Walter Johnson, pitching his first game of the season, hurled a three-hit shutout. With a crowd of 45,000 at Comiskey Park, the White Sox split a doubleheader with the Browns. St. Louis won the first game, 11 to 3 and Chicago the second, 10 to 0. At Navin Field, the Tigers and

Indians split a doubleheader with Cleveland winning the morning game, 9 to 8, and Detroit the afternoon contest, 11 to 3.

Sixty thousand fans, a new attendance record for a single day in Pittsburgh, came out to morning and afternoon games at Forbes Field. The Cubs took the morning game, 7 to 6, and the Pirates won the afternoon contest, 6 to 5. Both games went ten innings. Chicago's victory in the first game broke Pittsburgh's eleven-game winning streak. Cubs' shortstop Jimmy Cooney made an unassisted triple play in the first game.

At Sportsman's Park, the Cardinals defeated the Reds in both games of a doubleheader, 6 to 3 and 3 to 1, and took over third place in the standings from the Giants. Jesse Haines won his eighth in the first game. In Boston, the Robins swept a doubleheader from the Braves, 5 to 2 and 6 to 2. Thirty thousand fans were at the games at Braves Field.

The major leagues drew 360,000 people on Memorial Day. The eight American League games brought out 190,000, and the National League drew 170,000. Unfavorable weather, meanwhile, had forced 73 postponements in the major leagues so far that season. The National League had 42 games to make up and the American League 31. The Boston Braves led the list with 10.

Twenty-five thousand fans came out to Shibe Park in Philadelphia and watched the Yankees and Athletics play a doubleheader on Tuesday, May 31, 1927. Yankee third baseman Joe Dugan was out of the line-up after injuring his trick knee and twisting his ankle in the morning game the day before; Tony Lazzeri filled in for him at third base. In the last two days, Lazzeri had played second base, short stop, and third base. Waite Hoyt faced John Quinn in the first game, and Urban Shocker opposed Howard Ehmke in the second. All were right-handers.

Combs opened the first game with a walk. Koenig then grounded to Collins at second base, who threw to Boley, forcing Combs at second. With a count of three and two, Ruth hit a home run over the right field fence just inside the foul line. Gehrig then hit a sharp grounder that hopped over Poole's head into right field for a double. When Meusel singled to right, Gehrig raced home. The Yankees led 3 to 0.

Gehrig hit a home run off Quinn in the third making the score 4 to 1. The Yanks added another run in the fourth. In the fifth, Yankee catcher P. Collins hit a home run over the double-decked stand in left. Combs then singled. After Koenig tripled, Connie Mack brought Lefty Willis into the game. Willis walked Ruth and Gehrig. When Meusel singled, scoring Koenig, New York led 8 to 1. Hoyt gave up a run in the sixth, but the Yankees added two runs in the seventh. The Athletics scored one final run in the eighth.

Final score: Yankees 10, Athletics 3. (First game)

In the second game, with the score tied at two in the fifth, Shocker singled. When Combs doubled down the right field line, Shocker went to third. With runners at second and third, Koenig singled scoring Shocker and Combs. Ruth then hit a home run, his fifth in the last four days.

Already leading 8 to 2, the Yankees scored seven more in the sixth and went ahead 15 to 2. The Athletics scored one in the sixth, seventh, and eight. The Yankees finished the day's onslaught with three more runs in the eighth.

Final score: Yankees 18, Athletics 5. (Second game)

Yankee Notebook for Tuesday, May 31, 1927: It was the Yankees' first doubleheader sweep of the season . . . New York scored twenty-eight runs, made thirty-seven hits, and had a total of sixty-nine bases in the doubleheader . . . The Babe hit home runs fifteen and sixteen and was one game ahead of his 1921 record of 59 . . . Gehrig hit his twelfth home run and smacked a triple and a double . . . Collins, Lazzeri, and Koenig also hit home runs . . . Foxx homered for the Athletics.

In the second game, the Yankees went on a hitting rampage . . . Combs stroked two singles, two doubles, and a triple . . . Lazzeri homered, doubled, and singled twice . . . Even Shocker had three singles . . . Every player had one or more hits in the doubleheader, except Morehart . . . Hoyt (7-2) and Shocker (6-3) pitched complete games . . . Shocker was hit in the head by a pitch thrown by Rommel.

Five thousand fans came out to Shibe Park in Philadelphia to see the final game of the series with the Yankees on Wednesday, June 1, 1927.

Injuries plagued the Yanks. Bob Meusel suffered a painful charley horse in his right leg a day earlier. Urban Shocker, who was hit in the head by a pitch from Eddie Rommel, had a big bump on his skull. Pat Collins was cut on his forehead. Tony Lazzeri and Mark Koenig were bruised, and Joe Dugan had a twisted ankle.

Myles Thomas, a right-hander, started for the Yankees, and Rube Walberg, a left-hander, pitched for the Athletics. Koenig hit a home run into the left field stands in the first. As the game went along, Thomas pitched well and blanked the Athletics for six innings. With the score 1 to 0 in the Athletics' seventh, Simmons doubled down the third base line. Huggins came out of the dugout and argued with umpire Clarence Rowland that the ball was foul; Rowland almost tossed Lazzeri out of the game for arguing vehemently.

The score was tied at one in the ninth when Gehrig singled past Collins at second base. Gehrig was forced at second by Paschal. When Lazzeri hit a ground ball that went off Walberg's glove, Boley, the shortstop, knocked down the grounder and from both knees threw to Collins at second base in attempt to force Paschal; however, the throw was wild, and Paschal was safe. Huggins then sent Joe Dugan up to the plate to bat for Morehart. Dugan singled to center field. Paschal scored and the Yankees led 2 to 1. The Athletics did not score in the ninth.

Final score: Yankees 2, Athletics 1.

Yankee Notebook for Wednesday, June 1, 1927: The Yankees won four out of five in the series . . . Koenig's home run was his second . . . Gehrig had a double and single and took the lead in batting in the American League with a mark of .415 . . . Thomas (2-1) gave up six hits, allowed one run, walked one, and struck out one . . . Cochrane doubled and singled . . . Walberg limited the Yankees to five hits . . . Boley's error in the ninth set up Dugan's winning pinch hit.

Dugan was jeered with the taunt "I want to go home" when he came to the plate. The fans remembered the unfortunate episodes when Dugan was with the Athletics and left the team to return home . . . After the game, the Yankees returned to New York to begin a four game series with the Detroit Tigers at Yankee Stadium.

In Washington, D.C., Slim Harriss scattered seven hits as the Red Sox defeated the Senators, 6 to 1. Boston had ten hits off Firpo Marberry and Garland Braxton. The Senators left eleven men on base. At Navin Field, the Indians pounded the Tigers and won that afternoon, 14 to 1. Willis Hudlin was effective and won his sixth game. The Indians had twenty hits, including seven doubles and two triples. George Burns led the attack with four hits—one was his seventeenth double of the season.

At Forbes Field, the Phillies scored seven runs in the eighth and beat the Pirates, 7 to 4. Lee Meadows held the Phillies to only one hit over seven innings before Philadelphia erupted. Shucks Pruett pitched seven and Hal Carlson the final two frames. In Boston, the Robins topped the Braves, 6 to 2, and swept the four game series at Braves Field. Jumbo Jim Elliott held the Braves to four hits and one earned run. Babe Herman hit a three-run home run that clinched the game. Rain postponed the game between the Reds and Cardinals at Sportsman's Park.

After leaving Olean, New York thirty-seven years before, John McGraw, manager of the New York Giants, returned. He was welcomed and honored by the townspeople. In 1890, McGraw left the Olean team in the original New York-Pennsylvania State League after having made nine errors in one game. McGraw went on to sign with the Baltimore Orioles and played third base on one of the greatest baseball teams of all time. That day the Giants played McGraw's alma mater, St. Bonaventure College, in an exhibition game and won 12 to 2.

Major League Baseball Standings
June 1, 1927
American League

	Won	Lost	P.C.
New York	29	14	.674
Chicago	27	17	.614
Philadelphia	22	21	.512
Washington	19	20	.487
Cleveland	21	23	.477
St. Louis	19	22	.463
Detroit	18	23	.439
Boston	12	27	.308

National League

	Won	Lost	P.C.
Pittsburgh	26	13	.667
St. Louis	22	16	.579
New York	22	17	.564
Chicago	22	17	.564
Brooklyn	22	23	.489
Philadelphia	18	20	.474
Boston	13	21	.382
Cincinnati	12	30	.286

Chapter 16

Bob Meusel

When the Yankees opened Spring Training in Jacksonville, Florida on March 1, 1920 five players, Duffy Lewis, Harry Hannah, Frank O'Doul, Bill Piercy, and a highly touted rookie named Bob Meusel, were unsigned and had not yet reported. All were traveling from California and were expected any day. Within a few days Lewis, O'Doul, and Piercy reported, but for unexplained reasons it took one week before Hannah and Meusel arrived.

The 23-year-old Meusel made an impressive debut in his first workout with the Yankees at South Side Park. At 6'2" and 200 pounds, he hit the ball hard and far. Meusel also played third base rather well that day, although some thought he was too large a man to play there, a position that required agility. While many who observed him thought he was better suited for first base or the outfield, there was no room for Meusel at either of the positions. Miller Huggins went into Spring Training and the season with four outfielders, Duffy Lewis, Sammy Vick, Ping Bodie, and Babe Ruth, and a first baseman, Wally Pipp; all were experienced ball players.

Without an available position in the outfield or first base, Huggins played Meusel at third base, primarily to have his bat in the line-up. Like his teammate Babe Ruth, Meusel had a free-swinging motion. When making contact with the ball, Huggins told an interviewer that he knew of no slugger who could hit the ball harder than Meusel, except Ruth and possibly Joe Jackson.

About 50 miles south of San Francisco, California, in the Santa Clara Valley, lay San Jose. Spanish colonists founded the town in 1777 on the banks of the Guadalupe River, and after San Jose came under Mexican control in the 1820s, American settlers began to arrive from the east in the 1840s. In the years that followed, most of the people in San Jose were of European ancestry—mainly, English, German, Irish, and Italian.

In 1896, Charles Frederick Meusel, a teamster of German descent, lived in San Jose with his family. On July 19, 1896, his wife Mary (Smith) gave birth to the last of their six children—Robert (Bob) Meusel. Spending most of his life in Los Angeles, Bob was educated in public schools. After graduating from Los Angeles High School, Bob Meusel went to Arizona and played semi-professional baseball.

Back on the West Coast in 1917, he played briefly for Spokane before beginning his professional career in earnest with Vernon, California of the Pacific Coast League. Meusel batted .311 in 45 games at Vernon and before leaving for the Navy in 1918 played in only two games. While in the service, Meusel played baseball with other talented players on a very good team that even defeated the Chicago Cubs in an exhibition game.

Returning to Vernon in 1919, Meusel had a sensational season as a third baseman and outfielder, batting .337 in 163 games with 221 base hits, including 39 doubles, 14 triples, and 14 home runs. He also scored 113 runs and stole 21 bases. Looking to escape from the second division, the New York Yankees took an early interest in the young slugger.

On June 17, 1919, the Vernon Baseball Club sold Meusel to the Yankees for $10,000. As part of the remuneration ($4,500), the Yankees sent Hugh High and William Mitchell to Vernon, which agreed to accept additional players as payment for the balance due. The agreement stipulated that Meusel was to remain with Vernon until the close of the 1919 season.

After reporting to Spring Training in March 1920, Miller Huggins played Meusel at third base. As the baseball season progressed, his play at third base became a concern. Huggins finally conceded that he was ill suited for the position.

"Meusel is not a third baseman," Huggins told an interviewer.

After 45 games, Meusel was moved to the outfield, where he had an outstanding rookie year in 1920—batting .328, with 11 home runs, and 83 runs batted in.

The 1921 season was even better. Meusel batted .318 with 24 home runs and drove in 135 runs. His home run mark of 24 tied him for second behind Ruth's record of 59. Meusel's 135 run driven in was third in the league, behind Ruth's 171 and Harry Heilmann's (Detroit) 139. Meusel's performance helped the club win its first American League pennant.

Evident early in his career was another facet of Meusel's gifted talent, a powerful and accurate throwing arm. In fact, there were very few players that had a stronger arm. Meusel could throw to the bases or to home plate from any corner of the ballpark, whipping the ball like an infielder pegging to first base.

Casey Stengel, who played against Meusel in three World Series (1921-1923) as a member of the New York Giants, recalled: "He had lightnin' on the ball. I don't know what it was, but when he skipped the ball it skidded so crazy no catcher could handle it. He had to throw it on the fly all the way."

Opposing players respected Meusel's throwing ability, and even Ty Cobb would not try to score on a sacrifice fly. Meusel tied the American League mark in outfield assists in 1921 with 28 and led the league in 1922 with 24.

In the World Series loss to the Giants in 1921, Meusel batted only .200, but he did steal home in Game Two. Of note, Emil "Irish" Meusel, Bob's older brother, was an outfielder with the 1921 Giants. Irish, who was, of course, not Irish, but nicknamed because of his ruddy complexion and Irish looks, had a great series, batting .345, with 2 doubles, 1 triple, 1 home run, and 7 runs batted in.

Following the 1921 World Series, Meusel and Ruth, who had become close friends, went on a barnstorming tour in violation of baseball's rules and warnings by Commissioner Kenesaw Mountain Landis. On December 5, 1921, Landis handed Meusel and Ruth suspensions and fines. Both men were ineligible to play for the first five weeks of the 1922 season and fined their shares of the World Series.

Despite the suspensions to Ruth and Meusel, the Yankees finished the 1922 season in first place, one game ahead of the St. Louis Browns. However, Meusel had a disappointing year dropping to 84 runs batted in and 16 home runs from 135 and 24 a year earlier. In the Yankees' second consecutive loss to the Giants in the 1922 World Series, Meusel batted .300 but had only one extra base hit, a double.

The following season—1923—saw the Yankees win their first world championship. Meusel batted .313 with 91 runs batted in but hit only 9 home runs. In defeating the archrivals Giants in the 1923 World Series, Meusel led the Yankees with 8 runs batted in, including 2 triples and 1 double. Although the team failed to win the pennant in 1924, Meusel batted .325, with 120 runs driven in and 12 home runs.

For Meusel, 1925 turned out to be his best season as a Yankee; although batting only .290, he led the American League in runs batted in with 138 and in home runs with 33.

Nicknamed "Long Bob," Meusel was a gifted athlete; but his outward appearance was cold and undemonstrative. The press often described him as dour and colorless. Whether he took a third strike or hit a 450-foot home run, his expression never changed. In the outfield, Meusel hustled only when he wanted. At times he would run in on a fly ball, then slow down, and the ball would bounce in front of him. Other times Meusel would not run out ground balls.

His lack of hustle incensed the fans and coaches. Huggins talked to him about commitment, desire, and giving one's best. It did little good. Huggins was once asked what kind of attitude Meusel had?

"His attitude is just plain indifference," he answered.

Meusel lived in his world of solitude. The press reported that reputedly he said "Hello" to his teammates at the beginning of the season, "Goodbye" at the end, and little else in between.

Chapter 17

Detroit Tigers and Chicago White Sox

On Thursday, June 2, 1927, the Yankees began a long home stand in New York against the Detroit Tigers, Chicago White Sox, Cleveland Indians, and St. Louis Browns. Miller Huggins's biggest concern was the infield situation. Joe Dugan's injury had forced Huggins to move his players around. He played Tony Lazzeri at third base. Lazzeri played well there; however, Ray Morehart, who replaced Lazzeri at second base, had no hits in his last thirteen plate appearances.

With a crowd of 15,000 in the stands, Yankee left-hander Dutch Ruether opposed right-hander Tiger Ulysses Simpson Grant (Lil) Stoner. Born February 28, 1899 in Bowie, Texas, Stoner broke into the major leagues with the Tigers in 1922, winning 4 and losing 4, and posting a 7.00 era. After an absence in 1923, Stoner won 11 in 1924 and 10 in 1925. In 1926, he won 7 and lost 10 with a 5.46 era.

The Line-Ups

Tigers	Yankees
Jack Warner 3b	Earle Combs cf
Johnny Neun 1b	Mark Koenig ss
Heinie Manush cf	Babe Ruth rf
Bob Fothergill lf	Lou Gehrig 1b
Harry Heilmann rf	Cedric Durst lf
Charlie Gehringer 2b	Tony Lazzeri 3b
Jackie Tavener ss	Ray Morehart 2b
Larry Woodall c	John Grabowski c
Lil Stoner p	Dutch Ruether p

Ruether and Stoner pitched well.

With no score after five and one-half innings, Lazzeri, the Yankee third baseman, singled to right field in the sixth. Lazzeri went to third on a hit-and-run play when Morehart singled through the hole at short stop. When Grabowski forced Morehart at second base—Warner to Gehringer—Lazzeri scored.

The Yankees went ahead 2 to 0 in the seventh. Combs opened the inning with a single to center and raced to third when Koenig singled to right. On a three and two count, Ruth hit into a double play—Gehringer to Tavener to Neun—as Combs scored.

After Ruether gave up only his second single of the game to Tavener in the eighth, Woodall hit into a double play from Grabowski to Koenig. In the ninth with two outs, Neun, the Tigers' first baseman, walked and stole second. When Manush flied to center field, Combs raced back and made a catch with his hands high over his head to end the game.

Final score: Yankees 2, Tigers 0.

Yankee Notebook for Thursday, June 2, 1927: The win was the Yankees' fifth straight . . . Ruether (5-1) pitched masterfully; his curve and fastball were outstanding. The southpaw gave up two singles and two walks, both to Neun . . . Woodall was the only Tiger to pass second base . . . The Tigers' best batters, Manush, Fothergill and Heilmann, went hitless.

The Yanks had eight hits . . . Durst and Grabowski were the only Yankees without one . . . There were no extra base hits in the game . . . Gehrig had two singles and led the American League in batting at .420 . . . The Babe did not get the ball out of the infield . . . In the field, Combs made a backward running catch of Heilmann's fly to deep center in the second . . . Lazzeri had an error at third . . . The game was played in 1:31.

At Fenway Park in Boston, Ted Lyons held the Red Sox to eight scattered hits as the White Sox won the first game of that series, 7 to 2. With the victory, Lyons had won nine and lost two. The White Sox won nine of their last eleven games. In Washington, D.C., the Senators trounced the Browns, 11 to 2. After losing to the Red Sox twice in two days, manager Bucky Harris changed his line-up. Tris Speaker played first base and made twelve plays without an error. He figured in five double plays.

At Shibe Park, the Athletics won the opening game of the series from the Indians, 8 to 4. Lefty Pate, who relieved Samuel Gray in the fifth when the Indians loaded the bases with two outs, retired the side on one pitch.

In Cincinnati, the Giants opened a tour of the West with a victory over the Reds, 5 to 4 in twelve innings, at Redland Field. Rogers Hornsby's triple in the twelfth decided the game. Burleigh Grimes, who relieved Hugh McQuillan, pitched ten straight shutout innings for the Giants. Meanwhile at Forbes Field, with the score 3 to 3, the Pirates rallied for four runs in the seventh and went on to defeat the Phillies, 7 to 3. Carmen Hill held Philadelphia to five hits. One of the hits was Cy Williams's tenth home run with two runners on.

Yanks' skipper Miller Huggins sent Herb Pennock, a left-hander, to the mound at Yankee Stadium on Friday June 3, 1927. Tigers' manager George Moriarty countered with right-hander Ken Holloway. Joe Dugan and Bob Meusel were out of the line-up resting injuries. In their absences, Tony Lazzeri filled in again for Dugan at third base, and Cedric Durst played left field for Meusel. Ray Morehart, who had a timely hit in yesterday's victory, was at second base in place of Lazzeri.

In the second inning, Gehrig faced Holloway and hit a home run to right field. Pennock pitched well and kept the Tigers scoreless through six innings. With the nine scoreless innings against Ruether the day before, the Tigers had not scored in the last fifteen.

With the club leading 1 to 0 in the seventh, Koenig misplayed Heilmann's grounder. When Gehringer singled to center field, Heilmann raced from first to third. The next batter was Tavener, the Tigers' shortstop.

A small man at 5'5" and 138 pounds, Tavener already had two hits in the game, and Pennock worked carefully to him. With the count at one ball and two strikes, Tavener drove the ball deep to the outfield. Racing back to the bleachers, Ruth watched the ball sail over his head into the stands for a home run.

When Heilmann, Gehringer, and Tavener scored, the Tigers led 3 to 1.The Yankees threatened in the seventh. With two runners on base and two outs, Holloway faced Gehrig, who had hit a home run off him earlier. Gehrig, however, grounded out to the pitcher and the Yanks did not score. Neither team scored in the eighth and ninth.

Final score: Tigers 3, Yankees 1.

Yankee Notebook for Friday June 3, 1927: Pennock (5-2) pitched well except for the seventh when Tavener hit the home run. The southpaw gave up eight hits, walked two, and struck out two . . . Tavener's home run was the second of his career; his first home run also beat the Yankees last year at the Stadium . . . The Yanks had ten hits . . . Gehrig's home run was his thirteenth . . . Gehrig, Durst, and Pennock each had two hits . . . Shocker put on his uniform for the first time since he was hit in the head with a pitched ball . . . New York had won five-straight before that day's loss . . . Hoyt and Whitehill were scheduled to face each other the next day.

In Boston, Tommy Thomas won his tenth as the second place White Sox defeated the Red Sox, 5 to 1, in the second game of the series. Thomas gave up fourteen hits and hit a home run over the left field fence at Fenway Park with a runner on base. In the nation's capital, the Browns pounded three Senators' pitchers for thirteen hits and won, 8 to 4. Every Browns' player has at least one hit. At Shibe Park, the Indians scored three runs in the first off Jack Quinn and triumphed over the Athletics, 3 to 1. Cleveland hurler Jake Miller went the distance. The Athletics' lone tally was Al Simmons's sixth home run.

The first place Pirates defeated the Phillies with three home runs in a fifteen hit attack, 11 to 1. Vic Aldridge, the Pirates' starter, was sensational, giving up only one hit through eight innings, striking out seven. Glenn Wright, Paul Waner, and George Grantham each homered for Pittsburgh.

In Cincinnati, the Giants moved into second place as Zeke Barnes pitched a three-hit shutout against the Reds at Redland Field, 6 to 0. Rogers Hornsby, the Giants' second baseman, helped score three runs with a single, a double, and a sacrifice in four trips to the plate. At Wrigley Field, pitcher Guy Bush was hit hard as the Braves edged the

Cubs, 5 to 4. Rain postponed the game between the Robins and Cardinals at St. Louis.

Rain fell at Yankee Stadium as 5,000 faithful fans waited for the weather to clear on Saturday, June 4, 1927. The game between the Yankees and Tigers was scheduled to begin at 3:00 p.m. With rain still falling at 3:30 p.m., Ed Barrow decided to wait no longer and postponed the game. Jack Lenz announced the news to the crowd on his megaphone. Only one game was scheduled the next day. The postponed game would be played as part of a doubleheader when the Tigers returned to New York on August 3, 4 and 5.

That day at Fenway Park the White Sox scored two runs in the ninth without a hit and won their third straight over the Red Sox, 6 to 4. With the score 4 to 4, Del Lundgren walked three batters. When Baby Doll Jacobson misplayed Willie Kamm's liner to left with two outs, two runs scored. The victory moved the White Sox to within one game of the first-place Yankees.

At Griffith Stadium, the Browns scored four runs in the third off Walter Johnson and went on to defeat the Senators, 5 to 3. Elam Vangilder limited the Senators to seven hits. Browns' teammate Fred Schulte hit a home run in the fourth.

At Redland Field, Eppa Rixey held the Giants to five hits as the Reds won, 5 to 1. The Reds pounded Giants' starter Bill Clarkson for eighteen hits. The paid crowd was 3,400. In St. Louis, Flint Rhem scattered five hits and outpitched Dazzy Vance as the Cardinals shutout the Robins 4 to 0 on Bob O'Farrell Day at Sportsman's' Park. O'Farrell, the Cardinals' manager, was honored as the National League's most valuable player in 1926.

In Chicago, the Braves won their second in a row from the Cubs, 10 to 8, at Wrigley Field. Cubs' starter Charlie Root was hit hard in the first inning for four runs and driven from the mound in the seventh. Hack Wilson hit his tenth home run and Earl Webb his eighth for Chicago.

After yesterday's rain postponement, a crowd of 35,000 at Yankee Stadium in New York saw the final game of the series between the Yankees and Detroit Tigers on Sunday, June 5, 1927. Joe Dugan and Bob Meusel were again out of the line up; Tony Lazzeri played third base; Ben Paschal was in left field, and Ray Morehart filled in for Lazzeri at second base. Wilcy Moore, a right-hander, made his second start of the season for the Yanks.

Twenty-seven year old Earl Whitehill, a left-hander, from Cedar Rapids, Iowa pitched for the Tigers. Debuting with Detroit in September 1923, the five foot nine and half tall hurler went on to become very successful, averaging 15 victories a season from 1924 through 1926.

With no score after two innings, Moore walked Bassler in the third. When it began to rain heavily, the umpires stopped the game. Both teams took cover. Phil Scheck's groundskeepers covered the infield with tarpaulins. The crowd and players waited. After about one hour the rain stopped, the tarpaulins were removed, and the groundskeepers scattered saw dust and mopped up the puddles.

When the game resumed in the third, the Tigers scored a run and added another in the fourth. With Detroit leading 2 to 0 in the fourth, Whitehill walked Gehrig, who later scored after Paschal tripled to left center. After Lazzeri singled off Warner's shoes, Paschal made a delayed break for home. Tavener picked up the ball and threw home, but Bassler dropped the ball. Paschal was safe.

The game was tied at two.

Ruth came up in the sixth. Whitehall's first three pitches were called balls. The crowd was unhappy and voiced their disapproval. Ruth then hit Whitehall's next pitch into the right field bleachers for a home run.

With two outs in the Tigers' seventh, Moore gave up singles to Heilmann and Gehringer. When Tavener singled, Heilmann raced for home and slid into Grabowski, who was dazed slightly. On the play, Heilmann scored and the game was tied at three. With Gehringer on third and Tavener on first, Huggins brought in Myles Thomas, a right-hander, who walked Bassler. With the bases loaded, Whitehill flied out to Combs to end the scoring.

Combs walked in the Yankees' eighth. Whitehill then hit Koenig on the leg. With Koenig on first and Combs at second, Ruth, who hit a home run in the sixth, faced Whitehill. With the count three-and-two, the Babe singled. Combs scored and Koenig raced to third base. When Paschal hit a sacrifice fly to center field, Koenig tagged and scored. Thomas retired the Tigers in the ninth.

Final score: Yankees 5, Tigers 3.

Yankee Notebook for Sunday, June 5, 1927: Moore gave up twelve hits, walked two, and struck out one in 6 2/3. He was lucky at times. Twice the Tigers hit line drives to an infielder with two runners on base . . . Thomas (3-1) came into the game with the score tied in the seventh. Thomas did not give up a hit in 2 1/3, walking two, and striking out one . . . The Tigers left fourteen men on the bases . . . The Yankees had only six hits off Whitehill; Ruth and Lazzeri each had two . . . Ruth's home run was his seventeenth.

Gehringer made a fine play on Combs's pop fly, when he raced into right and made a one-handed catch with his back to the plate . . . Lazzeri and Morehart played well . . . The Yankees claimed Pat McNulty, an outfielder for the Indians, on waivers that day.

At Griffith Stadium in Washington, D.C., the Browns hammered Garland Braxton for twelve hits in six innings and routed the Senators, 9 to 1. Frank O'Rourke, the Browns' third baseman, led the attack with four hits. Tom Zachary limited the Senators to only six hits.

In St. Louis, 33,000 fans watched the Cardinals and Robins split a doubleheader as St. Louis won the first game, 8 to 0, and Brooklyn took the second, 6 to 1, at Sportsman's Park. Grover Cleveland Alexander scattered eight hits in the opener while his teammates pounded Jesse Petty. In the second contest, Robins' starter Bill Doak yielded only five hits.

With a crowd of 23,000 at Wrigley Field, Sheriff Blake limited the Braves to five hits as Chicago won 7 to 0. In Cincinnati, the Reds came from behind twice and edged the Giants, 10 to 9, at Redland Field. Billy Zitzmann's double with two on scored the tying and winning runs.

Major League Baseball Standings
June 5, 1927
American League

	Won	Lost	P.C.
New York	31	15	.674
Chicago	30	17	.638
Philadelphia	23	22	.511
St. Louis	22	23	.489
Cleveland.	22	24	.478
Washington	20	23	.465
Detroit	19	25	.432
Boston	12	30	.286

National League

	Won	Lost	P.C.
Pittsburgh	28	13	.683
St. Louis	24	17	.585
New York	24	19	.558
Chicago	23	19	.548
Brooklyn	23	25	.479
Philadelphia	18	22	.450
Boston	15	22	.405
Cincinnati	14	32	.304

ii

The Yankees were not scheduled on Monday, June 6, 1927. The Chicago White Sox were in town the next day for the start of a four game series. The White Sox trailed the Yankees by only one game in the standings, and the fans looked forward to seeing the two best pitching staffs in the American League.

Although it was early in the season, some considered that meeting the first crucial series for both clubs. White Sox manager Ray Schalk planned on using Alphonse (Tommy) Thomas, Red Faber, Ted Blankenship, and Ted Lyons. Miller Huggins went with Waite Hoyt, Urban Shocker, Dutch Ruether, and Herb Pennock. Thomas and Hoyt were expected to open the series in the Bronx.

At Fenway Park in Boston, Ted Lyons won his second game of the series as the White Sox pummeled the Red Sox, 10 to 2. The victory was Lyons's tenth. He had lost two. Chicago swept the series and won twelve out of the last fourteen games. John Clancy, the White Sox's rookie first baseman, had five hits that day.

In Philadelphia, Connie Mack revamped his line up. Mack replaced Jim Poole, the first baseman, with Jimmy Foxx, a third string catcher, and Bill Lamar, the left fielder, was benched in favor of Zach Wheat. Foxx and Wheat each had run-producing hits as the Athletics defeated the Indians, 4 to 1. Howard Ehmke held the Indians to only six hits over eight innings.

At Forbes Field, the Pirates came from behind and beat the Phillies, 7 to 5. With the score tied in the sixth, the Pirates scored two and went on to win. Paul Waner hit his fourth home run in the fifth. In St. Louis, the Cardinals took the series from the Robins, three games to one, with a 6 to 2 victory. Former Giant Bob McGraw pitched well after he gave up two runs in the second. At Wrigley Field, the Cubs beat the Braves, 4 to 3 in eleven innings. The Cubs tied the game against Larry Benton in the eighth and scored the winning run in the eleventh off George Mogridge.

The Giants played an exhibition game in Toledo, Ohio and defeated the Mudhens of the American Association. Bill Terry had a home run. Casey Stengel, the manager of the Mudhens, renewed old acquaintances with members of his former team.

With the Chicago White Sox in New York to play the Yankees for the first time that season there was a great deal of activity on the field before the game on Tuesday, June 7, 1927. Photographers were gathered at the visitors' dugout on the first base side. Posing on the steps was manager Ray Schalk and members of his pitching staff. Standing or leaning forward on an outstretched legs with arms crossed were Sarge

Connally, Elmer Jacobs, Tommy Thomas, Ted Lyons, Schalk, Charlie Barnabee and Red Faber. "Chicago" was embroidered on the jersey of their gray flannel uniforms.

Returning to New York for the first time in a Chicago uniform was Aaron Ward. His appearance on the field evoked warm memories for both him and the fans. Before being traded to the White Sox, Ward was the regular second baseman for the Yankees from 1917 through 1926, playing on the Yankees' pennant winning clubs in 1921, 1922, and on the franchise's first championship team in 1923.

Ward was a very good defensive second baseman and a capable hitter. However, with the arrival of Tony Lazzeri in 1926, Ward's playing time was reduced sharply; he appeared in only 22 games. After the 1926 season, Ward was traded to the White Sox for catcher John Grabowski and infielder Ray Morehart. Many Yankee fans were unhappy with the trade.

The pitchers that afternoon were right-handers Waite Hoyt and Tommy Thomas. Alphonse (Tommy) Thomas was born December 23, 1899 in Baltimore, Maryland. The 5'10" tall hurler debuted with the White Sox on April 17, 1926, and he went on to have an outstanding rookie season, winning 15 and losing 12 with a 3.80 era.

The Line-Ups

White Sox	Yankees
Alex Metzler cf	Earle Combs cf
Bill Hunnefield ss	Mark Koenig ss
Bill Barrett rf	Babe Ruth rf
Buck Crouse c	Lou Gehrig 1b
Bibb Falk lf	Cedric Durst lf
Willie Kamm 3b	Tony Lazzeri 3b
John Clancy 1b	Ray Morehart 2b
Aaron Ward 2b	Pat Collins c
Tommy Thomas p	Waite Hoyt p

Ruth came up to the plate in the Yankee fourth and ripped a fast ball into the right field bleachers. Gehrig then hit a line drive into the right field bleachers. The back-to-back home runs off Thomas gave the Yankees a 2 to 0 lead.

In the sixth, Gehrig opened the inning with a single. When Durst bounced a grounder between first and second base, Clancy gloved the ball and raced Durst to the bag. Durst won in a cloud of dust. On the play, Gehrig broke for third base and just beat Clancy's throw from across the diamond. Lazzeri then flied to Barrett in right. The White Sox outfielder made an excellent throw to Crouse, the White Sox catcher, in an attempt to nab Gehrig at the plate. When Crouse misplayed the ball, Gehrig slid in safely.

Clancy came up in the seventh and homered to left field off Hoyt. In the Yankees' half of the seventh, Collins lofted a home run to left field, giving the Yanks a 4 to 1 lead. Hoyt went on to retire the White Sox in the eighth and ninth innings.

Final score: Yankees 4, White Sox 1.

Yankee Notebook for Tuesday, June 7, 1927: Hoyt (8-2) scattered seven hits, walked three, and struck out four . . . For the White Sox, Clancy had three hits, including a home run that spoiled Hoyt's bid for a second shutout against Chicago. Coming up to bat in the ninth, Clancy had eight hits in a row. Five of his hits took place on Monday in Boston. However, when Clancy grounded to Koenig in the ninth, his streak ended.

Chicago's Thomas gave up six hits, including three home runs . . . Ruth hit his eighteenth . . . Gehrig also had a home run, his fourteenth, and a single. He led the American League with a .413 batting average . . . Collins's home run was his third . . . In the field, Morehart and Collins made errors . . . The fans gave Ward a nice reception when he came to bat in the second . . . Shocker and Faber were scheduled to pitch the next day.

At Shibe Park in Philadelphia, the Athletics defeated the Browns, 11 to 9. Ernie Wingard, who relieved Browns' starter Milt Gaston, leaped into the stands at the end of the third inning and punched a spectator who had been taunting him. In Washington, D.C., the Senators scored six runs in the second and four more in the fifth and triumphed over the Indians, 10 to 8, at Griffith Stadium. Cleveland's Johnny Hodapp hit a home run.

At Fenway Park, the Red Sox held off a late rally in the ninth by the Tigers and won, 6 to 5. Hal Wiltse held Detroit to two hits until the ninth, when the visitors scored four runs. Charlie Gehringer, the Tigers' second baseman, homered with two men on.

In Pittsburgh, Lee Meadows went the distance as the Pirates defeated the Giants, 9 to 6, at Forbes Field. Rogers Hornsby hit his 200th home run of his career in the third for the Giants. Bill Terry also homered. At Wrigley Field for the first time that season, the Robins slipped past the Cubs, 7 to 6. Jumbo Elliott, who relieved Buzz McWeeny, could not hold a 6 to 4 lead for Brooklyn. William L. Vecke, president of the Cubs, announced that infielder Jim Cooney and pitcher Tony Kaufmann were traded to the Phillies for pitcher Harold Carlson.

At Redland Field, Jakie May outpitched Shucks Pruett as the Reds won the opening game of the series from the Phillies, 5 to 1. In St. Louis, Charles G. Dawes, the Vice President of the United States, watched the Braves defeat the Cardinals, 12 to 5, at Sportsman's Park. Andy High hit two home runs and Frank Welch one for Boston.

With the temperature in New York in the upper 70's on Wednesday June 8, 1927, a crowd of 20,000 at the Stadium saw Yankee left-hander Dutch Ruether oppose the White Sox's Red Faber, a right-hander. That afternoon Miller Huggins again played Tony Lazzeri at third base for Joe Dugan, and Ray Morehart replaced Lazzeri at second. Cedric Durst played left field for Bob Meusel. Both Dugan and Meusel were in uniform.

Over the first eight innings, Ruether, Moore, and Giard were hit hard as Clancy, Falk, and Barrett hit home runs for the White Sox. The bright spot for the Yankees was Lazzeri, who homered in the second and eighth innings.

The Yankees came up in the ninth trailing 11 to 6. Faber took the mound to close out the game. Combs opened the ninth with a single. After Dugan fouled out, Ruth singled to right. Gehrig then smacked a double against the right field screen, scoring Combs. When Durst singled, Ruth and Gehrig crossed the plate.

Lazzeri came up with the Yankees down by two runs, 11 to 9. With two home runs already off Faber, manager Ray Schalk brought

George "Sarge" Connally, a right-hander, into the game. Batting against Connally, Lazzeri hit his third home run of the game, tying the game at eleven. He received a tremendous ovation from the fans as he circled the bases and crossed the plate.

The game went into extra innings.

Myles Thomas, a right-hander, retired the White Sox in the tenth and eleventh. When the Yankees came up in the bottom of the eleventh, Connally was still on the mound. Quickly, Durst opened with a triple against the bleachers in right field. Lazzeri was up next, and Schalk ordered him walked.

With Durst on third and Lazzeri on first and no one out, Schalk brought his outfielders in hoping to keep the winning run from scoring. Morehart, however, poked a single over Barrett's head in right, scoring Durst with the winning run.

Final score: Yankees 12, White Sox 11 (Eleven innings).

Yankee Notebook for Wednesday June 8, 1927: Ruether and Moore each went four innings and Giard one, giving up eleven runs and three home runs . . . Thomas (4-1) pitched the final two and did not allow a ball out of the infield . . . Lazzeri's three home runs were his fourth, fifth, and sixth. His first home run just dropped into the right field stands. The second went deep to the right field bleachers and rolled to the stands for an inside-the-park home run. The third sailed down the right field and fell a foot inside the white line and two feet inside the wire fence.

When Koenig left the game after aggravating an injury to his leg, Lazzeri moved to shortstop . . . Coming back from their own injuries, Dugan came into the game and played third base, and Meusel batted for Giard in the ninth . . . The Yankees announced that on September 8 the city's Italian-American sports fans would honor Tony Lazzeri at Yankee Stadium.

At Shibe Park in Philadelphia, Joe Boley and Jimmy Foxx helped the Athletics win their second in a row from the Browns, 7 to 5. Boley led the attack with four singles, and Foxx hit a home run in the fourth inning with no one on base. Zach Wheat had two doubles. In Washington, D.C., a ninth inning rally gave the Senators a 2 to 1 victory over the Indians. Washington's rookie pitcher Horace Lisenbee gave up eight hits. At Fenway Park, the Tigers evened the series with the Red Sox with a 5 to 3 victory. Bob Fothergill's home run in the sixth for Detroit was the deciding hit.

In Pittsburgh, Rogers Hornsby's home run off Vic Aldridge with two men on and two outs in the ninth gave the Giants their first victory over the Pirates, 8 to 7, at Forbes Field. George Grantham homered for Pittsburgh and Jack Cummings hit one for New York. At Sportsman's Park, Flint Rhem, Grover Cleveland Alexander, and Herman Bell were pounded for fourteen hits as the Braves defeated the Cardinals, 11 to 8.

Holding off a four-run rally in the ninth by the Phillies, the Reds won, 5 to 4, at Redland Field. In Chicago, home runs by Earl Webb and Hack Wilson paced the Cubs over the Robins, 3 to 2. Hal Carlson, newly acquired in a trade with the Phillies, gave up nine hits.

The Babe went to Fort Jay on Governors Island in Upper New York Bay on Thursday, June 9, 1927 and presented fifty-three autographed baseballs to Major General James H. McRae. One baseball would be given to the best amateur baseball player in each of the nation's fifty-three Citizen Military Training Camps, where thousands of young volunteers, mostly ages 16-19, spend four weeks of military training during the summer. Clowning for the photographers after the presentation, Ruth gave Gen. McRae a batting lesson.

Mark Koenig was still out of the line-up resting his injured leg, and Tony Lazzeri filled in at short stop. Ray Morehart replaced Lazzeri at second base. Joe Dugan was back at third base. New York's Herb Pennock, a left-hander, opposed Chicago's Ted Blankenship, a right-hander.

Pennock ran into trouble in the third after Crouse singled and scored on Blankenship's double to left center. A peculiar play followed when Metzler grounded to Pennock, who threw to Dugan. Blankenship was chased between third and second. Dugan threw to second, but his throw was wild. Blankenship went safely to third. Metzler, who was between first and second, was chased back to first by Morehart. Metzler was trapped but Collins who had been covering first had left the bag to protect the plate. With Both Blankenship and Metzler safe, Hunnefield then singled, scoring Blankenship. The White Sox led 2 to 0.

The White Sox added a run in the fourth. In the sixth, Morehart singled with one out and Ruth walked. With two runners on, Durst tripled to right center. Morehart and Ruth scored. The Yankees trailed 3 to 2.

Lazzeri opened the seventh with a single to center. After Dugan flied out, Collins drew a walk. Julie Wera ran for him. Huggins decided not to pinch-hit for Pennock and the Yankee southpaw singled to center. The crowd stood and cheered as Lazzeri scored the tying run. When Combs singled to center, Wera scored. With the Yankees leading 4 to 3, White Sox manager Ray Schalk brought in Bert Cole, a left-hander. Morehart hit Cole's first pitch down the third baseline, where it rolled to the stands and bounced away. As Falk chased the ball, Pennock and Combs scored. Morehart circled the bases for a home run.

Ruth then tripled over Falk's head in left. While at third base, the Babe took the first opportunity to head for home. Cole was so surprised that he threw the ball past Crouse. With Ruth's steal of home, the Yankees went ahead 8 to 3. Pennock retired the White Sox in the eighth and ninth.

Final score: Yankees 8, White Sox 3.

Yankee Notebook for Thursday, June 9, 1927: Pennock (6-2) went the distance, giving up only seven hits, five of which were bunched in the third and fourth innings. The Yankee southpaw walked two and struck out three . . . Morehart had three hits, including his first home run . . . Ruth and Durst tripled . . . Combs singled twice . . . Gehrig went hitless in four plate appearances . . . Lazzeri had one putout and five assists at shortstop . . . Koenig was not suffering from a charley horse as first reported but aggravated an injury to his leg suffered in Sunday's game with the Tigers.

In Philadelphia, Rube Walberg pitched a strong game as the Athletics won their fourth consecutive and third in a row from the Browns, 9 to 3, at Shibe Park. The Athletics had sixteen hits. Browns' starter Ernie Nevers was hit hard. Rallying for four runs in the top of the ninth at Fenway Park, the Tigers defeated the Red Sox, 6 to 4. Detroit's Bob Fothergill had a perfect day at the plate, hitting a home run, double, two singles, and a sacrifice fly. At Griffith Stadium, Walter Johnson was hammered for six hits in five innings as the Indians beat the Senators, 7 to 1. George Uhle kept the Senators scoreless after the first.

At Pittsburgh's Forbes Field, Joe Bush was knocked out of the box in the first without retiring a batter as the Giants pounded the Pirates, 12 to 1, with timely hits in the first, fourth, and sixth innings. In St. Louis, Jesse Haines scattered seven hits as the Cardinals beat the Braves, 6 to 1. Les Bell tripled and doubled for the Cards. At Wrigley Field, the Cubs scored two runs in the eighth and edged the Robins, 4 to 3. The win was Chicago's third in a row. The Cubs acquired Eddie Pick, the star third baseman of Kansas City of the American Association, for third baseman Howard Freigau and pitcher Luther Roy. In Cincinnati, Russ Wrightstone's triple in the ninth broke a 5 to 5 tie and gave the Phillies a 6 to 5 victory over the Reds.

On Friday, June 10, 1927, a crowd of 15,000 came out to Yankee Stadium to see the finale of the series with the Chicago White Sox. Ted Lyons, winner of seven in a row, went up against Urban Shocker. Both were right-handers. With the score tied at two, the White Sox came up in the fifth. Ward singled past Dugan and went to second on an out. The visitors went ahead by a score of 3 to 2 when Lyons surprised everyone in the ballpark when he tripled over Combs's head in centerfield, scoring Ward.

Falk's home run off Shocker in the eighth gave Chicago another run. Lyons, meanwhile, pitched scoreless ball, over the final five innings, limiting the Yankees to a total of five hits.

Final score: White Sox 4, Yankees 2.

Yankee Notebook for Friday, June 10, 1927: Shocker (6-4) started well but weakened in the fourth and fifth. The right-hander gave up nine hits, walked one, and struck out one . . . Lyons pitched magnificently for the White Sox in the last five innings during which only fifteen batters faced him . . . After Ruth walked to start the fifth and was out trying to reach second after a short wild pitch, no other Yankee reached first base . . . Of the five singles off Lyons, Gehrig and Dugan had two each and Lazzeri one . . . Lyons's victory was his eleventh in thirteen tries. With Koenig out, Lazzeri played shortstop again and Morehart was at second . . . Meusel returned to left field and had four putouts . . . Ruth committed an error in right field.

In Philadelphia, Ty Cobb hit a home run with Eddie Collins on base and the Athletics swept the four game series over the Browns, at Shibe Park. The score was 4 to 3. Eddie Rommel pitched well but needed help from Lefty Grove in the ninth with one out and the tying run on base. Grove retired Wally Schang and Otto Miller. At Griffith Stadium, Tris Speaker's double in the thirteenth led to the winning run as the Senators beat the Indians, 6 to 5.

With five runs in the twelfth inning at Fenway Park, the Tigers won their third straight for the first time that season defeating the Red Sox, 10 to 5. Hits off Charley Ruffing by Heine Manush, Harry Heilmann, and Lil Stoner helped the Tigers in the twelfth.

After scoring seven runs off Giants' starter Bill Clarkson in the fifth, the Pirates went on to beat the Giants, 13 to 4, at Forbes Field. Carmen Hill went the distance, giving up seven hits. The victory was Hill's seventh straight. Riggs Stephenson's sharp single to right with the bases loaded in the last half of the twelfth at Wrigley Field scored the winning run for the Cubs over the Robins, 5 to 4.

At Sportsman's Park, the Braves defeated the Cardinals, 11 to 8 in ten innings. St. Louis's Frankie Frisch's home run in the ninth with two men on had tied the score. In Cincinnati, the Reds won three out of four games from the Phillies with a victory, 9 to 3, at Redland Field.

Major League Baseball Standings
June 10, 1927
American League

	Won	Lost	P.C.
New York	34	16	.680
Chicago	32	20	.615
Philadelphia	28	22	.560
Washington	23	24	.489
Detroit	22	26	.458
Cleveland	23	26	.451
St. Louis	22	27	.449
Boston	13	34	.277

National League

	Won	Lost	P.C.
Pittsburgh	31	15	.674
Chicago	28	19	.596
St. Louis	26	20	.565
New York	26	21	.553
Brooklyn	23	30	.434
Boston	18	24	.429
Philadelphia	19	26	.422
Cincinnati	17	33	.340

Chapter 18

Cleveland Indians

With the Cleveland Indians in New York on Saturday, June 11, 1927, left-hander Garland Buckeye started for manager Jack McCallister. Yankee manager Miller Huggins sent right-hander Myles Thomas to the mound in the opening game of the series at the Stadium. Mark Koenig was still out with a leg injury, and Tony Lazzeri filled in again at shortstop. Ray Morehart was at second base.

The Line-Ups

Indians	Yankees
Charlie Jameison lf	Earle Combs cf
Ike Eichrodt cf	Ray Morehart 2b
Lew Fonseca 2b	Babe Ruth rf
George Burns 1b	Lou Gehrig 1b
Joe Sewell ss	Bob Meusel lf
John Hodapp 3b	Tony Lazzeri ss
Homer Summa rf	Joe Dugan 3b
Luke Sewell c	Pat Collins c
Garland Buckeye p	Myles Thomas p

With Morehart on third base in the third, Ruth came up to bat. The Babe hit what was considered the second longest home run at Yankee Stadium. Traveling further than a ball he hit two years earlier, the home run off Buckeye landed a dozen rows up in right center field in the section in front of the scoreboard.

The 30,000 fans in the ballpark and the Indians were in disbelief.

Thinking the bat was filled with a piece of lead, L. Sewell, the Indians' catcher, took the bat and looked at it suspiciously. After examining the end of it, balancing it in one hand and even sniffing it, Sewell found nothing illegal.

Ruth came up again in the fifth and blasted a home run, his twentieth of the season and the second of the game, into the bleachers, a few rows from the top. Apparently, upset by the home run, Buckeye walked Gehrig. After Meusel singled, McCallister replaced Buckeye with Benn Karr, a right-hander. Lazzeri then forced Meusel at second base. When Lazzeri attempted a steal of second, Gehrig suddenly raced home from third. Fonseca's return throw from Sewell was dropped by the Indian's catcher as Gehrig scored, giving the Yankees a 4 to 0 lead.

The Indians scored a run in the sixth when Combs lost Burns's ball in the sun. With a run in the home half of the sixth on singles by Thomas and Combs, and an error and an inside-the-park home run by Lazzeri in the seventh, the Yankees pulled ahead 6 to 1.

With a five run lead, Thomas went to the mound in the ninth. When a double, two walks, and a single made the score 6 to 3, Huggins called Wilcy Moore, a right-hander, into the game. With one out and the bases loaded, Moore got Jameison to ground out to Gehrig as a run scored. The game ended when Eichrodt fanned on three pitches.

Final score: Yankees 6, Indians 4.

Yankee Notebook for Saturday, June 11, 1927: Thomas (5-1) gave up eight hits, including three by Burns, in 8 1/3, while striking out four and walking seven . . . Still limping from his charley horse, Meusel made a great throw to catch Fonseca attempting to stretch a single into a double in the first . . . Ruth also made a good play when he made a jumping catch of J. Sewell's fly in the second . . . The Yanks had fourteen hits off Buckeye, Karr and Shaute; Meusel and Morehart had three each . . . Ruth's home runs were his nineteenth and twentieth . . . Lazzeri's four-bagger was his seventh.

From the American League Office in Chicago, President Ban Bancroft announced his decision on the protest filed by Connie Mack and the Athletics of the afternoon game on Memorial Day won by the

Yankees. Mack argued that when catcher Johnny Grabowski fell into the Athletics' dug out making a foul catch, the runners were entitled to as many bases as they could get, and Collins and Cobb should have crossed the plate.

The umpires ruled that each player could advance only two bases, and they allowed only Collins to score and held Cobb at third. Johnson agreed with the umpires' decision and did not allow the protest. He ruled that a ball in the dugout was out of play and allowing each runner two bases was correct.

At Shibe Park in Philadelphia, the Tigers scored four runs in the sixth and took a lead they never gave up, ending the Athletics' five-game winning streak in the opening game of the series, 6 to 5. The winning margin for Detroit occurred in the ninth on wild throws by Jimmy Dykes and Jimmy Foxx. The victory was the Tigers' fourth in a row. In Boston, the Browns routed the Red Sox, 10 to 5, at Fenway Park. St. Louis had seventeen hits off three Boston pitchers. At Griffith Stadium, Hollis Thurston scattered thirteen hits as the Senators triumphed over the White Sox, 9 to 4.

At Wrigley Field, Charlie Root bested Burleigh Grimes in a mound duel before a crowd of 35,000 as the Cubs beat the Giants, 2 to 1. Cubs' centerfielder Hack Wilson hit a home run and played well in the field. Eddie Roush's home run averted a shutout for New York. In St. Louis, Grover Cleveland Alexander won his fourth straight as the Cardinals defeated the Phillies, 4 to 2. The Cardinals were outhit eight to four but were aided by nine walks by Phillies' starter Shucks Pruett. At Forbes Field, the Robins scored four runs in the ninth and went onto beat the Pirates, 11 to 10. Dazzy Vance stopped a Pittsburgh rally in the ninth fanning Clyde Barnhart with the bases loaded.

Before the game at Yankee Stadium in New York on the afternoon of Sunday, June 12, 1927, 45,000 fans looked on as the Yankees celebrated the seventieth birthday of Joe Hornung, an old time baseball star. Hornung played the outfield for Buffalo, Boston, and Giants of the National League in the 1880's. During pre-game ceremonies, Yankee announcer George Levy presented Hornung with a check at home plate. The opposing pitchers that day were right-handers Waite Hoyt and Willis Hudlin.

George Willis Hudlin was born May 23, 1906 in Wagoner, Oklahoma. The 6 foot, 190 pound hurler debuted with the Indians on August 15, 1926. During the remainder of that season, he appeared in 8 games, starting 2. Hudlin won 1 and lost 3, compiling a respectable 2.81 era in 32 innings.

With the Yankees trailing 6 to 0, Huggins relieved Hoyt in the second. George Pipgras, a right-hander, came in and gave up a single to Burns. After stealing second and third, Burns tagged up and came home on J. Sewell's sacrifice fly, extending the Indians' lead to 7 to 0.

The Yankees scored two in the second with two outs on Lazzeri's double, a single by Wera, who had replaced Dugan, a hit by Grabowski and Pipgras's double. With Cleveland ahead 7 to 2 in the fifth, Combs tripled to center, scoring two runners. Leading by only three runs, Indians' manager Jack McCallister called George Uhle, a right-hander, into the game. Uhle retired the side.

After the Indians added a run in the seventh, the Yankees came up in the bottom of the inning. Ruth faced Uhle and hit his twenty-first home run into the middle of the right field bleachers. It was his third home run in two days. When Gehrig was called out on strikes, Huggins came out of the dugout and argued the call with home plate umpire McGowan.

With nobody on base in the eighth and the Indians ahead 8 to 5, the fans were surprised to see Pipgras hit a home run into the right field seats off Uhle. Down by two runs in the ninth, Morehart reached first on a slow grounder to J. Sewell at shortstop. When Gehrig's grounder to Spurgeon at second was misplayed, Morehart raced to third and scored when Durst, who had replaced Meusel, forced Gehrig at second base. With the score 8 to 7 in favor of the Indians, Lazzeri walked.

The noise from the crowd was deafening.

With two outs and the tying run on second, Mark Koenig, who had been out recovering from a leg injury, was sent to bat for Wera. The suspense was prolonged as Koenig fouled several pitches into the stands. On the next pitch, however, Koenig grounded out to Spurgeon for the final out.

Final score: Indians 8, Yankees 7.

Yankee Notebook for Sunday, June 12, 1927: Hoyt (8-3) lasted one and one-third innings, giving up six runs on five hits, walking one, and striking out one . . . In relief, Pipgras went 7 2/3, giving up only a run in the second and one in the seventh . . . Pipgras walked three, struck out three, and hit a batter, L. Sewell . . . Indian pitchers Hudlin and Uhle gave up thirteen hits . . . Ruth and Pipgras each homered and doubled . . . Combs tripled.

Ruth's home run was his twenty-first. Gehrig and Lazzeri have fourteen and seven, respectively, and the three led the American League. Behind them Ken Williams (Browns) and Al Simmons (Athletics) had six each. Hack Wilson of the Cubs led the National League with twelve.

At Griffith Stadium in Washington, D.C., Horace Lisenbee limited the White Sox to five hits as the Senators won, 6 to 1. Red Faber, who went seven innings, took the loss and Bert Cole finished. The loss was Chicago's second in a row. In Detroit, three singles in a row in the tenth inning gave the Tigers a victory over the Red Sox, 11 to 10. The winning pitcher was Ownie Carroll, who relieved Sam Gibson. Carroll pitched seven and one-third and drove in three runs with a triple and two singles while scoring two runs.

That day in St. Louis, Les Bell's home run in the ninth with Wattie Holm on base gave the Cardinals a victory over the Phillies, 5 to 4, at Sportsman's Park. Johnny Mokan, the Phillies' left fielder had a perfect day at bat with five hits in five trips. At Forbes Field, the Robins defeated the Pirates, 11 to 10. Manager Wilbert Robinson's fourth pitcher Norman Plitt drove in the go ahead run in the eighth. Joe Harris and Johnny Gooch homered for Pittsburgh.

In Cincinnati, the Braves evened their series with the Reds, 4 to 1. With a crowd of 45,000 at Wrigley Field, the Cubs edged the Giants, 7 to 6, winning their eighth straight. During the streak, Chicago won seven games by a one-run margin.

New York Giants' manager John McGraw traded shortstop Eddie Farrell, one of the top five leading batters in the National League, and pitchers Hugh McQuillan and Kent Greenfield to the Boston Braves.

In return, the Giants obtained catcher Zach Taylor, pitcher Larry Benton, and infielder Herb Thomas.

With the series tied at one game apiece in New York, the Yankees and Cleveland Indians played again at the Stadium on Monday, June 13, 1927. Shortstop Mark Koenig was out of the line-up, and Tony Lazzeri filled in again. Substituting for Lazzeri at second was Ray Morehart. In the outfield, Ben Paschal started in left for Bob Meusel.

For the Indians, Baby Doll Jacobson, whom the Indians had obtained from the Red Sox, was in uniform and played center field. Ike Eichrodt moved to right. Homer Summa went to the bench. Left-handers Herb Pennock and Joe Shaute opposed each other that afternoon.

After back-to-back home runs by Paschal and Lazzeri gave the Yankees an early lead, Indian manager Jack McCallister wasted no time in replacing Shaute with Benn Karr, a right-hander. Karr, however, gave up two more runs and the Yankees led 4 to 0.

In the third, Paschal hit his second home run deep into the left field seats. Paschal continued his timely hitting in the fifth when he doubled. After Lazzeri beat out an infield hit, Dugan then walloped a home run down the left field line. As Paschal, Lazzeri, and Dugan scored, the Yanks went ahead 8 to 0. On the mound, Pennock was pitching a one-hit game over the first five innings.

In the sixth, right-hander Emil Levsen, who replaced Karr, loaded the bases. When he walked Dugan, a run was forced home. Collins was the next batter, and the Yankee catcher homered off Levsen, making the score 13 to 0.

The Indians scored a run in the sixth, seventh, and eighth. With Garland Buckeye, a left-hander, on the mound in the eighth, Paschal tripled and scored on Collins's three-base hit. The day's scoring ended after the Indians' Bernie Neis homered with two men on in the ninth.

Final score: Yankees 14, Indians 6.

Yankee Notebook for Monday, June 13, 1927: Pennock (7-2) gave up ten hits, walking two, and striking out three . . . The Yankee lefthander held the Indians scoreless until the sixth . . . The Yankees had fifteen hits for a total of thirty-seven bases, including five home runs; Paschal had two and Lazzeri, Dugan, and Collins one each . . . Paschal also doubled and tripled, scored five runs and drove in three . . . Ruth and Gehrig had one hit a piece; a double . . . With the large lead, Huggins replaced the regulars as the game went on—Durst went to right field for Ruth, Gazella took over short for Lazzeri, and Wera replaced Dugan at third.

In Washington, D.C., General Crowder blanked the White Sox on three hits as the Senators won their third straight, 10 to 0. Ted Blankenship and Elmer Jacobs were battered as every Senator in the line-up had at least one hit. At Shibe Park, Eddie Collins pinch-hit in the ninth and started a rally for the Athletics that ended in a 7 to 6 win over the Tigers. Mickey Cochrane's single in the same inning with the bases loaded drove home the winning run. Lefty Grove, who pitched in relief, won. In Boston, Elam Vangilder pitched a five-hit shutout as the Browns defeated the Red Sox, 2 to 0. Vangilder helped himself with a home run over the left field fence in the fifth and a single that helped build a run in the third.

Although out hit thirteen to seven by the visitors, the Pirates defeated the Robins, 4 to 3, at Forbes Field. Returning after three weeks from an injury, Ray Kremer lasted into the eighth when the Robins scored two runs, making the score 4 to 3. Carmen Hill came in and stopped the rally. At Chicago's Wrigley Field, the Cubs won their ninth in a row trouncing the Giants, 6 to 2. Sheriff Blake scattered eleven hits and was assisted by the fielding of Hack Wilson in center.

Rain postponed the game between the Braves and Reds at Cincinnati, and wet grounds cancelled the Phillies and Cardinals at St. Louis.

Rain forced Ed Barrow to call off the game with the Cleveland Indians at Yankee Stadium on Tuesday, June 14, 1927. The game would be played when the Indians returned to New York on July 29, 30, 31 and August 1. In looking at the club's performance so far, Barrow and Huggins were satisfied. The Yankees were five games ahead of the second place White Sox and the club was playing well.

The development of Myles Thomas, George Pipgras, and Wilcy Moore strengthened the pitching corps. The infield of Lou Gehrig,

Tony Lazzeri, and Mark Koenig had improved. The reserves in the outfield and infield, Cedric Durst, Ben Paschal, Ray Morehart and Johnny Grabowski, added to the depth of the team.

Barrow and Huggins also knew that while the team was better balanced than in 1926, the opposition was stronger in 1927. At this time last year, the Yankees had a ten-game lead over the Athletics, compared to a five-game lead on that day. Both men knew that the Yankees needed to play well over the summer to repeat as American League champions.

Rain postponed all scheduled games in the American League. Meanwhile, in the National League at Wrigley Field in Chicago, the Cubs won their fourth in a row from the Giants, 4 to 3 in ten innings. The winning run was scored on Eddie Pick's hit down the first base line that the Giants argued was foul. Hack Wilson hit his thirteenth home run for Chicago. The Cubs had ten straight victories.

In Cincinnati, 900 fans, the smallest crowd at Redland Field in years, saw Jakie May hurl a four-hit shutout over the Braves, 1 to 0. Cuckoo Christensen's double scored Pee Wee Wanninger with the lone run of the game. Bunching hits off Alex Ferguson in the early innings, the Cardinals went on to defeat the Phillies, 6 to 4, at Sportsman's Park. Rain postponed the game between the Robins and Pirates at Pittsburgh.

Major League Baseball Standings
June 14, 1927
American League

	Won	Lost	P.C.
New York	36	17	.679
Chicago	32	23	.582
Philadelphia	29	23	.558
Washington	26	24	.520
Detroit	24	27	.471
St. Louis	24	27	.471
Cleveland	24	30	.444
Boston	13	37	.260

National League

	Won	Lost	P.C.
Pittsburgh	32	17	.659
Chicago	32	19	.627
St. Louis	29	20	.592
New York	26	25	.510
Brooklyn	25	31	.446
Boston	19	26	.422
Philadelphia	19	29	.396
Cincinnati	19	34	.358

Chapter 19

Mark Koenig

Yankee scout Bob Connery first saw Mark Koenig at Moose Jaw, Saskatchewan in the Western Canada League in 1921. Koenig was a 17-year-old, who had recently left his family and high school friends in California to make a career for himself in baseball. Despite Koenig's .202 batting average in the class D league in Canada, Connery saw potential in the young man and kept a close eye on him. Connery told Miller Huggins what he liked most about the boy was that he had courage and was a fighter; a kid who came back after making a mistake and played brilliantly.

Mark Anthony Koenig was born in San Francisco, California on July 19, 1904. Before moving to the West Coast at the turn of the century, his parents Charles and Stella Koenig, two brothers, and a sister lived in St. Louis, Missouri. Charles Koenig was a bricklayer as was his father William, who had immigrated to America from Germany.

As a youngster, Mark Koenig played baseball on the sandlots in San Francisco with another youngster and future major leaguer and teammate, Tony Lazzeri. Koenig attended Lowell High School, where he played the infield and pitched. After deciding that he wanted to play professional baseball, Koenig left Lowell before graduating and went to Canada.

When the Western Canada League disbanded half way through the season, Connery saw to it that Koenig signed with St. Paul of the American Association late in 1921. Over the next two seasons, he was farmed out from St. Paul for more experience; first to Jamestown in the Dakota League in 1922 (.253, 97 games) and then in 1923 to Des Moines in the Western League (.288, 156 games).

Koenig rejoined St. Paul as a utility infielder in 1924, but he played little, batting .267 in 68 games. He was considered a capable infielder, but his light hitting kept him from playing regularly. While unhappy about the role given him, Koenig was convinced that he could be an everyday regular and waited for an opportunity. It came in the post-season.

In 1924, the St. Paul Saints of the American Association played the Baltimore Orioles of the International League in what was billed as "The Little World Series." Before the opening game, the Saints' regular shortstop Danny Boone was injured during batting practice and was out for the series. The club's manager Nick Allen was frantic. Believing that Koenig was too inexperienced to take over for Boone, Allen looked for another available shortstop; however, Baltimore would not permit the Saints to bring someone from the outside when Koenig was already on the team. Taking advantage of the opportunity, Koenig had a sensational series.

There was a great deal of interest in Koenig after his performance in the Little World Series. A former scout of the Cincinnati Reds named Harry Strider lived in Minneapolis at the time, and he wrote a number of letters about Koenig to Garry Hermann, President of the Reds.

In one letter dated November 28, 1924, Strider wrote: "The object of this communication is to urge you to get an opinion on infielder Koenig of the St. Paul A.A. Team. This fine young player played shortstop for the Saints after Boone was hurt in the Little World Series, and covered himself with glory at the bat and in the field. I have also watched this man in several other games as a substitute and pinch hitter, and I firmly believe that he is a star in the making, and urge you to get a string attached to him."

Strider added: "He is a versatile player, playing any position in the infield, and has a wonderful arm. He could be converted into an outfielder, which I believe you are in more urgent need at the present time. He is a good batter, being a turn-around man (switch-hitter)."

When Koenig reported to the Saints in 1925, Allen, the team's manager, gave him the shortstop position. Boone moved to third base. As a regular for St. Paul in 1925, Koenig was superb, batting .308, with 153 hits, 35 doubles, 7 triples, and 11 home runs. He was also considered one of the best fielding shortstops in the league.

The Yankees followed Koenig's career closely. As a matter of fact, Bob Connery, who had scouted Koenig early on, became a baseball official with the St. Paul Club and he kept Barrow and Huggins apprised of Koenig.

After Huggins watched Koenig himself at St. Paul, he urged Barrow to obtain the young shortstop. Connery told Huggins six other major league clubs, including the Athletics, Browns, Senators, White Sox and Phillies, were also interested in him. In August 1925, Barrow obtained Koenig from St. Paul for $35,000 and three players.

After signing his contract, Koenig reported to the club. He was a big man for a shortstop at 6' and 180 pounds. Koenig threw right handed and batted from the left and right sides. Koenig played in his first game on September 8, 1925 and finished the season with the Yankees, playing in 28 games and batting .205.

There was an incident in Baltimore during that time that was noteworthy. During an exhibition game, Ruth was playing first base and Koenig was at short. Ruth had been ragging the rookie and was unhappy about a play that he thought Koenig should have made. Ruth and Koenig had words. Back in the dugout there was a pushing and shoving match between the two men that had to be broken up by the other players.

In the spring of 1926, Miller Huggins decided to make Koenig the regular shortstop along side another rookie, second baseman Tony Lazzeri. Many of the newspaper writers in New York felt that the Yankees couldn't win with two inexperienced players in the infield, but Huggins disagreed. He thought both Koenig and Lazzeri were extremely talented and would help the Yankees after a horrendous season in 1925.

When the season started, Koenig hit well but was unsteady in the field. The writers ripped into Koenig and Huggins's decision to play him. The youngster was sensitive and he took their comments to heart. Huggins called him into his office on more than one occasion to assure him that he was running the club, not the sports writers, and that as long as he wanted him at shortstop, Koenig was going to stay there. Lazzeri also helped him to adjust.

Off the field, Koenig became friends with Meusel, Hoyt, Pennock, and Gehrig, and he roomed with Benny Bengough in upper Manhattan. Gehrig would stop by their apartment and eat with the others two or three times a week. Meusel, Bengough and Koenig would often go over to the Gehrig home, where Lou's mother served them wonderful dinners.

As the club's regular shortstop, Koenig contributed to the club winning the pennant in 1926. He played in 147 games batting .271 with 167 hits, 26 doubles, 8 triples, 5 home runs, and 62 runs batted in. Huggins liked the fact that in 617 plate appearances, Koenig struck out only 37 times. He was erratic however in the field and was inclined to make errors and given to brooding.

The 1926 World Series with the Cardinals was a struggle for the Yankees and for Koenig, in particular, who many fans blamed for the team's loss in the seventh game. In the fourth inning, Koenig made an error on a double play ball, paving the way for the Cardinals to score what would later be the deciding run. Koenig felt responsible. After the game, he sat apart from the players, his head in his hands. The players tried to console him without success.

After the series some newspaper writers reported that the Cardinals were told before the World Series opened that Koenig was the weak link in the Yankees' defense and they "rode" him. The writers inferred that it had its intended affect, pointing out that Koenig made 4 errors, struck out 7 times, hit into 3 double plays, and batted only .125. Going into the 1927 season, Koenig was the regular shortstop. He was determined to redeem himself and to prove that he was a first-rate player in the eyes of the fans and teammates.

Chapter 20

Lindy! Lindy! Lindy!

The Yankees were not scheduled on Wednesday, June 15, 1927. At midnight the trading season closed, and from that time on no trades between the leagues were allowed, though it was permissible to obtain a player for the waiver price. If the Yankees wanted to claim a player, the club had to wait until every club lower in the league standings had passed up the player. Only at that time, could the Yanks make a deal with the other team.

The St. Louis Browns under their first year manager Dan Howley were in New York the next day to open a four game series. The Browns came to Yankee Stadium in sixth place and were playing better than last year at that time by five and one-half games.

At Shibe Park in Philadelphia, Ted Lyon's triple in the eighth off Lefty Grove gave the White Sox a victory over the Athletics, 6 to 4, in the first game of the series. Lyons's win was his major league leading twelfth and ninth in a row. Al Simmons drove in all of Philadelphia's runs in the first with his ninth home run with the bases loaded. Rain postponed the game between the Browns and Red Sox at Boston.

On a bright and sunny afternoon at Sportsman's Park, Jesse Haines shutout the Giants on two hits as the Cardinals won, 5 to 0. Before the game, 18,000 fans honored Rogers Hornsby, their former manager and player. He was presented with a watch as gratitude for leading the Cardinals to their first world championship in 1926. Hornsby was traded to New York after that season.

In Chicago, Charley Root won his eleventh as the Cubs crushed the Phillies, 12 to 5. Root scattered five hits until the ninth when Philadelphia scored five runs on six hits. At Forbes Field, Carmen Hill won his eighth in a row as the Pirates beat the Braves, 7 to 4. Hill gave up twelve hits but kept the Braves from scoring when they threatened. Pirate first baseman Joe Harris had three hits. The Pirates announced that veteran pitcher Joe Bush was unconditionally released, and Joseph Dawson, a right-hander, was purchased from Louisville for an unspecified amount of cash. In Cincinnati, Dazzy Vance bested Eppa Rixey in a mound duel as the Robins edged the Reds, 2 to 1.

There was an air of expectancy and excitement at Yankee Stadium in New York on Thursday, June 16, 1927 as 15,000 fans and 1,200 police waited for Colonel Charles A. Lindbergh. The festivities were part of the recent celebrations in Paris, London, Brussels, Washington, D.C. and New York honoring the young aviator's historic solo transatlantic flight the month before from Long Island to Paris.

Lindbergh was expected before the start of the game at 3:30 p.m.; however, when he did not arrive, Umpire George Hildebrand held up the game for twenty-five minutes. With Lindbergh still not at the stadium at 3:55 p.m., Hildebrand started the game. Waite Hoyt, a right-hander, started for the Yankees.

Opening the series for the St. Louis Browns was left-hander Tom Zachary. Jonathan Thompson Walton Zachary was born May 7, 1896 in Graham, North Carolina. The six foot-one hurler began his career with the Philadelphia Athletics in 1918 (2-0, 5.63 era). He joined the Senators in 1919, where he played through 1925. His best season for Washington was 1921 (18-16, 3.96 era). Traded to the Browns in 1926, Zachary won 14, lost 15, and posted 2 saves, compiling a 3.61 era.

The Line-Ups

Browns	Yankees
Frank O'Rourke 3b	Earle Combs cf
Ski Melillo 2b	Ray Morehart 2b
George Sisler 1b	Babe Ruth rf
Bing Miller lf	Lou Gehrig 1b
Harry Rice rf	Ben Paschal lf
Fred Schulte cf	Tony Lazzeri ss

Wally Gerber ss	Joe Dugan 3b
Wally Schang c	John Grabowski c
Tom Zachary p	Waite Hoyt p

Ruth came up to bat with Combs on second base and one out in the first inning. With two strikes, Zachary threw a pitch inside that the Babe blasted into the left center field bleachers for a home run. Gehrig came up next and belted a home run to almost the same spot. Howley wasted no time in replacing Zachary with Milt Gaston, a right-hander.

Dugan sparkled at third base in the third when he moved in front of Lazzeri and took a hit away from Gerber with a pretty one-handed pick-up. Meanwhile, the Yankees scored five more runs in the home half of the third on a hit by Paschal with the bases loaded, an error by Schulte on Lazzeri's fly ball, and a triple by Grabowski that cleared the bases. The Yankees led 8 to 0.

Gaston pitched well after the third inning, not allowing a hit. The Browns' only run of the day came in the seventh when Schulte homered.

Final score: Yankees 8, Browns 1.

As fans were walking on the field toward the outfield exits, there was a commotion at the left field gate and an automobile entered. Colonel Lindbergh's procession had finally reached Yankee Stadium. Earlier that day, the young aviator was honored at a rally by an estimated 200,000 people on the parade grounds adjoining Prospect Park in Brooklyn.

With the automobile's siren blowing, six police motorcycles escorted the car into a wall of hundreds of people. As scores of police formed a wedge through the crowd, Lindbergh smiled and waved in the back seat of the automobile.

When Harry M. Stevens, the Stadium's concessionaire, heard Lindbergh had arrived, he grabbed a hot frankfurter and hot dog roll and ran along the dark passageway under the stands to offer it to the flyer. Unfortunately, Stevens tripped and got sand over the hot dog and returned to get another.

With the crowd chanting "Lindy! Lindy! Lindy!" the car made its way slowly to the empty field boxes. Yankee owner Jacob Ruppert greeted the shy, slim young man. Both men shook hands. With Lindbergh waving to the crowd, the police cleared a small path and the automobile moved toward the exit.

By the time Stevens returned with another hot dog, Lindbergh had left.

Yankee Notebook for Thursday, June 16, 1927: Hoyt (9-3) went the distance, giving up seven hits, walking one, and striking out three . . . St. Louis's Zachary and Gaston gave up nine hits, including two home runs: Ruth's twenty-second and Gehrig's fifteenth, and doubles by Lazzeri and Grabowski . . . When told that Lindbergh had arrived after the game, Ruth remarked, "I had been saving that homer for Lindbergh and then he doesn't show up. I guess he thinks this is a twilight league."

In the field, Lazzeri and Combs made errors . . . Lazzeri, however, made a fine throw in the third to nab O'Rourke at the plate when he tried to stretch a triple into an inside-the-park home . . . Lazzeri also stole a base . . . Koenig did not play and was expected to be out of the lineup for some time. He hurt his leg again running to first base after batting for Wera on Sunday.

At Shibe Park in Philadelphia, Sarge Connally pitched a 4 to 0 shutout as the White Sox made it two in a row over the Athletics. Connally gave up eight hits and stranded nine. Bill Hunnefield and Bill Barrett hit home runs for Chicago. The White Sox picked up outfielder Bernie Neis from the Indians on waivers. In Washington, D.C., the Tigers rallied in the eighth and ninth innings and took the first of a four game series with the Senators, 6 to 1.

In the opening series at Fenway Park, the Red Sox narrowly defeated the Indians, 11 to 10. Boston used five pitchers and Cleveland three. The Red Sox had sixteen hits and the Indians fifteen.

In Pittsburgh, Lee Meadows held the Braves to six scattered hits as the league-leading Pirates won 6 to 0, at Forbes Field. Meadows's victory was his ninth against one defeat. Pittsburgh outfielder Paul Waner extended his consecutive hitting streak to nineteen games. Meanwhile, the Cubs won their twelfth game in a row as Hal Carlson faced his former team and routed the Phillies, 7 to 2, at Wrigley Field.

In St. Louis, the Giants ended a six game losing streak with a victory over the Cardinals, 10 to 5. Rogers Hornsby had three singles and a home run for four Giant runs. Teammate Bill Terry also had a home run plus a triple and single. At Redland Field, the Reds defeated the Robins for the first time that season, 10 to 1.

Fully recovered from being hit in the head in Philadelphia in May, right-hander Urban Shocker started for the Yankees at the Stadium on Friday, June 17, 1927. Opposing him was St. Louis Browns' left hander, Walter (Lefty) Stewart.

Born in Sparta, Tennessee, Walter Cleveland Stewart debuted as a 20-year-old for the Detroit Tigers in April 1921. After playing in only five games, he was sent to the minor leagues for more experience; Stewart spent six years trying to return to the major leagues. Obtained by the Browns, the left-hander had been recently called up from Toronto of the International League.

O'Rourke walked to open the game and went to second base on Collins's passed ball. After moving to third on a sacrifice, he scored on Sisler's fly to Paschal in left. Ruth limped to the plate in the first inning, a result of hurting his leg while striking out in Thursday's game. With a runner on first, he grounded to Mellilo, but could only take a few steps toward first base and was out on the double play. Huggins replaced Ruth with Cedric Durst in right field in the second.

With Stewart pitching very well, the Browns went to the home half of the fifth leading 1 to 0. In the fifth, Lazzeri and Dugan both singled. When Collins singled to left center, Lazzeri scored and Dugan advanced to third. Shocker then grounded to Sisler, who went to second for the force out. As Shocker raced to first base safely, avoiding the double play, Dugan scored. The Yankees went ahead 2 to 1.

The Browns tied the game in the seventh.

When the Yankees came up to bat in the eighth, right-hander Ernie Nevers was on the mound. Stewart had been lifted for a pinch-hitter. Morehart sent a slow roller close to the pitcher's mound. Nevers picked it up and threw wildly. The ball rolled toward the right field stands. As Morehart ran towards second, Rice, the right fielder, picked up the ball and made a bad throw to second that went into left field. When Miller, the left fielder, finally got to the ball, he kept Morehart on third. Durst then hit a sacrifice fly to Schulte in center, scoring Morehart. Shocker retired the Browns in the ninth.

Final score: Yankees 3, Browns 2.

Yankee Notebook for Friday, June 17, 1927: Shocker (7-4) gave up only four hits, walking three, and striking out one . . . The Browns left six men on the bases . . . The Yankees had nine hits; Combs, Collins, and Morehart had two apiece . . . There were no extra base hits in the game . . . Shocker had two sacrifices and Durst one . . . Lazzeri, Combs, and Dugan made good plays in the field in support of Shocker . . . The Babe was expected back in the line up the next day . . . With that day's victory, the Yankees had defeated the Browns six straight times.

At Griffith Stadium, Horace Lisenbee pitched another excellent game as the Senators beat the Tigers, 3 to 1. Bobby Reeves's single in the fourth drove in two runs and gave the Senators the lead. Meanwhile, the Washington Senators gave 37-year-old pitcher Stan Coveleski his unconditional release. Coveleski, a right-hander, developed arm trouble after the season opened and pitched only fourteen innings (2-1, 3.21 era).

Behind the strong pitching of Rube Walberg, who fanned seven and allowed only three hits after the third, the Athletics defeated the White Sox, 8 to 3, at Shibe Park. Charley Barnabe and Ted Blankenship pitched for Chicago. Right-hander Russell (Jing) Johnson, who last pitched for the Athletics' in 1919 (9-15, 3.61 era), rejoined the club. Johnson had been coaching Lehigh University for the past few years. He recently told Connie Mack that he wanted to try a comeback.

At Fenway Park, the Indians celebrated Bunker Hill Day with two victories over the Red Sox, 6 to 3 and 4 to 3. In the first game, Willis Hudlin's pitching, and his timely hitting, was decisive. In the second game, Walter Miller held Boston to two hits until the eighth, when the home team scored three runs with none out. Joe Shaute then came into the game and stopped the Red Sox.

Rallying for two runs in the ninth, the Braves went on to defeat the Pirates, 8 to 7, at Forbes Field. Paul Waner hit safely in his twentieth straight game. George Mogridge was the winning pitcher. In Chicago, Clarence Mitchell scattered six hits as the Phillies snapped the Cubs' twelve game winning streak, 12 to 2. Russ Wrightstone led the Philadelphia attack with a home run, a double, and a single. At Redland Field, Bill Doak pitched a complete game victory for the Robins over the Reds, 5 to 3. The Reds rallied for two runs in the ninth but fell short.

With a crowd of 25,000 at Yankee Stadium on Saturday, June 18, 1927, the St. Louis Browns sent Elam Vangilder, 31, from Cape Girardeau, Missouri to the mound. Miller Huggins went with Myles Thomas. Both were right-handed pitchers.

Trailing 2 to 0 in the first, Combs singled and Morehart was safe on Melillo's error. Gehrig came up and hit a long drive off Vangilder that landed in the right centerfield bleachers. As Combs, Morehart and Gehrig scored, the Yankees jumped ahead 3 to 2.

In the fifth, Gehrig tripled as the ball bounced off the wall of the left field stands. When Durst's hit landed in fair territory just back of third base, Gehrig scored easily. Koenig then walked and stole second. Vangilder walked Grabowski to get to Thomas, the Yankee pitcher. When Thomas singled into center field, scoring Durst and Koenig, the Yankees took a lead of 6 to 2.

After Thomas gave up a home run to Schang with Schulte on base in the sixth, the Browns loaded the bases on an error, a walk, and a hit. Huggins then replaced Thomas with Wilcy Moore, a right-hander, who retired Bing Miller to end the rally. With the club ahead 6 to 4, Moore escaped tight spots in the seventh and eighth. In the home half of the eighth with Morehart on base, Gehrig hit his second home run of the day into the right center field bleachers. Moore set down the Browns in the ninth.

Final score: Yankees 8, Browns 4.

Yankee Notebook for Saturday, June 18, 1927: Gehrig's home runs were his sixteenth and seventeenth . . . The Yankee first baseman trailed Ruth by five. The year before at the same time, Gehrig had only four home runs . . . Gehrig also drove in four runs and scored three . . . Dugan was the first Yankee thrown out of a game that season when he got into an argument with umpire Bill McGowan in the first at third base over a safe call on O'Rourke . . . With Dugan ejected, Lazzeri moved to third base, and Mark Koenig came in and played shortstop. Morehart stayed at second base.

Thomas (6-1) went 5 2/3 and gave up eight hits, walking six, and striking out two . . . Moore finished and gave up three hits in 3 1/3, walking two and striking out none . . . The Browns left fifteen men on the bases . . . The Yankees played poorly in the field as Morehart, Gehrig, and Koenig made errors . . . The loss was the Browns' seventh straight to the Yankees.

At Shibe Park in Philadelphia, Mickey Cochrane's inside-the-park home run earlier in that game and triple in the eighth with two on helped the Athletics defeat the White Sox, 6 to 2, and split the four-game series. Lefty Grove bested Tommy Thomas. In the nation's capital, General Crowder held the Tigers to four hits as the Senators won, 6 to 4. At Fenway Park, Del Lundgren scattered seven hits as the Red Sox evened their series with a victory over the Indians, 5 to 0. Arlie Tarbert, from Ohio State College, debuted in left field for Boston and played well.

After his visit to New York, Col. Charles Lindbergh flew to St. Louis in his plane "The Spirit of St. Louis." The celebrated aviator was given a parade and a reception. Later that day, he appeared at Sportsman's Park. Flanked by Commissioner Kenesaw Mountain Landis and Mayor Victor Miller, Lindbergh marched around the ballpark in front of a crowd of 37,000. Lindbergh stopped at the flagpole in centerfield.

With the "Star Spangled Banner" playing, Lindbergh first raised the American flag and then the Cardinals' world championship and National League pennants. At home plate, he shook hands with the players from each team and presented the Cardinals with their championship rings. With Grover Cleveland Alexander on the mound, the Cardinals defeated the Giants, 6 to 4. Jim Bottomley hit a home run for St. Louis.

At Forbes Field, the Pirates defeated the Braves, 7 to 4, in a game that saw Pittsburgh catcher Earl Smith and Boston manager Dave Bancroft get into a fight. In what was thought to be a long-standing baseball feud, Smith hit Bancroft in the jaw with his left fist. Bancroft fell to the ground unconscious and was carried off the field. He later required three stitches.

In Chicago, the Phillies scored six runs in the eighth and split the four-game series with a win over the Cubs, 7 to 2. Phillies' teammates Jimmy Wilson and Fresco Thompson each stole home in the eighth. Wet grounds postponed the game between the Robins and Reds at Cincinnati.

With the get-away game between the St. Louis Browns postponed because of wet grounds in New York on Sunday, June 19, 1927, the Yankees left that evening for Boston to play a five game series with the Red Sox at Fenway Park.

Miller Huggins told reporters that Bob Meusel and Mark Koenig would be given all the time they needed to completely recover from injuries; Meusel had a charley horse and Koenig a sore thigh. Although still bothered with a twisted knee, Babe Ruth was expected to play the next day.

While the Yanks were idle, the Tigers evened the four game series with the Senators with a victory, 5 to 1, at Griffith Stadium. Ken Holloway scattered eight hits for Detroit. At Dunn Field, Ted Lyon's nine game winning streak ended as the Indians edged the White Sox, 3 to 2. Joe Shaute limited Chicago to four hits. The loss was the White Sox's ninth in their last twelve games.

At Sportsman's Park in St. Louis, the Giants ended their road trip with a 4 to 3 win over the Cardinals. Home runs by Rogers Hornsby and Randy Reese accounted for three of New York's runs. Bill Terry's sacrifice fly in the ninth scored the winning run. At Wrigley Field, a crowd of just under 45,000 people saw the Cubs and Pirates battle each other as the home team won 14 to 7. The victory cut the Pirates' lead to one game. Charlie Root won his twelfth. In Cincinnati, Phillies' pitcher Jack Scott pitched both games of a doubleheader against the Reds, winning the first game, 3 to 1, and losing the second contest, 3 to 0. The Braves and Robins were rained out at Brooklyn.

Major League Baseball Standings
June 19, 1927
American League

	Won	Lost	P.C.
New York	39	17	.696
Chicago	34	26	.567
Philadelphia	31	25	.584

Washington	28	26	.519
Detroit	26	29	.473
Cleveland	27	32	.458
St. Louis	24	30	.444
Boston	15	33	.278

National League

	Won	Lost	P.C.
Pittsburgh	35	19	.648
Chicago	35	21	.625
St. Louis	31	22	.586
New York	28	27	.509
Brooklyn	27	32	.458
Boston	20	29	.408
Philadelphia	22	32	.407
Cincinnati	21	37	.362

ii

Rain canceled the game between the Yankees and the Boston Red Sox at Fenway Park on Monday, June 20, 1927. A doubleheader was scheduled for the next day and another on Wednesday. Working out with the Yankees was Joe Styborski, a right-hander from Penn State. The scouting report on Styborski was that he had a good fast ball and could hit; however, it was expected that the Yankees would send him to the minor leagues for more experience.

There were no games played in the American League. The only game played in the National League was at Wrigley Field, where the Pirates blanked the Cubs, 4 to 0. Lee Meadows scattered four hits and recorded his second straight shutout. Johnny Gooch, the Pirates' catcher, had a home run in the sixth with two men on. Teammate Paul Waner had two hits, running his consecutive hitting streak to twenty-three games.

It was Tony Lazzeri Day at Fenway Park in Boston on Tuesday, June 21, 1927 as a crowd of 20,000 came out to watch the Red Sox and the

Yankees. In that day's doubleheader, left-hander Herb Pennock and Waite Hoyt, a right-hander, opposed right-handers Fred Wingfield and Tony Welzer.

First Game
The Line-Ups

Yankees	Red Sox
Earle Combs cf	Bill Regan 2b
Ray Morehart 2b	Fred Haney 3b
Babe Ruth lf	Arlie Tarbert lf
Lou Gehrig 1b	Ira Flagstead cf
Cedric Durst rf	Phil Todt 1b
Tony Lazzeri ss	Buddy Meyer ss
Joe Dugan 3b	Wally Shaner rf
Pat Collins c	Grover Hartley c
Herb Pennock p	Fred Wingfield p

Combs opened the game with a triple. Wingfield then gave up three singles and three runs before retiring the side. Leading 3 to 0 in the fourth, Collins, the Yanks' catcher, scored two men with a single to left field. Collins then crossed the plate on Combs's single. The Yankees led 6 to 0.

In the sixth, Combs again sent Collins home with a single. Meanwhile, over the first seven, Pennock allowed the Red Sox only three hits. In Boston's home half of the eighth, Wingfield and Regan singled. When Haney's drive bounced past Durst in right, Wingfield and Regan scored. Haney ended up at third. When Dugan threw out Tarbert, Haney scored Boston's third and last run. Pennock retired the Red Sox in the ninth.

Final score: Yankees 7, Red Sox 3 (First game).

Before the start of the second game, a delegation of Italian admirers presented Lazzeri with a jeweled ring. Gehrig came to the plate in the first inning with two runners on and hit a long drive that sailed over the fence in center field. The home run off Welzer gave the Yankees a 3 to 0 lead.

The Yanks were ahead 3 to 1 in the third after Combs tripled, his second of the doubleheader, and scored when Shaner dropped Morehart's easy fly ball in right. Two more runs scored on Ruth's double, two walks, and a sacrifice fly by Dugan. Gehrig's double in the fourth drove in another run making the score, 7 to 1.

Jack Russell, a right-hander, replaced Welzer in the sixth and held the Yankees to one hit. Hoyt pitched very well, not allowing a runner to reach second base over the final seven innings.

Final score: Yankees 7, Red Sox 1 (Second game).

Yankee Notebook for Tuesday, June 21, 1927: With two victories that afternoon, the Yankees had won six consecutive games . . . Pennock (8-2) gave up six hits in the first game, walking none, and striking out two . . . The Yankees had a total of thirteen hits off Wingfield; Combs and Collins had three each and Ruth and Lazzeri two apiece . . . In the field, Morehart and Lazzeri made errors.

In the second game, Hoyt (10-3) limited the Red Sox to five hits, walking three, and striking out five . . . Overall, Pennock and Hoyt gave up only eleven hits . . . The Yankees had nine hits off Welzer and Russell . . . Gehrig's home run in the second game was his eighteenth . . . Gehrig and Ruth doubled . . . Combs tripled . . . Ruth was still limping; however, he played all of the first game and six innings of the second; Ben Paschal replaced Ruth in left field . . . As part of the festivities for Lazzeri that evening, his fans gave him a dinner at the Elks Hotel.

A crowd of 25,000 at Shibe Park in Philadelphia saw the Athletics split a doubleheader with the Senators as they lost the first game, 5 to 4, and won the second, 8 to 2. In the opener, Washington scored three runs off Eddie Rommel in the first and never lost the lead. In the finale, Philadelphia had nine hits and eight runs off Walter Johnson. Athletics' Rube Walberg scattered five hits. Rain postponed the game between the Browns and White Sox at Chicago.

At the Polo Grounds, rookie catcher Frank Hogan hit a home run in the tenth inning as the Braves beat the Giants 7 to 5. The home run was Hogan's second of the day. In Pittsburgh, second baseman Hughie Critz singled Ethan Allen home in the tenth as the Reds beat the Pirates, 7 to 6. At Brooklyn's Ebbets Field, Dazzy Vance gave up only five hits to the Phillies as the Robins won 7 to 3. Meanwhile, the Cardinals took two from the Cubs at Sportsman's Park, 6 to 5 and 12 to 3. Jesse Haines and Flint Rhem won. Charlie Root and Jim Brillheart took the losses.

The doubleheader at Fenway Park in Boston on Wednesday, June 22, 1927 saw Yankee right-handers Myles Thomas and Urban Shocker oppose Boston's left-hander Hal Wiltse, who had already beaten the Yankees twice, and right-hander Charlie Ruffing.

In the first game, the Red Sox took a 3 to 2 lead into the top half of the fifth inning. With Ruth at the plate, Wiltse delivered a pitch that the Babe hit for a home run over the top of the centerfield fence. At three-all in the bottom of the fifth, the Red Sox's Tobin doubled off Thomas and scored on Regan's single. When Carlyle doubled, Regan raced to third. At that point, Huggins called for Wilcy Moore, a right-hander, who came in and retired the side.

With the Red Sox leading 4 to 3 in the seventh, Combs drove in a run with a double. Later in the inning with Moore on third, Bob Meusel, who batted for Morehart, hit a sacrifice fly. Moore tagged up and scored. Ruth then came up again and hit his second home run of the game, a long drive that went through an open space between the right field bleachers and hit a garage. As Combs and Ruth scored, the Yankees led 7 to 4. Moore pitched a scoreless seventh, eighth, and ninth.

Final score: Yankees 7, Red Sox 4 (First game)

Ruffing opened the second game walking Combs and Ruth. Trying to stop Combs from stealing third, Ruffing threw to Myer, the short stop. When Myer's relay throw to third base was wild, Combs scampered home. On the play, Ruth went from first to third. Ruffing then walked Gehrig. After Myer at short caught Durst's line drive, he threw the ball beyond Todt's reach in an attempt to double Gehrig. As the ball went into the outfield, Ruth came home. The Yankees led 2 to 0.

In the fifth, Ruffing walked Grabowski, who was sacrificed to second by Shocker. With two outs, Morehart lofted a short fly behind the shortstop. Myer ran back, caught it momentarily, and dropped it. Grabowski scored on what the official scorer called a two-base hit. The Red Sox scored two in the bottom of that inning.

Shocker went into the ninth ahead 3 to 2.

After Todt opened with a double, Huggins decided to replace Shocker with right-hander Wilcy Moore. Moore threw out Myer when the Red Sox's shortstop sacrificed. When Moore fielded Regan's roller, he went after Todt, who was scrambling back to third. Moore's throw sailed over Dugan's head. Todt got to his feet and raced for home plate. Lazzeri, who was backing up Dugan, fielded the ball and threw to Grabowski, who tagged out Todt at the plate. The game ended when Moore retired the next batter.

Final score: Yankees 3, Red Sox 2 (Second game)

Yankee Notebook for Wednesday, June 22, 1927: Ruth's two home runs in the first game were his twenty-third and twenty-fourth . . . Combs had two singles and a double . . . Paschal and Lazzeri also doubled . . . Thomas, Dugan, and Meusel sacrificed . . . On the hill, Moore (6-4) won the first game and saved the second . . . After relieving Thomas in the opening game, Moore pitched 4 2/3 and gave up only three hits.

In the second game, Shocker (8-4) went eight innings and gave up six hits, walking two, and striking out one . . . Moore replaced Shocker with none out in the ninth and did not give up a hit . . . For the Red Sox, Ruffing gave up only three hits and was the victim of errors by teammates in the first . . . Ruffing walked eight and struck out seven . . . Morehart and Dugan doubled . . . Gehrig went hitless in the doubleheader . . . On the base paths, Combs and Gehrig, who walked, each stole a base . . . The two victories that day gave the Yankees an eight-game winning streak.

At Shibe Park, the Athletics and Senators split a doubleheader as Washington won the first game, 4 to 2, and Philadelphia the second, 13 to 7. Horace Lisenbee, who faced the Athletics for the first time, won his ninth giving up six hits. In the second contest, the Athletics knocked General Crowder out of the box in the second. Al Simmons had two home runs.

In a doubleheader at Comiskey Park between the White Sox and Browns, St. Louis won the first game, 3 to 2 in ten innings, and Chicago took the second, 8 to 5. Lefty Stewart beat Sarge Connally in the opener. Tommy Thomas defeated Milt Gaston in the finale. Thomas's victory was his eleventh. Wally Schang and Aaron Ward hit home runs.

Down 5 to 0, the Pirates scored five runs in the second to tie and went on to defeat the Reds, 11 to 9, at Forbes Field. Ray Kremer was knocked out in the second and replaced by Johnny Morrison. Carmen Hill, who replaced Morrison, was the winning pitcher.

In St. Louis, the Cardinals strengthened their hold on second place by pounding the Cubs, 11 to 5, at Sportsman's Park. Grover Cleveland Alexander, who volunteered to pitch out of turn, scattered six hits, while teammates battered three Cubs' pitchers for sixteen hits. Jim Bottomley homered for St. Louis. Hack Wilson hit his fourteenth for Chicago. Rain postponed the games between the Braves and Giants at the Polo Grounds and Phillies and the Robins at Ebbets Field.

On a sultry afternoon at Fenway Park, the Yankees and Boston Red Sox played the final game of the series on Thursday, June 23, 1927. The starting pitchers were left-hander Dutch Ruether and Del Lundgren, a right-hander. Carl Leonard Lundgren, 27, from Lindsborg, Kansas began his major league career with the Pittsburgh Pirates in 1924 (0-1, 6.35 era) and spent 1925 in the minors before coming over to the Red Sox in 1926 (0-2, 7.55 era).

With the Red Sox leading 4 to 2, the Yankees came up in the second against Lundgren. After Ruth drove in two runs with a single, Gehrig hit a home run over the left center field fence. The Yankees ended the inning with a 7 to 2 lead. In the next frame, Ruether drove in two more runs with a double off right-hander Danny MacFayden.

In the fourth, Combs went to his right to make a spectacular backhand catch of Shaner's line drive. With MacFayden on the mound, Gehrig came up again in the sixth and hit another home run that landed in the right field bleachers. When Gehrig crossed the plate, the Yanks led 10 to 2.

In the seventh, Ruth split one of Hartley's fingers with a foul tip.

When the catcher came out of the game, Red Sox manager Bill Carrigan went behind the plate and kept the pitcher warm while a new catcher was getting ready. Before returning as manager in 1927, Carrigan was the player-manager of the Red Sox from 1913 to 1916. Under Carrigan, the Red Sox won the World Series in 1915 and 1916. Ruth was a member of those championship teams.

The Boston fans urged Carrigan to stay in the game and do the catching. When Carrigan threw the ball to second on one bounce, the Babe took his former manager by the arm and led him back to the Red Sox dugout.

In the eighth, Gehrig faced MacFayden once again. And again Gehrig homered. This time the ball landed in the right center field bleachers, a little further to the right than the last one. Ruether held the Red Sox scoreless over the final eight innings.

Final score: Yankees 11, Red Sox 4.

Yankee Notebook for Thursday, June 23, 1927: Gehrig's three home runs were his nineteenth, twentieth, and twenty-first, and he was three behind Ruth for the major league lead . . . The only other player that hit three home runs in one game that season was teammate Tony Lazzeri . . . Gehrig drove in five runs and scored three . . . In total, the Yanks had fifteen hits off Lundgren and MacFayden . . . Every Yankee starter except Collins had at least one hit; Gehrig had four hits, Ruether three, and Combs and Dugan two each.

On the mound, Ruether improved to a record of six wins and one loss, giving up nine hits, walking two, and striking out two . . . The win was the Yankees' fifth straight over Boston and the club's ninth consecutive victory . . . The Yanks had won twenty out of their last twenty-four games and led the second-place Athletics by ten games . . . The Yankees were scheduled to play the Springfield Club of the Eastern League in an exhibition game the next day and return to Yankee Stadium on Saturday to play a doubleheader against the Athletics . . . Another doubleheader was scheduled with Philadelphia on Sunday.

Starting his first game of the season, Lefty Willis of the Athletics held the Senators scoreless after the first inning at Shibe Park as Philadelphia took the final game of the series with Washington, 4 to 1. Al Simmons led the Athletics' attack with three hits, including his third home run in the last two days.

At Comiskey Park, the Tigers defeated the White Sox, 6 to 5 in eleven innings. The loss dropped Chicago to third place. Detroit scored the winning run off Ted Lyons, who allowed six hits. In Cleveland, the Indians took the first game of the series from the Browns, 7 to 2, in a game halted by rain in the sixth. Willis Hudlin was the winning pitcher.

In St. Louis, the Cardinals nosed out the Reds, 4 to 3, at Sportsman's Park as Frankie Frisch scored the winning run in the fifth. The victory was St. Louis's fourth straight and put them two games behind the league leading Pirates. Bob McGraw allowed eight hits and was the winning pitcher. At Ebbets Field, Bobby Barrett's home run and triple gave southpaw Jesse Petty and the Robins a victory over the Phillies, 3 to 1. In New York, the Giants swept a doubleheader from the Braves, 6 to 2 and 9 to 6. Freddie Fitzsimmons and Don Songer won.

With most of the regulars having gone back to New York from Boston on Friday, June 24, 1927, a makeshift team of Yankees played an exhibition game in Springfield, Massachusetts defeating the Ponies of the Eastern League, 8 to 7.

Yankee manager Miller Huggins tried out Roy Chesterfield, Joe Styborski, and Joe Giard on the mound. In the field, Lou Gehrig was in right and Babe Ruth played first base. Ruth put on a show for the crowd. The Babe hit a home run over the right field fence in the first; singled in the third; hit another home run over the left field fence in the fifth, and batting right-handed, doubled into left field in the seventh.

Coming up in the ninth, however, the Babe grounded out and pulled up lame. He had wrenched his knee again. Gehrig had one hit—a home run over the center field fence—in the ninth. The Yankees actually scored two in that inning for a total of ten runs, but the game was called when about 500 boys raced onto the field in the bottom of the ninth wanting autographs.

Before leaving Springfield, Ruth discovered that his favorite bat and eight others had disappeared from the dugout. The Babe offered a $25 reward for its return and offered a duplicate bat in its place with no questions asked.

At Comiskey Park in Chicago, the Tigers collected sixteen hits, knocked Red Faber out of the game in the sixth inning, and made it two-straight over the White Sox with a victory, 9 to 4. Tigers' starter Rip Collins was helped by two double plays that broke up Chicago rallies. In Boston, Hollis Thurston's pitching and hitting helped the Senators defeat the Red Sox, 5 to 3, at Fenway Park. Thurston gave up eight hits in a complete game effort and drove in three runs with a double and two singles. At Cleveland's Dunn Field, the Browns evened the series with the Indians in a ten-inning game, winning 2 to 1.

The Athletics were not scheduled, but there was news from Pennsylvania that affected the franchise. The Pennsylvania Supreme Court sustained a lower court decision that banned professional Sunday baseball in Philadelphia. The lower court had declared Sunday baseball "a worldly employment" in violation of the Sunday law of 1794. The basis for the legal action was the game between the Athletics and White Sox on Sunday, August 26, 1926.

"We cannot imagine anything more worldly or unreligious than professional baseball as it is played today," wrote the Pennsylvania Supreme Court in its seven-to-two majority decision.

At Forbes Field, Charlie Root held the Pirates to seven hits as Chicago defeated the home team, 4 to 2. The deciding run was scored in the fourth on Riggs Stephenson's double, Charlie Grimm's single, and a sacrifice fly by Gabby Hartnett. In St. Louis, the Cardinals moved to within one game of the Pirates as they beat the Reds, 3 to 2. Bill Sherdel held the visitors to six hits. That afternoon was Ladies' Day, and a new record was set as 11,527 women were admitted free.

At Ebbets Field, four errors by the Robins helped the Braves win, 5 to 3. Jumbo Jim Elliott pitched good enough to win, but was the victim of poor fielding. At the Polo Grounds, the Giants and Phillies split a doubleheader with New York winning the first game, 7 to 3, and Philadelphia taking the second, 6 to 5, in ten innings.

John A. Heydler, President of the National League, fined Pirate catcher Earl Smith $500 and suspended him for thirty days for his attack on Dave Bancroft, manager of the Boston Braves on June 18. Heydler described Smith's action as "a vicious and brutal assault on a player of a competing club."

That night the first professional baseball game played under floodlights powered by electricity took place at Lynn, Massachusetts. The experiment was arranged by engineers from the General Electric Company and played on their athletic field. A crowd of 5,000, including the Washington Senators and Boston Red Sox, were in the stands watching Lynn and Salem of the New England League.

Seventy-two projectors mounted on 5-foot poles supplied 26,300,000-beam candlepower. The players on the field and members of the crowd agreed there was no problem either playing or watching the game under the lights. Representatives from several of the major league clubs predicted that night baseball would soon be added to the schedules.

Major League Baseball Standings
June 24, 1927
American League

	Won	Lost	P.C.
New York	44	17	.721
Philadelphia	34	27	.567
Chicago	36	29	.547
Washington	31	29	.517
Detroit	28	29	.491
Cleveland	28	33	.459
St. Louis	26	32	.448
Boston	15	45	.250

National League

	Won	Lost	P.C.
Pittsburgh	37	21	.638
St. Louis	36	22	.621
Chicago	36	25	.590
New York	31	29	.517
Brooklyn	29	33	.468
Boston	22	31	.415
Philadelphia	23	35	.397
Cincinnati	22	40	.355

Babe Ruth

Lou Gehrig

Babe Ruth, Miller Huggins and Lou Gehrig

Babe Ruth and Ty Cobb

Connie Mack and Miller Huggins

Earle Combs, Babe Ruth and Bob Meusel

Earle Combs

Miller Huggins and Babe Ruth

Babe Ruth and Edward Grant Barrow

Herb Pennock

Waite Hoyt

Walter Ruether

Wilcy Moore

Urban Shocker

Joe Dugan

Lou Gehrig, Mark Koenig, Tony Lazzeri and Joe Dugan

Tony Lazzeri

Bob Meusel

George Pipgras

Pat Collins

Mark Koenig

Chapter 21

Home Run Derby

With a crowd of 55,000 at Yankee Stadium in the Bronx on Saturday, June 25, 1927, the Yankees and the Philadelphia Athletics opened a six game series, which included doubleheaders on that day and the next. The pitching match-ups were left-handers Herb Pennock and Lefty Grove in the first game, and Waite Hoyt, a right-hander, and left-hander Rube Walberg in the second.

When the Babe got off the train Friday night he could hardly walk. He had wrenched his knee in the exhibition game at Springfield. Ruth told Miller Huggins he was fine and could play. It was the first time in a month that Huggins had all the regulars in the line-up.

First Game
The Line-Ups

Athletics	Yankees
Max Bishop 2b	Earle Combs cf
Walt French rf	Mark Koenig ss
Bill Lamar lf	Babe Ruth rf
Al Simmons cf	Lou Gehrig 1b
Sammy Hale 3b	Bob Meusel lf
Jimmy Dykes 1b	Tony Lazzeri 2b
Cy Perkins c	Joe Dugan 3b
Joe Boley ss	John Grabowski c
Lefty Grove p	Herb Pennock p

The Yanks came up in the bottom of the ninth trailing 7 to 2. Grove was pitching when Meusel led off and singled. Then Lazzeri doubled. With runners at the corners, Dugan hit a ball into the right field corner for a double, scoring both runners. With the Athletics' lead trimmed to 7 to 4, Manager Connie Mack replaced Grove with Joe Pate, a left-hander. After Pate retired Grabowski for the first out, he then walked Pat Collins, who batted for Pennock. With the crowd cheering loudly, Huggins sent Julie Wera in to run for Collins.

With runners at first and second, Combs hit a ball down the left field line that was fair by inches. As the ball bounced into the left field boxes, Dugan scored making the score 7 to 5. With Wera on third and Combs on second with one out, Mike Gazella, who was playing short stop, hit a long sacrifice fly that scored Wera, and the Yanks were down by one. The Babe came up, but Pate walked him.

Amid thundering cheers, Gehrig batted with two outs and Combs and Ruth on the bases. The count went to three and two. Pate then struck Gehrig out with a curve ball. With the game over, the Athletics rush to the mound and congratulated Pate.

Final score: Athletics 7, Yankees 6 (First game)

In the second game, the Athletics scored a run off Hoyt in the first on Lamar's inside-the-park home run. The Yankees tied the score off Walberg in the fifth when Hoyt walked and later came home on a sacrifice and Paschal's single. The Yankees went ahead in the sixth, 2 to 1, after Lazzeri tripled to the centerfield stands and came home on a squeeze play with Dugan at the plate.

Over the first seven innings, Hoyt had pitched very well, giving up only three hits. However, the Athletics scored three runs in the eighth after French singled off Hoyt's glove scoring Boley and Lamar tripled, sending French and Bishop home. In the eighth trailing 4 to 2, the Yankees faced left-hander Joe Pate, who had relieved Walberg. Pate kept the Yanks from scoring in the eighth and ninth.

Final score: Athletics 4, Yankees 2 (Second game)

Yankee Notebook for Saturday, June 25, 1927: The doubleheader loss was the Yankees' first of the season and ended the team's nine-game winning streak . . . Grove struck out nine in the opener; Gehrig fanned three times . . . Pennock (8-3) gave up fourteen hits, walked two, and struck out four . . . At the plate, Gehrig, Lazzeri, Dugan, and Combs each doubled . . . Koenig came out of the game early and Lazzeri went from second to short. Lazzeri later moved back to second and Gazella played short . . . The Yankees made an unusual double play when Pennock threw to Dugan at third, who then pegged the ball to Gehrig to double up Perkins at first base . . . Pennock, Dugan, and Gazella made errors.

Hoyt (10-4) was the losing pitcher in the second game. He gave up eight hits, walking none, and striking out one . . . For the Athletics, Walberg yielded only five hits, and Pate did not allow a hit in the final two innings . . . The only extra base hit for the Yanks was Lazzeri's triple.

Ruth's favorite bat, which had disappeared from the dugout in Springfield, was found. A man hitting pop flys on a sandlot noticed that the bat he was using was heavier than usual. Upon closer inspection, he noticed that Ruth's name was burned on the bat. He promptly returned it to the Springfield baseball club. The local authorities started an investigation to find out how Ruth's bat got to the sandlot.

In Boston, big rallies in the sixth and ninth innings helped the Senators defeat the Red Sox, 8 to 3, at Fenway Park. Bump Hadley pitched 6 1/3, giving up two runs and Garland Braxton hurled the final 2 2/3, yielding one hit, a home run by Wally Shaner in the ninth. At Comiskey Park, Ken Holloway scattered seven hits as the Tigers made it three straight over the White Sox, 4 to 0. Jackie Tavener homered for Detroit. Rain postponed the game between the Indians and Browns at Cleveland.

At Sportsman's Park, the Cardinals finished the day one-half game behind the Pirates in the National League after splitting a doubleheader with the Reds, with St. Louis winning the first game, 3 to 2, and losing the second, 10 to 7. In Pittsburgh, the Cubs won their second straight from the Pirates, 6 to 4. Hack Wilson, the league's home run leader, hit his fifteenth for Chicago. Teammate Eddie Pick also homered. Kiki Cuyler hit a four-bagger for Pittsburgh.

In Philadelphia, the Giants won the final game of the series against the Phillies, 6 to 3. Bill Terry hit a home run in the ninth for his fourth hit of the game. Rogers Hornsby singled, doubled, and tripled. At Ebbets Field, the Robins and Braves split a twin bill that day as Brooklyn won the first game, 4 to 3, and Boston the second, 7 to 3.

On Sunday, June 26, 1927, a crowd of 61,000 fans at Yankee Stadium in New York watched the Yankees and Philadelphia Athletics play their second doubleheader in two days. Suffering from a strained ligament in his right knee, Miller Huggins kept Babe Ruth out of the line-up. He was expected to be out a couple of days.

Before the game, fans of Johnny Grabowski from Schenectady, New York presented him with a check for $1,300. Also that day, another college pitcher tried out for the Yankees. His name was Donald Miller, a right-hander, from the University of Michigan.

On the mound, Myles Thomas and Jack Quinn opposed each other in the first game, and Sam Gray and Wilcy Moore pitched the second. All were right-handers. Coming to bat in the third inning of the opener, the Yankees trailed 2 to 0. After Thomas walked and Combs tripled, the Yanks were down by one run. The Athletics added a run in the fifth. When Dugan tripled in the bottom of the fifth and scored on Grabowski's sacrifice fly to French in right field, the Yankees trailed 3 to 2.

Quinn, meanwhile, pitched very well. When the Athletics came up in the ninth, Joe Giard, a left-hander, was on the mound. Philadelphia added a run on Simmons's double, and a single by Hale. Quinn retired the Yanks in the ninth.

Final score: Athletics 4, Yankees 2. (First game)

In the second game, the Yankees scored five runs off Gray in the first on two errors by Bishop; singles by Morehart and Durst, and a double by Meusel. Replacing Gray in the second was a 23-year old right-hander named Neal Baker, a recent graduate from the University of Texas. It was Baker's major league debut.

Baker and Moore pitched scoreless ball over the next three innings. In the fifth, the Athletics scored a run and the Yankees answered with one in the bottom of that inning to make the score 6 to 2. Philadelphia added a run in the sixth. With left-hander Joe Pate on the mound in the seventh, Gehrig hit a home run that sailed into the right centerfield stands. Moore retired the Athletics in the eighth and ninth.

Final score: Yankees 7, Athletics 3 (Second game)

Yankee Notebook for Sunday, June 26, 1927: In the first game, Thomas (6-2) gave up eleven hits in eight innings, walking four, and striking out two . . . Giard pitched one inning and gave up two hits . . . Combs had a double and triple and Dugan doubled . . . Gehrig struck out three times . . . In the field, Lazzeri made two errors at short . . . Quinn held the Yankees to six hits and hit Thomas with a pitch.

Moore (7-4) pitched well, holding the Athletics to five hits in the second game. He walked three and struck out five . . . The Yankees had eleven hits . . . Gehrig's home run was his twenty-second. The young slugger trailed Ruth by two . . . Gehrig also singled . . . Durst and Meusel doubled . . . Lazzeri made a one-handed stop of Simmons's grounder in back of second and another fine play in deep short in the sixth . . . Meusel made an error in left . . . Cobb got a hand from the crowd when he batted for Boley in the sixth . . . The first game was played in 1:50 and the second in 1:45.

At Griffith Stadium in Washington, D.C., the Senators scored eight runs in the fourth and went on to defeat the Red Sox for the third straight time, 8 to 7. Goose Goslin homered for Washington. In Chicago, the White Sox beat the Tigers with a six-run rally in the seventh inning, 9 to 7. Earl Whitehill, the Tigers' starter was knocked out of the box in the seventh. Replacing Tommy Thomas in the fifth, Sarge Connally was the winning pitcher. At Dunn Field, the Indians and Browns split a doubleheader as George Uhle bested Lefty Stewart in the first game, 2 to 0. Milt Gaston triumphed over Garland Buckeye, 7 to 3, in the finale.

In St. Louis, the Pirates took the series opener from the Cardinals, 9 to 3, at Sportsman's Park and increased their first-place lead to one and one-half games. Pirate right fielder Paul Waner had a double and two singles. Carmen Hill was the winning pitcher. At Redland Field, despite five errors by his teammates, Adolfo Luque held on to beat the Cubs, 8 to 5. The Reds scored three runs in the eighth for the winning margin. With a crowd of 22,000 at Ebbets Field, Dazzy Vance scattered six hits and struck out six as the Robins routed the Giants, 7 to 1.

Babe Ruth was out of the line-up resting his knee when the Yankees and Philadelphia Athletics met again at Yankee Stadium on Monday, June 27, 1927. With a small crowd watching, southpaw Dutch Ruether opposed right-hander Howard Ehmke.

Combs opened the Yankees' first with a home run into the front row in right field. After Ehmke hit Meusel with a pitch in the fourth, Lazzeri hit a ball that landed just fair in the left field stands for a home run. The Yankees added two runs in the sixth and one in the eighth. Ruether pitched well, scattering only four hits.

The Athletics came up in the ninth inning trailing 6 to 0. With one out, Lamar beat out a hit. Simmons then beat out a grounder to Lazzeri. Galloway walked. With the bases loaded, Ruether walked Dykes, forcing home Lamar. Eddie Collins came up and batted for the pitcher Jing Johnson, who had replaced Ehmke in the eighth.

When Ruether threw ball one to Collins, Huggins decided to bring in left-hander Herb Pennock. The southpaw faced Collins, who flied to Durst in right, scoring Simmons. With two outs, Boley grounded to Dugan and the game ended.

Final score: Yankees 6, Athletics 2.

Yankee Notebook for Monday, June 27, 1927: The victory gave the Yankees a nine game lead over the second-place Athletics . . . Combs's home run was his first and Lazzeri's ninth . . . The Yankees had eight hits but left eleven men on . . . Gehrig had one hit, a single, and led the American League with a .392 mark.

Ruether (7-1) went 8 1/3 innings, giving up seven hits, walking two, and striking out one . . . Pennock did not allow a hit in 2/3 of an inning . . . Ehmke hit Dugan in the second and Meusel in the fourth . . . On a negative note, Lazzeri's shoulder was sore and he had difficulty throwing the ball to first base . . . The Yankees announced that right-hander Roy Chesterfield was released on option to Chattanooga, Tennessee.

At Fenway Park in Boston, three runs in the seventh and four in the eighth gave the Senators the winning margin over the Red Sox, 9 to

8. Twenty-year old rookie left-hander Bobby Burke won in relief. In Detroit, the Tigers bunched five of their six hits in the sixth inning and defeated the Browns, 4 to 2. Sam Gibson went the distance for the Tigers.

In Chicago, the White Sox and Indians split a doubleheader as the hometeam won the first game, 7 to 2, and the visitors the second, 12 to 4. Ted Lyons held the Indians to six hits in game one. George Grant gave up nine hits to the White Sox in the second.

With a victory over the Pirates at Sportsman's Park, 7 to 5, the Cardinals moved within one-half game of first place. Frankie Frisch had two hits for St. Louis and he stole his twenty-second base. Teammates Jim Bottomley stroked two doubles and a single and Ray Blades hit a home run.

At Redland Field, the Cubs pounded Jakie May and Ray Kolp and beat the Reds, 11 to 4. Jim Brillheart went the distance giving up eight hits. In New York, Phillies' right-hander Claude Willougby scattered six hits and blanked the Giants, 6 to 0, at the Polo Grounds.

With the Philadelphia Athletics leading the Yankees in the series 3 to 2, Miller Huggins sent right-hander Urban Shocker to the mound on Tuesday, June 28, 1927. Rube Walberg, a left-hander, pitched for the Athletics.

The Yankees already had 3 to 0 lead when Paschal came up in the third and beat out a hit. Then Gehrig hit a home run into the exit gate in the right field bleachers, and the Yankees led 5 to 0. The Yanks scored one run in the fifth and three more runs in the eighth. Going to the Athletics' ninth, the Yanks had a comfortable 9 to 0 lead. Shocker had pitched brilliantly, giving up only four hits.

Lamar opened the ninth with a single and scored on Simmons's triple. After Dykes and Foxx reached base, Huggins replaced Shocker with Wilcy Moore, a right-hander. When Boley and Cobb singled, Huggins replaced Moore with left-hander Herb Pennock. Bishop's sacrifice fly made the score 9 to 6. Perkins walked. Hale reached base safely and stole second base. When Morehart threw away Lamar's grounder, Perkins and Hale dashed for home. The score was 9 to 8.

Huggins then brought in Myles Thomas, a right-hander, who got Simmons to fly to Combs for the second out. The game ended after Cochrane grounded out to Morehart.

Final score: Yankees 9, Athletics 8.

Yankee Notebook for Tuesday, June 28, 1927: The Yankees and Athletics split the six game series . . . Gehrig's home run was his twenty-third. The Yankee first baseman trailed Ruth by one . . . The home run was Gehrig's 100th hit of the season, and he was the first player in the American League to reach that mark . . . Shocker (9-4) went eight innings, giving up nine hits, walking one, and striking out three . . . Walberg, Johnson, Rommel, and Pate pitched for the Athletics . . . Rommel hit Shocker in the head for the second time that season . . . Simmons made a remarkable backhand catch of Gehrig's drive at top speed in the first.

In Boston, General Crowder allowed only two singles as the Senators shutout the Red Sox, 4 to 0 at Fenway Park. It was Boston's tenth consecutive loss. At Comiskey Park, White Sox's coach Russell "Lena" Blackburne, who ran the club after manager Ray Schalk was forced to leave the game, inserted himself as a pinch-hitter. He singled home the tying run and scored the winning run as Chicago nosed out Cleveland, 8 to 7. Blackburne last played in the major leagues in 1919 with the Phillies.

At Navin Field, the Tigers took both games of a doubleheader from the Browns, 9 to 3 and 6 to 3. Harry Heilmann had three triples, a double, and a single in eight times at bat in the twin bill.

In St. Louis, the Pirates increased their lead to one and one-half games with a victory over the Cardinals, 9 to 8, at Sportsman's Park. Pittsburgh tied the score in the sixth and then scored the winning run in the seventh. Vic Keen hit Pirates' shortstop Glenn Wright in the head. Wright was unconscious for a few minutes and was helped off the field by teammates. An examination showed he was not badly injured.

At Redland Field, the Reds took two out of three in their series with the Cubs with a victory, 8 to 1. In Philadelphia, spitballer Clarence Mitchell gave up twelve hits but held the Giants as the Phillies won, 7 to 3.

Major League Baseball Standings
June 28, 1927
American League

	Won	Lost	P.C.
New York	47	20	.701
Philadelphia	37	30	.552
Chicago	38	31	.551
Washington	35	29	.547
Detroit	32	30	.516
Cleveland	30	36	.455
St. Louis	27	36	.429
Boston	15	49	.234

National League

	Won	Lost	P.C.
Pittsburgh	39	23	.629
St. Louis	38	25	.603
Chicago	38	27	.585
New York	32	32	.500
Brooklyn	31	34	.477
Boston	23	32	.418
Philadelphia	25	36	.410
Cincinnati	25	42	.3573

ii

With his right knee heavily bandaged, Babe Ruth was back in the line-up for the first of a four game series with the Boston Red Sox at Yankee Stadium in New York on Wednesday, June 29, 1927. Mark Koenig was out resting his injured leg, and Miller Huggins played Tony Lazzeri at shortstop and Ray Morehart at second base. On the mound, right-hander George Pipgras started for the Yankees. Hal Wiltse, a left-hander, opened for the Red Sox.

The Line-Ups

Red Sox	Yankees
Jack Tobin rf	Earle Combs cf
Red Rollings 3b	Ray Morehart 2b
Roy Carlyle lf	Babe Ruth rf
Bill Regan 2b	Lou Gehrig 1b
Phil Todt 1b	Bob Meusel lf
Buddy Meyer ss	Tony Lazzeri ss
Wally Shaner cf	Joe Dugan 3b
Grover Hartley c	John Grabowski c
Hal Wiltse p	George Pipgras p

A single, Dugan's wild throw, and Shaner's triple gave the Red Sox an early 2 to 0 lead. The Yankees scored one run in the third after Wiltse walked Morehart and Ruth doubled. New York tied the score in the fourth after Pipgras tripled scoring Lazzeri, who had singled.

With the score tied at two, Gehrig hit a home run off Wiltse into the right field bleachers. The Yankees added four in the seventh as Ruth opened with a single and Meusel walked. Lazzeri forced Meusel. Dugan came up and tripled to left center, scoring Ruth and Lazzeri. Grabowski then hit a three-bagger to deep right center bringing Dugan home. Pipgras's single scored Grabowski.

The Yanks scored their final run in the eighth. Ruth singled and was forced by Gehrig. After Gehrig raced to third on Meusel's single, both runners attempted a double steal. Gehrig, who had edged far off third, scored safely at the plate under Regan's return throw to Hartley.

Final score: Yankees 8, Red Sox 2.

Yankee Notebook for Wednesday, June 29, 1927: Gehrig's home run tied Ruth with twenty-four . . . Ruth had four hits, a double and three singles, in five appearances at the plate . . . Going the opposite way, the Babe slapped a single through short in the seventh, driving home his second run of the game . . . Combs, Meusel, Lazzeri, and Pipgras each had two hits.

Pipgras (1-0) pitched exceptionally well, mixing his pitches effectively. He gave up only three hits, striking out six, and walking four . . . Only one Red Sox batter reached first base in the last four innings . . . The Yankees had fifteen hits . . . Hoyt was at the Stadium but had a sore elbow on his pitching arm . . . The loss was Boston's eleventh straight.

In the nation's capital, the Senators moved into second place and dropped the Athletics to fourth as they won, 5 to 3. Sloppy Thurston pitched well but needed help from Firpo Marberry in the eighth. The losing pitcher was Lefty Grove. Sam Gray and Joe Pate also pitched. Mickey Cochrane homered with a man on in the eighth. At Navin Field, the Tigers swept the four game series from the Browns with a victory, 9 to 3. Detroit scored four in the sixth and five in the eighth. Tiger outfielder Bob Fothergill homered in the eighth. In Chicago, Ted Blankenship blanked the Indians, 5 to 0, as Chicago beat Cleveland in the first game of a doubleheader. The Indians won the second game, 8 to 6.

Rallying for five runs in the eighth at Sportsman's Park, the Cardinals evened the series at two apiece by taking the final game from the Pirates, 10 to 9. St. Louis shortstop Specs Toporcer's double brought home the winning run. With the victory, the Cardinals closed within one-half game of the Pirates in the National League.

At Redland Field, the Cubs edged the Reds, 2 to 1 in ten innings, as Chicago and Cincinnati split the four game series. In Philadelphia, errors by Babe Herman and Butch Henline helped the Phillies score four runs against the Robins and win, 5 to 4. The Giants and Braves were postponed because of rain in Boston. Joe Bush, who was released by the Pirates and had tried out with the Phillies, signed with the Giants.

On Thursday, June 30, 1927, 3,000 fans, the second smallest crowd of the season at Yankee Stadium, watched the Red Sox's Slim Harriss face the Yankees' Myles Thomas. Both were right-handers. Coming into the game, the Yankees had won four in a row, while Boston looked to end an eleven-game losing streak.

Harriss's first batter in the home half of the first inning was Combs, who tripled. Ruth walked. With runners at the corners, Gehrig hit a long drive into the right field seats for a home run. The Yankees added two runs in the second. With the club leading 5 to 0, Boston came up in the third. A shaky Thomas gave up six runs, two of them on Shaner's home run with a runner on. With two outs, Huggins brought in right-hander Wilcy Moore, who retired the side.

Gehrig tied the game at six in the third after he singled, stole second, and scored on Lazzeri's hit to left. Tony Welzer, a right-hander, replaced Harriss. The game was decided in the fourth. The scoring began with Morehart's single. Then Ruth homered into the right field bleachers making the score, 9 to 6. The Yankees added one run in the fifth and three more in the sixth. Moore allowed only three hits after the third.

Final score: Yankees 13, Red Sox 6.

Yankee Notebook for Thursday, June 30, 1927: Gehrig's home run was his twenty-fifth. He took over the major league lead until Ruth homered in the fourth to tie him . . . Ruth and Gehrig were five games behind the Babe's record of 1921 . . . Gehrig also doubled and singled . . . Ruth doubled . . . Meusel had two doubles and a single . . . The Yankees had nineteen hits off Harriss and Welzer.

Thomas lasted only 2 2/3, giving up six runs and six hits. He walked two and struck out none . . . Moore (8-4) pitched three-hit ball over the final 6 1/3 innings, walking one, and striking out eight . . . In the field, Morehart, Ruth, and Dugan made errors . . . Hoyt's elbow showed improvement, and he was expected back in the rotation in a couple of days.

In Washington, D.C., Goose Goslin's single in the ninth scored Sam Rice with the winning run, giving the Senators their second straight victory over the Athletics, 6 to 3, at Griffith Stadium. Firpo Marberry was the winning pitcher. At Dunn Field, Charlie Gehringer's home run started a three-run rally in the eighth and gave the Tigers a victory over the Indians, 6 to 5. George Uhle, who was beaten for the fifth time by the Tigers, took the loss. In the opening game of the series at St. Louis, the White Sox defeated the Browns, 5 to 1. It was Tommy Thomas's sixth victory over the Browns.

At Braves Field, the Giants and Braves split a doubleheader with Boston winning the first game, 6 to 1, and New York the second, 11 to 6. Bob Smith scattered six hits in the opener. Don Songer was the winning pitcher in the finale. The Robins and Phillies were postponed because of rain in Philadelphia.

The talk by the fans and players was about Lou Gehrig. Tied with Babe Ruth with twenty-five home runs, Gehrig was red hot with three home runs in the last three games and four in the last five. The game that afternoon on Friday, July 1, 1927 with the Red Sox saw Herb Pennock, a left-hander, oppose right-hander Danny MacFayden.

In the first inning, Combs hit a long drive over the running track in left center in Yankee Stadium and came all away around for a home run. After Ruth singled to right, Gehrig drove MacFayden's pitch into the right field bleachers. Meusel then tripled to right. Dugan's single scored Meusel. The Yankees led 4 to 0.

The Red Sox came back with three runs in the third making the score 4 to 3. In that inning, Pennock was hit by Rogell's liner. The ball caromed off the Pennock's stomach and rolled over to Dugan, who threw Rogell out. Pennock went down to the ground and both teams rushed to the mound to help him. It took him five minutes to recover and throw the ball to the plate.

The Yankees answered with two runs in the fourth. In the fifth, Shaner reached second when Meusel made an error on his fly ball. When MacFayden singled, Shaner scored. Tobin then hit safely sending MacFayden to third. Huggins then called Bob Shawkey, a right-hander, in from the bullpen in left field. Pennock departed. Shawkey kept the Red Sox from scoring further and the inning ended with the Yankees leading 6 to 4. The Yanks added a run in the seventh. Shawkey pitched well giving up only three hits the rest of the way.

Final score: Yankees 7, Red Sox 4

Yankee Notebook for Friday, July 1, 1927: The victory was the Yankees' sixth straight . . . Gehrig's home run was his twenty-sixth . . . For the first time since 1922, another player other than Ruth led the majors with home runs at that point in the season . . . Combs's home run was his second . . . Overall, the Yankees had twelve hits. Gehrig, Dugan, and Gehrig doubled . . . Ruth singled twice . . . Meusel tripled.

Pennock (9-3) went 4 1/3, giving up four runs and six hits. He walked none and struck out one . . . Shawkey was very effective, pitching 4 2/3, giving up three hits, walking one, and striking out two . . . Combs, Meusel, and Grabowski made errors . . . The loss was Boston's thirteenth in a row.

At Griffith Stadium in Washington, D.C., Bump Hadley limited the Athletics to three hits as the Senators won, 2 to 1. The win was the Senators eighth straight. The loss was Philadelphia's sixth in a row. In St. Louis, 500 fans, the smallest crowd of the year at Sportsman's Park, saw the Browns end their five game losing streak defeating the White Sox, 14 to 12. The Browns had eighteen hits and two home runs. At Dunn Field, the Tigers won for the tenth time in the last eleven games with a victory over the Indians, 10 to 5. Detroit scored six runs in the third to decide the game. Charlie Gehringer had four hits.

At Pittsburgh's Forbes Field, Carmen Hill scattered six hits as the Pirates defeated the Reds, 5 to 1. Hill's triple with two men on in the second gave the home team the lead. In Chicago, the Cubs hammered Flint Rhem and went on to beat the Cardinals, 6 to 2. Hal Carlson limited the Cardinals to five hits. With two runs in the ninth, the Phillies won over the Robins, 7 to 6, at Baker Bowl. Meanwhile at Braves Field, the Giants and Braves split a doubleheader with Boston winning the first game, 7 to 6, and New York taking the second, 4 to 1.

Looking to sweep the Red Sox in the final game of the series, Yankee skipper Miller Huggins sent left-hander Dutch Ruether to the mound on Saturday, July 2, 1927. Red Sox Manager Bill Carrigan went with young right-hander Jack Russell. Eighteen thousand fans were at Yankee Stadium to cheer the Yanks.

Morehart, the Yankees' second baseman, tripled in the first and was out at the plate on an attempted double steal. Russell held the Yanks from scoring over the first four innings. With the Red Sox leading 2 to 0, the Yankees came up in the fifth. Lazzeri doubled to deep left. He moved to third when Dugan rolled a hit between third and short.

Collins's out scored Lazzeri, and Dugan went to second. After Ruether fanned, Combs singled sending Dugan home, tying the score at two.

Ruth opened the sixth with a single to right but was forced at second by Gehrig. Meusel then slashed a double that hit the third base bag, raising a cloud of chalk dust. The ball went down the left field line and caromed off the stands. Tarbert, the left fielder, had some difficulty fielding the ball. Gehrig raced home with the go ahead run.

Rogell's line drive in the seventh knocked Ruether on his back, but he caught the ball and got up smiling. The Yankee left-hander was so tough that the Red Sox were able to get only six men to first base in the last six innings.

Final score: Yankees 3, Red Sox 2.

Yankee Notebook for Saturday, July 2, 1927: It was the Yankees' seventh straight victory and the sixteenth in the last nineteen . . . With that day's win, New York opened a nine and one-half game lead over the second place Senators . . . Ruether (8-1) pitched well, giving up two runs on seven hits, walking three, and striking out two. The left-hander had beaten Boston four times that season; two of them by shutouts . . . There were no home runs . . . Ruth and Gehrig only had a single between them . . . The Yankees left for Washington to play a single game the next day before returning to New York to play the Senators in a doubleheader on July 4th.

That day, the Senators won their ninth straight with a victory over the Athletics, 4 to 2, at Griffith Stadium. Bob Burke, who started his first game for Washington, allowed eight hits. Firpo Marberry relieved him in the ninth. In St. Louis, Bibb Falk's home run in the tenth inning gave the White Sox a victory over the Browns, 6 to 5. Aaron Ward's home run with two on in the sixth had tied the score. At Dunn Field, the Tigers swept the series over the Indians with a 6 to 1 win. Detroit scored three runs off Willis Hudlin in the fifth to decide the contest. The winning pitcher was Sam Gibson.

Coming from five runs behind in the seventh, the Pirates rallied in the ninth and beat the Reds, 7 to 6, at Forbes Field on Clyde Barnhart's home run with Pie Traynor on base. Heinie Groh, who had been recently obtained from the Giants, had two singles and scored a run. Mike Cvengros, who followed Lee Meadows and Johnny Morrison, was the winning pitcher.

In Chicago, the Cubs defeated the Cardinals, 7 to 4, and moved into second place. At Braves Field, the Giants and Braves played their third consecutive doubleheader as New York won the first game, 4 to 1, and Boston the second, 2 to 1. With 15,000 fans at Philadelphia, the Robins took both games of a doubleheader from the Phillies, 7 to 5 and 3 to 0.

Major League Baseball Standings
July 2, 1927
American League

	Won	Lost	P.C.
New York	51	20	.718
Washington	39	29	.574
Chicago	41	33	.554
Detroit	36	30	.545
Philadelphia	37	34	.521
Cleveland	31	40	.437
St. Louis	28	39	.418
Boston	15	53	.221

National League

	Won	Lost	P.C.
Pittsburgh	41	24	.631
Chicago	41	27	.603
St. Louis	39	27	.591
New York	35	35	.500
Brooklyn	33	36	.478
Boston	26	35	.426
Philadelphia	27	38	.415
Cincinnati	25	45	.357

Chapter 22

Waite Hoyt

In the summer of 1915, Miller Huggins was 36-years-old and the player-manager of the St. Louis Cardinals. He knew then that his career as an every day ballplayer was coming to an end, and he had already thought about turning second base over to a talented 20-year-old Texan named Rogers Hornsby. Without knowing it at the time, the professional baseball career of another very talented youngster was beginning that summer: a right-handed pitcher that Huggins would later manage and grow fond of. His name was Waite Hoyt.

In August 1915, Waite Hoyt was 15-years-old. As a star high school pitcher at Erasmus Hall in Brooklyn, he was five feet ten and one-half inches tall and weighed 165 pounds. Impressed with the boy's motion and control on the mound, John J. McGraw, the manager of the New York Giants drew up a contract with Waite's father—Addison Hoyt, an old-time vaudeville minstrel—for his club to have the services of the young right-hander when he was old enough.

When Addison Hoyt later signed the contract, his son Waite became the youngest ball player of that time ever placed under any form of contract by a big league club. Working out at the Polo Grounds in a Giants' uniform after school, the players soon nicknamed the good-looking youngster with pink cheeks, blond hair and brown eyes, "Schoolboy."

Waite Charles Hoyt was born September 9, 1899 in Brooklyn, New York to Louise and Addison Hoyt. Young Waite attended public schools in the Flatbush section of Brooklyn and started out as a third baseman, later shifting to second base.

One cold winter day, young Waite was skating in Prospect Park when an acquaintance came over and asked if he wanted to join his ball club, the Wyandottes. Interested in the new uniforms the players were to wear, Hoyt was eager to join. When he asked what position was open, Waite was told that the team was looking for a pitcher.

"Just your man, I can pitch," Hoyt replied.

Hoyt had never pitched before.

The Wyandottes entered the Brooklyn Eagle, the Brooklyn Times, and the Prospect Park Leagues. They played four or five games a week. Hoyt pitched most of the games, and the team won several local championships. Later Hoyt attended Erasmus Hall High School and pitched for the team. In the spring of 1915, he was only a second string pitcher but soon pitched sensationally and attracted the interest of people in professional baseball.

Waite's father Addison was offered and declined contracts for his son with New Haven of the Colonial League and Brooklyn of the Federal League; he did not have Waite accept a tryout with the St. Louis Browns. The Hoyt family felt Waite was too young to become a professional baseball player.

In July 1915, two former ballplayers with the Brooklyn Robins, Nap Rucker and Jack Coombs, invited Waite to daily workouts at Ebbets Field, which was close to the Hoyt home. Hoyt's family agreed. After weeks of working out, the Robins did not take an interest in the youngster. However, Charley Dooin, who scouted for the New York Giants, saw him and was interested.

During a series between the Robins and Giants in Brooklyn in August 1915, Dooin called McGraw's attention to Hoyt. The Giant's manager invited him to the Polo Grounds for a tryout. This was an opportunity the Hoyt family could not pass up. McGraw liked what he saw and signed the youngster. While under contract to the Giants, Hoyt won three games for Erasmus Hall in April 1916, including two no-hitters within four days.

Hoyt quit school shortly thereafter hoping to gain pitching experience in the minor leagues. From that moment on Hoyt moved in adult circles and baseball became his life. McGraw farmed Hoyt to

Mt. Carmel in the Pennsylvania State League, where he pitched in six games including an entire nineteen-inning affair, allowing nine hits and one walk.

When the league disbanded later in the season, he returned to New York. The Giants then loaned him to Hartford of the Eastern League in June 1916, but he was recalled after the club and the Giants became embroiled in a contract dispute. McGraw then sent him to Lynn of the Eastern League.

In February 1917, 16-year-old Hoyt went with the Giants to Marlin, Texas for Spring Training. Afterwards, McGraw sent him to Memphis of the Southern Association. While with that club in May 1917, O.B. Keeler, a reporter for *The New York American*, watched him pitch against Atlanta.

"He cuts loose his fast one—his best bet—with a sweeping overhand motion that permits him to get all his weight into the delivery, and the ball comes over with a wicked hop, from a downward slant," reported Keeler. "His change of pace is good; plentifully good enough. His curve is all it should be. His motion is easy and very, very swift with men on bases. And he plays ball as if he loves to play ball, which he does."

Later that season, Hoyt was sent to Montreal of the International League. In 1918, John McGraw assigned Hoyt to Nashville and in the summer of that year he was called up to the big club. Finally, on July 24, 1918, Waite Hoyt made his major league debut with the Giants at the age of eighteen. Pitching one inning against the St. Louis Cardinals, he gave up no hits and struck out two.

Hoyt never pitched for the Giants again.

After his debut that day, McGraw told Hoyt he was sending him to the minor leagues again. McGraw had bought Fred Toney from the Reds and to make room for him on the roster, Hoyt was sent to Newark of the International League. After a few games at Newark, McGraw informed Hoyt that he was moving again. The Giants had used three options on Hoyt and could not farm him out again, and he was traded to Rochester for Ross Youngs and George Kelly. Tired of the minors, Hoyt told McGraw that he would not report.

McGraw did not believe him.

When Hoyt did not show up at Rochester, his contract was sold to New Orleans. But Hoyt did not report to New Orleans either; instead, he joined the Baltimore Drydocks, an independent baseball team, which had a strong shipyard team during the war. On occasion, the Baltimore team played major league clubs on Sundays. Hoyt pitched very well for his new team. In one memorable game, he pitched against the Cincinnati Reds and won 1 to 0, allowing only four hits. Scouts began to watch him and several offers came.

Hoyt's catcher at the time was Norman McNeil, who belonged to the Boston Red Sox. While in Washington D.C. in the summer of 1919, McNeil told Red Sox manager Ed Barrow about Hoyt. Barrow told McNeill to bring him to the ballpark. Hoyt came and pitched batting practice. Barrow was impressed and bought Hoyt's contract from New Orleans.

A few days later, Barrow wired Hoyt and told him to meet him at the ballpark at 11:00 am. When Barrow arrived, he found Hoyt waiting for him. Hoyt had been there since 9:00 am. Barrow offered the young man a contract, but Hoyt had some demands. Tired of being assigned to the minors and playing for poor clubs, Hoyt wanted it written his contract that he would not be farmed out and that he would start regularly after that.

Barrow was taken aback by the 19-year-old, but he knew that Hoyt had walked out on McGraw and might do the same to him. Barrow gave him a standard contract to sign and his word that he wouldn't send him to the minors. Barrow told Hoyt he would get a chance to start. Hoyt took Barrow at his word and signed.

Waite Hoyt reported to the Boston Red Sox in July 1919. He remembered the day he was introduced to the players in the clubhouse by Ed Barrow.

"I had met Sad Sam Jones . . . Stuffy McInnis . . . Ossie Vitt . . . Harry Hooper . . . Mike McNally . . . and now we came to Ruth's locker. The big fellow had his back to us, pulling up the heavy socks we wore in those days. When he turned and looked up, I saw a wide, swarthy, rather homely face, expectant eyes and a wave of black, curly hair that dripped down over his forehead like a bottle of spilled ink."

'This is Waite Hoyt, our new pitcher,' said Barrow.

'A little young to be up here, aren't you?" the Babe cracked.

'I'm the same age you were when you got here, Babe,' I retorted, trying to be matter of fact about it all.

'Good luck, keed,' he said, with a trace of a smile as he turned back to getting dressed."

Barrow started Hoyt against Ty Cobb and the Detroit Tigers at Fenway Park. Hoyt was nervous and had a sleepless night but won that day 2 to 1 in extra innings. The game ended in a brawl between the umpires and Tiger players under the stands over a decision that gave the Red Sox the winning run.

Hoyt was ecstatic but had no money to call or wire his father in Brooklyn. Meanwhile, Addison Hoyt had to phone *The New York Journal* to learn that Waite had won. Waite Hoyt sat alone at Fenway that evening and took in the day's events. He realized that he had to go back out on the mound in four days and do it again.

In his next start, Hoyt defeated the Cleveland Indians, 6 to 4. In his third appearance he won again, this time against the St. Louis Browns. Overall in 1919, Hoyt made eleven starts for the Red Sox. He won 4 and lost 6, with 1 shutout and a 3.26 era.

The next year, Hoyt started 22 games for Boston. He shut out the Yankees and beat the Senators before an operation hospitalized him for thirteen weeks. That season he won 6 and lost 6, with 2 shutouts and posted a 4.39 era. The Red Sox finished in the second division in 1920.

While with the Red Sox, Hoyt learned his skills and gained valuable experience. He went on to develop an outstanding curve ball, excellent fast ball, and one of the best change of paces in the game.

Hoyt pitched a memorable game against the Yankees on September 24, 1919. The Yankees had scored against him in the first inning, but a home run by Babe Ruth tied it up in the ninth. Hoyt did not allow a Yankee player to reach first base from the second to the twelfth—eleven perfect innings—until Wally Pipp tripled and scored on Del Pratt's sacrifice fly in the thirteenth. Hoyt got little recognition because Ruth's home run that day off Hank Thormahlen was his twenty-eighth of the season and broke the major league record established by Buck Freeman. (Ruth hit one more that season for twenty-nine.)

During his time with the Red Sox, Hoyt developed a close friendship with Ruth. A year later, the Babe was traded to the Yankees. Hoyt was unhappy, both personally and professionally.

"The surest way to becoming a winning pitcher," said Hoyt "is to be on the same team with the Babe. Once he left the Red Sox I went around insulting Boston officials so they would trade me, preferably to the Yankees."

Hoyt's wish came true.

By 1920, Ed Barrow had left the Red Sox and became the business manager for the New York Yankees. He asked his old employer about Hoyt's availability. When told that he could be obtained, Barrow put a deal together. On December 15, 1920 the Yankees obtained Waite Hoyt, Wally Schang, Mike McNally, and Harry Harper for Del Pratt, Muddy Ruel, Sammy Vick, and Hank Thormahlen.

Waite Hoyt's first season with the Yankees in 1921 was a huge success. That year the Yankees won their first American League championship and Hoyt was a major contributor, winning 19 and losing 13, with a 3.10 era. He was also sensational in the World Series against the Giants.

In Game Two of the '21 World Series, Hoyt pitched a 3 to 0 shutout, allowing only two hits. In Game Five, Hoyt won 3 to 1, giving up six hits. In Game Eight, he lost 1 to 0 on an unearned run in the first when a grounder went through the legs of shortstop Roger Peckinpaugh. For the series, Hoyt pitched three complete games and did not allow an earned run in twenty-seven innings—a feat that tied Christy Mathewson's 1905 record.

In 1922, Hoyt won 19 games for the second season in a row. In the World Series he relieved in the first game and lost the third game. In his third year with the Yankees in 1923, Hoyt won 17 and started Game One of the Word Series. He won 18 in 1924 and 11 in 1925, when the club fell apart.

Hoyt's 16 victories in 1926 were instrumental in the Yankees rebounding and winning their fourth pennant. In the '26 World Series against the Cardinals, Hoyt struck out eight in winning the fourth game. In the memorable seventh game of that series, he gave up three unearned runs in the fourth and left for a pinch hitter in the bottom of the sixth with the Cardinals leading 3 to 2. Later, in the bottom of the seventh, the historic confrontation between Lazzeri and Alexander took place with the Cardinals going on to win the series.

Waite Hoyt was highly intelligent, articulate, and possessed a very good sense of humor. He was also good-looking, popular, and always took an interest in his appearance. On February 1, 1922, Hoyt married Dorothy Pyle. Having no occupation other than a ball player, he figured one day he might have to do something else for a living. Hoyt talked it over with his father-in-law who operated the Harry T. Pyle Mortuary at 1925 Church Avenue and decided to learn the undertaking business. He started working in the business in 1924 and did everything but embalming. Later the famed *New York Times* columnist John Kieran gave Hoyt the nickname "The Merry Mortician."

During those raucous years of the 20's, Huggins thought Hoyt was a model player; someone who followed the training rules, and he often pleaded with the other Rule breakers to act like him. Hoyt, however, did a good job of fooling his manager. He later admitted that he enjoyed the bright lights as much as Ruth and the others but acted alone. Hoyt could get back to the Yankee hotel by 6 a.m., take a quick shower, change clothes and be in the dining room wearing a tie and jacket at 7:30 a.m. to greet Huggins, looking as if he had slept for eight hours.

It was at that time that Hoyt coined the famous phrase, "It's great to be young and a Yankee."

Chapter 23

Record Crowd

Having won nine straight victories that moved them into second place, the Washington Senators hosted the New York Yankees in the nation's capital on Sunday, July 3, 1927. With 30,000 fans at Griffith Stadium, right-handers Urban Shocker and Horace Lisenbee opposed each other that afternoon.

The Line-Ups

Yankees	Senators
Earle Combs cf	Sam Rice rf
Ray Morehart 2b	Bucky Harris 2b
Babe Ruth rf	Tris Speaker cf
Lou Gehrig 1b	Goose Goslin lf
Bob Meusel lf	Joe Judge 1b
Tony Lazzeri ss	Muddy Ruel c
Joe Dugan 3b	Ossie Bluege 3b
John Grabowski c	Bobby Reeves ss
Urban Shocker p	Horace Lisenbee p

Ruth faced Lisenbee in the first and hit the longest home run ever to land in the center field bleachers at Griffith Stadium. In the bottom half of the inning, Goslin homered with a runner on and the Senators led 2 to 1. Both teams scored in the third and were tied at three. After Shocker twisted an ankle in the third, Myles Thomas, a right-hander, came in to pitch.

The Senators came to bat in the fifth. A double by Speaker, a walk to Goslin, a double by Judge, and Ruel's single gave the Senators a 6 to 3 lead. After Bluege singled, Huggins brought in left-hander Joe Giard, and he retired the Senators.

Morehart made an unbelievable play in the sixth. Racing to the other side of second and while still in the air after the catch, he made an accurate throw to first base, beating Reeves, a very fast runner. The Yankees scored a run in the seventh, and Lazzeri's homer into the left-field stands to open the eighth off southpaw Garland Braxton cut the Senators' lead to 6 to 5. After Grabowski left for a pinch-hitter in the top of the eighth, Bengough caught the bottom half of that inning.

With Gehrig on base with one out in the ninth, Firpo Marberry, a right-hander, relieved Braxton. Marberry retired Lazzeri and Meusel to end the game.

Final score: Senators 6, Yankees 5.

Yankee Notebook for Sunday, July 3, 1927: The loss ended the Yankees' seven-game winning streak . . . Ruth's home run was his twenty-sixth . . . The Babe and Gehrig were tied for the most home runs in the majors . . . Lazzeri's home run was his tenth . . . Gehrig had two hits, a double and triple . . . Combs also doubled . . . Meusel had a stolen base . . . After relieving Shocker, who went 2 1/3, Thomas (6-3) gave up three runs on five hits in two innings . . . Giard pitched scoreless ball over the final 2 1/3, giving up only three hits.

At Navin Field in Detroit, the Tigers' seven-game winning streak ended as the Indians edged the hometeam, 10 to 9. With help from Benn Karr, Garland Buckeye was the winning pitcher. Harry Heilmann homered for Detroit. In St. Louis, the White Sox scored eight runs in the seventh and beat the Browns, 14 to 7. Browns' left fielder Ken Williams hit two home runs. White Sox left fielder Bibb Falk also homered.

In Cincinnati, a double by Hughie Critz scored Ethan Allen with the deciding run as the Reds beat the Pirates, 5 to 4, at Redland Field. With the loss, Pittsburgh's lead was cut to one-half game over the Cubs. Joe Cronin, filling in for the injured Glenn Wright at short, made three errors in the sixth helping the Reds score three runs.

At Ebbets Field, the Robins won a doubleheader from the Phillies, 6 to 1 and 6 to 5 in eleven innings. At the Polo Grounds, Eddie Roush's timely hits in both games helped the Giants sweep a doubleheader from the Braves, 6 to 5 and 8 to 7.

On Monday, July 4, 1927 more than 74,000 fans, the largest crowd in baseball history, were at Yankee Stadium in New York to watch a holiday doubleheader between the Yankees and Washington Senators. With every seat in the grandstands and bleachers filled, people overflowed into the aisles and runways and were even on the rafters. After standing on line for an hour or more outside the Stadium, thousands were eventually turned away.

The Yanks started right-handers George Pipgras and Wilcy Moore. The Senators countered with right-handers Hollis Thurston and General Crowder.

First Game
The Line-Ups

Senators	Yankees
Sam Rice rf	Earle Combs cf
Stuffy Stewart 2b	Ray Morehart 2b
Tris Speaker cf	Babe Ruth rf
Goose Goslin lf	Lou Gehrig 1b
Joe Judge 1b	Bob Meusel lf
Muddy Ruel c	Tony Lazzeri ss
Ossie Bluege 3b	Joe Dugan 3b
Bobby Reeves ss	Pat Collins c
Hollis Thurston p	George Pipgras p

Already leading 1 to 0, Collins homered with a man on base in the second for New York. That lead was cut when the Senators scored one run off Pipgras in the third. However, the Yankees exploded for five runs in the fourth as follows: Lazzeri singled past Reeves. Dugan singled to left. Collins hit one past Bluege, scoring Lazzeri. When Thurston could not field Pipgras's bunt, the bases were loaded. Combs's sacrifice fly scored Dugan. A balk by Thurston sent Collins home. After a walk to Ruth and a base hit by Gehrig, Meusel doubled home two more runs. Walter Johnson, a right-hander, then replaced Thurston and retired the side. The Yankees led 8 to 1.

Pipgras pitched well as the game went on.

The Yankees came up in the eighth with Johnson on the mound and one out. Combs tripled; Morehart doubled, and Ruth singled. Then with two on, Gehrig hit a home run. Pipgras retired the Senators in the ninth.

Final score: Yankees 12, Senators 1 (First Game)

The Yankees continued their scoring barrage in the second game with four runs in the first, one in the second, and two in the fifth. Moore gave up one in the top half of the fifth, and New York went into the home half of the sixth leading 7 to 1.

It became worse for Washington.

Right-hander Firpo Marberry, who had replaced Crowder in the first, was on the mound. Marberry walked Ruth and Gehrig. Both scored on Meusel's triple. Lazzeri then doubled, scoring on Dugan's sacrifice bunt. With Grabowski on base, Moore sacrificed, and Combs doubled for one more run.

After Marberry walked Morehart, Bobby Burke, a left-hander, came in and walked Ruth. With the bases loaded, Gehrig hit another home run. When the inning ended, the Yankees led 16 to 1.Three more runs in the seventh, and two in the eighth completed the scoring for the Yanks.

Final score: Yankees 21, Senators 1 (Second Game)

Yankee Notebook for Monday, July 4, 1927: In the doubleheader, the Yankees scored thirty-three runs on thirty-three hits for a total of sixty-nine bases . . . Gehrig had four hits in the twin bill, a single, double, and two home runs—numbers twenty-seven and twenty-eight . . . At the end of the day, Gehrig led Ruth in home runs by two . . . The Babe had five hits in the doubleheader; four singles and a triple . . . Dugan had four hits in the first game, and Lazzeri had four in the finale . . . Collins, Wera, and Lazzeri also homered . . . Pipgras (2-0) gave up nine hits, walked three, and struck out three in the first game.

In the second contest, Moore (9-4) yielded ten hits, walking one, and striking out three . . . An X-ray revealed Urban Shocker had broken a small bone in his right ankle during Sunday's game at Washington. The injury happened while the pitcher was running from first to third. Shocker was expected to be out for at least two weeks.

At Fenway Park in Boston, Lefty Grove struck out ten and gave up only six hits in the first game of a doubleheader as the Athletics defeated the Red Sox, 10 to 3, but lost the second game, 11 to 3. Red Sox's Hal Wiltse scattered five hits in the finale. Boston's victory snapped a fifteen-game losing streak. Limiting the White Sox to a total of eight hits in morning and afternoon games at Dunn Field, the Indians won both, 2 to 0 and 6 to 2. At Sportsman's Park, the Browns and Tigers split a doubleheader. St. Louis won the first game, 8 to 4, and Detroit took the second, 10 to 8.

Sixty-thousand people came out to morning and afternoon games at Forbes Field as the Pirates took both games from the Cardinals, 7 to 2 and 6 to 4. Lee Meadows out pitched Grover Cleveland Alexander in the first game. Carmen Hill won the second contest. Playing morning and afternoon games at Wrigley Field, the Cubs took both from the Reds, 2 to 1, in ten innings, and 6 to 3. Watching the games were 12,000 fans in the morning and 29,000 in the afternoon.

With a crowd of 30,000 at Ebbets Field, the Giants swept the Robins in a doubleheader, 4 to 3 in eleven innings and 9 to 4. At Baker Bowl, the Braves took both games of a doubleheader from the Phillies, 5 to 4 and 8 to 2.

Before leaving on a road trip to the West, the Yankees and Washington Senators played the final game of the series in New York on Tuesday, July 5, 1927. Pitching that day was Yankees' right-hander Waite Hoyt, who was returning from a sore elbow suffered the previous week. Bump Hadley, a right-hander, pitched for the Senators.

Hoyt only pitched to two batters, Rice and Harris, who reached base on a single and error by Morehart, respectively. After Hoyt threw one ball to Speaker, Huggins removed him. Left-hander Joe Giard came in and was greeted with a double by Speaker and a home run by Goslin. The Senators led 5 to 0.

After the Senators tallied one in the third on Ruel's home run to left, the Yankees came back and scored two in the third and one in the fourth making the score 6 to 5. In the seventh, Gehrig tripled and scored on Meusel's sacrifice fly, tying the game at six. Right-hander Bob Shawkey, who relieved Giard in the second, pitched exceptionally well.

Shawkey retired the Senators in the ninth, and the Yankees came up in the last of that inning with the game tied at six. On the mound was right-hander Horace Lisenbee, who had relieved Garland Braxton in the sixth. Lisenbee retired Gehrig and Meusel on fly balls.

With two outs, Lazzeri came up to bat.

On a count of two balls and one strike, Lazzeri hit a drive to left field that landed in fair territory by a few feet for a home run.

Final score: Yankees 7, Senators 6.

Yankee Notebook for Tuesday, July 5, 1927: The Yankees had ten hits off Hadley, Braxton, and Lisenbee . . . Lazzeri had a single, double, and home run . . . Gehrig singled twice and tripled . . . Morehart had a base hit and a three-bagger . . . Shawkey (2-1) went 7 2/3 and gave up only four hits, walking three and striking out four . . . Hoyt faced two batters and Giard lasted only 1 1/3 . . . By the end of the day, Gehrig led the league with a .399 batting mark; Meusel was fourth at .373, and Ruth was fifth, batting .366.

With two outs in the ninth at Fenway Park in Boston, second baseman Bill Regan's double scored the winning run as the Red Sox defeated the Athletics, 6 to 5. The Red Sox had sixteen hits off Lefty Willis, Joe Pate, and Lefty Grove. Phil Todt's throw to first base in the seventh hit umpire Tommy Connolly and broke his nose.

At Sportsman's Park, the Browns pounded out twenty hits against the Tigers and won, 17 to 8. George Sisler had three hits and stole three bases including home. Milt Gaston, Bing Miller, Harry Rice, and Fred Schulte homered for St. Louis. Charlie Gehringer hit a home run with the bases loaded for Detroit.

Well-known lawyer Clarence Darrow offered his services and those of his staff to the Philadelphia Athletics in taking to the Supreme Court the test case that forbid Sunday baseball in Pennsylvania. The offer was made by telegram from the Association Opposed to Blue Laws.

In Pittsburgh, the Pirates held on to a one-half game lead with a 14 to 2 victory over the Cardinals at Forbes Field. Facing four St. Louis pitchers, the Pirates' scored twelve runs in the fourth and fifth innings. Vic Aldridge limited the Cardinals to five hits. Closing the home stand at Wrigley Field, the Cubs won their seventh in a row, 8 to 5, over the Reds. Driving Adolfo Luque from the mound in the eighth, the Cubs scored three runs to clinch the contest. In Philadelphia, rookie southpaw Lester Sweetland won his major league debut as the Phillies rallied for two runs in the ninth and defeated the Braves, 5 to 4.

Major League Baseball Standings
July 5, 1927
American League

	Won	Lost	P.C.
New York	54	21	.720
Washington	40	32	.556
Chicago	42	35	.545
Detroit	37	33	.529
Philadelphia	38	36	.514
Cleveland	34	40	.459
St. Louis	30	41	.423
Boston	17	54	.239

National League

	Won	Lost	P.C.
Pittsburgh	44	25	.638
Chicago	45	27	.625
St. Louis	39	31	.557
New York	39	35	.527
Brooklyn	35	38	.479
Boston	28	38	.424
Philadelphia	28	42	.400
Cincinnati	26	48	.351

ii

The Yankees were not scheduled on Wednesday, July 6, 1927. With the three game sweep of the Senators in New York, the club led the race in the American League by 12 1/2 games. Since May 29th, the team won thirty out of thirty-eight games and had winning streaks of nine and seven in a row.

The Yankees were scheduled to play an exhibition game with the Toronto Maple Leafs of the International League on Thursday and doubleheaders with the Tigers at Detroit on Friday and Saturday.

That afternoon Ty Cobb stole home in a triple steal in the first game of a doubleheader as the Athletics beat the Red Sox, 5 to 1, at Fenway Park. The Athletics also won the second game, 7 to 6. Al Simmons and Jimmy Dykes homered for Philadelphia in the opener. Fracturing his left wrist and a rib, Browns' centerfielder Fred Schulte was taken to the hospital after he ran into a concrete bleacher wall at Sportsman's Park as the Tigers beat the home team, 9 to 8. Schulte was scheduled to be out indefinitely. Jackie Tavener homered for the Tigers.

Clearing waivers, the Browns sent left-hander Tom Zachary to the Senators in exchange for Alvin (General) Crowder, a right-hander. Zachary was traded to the Browns from the Senators in 1925. Crowder came to the Senators from the Southern Association in 1926.

At Baker Bowl in Philadelphia, the Phillies moved into sixth place after defeating the Braves in a doubleheader, 6 to 4 and 5 to 3. Dutch Ulrich gave up only three hits after relieving Tony Kaufmann in the first inning of the first game. Jack Scott kept the Braves in check in the second contest.

At Ontario, Canada on Thursday, July 7, 1927, the Yankees were beaten in an exhibition game, 11 to 7, by the Toronto Maple Leafs of the International League. The Maple Leafs scored seven runs in the sixth off Don Miller, a former pitcher at Dartmouth. Miller had entered the game after Joe Styborski of Pennsylvania State went the first five. Mike Gazella homered in the seventh with Lou Gehrig on base.

At Sportsman's Park in St. Louis, the Tigers pounded Ernie Wingard and took the final game of the series from the Browns, 9 to 6. Ken Holloway, who relieved Rip Collins in the ninth, stopped a Browns' rally.

With rain falling in the ninth at Forbes Field, the game was called and the Cubs defeated the Pirates, 2 to 1. With the victory, Chicago took over first place from Pittsburgh by one-percentage point. Hal Carlson was the winning pitcher, and Joe Dawson took the loss. At Boston, in the opening game of the series, the Cardinals snapped a six-game losing streak by beating the Braves, 12 to 1. Bill Sherdel limited Boston to five hits.

In New York, Dazzy Vance and the Robins defeated the Giants in the series opener, 3 to 2, and at Baker Bowl in Philadelphia, the Reds took the opening game of the series by beating the Phillies, 11 to 4. Red Lucas had a shutout until the ninth when he allowed four runs.

With 25,000 fans at Navin Field in Detroit on Friday, July 8, 1927, the Yankees and Tigers played a doubleheader. Southpaw Dutch Ruether opposed right-hander Lil Stoner in the first game, and George Pipgras, a right-hander, faced left-hander Earl Whitehill in the finale.

First Game
The Line-Ups

Yankees	Tigers
Earle Combs cf	Jack Warner 3b
Ray Morehart 2b	Charlie Gehringer 2b
Babe Ruth lf	Heinie Manush cf
Lou Gehrig 1b	Bob Fothergill lf
Bob Meusel rf	Harry Heilmann rf
Tony Lazzeri ss	Johnny Neun 1b
Joe Dugan 3b	Jackie Tavener ss
John Grabowski c	Larry Woodall c
Dutch Ruether p	Lil Stoner p

With the score tied at three in the second, the Tigers pounded Ruether for three triples and knocked him out of the game. Right-hander Myles Thomas relieved him. After two innings the Tigers led 6 to 3. The Yankees pulled within one run of the Tigers in the third. Detroit, however, went on to score two in the fifth and two more in the sixth off Thomas, who was forced from the game in the seventh. Left-hander Joe Giard came in and pitched to one batter, retiring the side. After Giard left for a pinch-hitter, right-hander Bob Shawkey hurled the eighth. Despite tallying one run in the sixth and two in the seventh, the Yankees could not overtake the Tigers.

Final score: Tigers 11, Yankees 8 (First game)

In the second game, Ruth came up in the third with Combs and Morehart on and the Yankees leading 3 to 2. The Babe hit a long drive to deep center field for an inside-the-park home run making the score 6 to 2. When Pipgras lost control and began to walk batters in the third, Huggins called in right-hander Wilcy Moore. With two outs, Moore retired the side.

The Yankees scored two more in the fourth. The Tigers tallied two in the seventh. The Yanks added two more runs in the eighth and went ahead 10 to 4. When the Tigers scored three runs off Moore in the eighth with none out, Huggins brought in left-hander Herb Pennock, who retired the side. In the ninth, Detroit scored one run and posed a serious threat with two men on and one out, but Pennock got the final two outs.

Final score: Yankees 10, Tigers 8 (Second game)

Yankee Notebook for Friday, July 8, 1927: In losing the first game, Ruether (8-2) gave up five hits in 1 1/3, walking one and striking out none . . . Thomas went 5 1/3, Giard 1/3, and Shawkey 1 . . . The Yankees had fourteen hits . . . Combs, Gehrig, and Lazzeri had three hits apiece . . . Dugan doubled . . . Combs and Gehrig tripled . . . Lazzeri hit his thirteenth home run . . . Combs stole two bases . . . Dugan and Lazzeri made errors.

In the second game, Pipgras (3-0) went 2 1/3, Moore 4 1/3, and Pennock 2 . . . Ruth's home run was his twenty-seventh . . . Combs had two doubles . . . On the base paths, Ruth and Lazzeri each stole a base . . . The Yankees and Tigers were scheduled to play another doubleheader the next day.

Yielding to the pleas of American League owners, Ban Johnson, 61, resigned in New York as President. Johnson, who founded the American League, had thirty-four years of service in baseball, which went back to when he and Charles Comiskey took over the Western

League in 1893. The resignation was effective November 1, 1927. No successor was named.

At Dunn Field in Cleveland, the Senators won a doubleheader over the Indians by scores of 7 to 4 and 4 to 3. Washington's Goose Goslin and Nick Cullop homered in the first game. Cleveland's George Burns had his thirty-first and thirty-second doubles in the second. In St. Louis, Lefty Grove allowed eight hits and struck out seven at Sportsman's Park as the Athletics defeated the Browns, 7 to 5. Al Simmons tripled and homered. Ty Cobb scored two men with a double in the seventh. At Comiskey Park, the White Sox fell to fourth place after losing to the Red Sox, 11 to 5. Thirteen hits by Boston coupled with four Chicago errors gave the Red Sox the victory.

At Forbes Field in Pittsburgh, Charlie Root pitched a one hitter against the Pirates as the Cubs defeated Lee Meadows and won, 1 to 0. The victory was Root's fifteenth. Johnny Gooch, the Pirates' catcher, spoiled the no-hitter when he singled to left with two outs in the eighth. The win gave the Cubs a game and a half lead.

In Boston, Kent Greenfield pitched well as the Braves beat the Cardinals, 3 to 2. At Baker Bowl, Hughie Critz broke a five-all-tie by scoring two runs with a double as the Reds won their second straight from the Phillies, 8 to 5 in eleven innings. In New York, the Giants beat the Robins 6 to 2.

With fans crowding into the grandstands, climbing into temporary bleachers erected in the outfield and spilling onto the field, 30,000 crammed into Navin Field on Saturday, July 9, 1927. Eager to watch the Yankees and Tigers battle each other in a doubleheader, the turnout was the biggest ever at the Tigers' ballpark. Pitching for New York in the doubleheader were right-handers George Pipgras and Urban Shocker. Ken Holloway and Sam Gibson were on the mound for Detroit.

With one man on base in the first, Ruth hit a home run off Holloway into the centerfield bleachers. The Babe then doubled in the second frame, driving in another run. Coming up again in the fourth, Ruth hit his second home run that sailed into the centerfield bleachers. Right-hander Ownie Carroll then replaced Holloway and retired the side. The Yankees led 8 to 3.

When the Tigers erupted for four runs in the fifth making the score 8 to 7, Huggins brought in right-hander Wilcy Moore. Moore retired the Tigers. Home runs by Dugan and Meusel helped the Yankees score two runs in the sixth and three each in the seventh, eighth, and ninth.

Final score: Yankees 19, Tigers 7. (First game)

In the second game, Shocker lasted only 2 1/3 before being replaced by left-hander Joe Giard as the Tigers took a 6 to 0 lead after three. Three more runs in the fourth extended their lead to 9 to 0. With two Yankees on base in the fifth, Lazzeri hit a home run; however, the Tigers weren't finished. Detroit scored four in the fifth and one more in the sixth off Waite Hoyt. The day's scoring ended with the Yankees' final tally in the seventh. After Hoyt retired Detroit in the seventh, the game was called because of darkness.

Final score: Tigers 14, Yankees 4 (Second game)

Yankee Notebook for July 9, 1927: With home runs twenty-eight and twenty-nine, Ruth regained the home run lead from Gehrig . . . The Babe also had two doubles and a single for a total of 13 bases . . . The Yanks had 20 hits in the first game . . . Lazzeri had four singles . . . Dugan homered, doubled, singled twice, and drove in four runs . . . Meusel's home run was his fourth and Dugan's second . . . Pipgras (4-0) lasted only four innings and received credit for his second victory in two days . . . The Yankee right-hander gave up seven hits, walked four, and struck out none . . . Moore went five innings and surrendered only four hits . . . Combs and Meusel each stole a base.

In the second game, Shocker (9-5) gave up five hits, walked two, and struck out none in 2 1/3 . . . Giard went three innings and yielded ten hits . . . Hoyt pitched 1 2/3, giving up one hit . . . Gibson limited the Yankees to nine hits and struck out five . . . Lazzeri's home run was his fourteenth . . . Meusel and Ruth doubled . . . Gehrig (.398), Ruth (.372) and Meusel (.368) were first, third, and fifth in batting in the American League.

Taking both games of a doubleheader from the Indians at Dunn Field in Cleveland, the Senators won 6 to 5 in thirteen innings and 3 to 2. Dividing a doubleheader at Comiskey Park, the Red Sox won the opener, 2 to 1, as Charlie Ruffing scattered four hits. The White Sox took the finale 5 to 0 on Elmer Jacobs's seven hit shutout. In St. Louis, home runs by Milt Gaston and Harry Rice led the Browns to a 7 to 5 victory over the Athletics at Sportsman's Park. Al Simmons homered for Philadelphia.

Twenty thousand fans at Forbes Field saw Vic Aldridge blank the Cubs, 4 to 0, on two hits as the Pirates closed within one-half game, or two percentage points, of first place. Playing the Braves at Boston, the Cardinals took both games of a doubleheader, 6 to 3, and 4 to 2. With a crowd of 45,000 at the Polo Grounds, the Giants and Robins split a twin bill as Brooklyn won the first game 7 to 5 and New York the second, 1 to 0. In Philadelphia, Cy Williams's double in the eighth drove in three runs and gave the Phillies a 12 to 11 victory over the Reds.

On a bright and sunny day, a crowd of 30,000 overflowed Navin Field to see the Yankees' Babe Ruth and Lou Gehrig on Sunday, July 10, 1927. Left-hander Herb Pennock started for New York. Earl Whitehill, a left-hander, pitched for Detroit.

The Tigers took an early lead in the first as Gehringer singled, stole second base, and scored on Manush's base hit. The Yankees tied the score in the second as Gehrig was hit by a pitch, moved to third on successive outs, and scored on Dugan's single. In the third, Warner homered to left field off Pennock. The Tigers led, 2 to 1.

Gehrig doubled against the centerfield fence in the fourth. It could have been a home run, however, ground rules were in effect because of the crowd on the field. Gehrig was stranded and the Yanks did not score. The Tigers scored four more runs in the bottom of the fourth, highlighted by doubles by Heilmann and Whitehill. Shortstop Tavener stole second, third, and home on three successive pitches that inning.

As the game went on, Whitehill's curve balls baffled the Yankees. In the seventh, Grabowski walked and Julie Wera, batting for Pennock, was hit by a pitched ball. When Morehart doubled, Grabowski scored. The Yankees trailed 6 to 2. There was no further scoring until the ninth when Morehart singled, went to second on a balk, and scored on a wild pitch.

Final score: Tigers 6, Yankee 3.

Yankee Notebook for Sunday, July 10, 1927: Pennock (8-4) gave up nine hits, walked two, and struck out none . . . Pipgras and Thomas each pitched one inning and did not allow a hit . . . The Yankees managed ten hits off Whitehill, who struck out six . . . Ruth was hitless in five trips to the plate and hit only one ball out of the infield . . . Morehart had three hits and Dugan and Pennock two each . . . Combs and Dugan made errors . . . On his way to left field, Ruth was stopped several times by boys who ran out to him for autographs. The Babe signed their programs and baseballs.

In a rain-shortened game called after seven innings in Cleveland, the Senators overcame a seven-run lead by the Indians and won, 10 to 9, at Dunn Field. Sam Rice led Washington's attack with two singles, a double, and a triple. At Comiskey Park, Tommy Thomas won his thirteenth as the White Sox defeated the Red Sox, 4 to 1. In a wild game at Sportsman's Park, the Athletics collected twenty hits off three Browns' pitchers and won, 14 to 11. Philadelphia's Al Simmons stole home in the fifth, and Sammy Hale hit for the circuit in the ninth.

With 30,000 cheering fans at the Polo Grounds, the Giants' Virgil Barnes threw a one-hit shutout over the Cardinals, 5 to 0, in the opening game of the doubleheader as the visitors took the second game, 7 to 3. Bob O'Farrell had the only hit for the Cardinals in the opener. St. Louis' rookie shortstop Henry Schuble homered in the finale. In Brooklyn, the Cubs blanked the Robins, 1 to 0, as Guy Bush gave up only five hits. Ed Pick blasted a home run in the seventh over the right field wall.

The Yankees and Tigers finished their series at Navin Field in Detroit on Monday, July 11, 1927. Right-handers Waite Hoyt and Lil Stoner pitched. Miller Huggins was anxious to see how Hoyt would fare against Detroit. Hoyt was recovering from a sore elbow and faced only two batters in his last start.

Greeted by a single and a double, Hoyt gave up two runs in the first. The Yankees pulled within one run in the fifth after Collins hit a home run over the left field fence. With Detroit leading 2 to 1, Gehrig came up in the sixth and began a five-run rally with a double. The Tigers added a run in the bottom half of that inning. The Yankees led 6 to 3.

Stoner was on the mound in the seventh as the Yankees scored twice, highlighted by Gehrig's home run with no one on base that sailed into the bleachers between right and center field. The home run was Gehrig's twenty-ninth.

Hoyt, who allowed only one hit between the first and seventh, weakened and gave up two runs in the eighth. Huggins then decided to replace Hoyt with right-hander Bob Shawkey. With two outs, Shawkey retired the Tigers and pitched a scoreless ninth.

Final score: Yankees 8, Tigers 5.

Yankee Notebook for Monday, July 11, 1927: In the victory over Detroit, Gehrig had two hits—a double, and home run . . . . Collins hit his sixth home run . . . The Yanks had twelve hits off Stoner, Hawkins, and Holloway . . . Ruth went hitless in four trips to the plate . . . Meusel, Lazzeri, Collins, and Hoyt had two hits apiece . . . Hoyt drove in three . . . Lazzeri and Meusel each stole a base.

Hoyt (11-4) pitched 6 2/3 and gave up six hits, walked three, and struck out one. He also hit Manush . . . Shawkey went 2 1/3, yielding three hits with one strike out . . . Morehart had two errors at second base . . . The Yankees left for Cleveland, Ohio after the game.

At Dunn Field, Bucky Harris, the Senators' player-manger, stole home in the tenth inning with the winning run that beat the Indians, 3 to 2. With the victory Washington won six straight from Cleveland. In Chicago, Bill Barrett's daring base running with two outs in the ninth gave the White Sox a 7 to 6 win over the Red Sox. At Sportsman's Park, Ty Cobb's three hits, including a home run with a man on, helped the Athletics defeat the Browns, 7 to 6.

At Baker Bowl, the Cardinals gained one-half game over the idle Pirates and Cubs by taking the opening game of the series against the Phillies, 7 to 0. Grover Cleveland Alexander scattered seven hits. Wet grounds postponed the game between the Cubs and Braves at Boston.

Major League Baseball Standings
July 11, 1927
American League

	Won	Lost	P.C.
New York	57	24	.704
Washington	46	32	.590
Chicago	45	37	.549
Detroit	42	36	.538
Philadelphia	43	37	.538
Cleveland	34	46	.425
St. Louis	31	46	.403
Boston	19	59	.244

National League

	Won	Lost	P.C.
Chicago	48	28	.632
Pittsburgh	45	27	.625
St. Louis	44	33	.571
New York	42	38	.525
Brooklyn	37	41	.474
Philadelphia	31	45	.408
Boston	29	43	.403
Cincinnati	28	49	.364

Chapter 24

Ruth and Gehrig Hit 30th

It was a hot sultry summer day in Cleveland, Ohio on Tuesday, July 12, 1927. That day the Yankees visited Dunn Field for the second series of the season. Last there on May 18 through 22, the Indians and Yankees split four games. Right-hander Urban Shocker faced Joe Shaute, a left-hander.

The Line-Ups

Yankees	Indians
Earle Combs cf	Charlie Jamieson lf
Ray Morehart 2b	Freddy Spurgeon 2b
Babe Ruth rf	Homer Summa rf
Lou Gehrig 1b	George Burns 1b
Bob Meusel lf	Joe Sewell ss
Tony Lazzeri ss	Luke Sewell c
Joe Dugan 3b	Ike Eichrodt cf
John Grabowski c	Johnny Hodapp 3b
Urban Shocker p	Joe Shaute p

The Yankees took an early 3 to 0 lead in the third after Combs tripled, Morehart doubled, Ruth walked, and Gehrig and Meusel doubled. Over the next three innings Shocker and Shaute pitched well.

The game went into the seventh. The Yanks went ahead 4 to 0 when Grabowski singled, moved to second on Shocker's sacrifice, and scored on a base hit by Morehart. Shocker, meanwhile, was pitching an excellent game.

Still leading 4 to 0, the Yanks came to bat in the ninth. Grabowski reached base on an error by Hodapp, the third baseman, and advanced to second on Shocker's third sacrifice. Morehart's third hit of the game sent Grabowski home with the Yankees' fifth run. Ruth then came to the plate and hit a home run off Shaute that sailed over the right field fence.

Shocker retired the Indians in the bottom of the ninth. After the last batter of the game hit a slow grounder, Shocker fielded the ball and twisted his ankle. He had to be carried off the field.

Final score: Yankees 7, Indians 0.

Yankee Notebook for Tuesday, July 12, 1927: Ruth's home run was his thirtieth and gave him one more than Gehrig . . . The Yankees had fourteen hits: Combs, Gehrig, Dugan, and Grabowski each had two . . . Gehrig singled and doubled . . . Morehart doubled twice and singled . . . Meusel had a two-base hit and a triple.

Shocker (10-5) scattered seven hits in a complete game shutout, striking out one and walking one. He also hit a batter—Burns . . . Only two Indians reached third base; one was thrown out at the plate and the other was stranded when the game ended . . . Shocker was helped by good fielding from Ruth, Gehrig, and Lazzeri.

In Detroit, the Senators won their seventh in a row by defeating the Tigers, 9 to 6, at Navin Field in the opening game of the series. Sam Rice's double in the eighth clinched the game. Scoring eight runs in the sixth and seventh at Comiskey Park, the White Sox went on to beat the Athletics, 8 to 5. Winning pitcher Sarge Connally had four hits in four at bats. At Sportsman's Park, George Sisler's home run in the ninth with two men on gave the Browns a 6 to 5 win over the Red Sox. Scoreless until the ninth, Boston rallied for five runs at the top of that inning before falling short in their effort to tie the game.

In oppressive heat at Braves Field, the Cubs took the opening game of the series from the Braves, 6 to 2. Chicago's Sheriff Blake scattered only three hits. At Ebbets Field, the Pirates beat Brooklyn, 2 to 1. Pittsburgh's Carmen Hill allowed six hits, and Brooklyn's Dazzy Vance struck out eleven.

At Philadelphia, the Cardinals won their third in a row with a victory over the Phillies, 9 to 6. Left fielder Cy Williams hit his sixteenth home run in the ninth for the home team. At the Polo Grounds, Rogers Hornsby hit his sixteenth home run with Freddie Lindstrom on base as the Giants defeated the Reds, 3 to 2.

With baseball fans across the country following closely the home run race between Babe Ruth and Lou Gehrig, the Yankees and Indians played again at Dunn Field on Wednesday, July 13, 1927. Left-hander Dutch Ruether opposed right-hander Willis Hudlin.

Trailing 3 to 2, the Yankees came up to bat in the eighth against Hudlin. With Morehart on base, the Babe hit a long drive that hit the fence in right center for a double. As Morehart scored the tying run, Ruth ended up at third when Eichrodt's throw was wild. With one out and Ruth on third, Gehrig walked. When Meusel grounded to short, Ruth broke for the plate. Shortstop Joe Sewell threw to his brother Luke, the Indians' catcher. Ruth was out at home.

With Gehrig and Meusel on the bases, Lazzeri smacked a triple down the right field line. Both runners scored and the Yanks led by two. Ruether retired the Indians without a hit in the eighth and ninth.

Final score: Yankees 5, Indians 3.

Yankee Notebook for Wednesday, July 13, 1927: The Yankees had nine hits off Hudlin . . . Ruth went four-for-four with a double and three singles . . . Gehrig went hitless in three plate appearances, but ended the day second in the league in batting with a mark of .393; Al Simmons of the Athletics' topped the league at .401 . . . Meusel doubled and Lazzeri tripled . . . Ruether (9-2) gave up eight hits, walking none, and striking out none . . . Spurgeon homered and doubled for the Indians . . . After the game, Ruether went to New York where his wife had undergone an operation.

At Navin Field, the Tigers took both games of a doubleheader from the Senators, 7 to 3 and 13 to 9. Detroit's Johnny Neun stole home in each game. Teammate Harry Heilmann had five hits in five at bats in the second game and a total of seven hits in the doubleheader. After having four hits the day before, George Sisler had four more against the Red Sox as the Browns won, 14 to 3.

On Eddie Collins Day at Comiskey Park, the Athletics defeated Ted Lyons and the White Sox, 7 to 5. Collins, the former manager of the White Sox, was presented with an automobile. The game was delayed a half-hour by rain.

After losing the first game of a doubleheader to the Braves at Braves Field, 6 to 3, the Cubs took the second, 4 to 1, as Charlie Root won his sixteenth. The victory, coupled with Pittsburgh's loss, kept Chicago in first place by eleven percentage points. In a sweltering heat at Ebbets Field, a crowd of 6,000 watched the Robins tie the Pirates in the ninth and win, 2 to 1 in the eleventh. With a 9 to 7 victory over the Phillies at Baker Bowl, the Cardinals ended the day two and one-half games behind the Pirates.

Under cloudy skies and the temperature around 90-degrees in Cleveland, the Yankees and Indians met again on Thursday, July 14, 1927. The Indians came into the game with eight straight losses. That afternoon Wilcy Moore, a right-hander, faced left-hander Walter Miller.

Errors by Lazzeri and Morehart in the first inning gave the Indians two runs. The Indians went ahead 4 to 0 in the third after Surgeon beat out a bunt, Summa sacrificed, Burns doubled, and Joe Sewell singled.

In the fourth, Meusel singled and scored after Koenig, who had replaced Lazzeri at short after he hurt his shoulder, doubled. With the Indians leading 4 to 1, Moore was lifted for a pinch-hitter in the seventh. Right-hander George Pipgras hurled the last two innings. Miller pitched well for the Indians holding the Yankees scoreless for the remainder of the game.

Final score: Indians 4, Yankees 1.

Yankee Notebook for July 14, 1927: Cleveland's Miller gave up ten hits . . . Ruth and Gehrig went hitless . . . Meusel had two singles and a triple; Combs smacked three singles; and Koenig doubled and singled . . . Gehrig struck out with the bases loaded in the third . . . Moore (9-5) went six innings, giving up eight hits, walking none, and striking out none . . . Pipgras went two and gave up no hits. He walked none and struck out two . . . In the field, the Yankees made five errors—Morehart (2), Meusel, Lazzeri, and Koenig.

At Sportsman's Park in St. Louis, the Browns took the third straight game of the series from the Red Sox, 4 to 2. Browns' pitcher Lefty

Stewart singled home the winning run in the seventh. With the Tigers leading the Senators 2 to 0 in the third at Detroit, rain caused a postponement of the game. Rain also canceled the game between the Athletics and White Sox at Chicago.

With Commissioner Landis on hand at Braves Field, Bob Osborn held the Braves to seven hits as the Cubs won their third straight game over the Braves, 6 to 1. In Brooklyn, Kiki Cuyler's hit in the ninth gave the Pirates a 6 to 5 win over the Robins . . . At the Polo Grounds, the Reds and Giants played a twin bill as Cincinnati won both games, 8 to 6 and 8 to 3. Wally Pipp's home run in the ninth won the first game. In Philadelphia, the Cardinals' four game winning streak ended as the Phillies pounded Flint Rhem and won, 7 to 3.

As temperatures reached into the mid-90s at Dunn Field in Cleveland, the Yankees and Indians played the fourth and final game of the series on Friday, July 15, 1927. The opposing pitchers on that hot and oppressive day were right-handers Waite Hoyt and George Uhle.

The Indians led 9 to 3 when the Yankees came to bat in the eighth. Uhle was on the mound. After Morehart and Ruth walked, Gehrig singled home one run. When Meusel doubled, Ruth and Gehrig scored. The Yankees trailed 9 to 6. At that point, Indians' manager Jack McCallister brought southpaw Garland Buckeye in with none out. Buckeye retired the side.

Batting for Thomas in the ninth, Ben Paschal doubled off Buckeye. After Combs grounded out, Lazzeri singled to center, scoring Paschal. Ruth walked. Lazzeri stole third and scored on Gehrig's sacrifice fly to left. With the score 9 to 8 and two outs, Meusel doubled, scoring Ruth. The game was tied.

Right-hander Willis Hudlin replaced Buckeye. When Koenig singled, Meusel came home and the Yanks went ahead 10 to 9. Right-hander Bob Shawkey pitched the ninth, holding the Indians scoreless.

Final score: Yankees 10, Indians 9.

Yankee Notebook for Friday, July 15, 1927: In the come-from-behind victory, the Yankees had fifteen hits, including six doubles—Meusel (2), Collins, Combs, Morehart, and Paschal . . . Meusel and Koenig had three hits each . . . Ruth had one hit and scored two runs . . . Gehrig singled twice and scored one run . . . Ruth and Dugan had errors in the field.

Hoyt lasted 4 1/3 innings, giving up eight hits, walking none, and striking out none . . . Pipgras, Thomas, and Shawkey followed Hoyt . . . Thomas (7-3) was credited with the win. He went two innings and gave up two hits and walked one . . . The Yankees were scheduled to return to Cleveland from August 20 through 22 for their final visit of the season.

By scores of 3 to 1 and 13 to 10, the Athletics swept a doubleheader from the White Sox at Comiskey Park. Philadelphia's Al Simmons led the American League in batting at .400. Sweeping the four game series at St. Louis, the Browns defeated the Red Sox, 3 to 2, for the tenth straight time. Rain postponed the two games scheduled between the Senators and Tigers at Detroit.

Before traveling to New York to play the Giants, the Cubs won their fourth out of five games played with the Braves at Boston with a victory, 9 to 5. Meanwhile, with 5,000 fans sitting in a sweltering heat at Ebbets Field, the Pirates won that final meeting of the series with the Robins, 5 to 2. Pirate teammates Paul Waner, Joe Harris, and Clyde Barnhart led the league in batting at .391, .375 and .364, respectively.

Trailing by seven runs, the Cardinals rallied for eight runs over the final four innings against the Phillies and won, 9 to 7, at Baker Bowl. At the Polo Grounds, Burleigh Grimes scattered four hits as the Giants defeated the Reds, 4 to 1.

Major League Baseball Standings
July 15, 1927
American League

	Won	Lost	P.C.
New York	60	25	.706
Washington	47	34	.580
Philadelphia	46	38	.548
Detroit	44	37	.543
Chicago	46	40	.535

St. Louis	35	46	.432
Cleveland	35	49	.417
Boston	19	63	.232

National League

	Won	Lost	P.C.
Chicago	52	29	.642
Pittsburgh	48	28	.632
St. Louis	47	34	.580
New York	44	41	.518
Brooklyn	38	44	.463
Philadelphia	32	48	.400
Boston	30	47	.390
Cincinnati	31	51	.378

ii

On a hot and sweltering afternoon, 10,000 fans, the largest crowd of the season at Sportsman's Park, came out to see Babe Ruth and Lou Gehrig on Saturday, July 16, 1927. Losers of seven in a row to the Yankees, St. Louis sent right-hander Sad Sam Jones to the mound. Left-hander Herb Pennock pitched for New York.

The Line-Ups

Yankees	Browns
Earle Combs cf	Frank O'Rourke 2b
Ray Morehart 2b	Herschel Bennett rf
Babe Ruth lf	George Sisler 1b
Lou Gehrig 1b	Bing Miller lf
Bob Meusel rf	Harry Rice cf
Mark Koenig ss	Spencer Adams 3b
Joe Dugan 3b	Steve O'Neill c
John Grabowski c	Wally Gerber ss
Herb Pennock p	Sam Jones p

The Yankees took an early lead. After Gehrig singled and stole second to start the second, Koenig singled. Both runners scored when Dugan's ball went past Rice in center for an error. In the third, the Yankees went ahead 3 to 0 when Combs doubled and Morehart walked. When Combs was doubled up on Ruth's fly to Rice, Morehart took second and scored on a base hit by Gehrig. The Browns scored two in the fifth.

Going to the top of the seventh, the Yankees led 3 to 2. With one out, Combs and Morehart singled. Ruth walked. With the bases loaded, Gehrig doubled to right, sending Combs and Morehart home. Pennock set down the Browns in the final three frames.

Final score: Yankees 5, Browns 2.

Yankee Notebook for Saturday, July 16, 1927: Pennock (9-4) pitched a complete game and gave up only six hits . . . The Yankees had eleven hits off Jones . . . Gehrig and Morehart had three hits each and Combs and Dugan two . . . Gehrig's three hits drove in three runs. He also scored one . . . Ruth went hitless in three plate appearances, hitting into two double plays in his first two times at bat . . . The victory was the Yankees' eighth straight over the Browns.

In the opening game of the series at Comiskey Park, the White Sox defeated the Senators, 7 to 5. After Chicago's Ted Blankenship was knocked out of the game, Sarge Connally came in and kept the Senators from further scoring. The Senators announced they would celebrate Walter Johnson's twenty years in major league baseball on August 2.

At Navin Field, the Athletics took an early lead in the first inning against the Tigers and went on to win 9 to 3. In Cleveland, the Red Sox swept a doubleheader from the Indians, 6 to 3 in twelve innings and 5 to 4. Ten double plays were made in the twin bill.

At Baker Bowl, the Phillies took both games of a doubleheader from the Pirates, 11 to 10 and 11 to 9. Cy Williams hit a home run in each game, numbers seventeen and eighteen. With 16,000 fans at Ebbets Field, Jesse Petty outpitched Grover Cleveland Alexander as the Robins won the first game of a doubleheader from the Cardinals, 3 to 0, but lost the second, 9 to 2.

In New York, the Giants won a pair from the Cubs, 6 to 5 and 4 to 2, with 30,000 fans on hand. Travis Jackson won the first game in the eighth with a bases loaded home run. In Boston, the Reds moved out of last place with a victory over the Braves, 3 to 2. Rain caused the cancellation of the second game in the third inning.

Under sunny skies at Sportsman's Park in St. Louis, Missouri, 18,000 fans came out to the ball park on Sunday, July 17, 1927. In that afternoon's contest, two right-handers faced each other—Urban Shocker for New York and Milt Gaston for St. Louis.

The Browns led 4 to 3 in the Yankees' half of the eighth inning when Gehrig hit a ball into the centerfield bleachers for a home run. With the score tied at four, Meusel then homered into the left field seats sending the Yankees ahead. After Shocker gave up two home runs in the seventh, Wilcy Moore relieved. Moore pitched a scoreless eighth and ninth.

Final score: Yankees 5, Browns 4.

Yankee Notebook for Sunday, July 17, 1927: Gehrig's thirtieth home run tied Ruth again for the home run lead . . . With that day's blast, Gehrig had hit one in every American League Park . . . Meusel's home run was his fifth . . . Gaston, who went the distance, surrendered seven hits; Combs and Meusel had two hits each . . . Ruth singled in two official plate appearances.

Shocker left the game trailing by a score of 4 to 3 after 6 1/3. He yielded seven hits, struck out seven, and walked five . . . Moore (10-5) came on in relief and went 2 2/3, giving up two hits, striking out four, and walking one . . . Gehrig and Meusel made errors . . . The Browns left ten men on the bases. O'Neill, the St. Louis catcher, threw out three Yankee runners.

At Comiskey Park in Chicago, Tris Speaker's two doubles led a seventeen hit attack as the Senators defeated the White Sox, 7 to 4. Walter Johnson went the distance. In Detroit, Philadelphia's Jimmy Dykes fumbled Bernie DeViveiro's surprise bunt in the ninth and Marty McManus scored the winning run as the Tigers took the second game of the series from the Athletics, 5 to 4. Rain postponed the game between the Red Sox and Indians at Cleveland.

Scoring three runs in the ninth off Dazzy Vance at Ebbets Field, the Cardinals came from behind on Johnny Schulte's triple and defeated the Robins, 5 to 3. The game was delayed because of a heavy shower at the start of the game. Wet grounds postponed the game between the Cubs and Giants at New York.

It was Ladies' Day at Sportsman's Park in St. Louis on Monday, July 18, 1927. On a sunny and hot afternoon, 1,996 women and 900 members of the Citizens' Military Training Camps were admitted free. With 7,556 paid customers, the total attendance to see the third game of the series between the St. Louis Browns and the Yankees was 18,452.

Yankee right-hander George Pipgras opposed the Browns' Ernie Wingard, a left-hander. With the score tied at 1 to 1 in the seventh, the Yankees erupted for six runs on five hits, two errors, a double steal, and a walk. Wingard was knocked out of the game, and right-hander Ernie Nevers came in.

Leading 7 to 1, the Yankees added three more runs in the eighth, which included a home run by Gehrig into the left field bleachers. The Browns rallied for five runs in the ninth, highlighted by George Sisler's bases loaded home run over the right field pavilion—but St. Louis fell short.

Final score: Yankees 10, Browns 6.

Gehrig's thirty-first home run gave him one more than the Babe; however, Ruth was still the idol of the young fans. After the game, youngsters mobbed Ruth at the exit gate at Sportsman's Park, asking him to sign baseballs, scorecards, autograph books, and pieces of paper. Meanwhile, Gehrig walked out of the gate and up the street alone.

No one approached him for an autograph.

Yankee Notebook for Monday, July 18, 1927: That afternoon the Yankees had twelve hits . . . Combs had two doubles and Meusel one . . . Gehrig sacrificed twice and Grabowski once . . . Pipgras (5-0) went the distance. He pitched well before giving up five runs in the ninth. The Yankee right-hander yielded a total of twelve hits, walking three, and striking out three. He also balked . . . In the field, Meusel and Koenig each stole a base . . . The loss was the Browns' tenth straight to the Yankees.

In Chicago, Bump Hadley limited the White Sox to six hits as the Senators won, 5 to 1, at Comiskey Park. With a four-for-four day, including a home run, Bob Fothergill led the Tigers to victory over the Athletics, 5 to 3 at Navin Field. Sam Gibson beat Lefty Grove. In the first inning, Ty Cobb doubled for his 4,000th hit.

At Dunn Field, the Red Sox and Indians split a doubleheader as Boston won the first game, 14 to 5 and Cleveland the second, 4 to 0. Indian first baseman George Burns hit his thirty-eighth and thirty-ninth doubles—one more than his record mark in 1926.

At Baker Bowl, the Pirates went into first place by one point after taking both games of a twin bill from the Phillies, 9 to 7 and 6 to 5. Three runs off Tony Kaufmann in the fifth of the opener broke a 5-to-5 deadlock. In the finale, Carmen Hill, who relieved Lee Meadows in the ninth when the Phillies drew within one, retired Cy Williams and Freddy Leach to end the game.

In New York, the Cubs and Giants split a doubleheader as Chicago won the first game, 6 to 4 in ten innings and New York the second, 3 to 2. At Braves Field, Hughie Critz's three hits, including a home run, led the Reds to a 3 to 2 victory in ten innings over the Braves. Rain postponed the game between the Cardinals and Robins at Brooklyn.

Tuesday, July 19, 1927 was another very hot and humid afternoon in St. Louis, Missouri, where the Browns and Yankees played the finale of their four-game series. Two left-handers opposed each other: Dutch Ruether for New York and Walter Stewart for St. Louis.

The Yankees jumped off to a quick lead in the second when Meusel's grounder to Gerber at short was misplayed and Koenig singled. With two outs, Ruether singled Meusel home. When Miller let the ball get by him in left, Koenig scored. Lazzeri opened the third with a triple and scored on Ruth's base hit. Just missing a home run by inches, Gehrig tripled off the sign in left. The Babe scored. When Meusel doubled, Gehrig scored. Win Ballou, a left-hander, replaced Stewart.

Another run in the sixth gave the Yankees a 6 to 0 lead. After Ruether gave up one run and showed signs of weariness in the seventh, Huggins brought in right-hander Wilcy Moore. With one out and O'Neill and Gerber on the bases, Moore walked Ken Williams, who batted for the pitcher Ballou. With the bases loaded, Moore then retired the side by striking out O'Rourke and taking Gehrig's toss of Bennett's grounder. General Crowder pitched the eighth for St. Louis. Moore retired the Browns in the eighth and ninth.

Final score: Yankees 6, Browns 1.

Yankee Notebook for Tuesday, July 19, 1927: Ruether (10-2) went six and one-third innings, giving up seven hits. The southpaw did not walk or strike out a batter . . . Moore pitched two and two-third innings. He did not yield a hit, walking one, and striking out two . . . The Yankees reached Stewart and Ballou for ten hits . . . Crowder did not give up a hit . . . Meusel doubled and Lazzeri and Gehrig tripled . . . Wera substituted for Dugan at third again but went hitless in four at bats . . . The game was played in 1:53 . . . The victory was the Yankees' eleventh straight over the Browns.

Knocking Elmer Jacobs out of the game in the sixth after scoring two runs, the Senators went on to beat the White Sox, 4 to 3, at Comiskey Park in Chicago. Firpo Marberry, who relieved Hollis Thurston, did not give up a hit over the final four and two-third innings. Scoring seven-runs in a spectacular ninth inning rally at Navin Field, the Tigers defeated the Athletics, 10 to 9. At Dunn Field, the Red Sox and Indians split a twin bill with Cleveland winning the first game, 4 to 2, and Boston the finale, 6 to 5.

At the Polo Grounds, a crowd of 25,000 cheered John J. McGraw as he was honored on his silver jubilee as manager of the Giants. Honoring him that afternoon was Commissioner Landis, President John A. Heydler of the National League, Mayor Jimmy Walker, Colonel Jacob Ruppert, Commander Richard E. Byrd, and Charles A. Stoneham. The Giants later lost to the Cubs, 8 to 5.

Winning for the third time in a row at Braves Field, the Reds defeated the Braves, 8 to 2. Eppa Rixey held the home team to six hits. Rain postponed the Cardinals and Robins at Brooklyn and Pirates and Phillies at Philadelphia.

Before going to Chicago to open a series with the Chicago White Sox, the Yankees stopped at St. Paul, Minnesota for an exhibition game with the St. Paul Club of the American Association on Wednesday, July 20, 1927. On the way to St. Paul, the train went through towns named Hannibal, Keokuk, and Burlington. At every stop, crowds came out to the train station to see Babe Ruth. The Babe would always step on the platform and say a few words.

At St. Paul, 15,000 fans cheered as the Yankees won, 9 to 8. Ruth hit three doubles into the crowd which surrounded the field. Gehrig hit a double up against the left field fence. Thrilling the fans at the ball park, Ruth pitched the ninth inning.

Bunching hits in the second and sixth at Comiskey Park in Chicago, the Senators took the final game of the series, 5 to 3. Tom Zachary weakened in the eighth and Garland Braxton came in. Washington won four out of five games in that series.

In New York, Mel Ott's ninth inning home run with one man on gave the Giants a come-from-behind victory over the Cubs at the Polo Grounds, 5 to 4. Travis Jackson homered twice for the Giants. At Baker Bowl, the Pirates split a doubleheader with the Phillies as Philadelphia won the first game, 4 to 3, and Pittsburgh the second contest, 6 to 5. The victory, coupled with the Cubs' loss, moved the Pirates back into first place. Pirates' center fielder Lloyd Waner had five straight hits in the finale.

A mid-week crowd of 13,000 at Ebbets Field saw the Robins and Cardinals split a twin bill as Brooklyn's ace Jesse Petty outpitched Flint Rhem in the opener, 2 to 1, and St. Louis took the second, 3 to 1. After losing the first game of a doubleheader to the Reds, 4 to 2, Joe Genewich of the Braves held the visitors to four hits as Boston defeated Cincinnati, 2 to 1, at Braves Field.

Major League Baseball Standings
July 20, 1927
American League

	Won	Lost	P.C.
New York	64	25	.719
Washington	51	35	.593
Detroit	47	38	.553
Philadelphia	47	41	.534
Chicago	47	44	.516
St. Louis	35	50	.412
Cleveland	37	53	.411
Boston	23	65	.261

National League

	Won	Lost	P.C.
Pittsburgh	51	31	.622
Chicago	54	33	.621
St. Louis	50	36	.571
New York	48	43	.527
Brooklyn	40	47	.460
Philadelphia	35	51	.407
Cincinnati	35	52	.402
Boston	31	51	.378

Chapter 25

Home Run Battle

On a warm afternoon under cloudy skies, a crowd of 18,000 watched the Chicago White Sox and New York Yankees open a four game series at Comiskey Park on Thursday, July 21, 1927. Right-handers Waite Hoyt and Sarge Connally faced each other.

The talk in Chicago and around baseball was the home run battle between Babe Ruth and Lou Gehrig. With thirty-one home runs—one more than Ruth—fans were asking if Gehrig would become the new home run champion and wondered if he could break Ruth's magic mark of 59 home runs in one season.

The Line-Ups

Yankees	White Sox
Earle Combs cf	Willie Kamm 3b
Mark Koenig ss	Bill Hunnefield ss
Babe Ruth lf	Alex Metzler cf
Lou Gehrig 1b	Bill Barrett rf
Bob Meusel rf	Bibb Falk lf
Tony Lazzeri 2b	Bud Clancy 1b
Julie Wera 3b	Harry McCurdy c
John Grabowski c	Moe Berg 2b
Waite Hoyt P	Sarge Connally P

Connally and Hoyt pitched well in the early and middle innings. The only run came in the fourth on a hurried throw by Lazzeri to catch Clancy on a tapper to short. As the game went into the late innings,

Connally held the Yankees to one hit, a ball popped into left for a double by Gehrig, who was trying to duck out of the way of a fast ball.

Going to the Yankees' eighth, the White Sox still led 1 to 0. Lazzeri tripled to deep right center field. Ben Paschal, pinch-hitting for Wera, then hit a Texas league double into left that scored Lazzeri with the tying run. When Combs was hit with a pitched ball, there were runners on first and second.

Koenig then singled, driving Paschal home. On the throw to third to nab Combs, who slid in safely, Koenig raced to second. When Koenig was trapped off second, Combs raced for the plate and scored after McCurdy dropped Hunnefield's throw. Ruth then doubled scoring Koenig, making the score 4 to 1 in favor of the Yanks.

Hoyt retired the White Sox in the eighth and ninth.

Final score: Yankees 4, White Sox 1.

Yankee Notebook for Thursday, July 21, 1927: Hoyt (12-4) pitched a very strong game. He gave up seven hits—all singles—walked one and struck out two . . . Falk and Clancy had two hits apiece . . . Hoyt hit a batter—Metzler . . . Connally struck out seven and gave up only five hits, but four were for extra bases . . . Connally also hit Combs with a pitch . . . Gehrig, Paschal, and Ruth doubled . . . Lazzeri tripled . . . In the field, Lazzeri and Meusel committed errors . . . The game was played in 1:41.

At Sportsman's Park in St, Louis, Herschel Bennett's double in the ninth sent three runners home as the Browns edged the Senators, 5 to 4, in the first game of a doubleheader. In the second contest, wind and darkness caused the game to be called in the seventh with the score tied at two. In the opening game of the series at Detroit's Navin Field, the Tigers beat the Red Sox, 7 to 3.

In Cleveland, the Athletics took the first game of the series from the Indians, 8 to 3. In the sixth, Ty Cobb reached first on an error, stole second, and took third on an out. Cobb came home on Baby Doll Jacobson's bad throw to the plate from center.

At Braves Field, timely hitting and spectacular fielding helped the Braves win both games of a doubleheader from the Pirates, 2 to 1 and 5 to 2. The losses dropped Pittsburgh to second place, seven percentage points behind Chicago. At Baker Bowl, the Phillies took the opening game of a three game series from the Cubs, 7 to 3.

In New York, Al DeVormer's wild throw to third base in the ninth gave the Cardinals the winning run over the Giants, 7 to 6. At Ebbets Field, in the opener of a four game series, the Reds defeated the Robins, 2 to 1, in thirteen innings.

A brisk and chilly wind under sunny skies swept through Chicago, Illinois on Friday, July 22, 1927. The crowd of 30,000 at Comiskey Park was cold and tried hard to stay warm. The game's pitchers were right-hander Ted Lyons, who was looking for his fifteenth victory, and left-hander Herb Pennock. Earle Combs, who had been hit by a pitch thrown by Sarge Connally the day before, was replaced by Cedric Durst, and Julie Wera was at third again for Joe Dugan, who was resting his knee.

Pennock was hit hard.

Behind 5 to 0, Huggins lifted him for a pinch-hitter in the seventh. Myles Thomas, a right-hander, came on in relief and quickly gave up a home run to Falk with a man on. With the White Sox leading 7 to 1, the Yankees came up in the eighth inning. They picked up one run on Ruth's single and Gehrig's double. The Yanks scored three more runs in the ninth highlighted by Ruth's triple with two runners on, but Lyons ended the rally.

Final score: White Sox 7, Yankees 5.

Yankee Notebook for Friday, July 22, 1927: Lyons won his fifteenth for Chicago, giving up thirteen hits . . . Durst and Gehrig doubled and Ruth tripled . . . Pennock (10-5) went six innings, giving up ten hits. He walked none and struck out one . . . Thomas pitched two innings and gave up three hits, including Falk's home run. The right-hander walked one . . . Barrett had four hits in four plate appearances . . . Gazella went to third for Wera during the game . . . Lazzeri made three errors at shortstop.

Despite being outhit in the doubleheader by the Senators, the Browns won both games in St. Louis, 7 to 6 and 3 to 2. Rain halted the game between the Indians and Athletics at Dunn Field after the second inning with the score tied at 1 to 1.

At Braves Field, triples by the Waner brothers helped the Pirates rally in the seventh for four runs and defeat the Braves, 5 to 2. The victory coupled with the Cubs' loss at Baker Bowl lifted Pittsburgh back into first place. In Philadelphia, the Phillies made it two straight over the Cubs, 6 to 5.

In New York, errors by Andy Reese and Zach Taylor hurt the Giants as the Cardinals won, 7 to 4. At Brooklyn's Ebbets Field, Red Lucas pitched a one-hitter and faced only twenty-eight men as the Reds won the second game of that series from the Robins, 3 to 0.

Thirty thousand fans came out to Comiskey Park in Chicago and cheered the White Sox and Yankees on the afternoon of Saturday, July 23, 1927. Many hoped to see Babe Ruth and Lou Gehrig hit home runs in an epic battle that fascinated baseball fans around the nation. The mound opponents were Urban Shocker of New York and Chicago's Ted Blankenship, both right-handers.

With Blankenship and Shocker pitching well, the game moved into the seventh inning with the White Sox ahead 2 to 1. In that inning, Grabowski singled with one out, and Julie Wera came in and ran for him. Blankenship then walked Combs, who batted for Shocker. Durst also walked. With the bases loaded, Koenig came to the plate and tripled to deep left center, scoring Wera, Combs, and Durst.

Bert Cole, a left-hander, replaced Blankenship. With Koenig on third, Cole walked Ruth. Gehrig then lofted a long sacrifice fly to center and Koenig scored the fourth run of the inning. Wilcy Moore, a right-hander, pitched the seventh, eighth, and ninth and held the White Sox scoreless.

Final score: Yankees 5, White Sox 2.

Yankee Notebook for Saturday, July 23, 1927: The Yankees scored four runs in the seventh on two hits . . . Blankenship, Cole, and Jacobs gave up a total of ten hits: Koenig, Gehrig, and Gazella each had two . . . Gehrig doubled and Koenig tripled . . . Ruth also singled . . . Shocker (11-5) pitched six innings, giving up seven hits. He walked one and struck out none . . . Moore gave up two hits in three innings, walking one, and striking out three.

The Yankees were scheduled to play their final game of the road trip in Chicago the next day . . . The club planned on stopping over at Johnston, Pennsylvania for an exhibition game before returning to New York.

At Sportsman's Park in St. Louis, the Senators knocked Walter Stewart out of the box in an eighth-inning rally and went on to beat the Browns, 9 to 8. Washington center fielder Tris Speaker homered, tripled, and singled twice in five plate appearances. In Detroit, Earl Whitehill limited the Red Sox to four hits as the Tigers won their fifth in a row, 3 to 2. Rain postponed a doubleheader between the Athletics and Indians at Cleveland.

In Boston, the Pirates stayed in first place by capturing the second game of a doubleheader from the Braves, 4 to 3. The game was stopped by rain as the seventh inning was about to begin. Pittsburgh had dropped into second place temporarily when they lost the opener of the twin bill, 6 to 2. Rain postponed the Cubs and Phillies at Philadelphia and a doubleheader between the Reds and Robins at Brooklyn.

On a warm sunny afternoon in Chicago, 50,000 fans came out to Comiskey Park to see the finale of the series between the Yankees and White Sox on Sunday, July 24, 1927. The Yankees had won two of the three games.

Pitching that day were right-handers George Pipgras and Tommy Thomas. Ruth came up in the first and tripled to deep center. When Gehrig singled to right, the Babe trotted home. Coming to the plate again in the third, Ruth hit a home run off Thomas into the right field stands. The White Sox scratched out a run in the fourth and one in the sixth to tie the score.

Going to the seventh with the game tied at two, Thomas walked Collins. When Pipgras sacrificed, Collins moved to second base. Koenig, the star of the game the day before, then singled, sending Collins home with the go-ahead run for New York. Meanwhile, Huggins had Wilcy Moore warming up in the bullpen from the seventh inning on.

When Falk opened the ninth with a single off Pipgras, Huggins brought Moore in. With Falk advancing no further than second, Moore went on to retire the side and end the game.

Final score: Yankees 3, White Sox 2.

Yankee notebook for Sunday, July 24, 1927: The Babe had three hits that day, a single, triple, and home run . . . It was Ruth's thirty-first home run and tied him again with Gehrig for the home run lead . . . Gehrig singled and had an extra base hit taken away by Barrett in right . . . Lazzeri and Meusel doubled . . . Pipgras (6-0) went eight innings before Moore relieved him in the ninth. Pipgras gave up eight hits, walking three, and striking out two . . . Moore did not yield a hit . . . For the White Sox, Thomas gave up seven hits and struck out seven.

The Yankees pulled off two double plays; both from Gehrig to Koenig and back to Gehrig . . . Each team left six men on the bases . . . All the regulars started for the Yanks, except Dugan . . . Gazella played third base . . . The Yanks reported that Wera had a bruised shoulder . . . After the game, both the Yankees and White Sox left on the same train for the trip east.

At Sportsman's Park in St. Louis, the Senators scored nine runs in the seventh and crushed the Browns 14 to 6. Twelve of Washington's fifteen hits came in the sixth and seventh innings. In Cleveland, poor defensive play hurt the Athletics as the Indians won a doubleheader by scores of 9 to 6 and 5 to 2. In the final game of the series at Navin Field, the Red Sox held off the Tigers and won, 8 to 7. Harry Heilmann's single in the eighth extended his successive hitting streak to nine.

In New York, the Pirates and Giants split a doubleheader as Pittsburgh won the opener, 11 to 6, and New York the second game, 9 to 3. At Ebbets Field, the Cubs and Robins played a twin bill as Brooklyn won the first game, 3 to 2 in ten innings, and Chicago the finale, 7 to 1. In Cincinnati, Rube Bressler's two triples and a single led the Reds to a victory over the Cardinals, 9 to 4.

On the last leg of the trip back to New York, the Yankees stopped at Johnstown, Pennsylvania on Monday, July 25, 1927 for an exhibition game against the Johnstown Club of the Middle Atlantic League. The Yankees lost 7 to 5. With the road trip that ended, the Yankees won thirteen and lost five. The Senators also played very well, winning nine of its first eleven games on the road, but did not pick up any ground.

"We win and we win," said Joe Judge of the Senators. "But the Yanks don't even pause for a breath. How can you jump a team when you can't even catch up to it?"

The consensus in the baseball world was that the Yankees had 'clinched' the American League Pennant. However, it would take a few more weeks to capture the flag mathematically.

At Shibe Park in Philadelphia, Jimmy Dykes's home run off Lil Stoner's first pitch in the thirteenth inning gave the Athletics a 6 to 5 victory over the Tigers in the first game of that series. In Boston, the Red Sox hammered George Uhle in the first five innings and beat the Indians, 10 to 7.

In New York, a home run by Andy Reese and Larry Benton's outstanding pitching gave the Giants a 1 to 0 victory over the Pirates at the Polo Grounds. The loss moved the Cubs back into first place in the National League. At Redland Field, the Reds won a doubleheader from the Cardinals by scores of 3 to 2 and 4 to 3.

Major League Baseball Standings
July 25, 1927
American League

	Won	Lost	P.C.
New York	67	26	.720
Washington	53	38	.582
Detroit	49	40	.551
Philadelphia	49	43	.533
Chicago	48	47	.505
St. Louis	38	52	.422
Cleveland	39	55	.415
Boston	25	67	.272

National League

	Won	Lost	P.C.
Chicago	55	36	.604
Pittsburgh	54	36	.600
St. Louis	52	39	.571
New York	50	46	.521
Brooklyn	41	50	.451
Cincinnati	40	52	.435
Philadelphia	37	51	.420
Boston	34	53	.391

ii

Losers of eleven straight games to the Yankees, the St. Louis Browns visited Yankee Stadium in New York to play a doubleheader on Tuesday, July 26, 1927. With 20,000 fans at the ballpark under sunny skies and temperatures in the low-80s, the Browns sent right-handers Milt Gaston and Sad Sam Jones to the mound. Miller Huggins went with left-hander Dutch Ruether and right-hander Waite Hoyt.

First Game
The Line-Ups

Browns	Yankees
Frank O'Rourke 2b	Earle Combs cf
Herschel Bennett rf	Mark Koenig ss
George Sisler 1b	Babe Ruth rf
E. Miller lf	Lou Gehrig 1b
Harry Rice cf	Bob Meusel lf
Otto Miller 3b	Tony Lazzeri 2b
Steve O'Neill c	Mike Gazella 3b
Wally Gerber ss	John Grabowski c
Milt Gaston p	Dutch Ruether p

With one on and one out in the first, Ruth hit a home run off Gaston into the right field bleachers. O'Neill, the Browns' catcher, did not have a chance to face Ruether until the fifth inning, even though he was seventh in the batting order. Gerber, the shortstop, got mixed up and batted out of turn in the second, making the third out. Then he had to bat again in the third in his own place to start that inning.

Adding three more runs in the third and two in the fifth, the Yanks came up in the sixth leading, 7 to 1. With Gaston still pitching, Ruth hit his second home run into the right field bleachers. Except for the one run the Browns scored in the fourth, Ruether was in total control. In the home half of the eighth, the Yankees added insult to injury, exploding for seven runs on six hits, three walks, and one error—all with Gaston still on the mound. Ruether retired the Browns in the ninth.

Final score: Yankees 15, Browns 1. (First game)

In the second game, the Browns bunched five hits in the first three innings off Hoyt and took a 2 to 0 lead into the home half of the third. In that inning, Koenig doubled and Ruth singled, bringing Gehrig to the plate. With two runners on, Gehrig cracked a home run off Jones into the right field bleachers. The Yankees led 3 to 2.

After Ski Melillo pinch-hit for Jones, Ernie Wingard, a left-hander, came in to pitch the home half of the seventh. With the score 3 to 2, the Yankees erupted for nine runs on seven hits, three errors, and a walk making the score 12 to 2. The Browns scratched out a run in the ninth.

Final score: Yankees 12, Browns 3 (Second game)

Yankee Notebook for Tuesday, July 26, 1927: In the first game, the Yankees had fourteen hits . . . Ruth had a perfect four-for-four day at the plate with two home runs—numbers thirty-three and thirty-four—and two singles . . . The Babe's two homers gave the Yankees one hundred for the season . . . Koenig, Gehrig, Meusel, and Grabowski stroked two singles each . . . Ruether (11-2) went the distance, giving up one run and six hits. The left-hander walked one and struck-out six. He also hit E. Miller . . . After Ruether yielded one run in the fourth, only two Browns got as far as second base . . . Meusel had a stolen base.

In the second game, Hoyt (13-4) gave up eight hits, walking one and striking out two . . . Bennett, Rice, and Williams each doubled . . . Jones and Wingard gave up thirteen hits . . . Ruth had three singles and Gehrig doubled and homered—his thirty-second . . . Ruth led Gehrig in the home run battle—thirty-three to thirty-two and was five home runs behind the pace he set in 1921 when he hit fifty-nine.

Ruth had two straight hits in the second game. With the four in game one, he had six hits in a row before he was retired . . . Combs also doubled and tripled, and Meusel had two singles . . . Collins behind the plate gave up stolen bases to Sisler and Williams . . . The Browns made four errors . . . With the losses, St. Louis dropped thirteen in a row to New York.

Returning to Griffith Stadium in Washington, D.C., the Senators defeated the White Sox in a doubleheader, 5 to 1 and 6 to 5, in eleven innings. Trailing in the second game, Washington tied the score in the ninth and then won in extra innings. In Philadelphia, the Tigers and Athletics split a twin bill at Shibe Park as Detroit won the opening game, 10 to 4, and Philadelphia the second, 5 to 2. At Boston's Fenway Park, a seven-run rally in the third inning off Charlie Ruffing gave the Indians a win over the Red Sox, 7 to 2.

Trailing in the eighth to the Robins at Forbes Field, the Pirates rallied for two runs and won, 6 to 5. Former Pirate Max Carey had three hits, scored three runs, and stole three bases—one of them home. In Cincinnati, the Reds won their six straight and swept the four game series from the Cardinals, 11 to 10.

Despite the threat of rain, the game between the Yankees and St. Louis Browns on Wednesday, July 27, 1927 went on as scheduled at Yankee Stadium in the Bronx. With a small crowd at the ballpark, left-handers Win Ballou and Herb Pennock opposed each other.

Rain halted the game in the second. When the Yankees came up in the third, the club trailed 1 to 0. Koenig tripled in that inning and scored on Ruth's roller to second. Managing only two hits off Ballou, the Yankees came up in the sixth with the score tied at one.

After Ballou walked Ruth with one out, Gehrig came to the plate and hit a home run into the right field seats giving the Yankees a 3 to 1 lead. After Meusel was retired, Lazzeri batted and blasted a home run into the left field seats making the score 4 to 1. From the second inning on, Pennock gave up only one hit.

Final score: Yankees 4, Browns 1.

Yankee Notebook for Wednesday, July 27, 1927: Gehrig's thirty-third home run tied him again with Ruth . . . Lazzeri's homer was his fifteenth . . . The Babe singled and scored a run . . . Twice Ruth flung down his bat in disgust when Ballou walked him. Two other times he did not get anything good and hit high fly balls.

Pennock (11-5) was masterful. He gave up only three hits, walked one, and struck out three . . . The Yankee left-hander set down the Browns in seven of the nine innings; only three of the twenty-one men he faced in those seven frames were able to hit the ball out of the infield . . . With so many balls hit in the infield, Gehrig had twelve putouts . . . Ballou gave up only six hits for St. Louis . . . The game was played in 1:45.

Scoring three runs in the tenth at Griffith Stadium, the White Sox defeated the Senators, 7 to 4. Ted Lyons went the distance for Chicago. In Philadelphia, Earl Whitehill outpitched Sam Gray at Shibe Park as the Tigers beat the Athletics, 3 to 1. Harry Heilmann hit a home run for Detroit in the sixth. Rain postponed the game between the Indians and Red Sox at Boston.

In an exciting pitching duel between Dazzy Vance and Vic Aldridge at Forbes Field, the Pirates won over the Robins, 2 to 1. With the Cubs losing, the Pirates held first place. With 28,000 fans at Wrigley Field, Bill Terry smacked a double to left center field with the bases loaded in the ninth, giving the Giants a victory over the Cubs, 6 to 4.

In St. Louis, Ray Blades's single, with the bases filled and two outs in the eleventh, drove in the winning run as the Cardinals beat the Phillies, 9 to 8. At Redland Field, the Reds moved into fifth place after splitting a twin bill with the Braves as Boston won the first game, 7 to 2, and Cincinnati took the second, 5 to 2.

The home run battle between Ruth and Gehrig was the talk of baseball. Going into the final game of the series with the Browns in New York on Thursday, July 28, 1927, Ruth and Gehrig were tied for the major league home run lead with thirty-three. That afternoon a crowd of 10,000 was at Yankee Stadium in New York on a sweltering day. Right-handers Urban Shocker and Elam Vangilder pitched.

After the Browns took an early 3 to 0 lead in the first, the Yankees came to bat in the home half of that inning. After scoring five runs on three walks and three hits, a triple by Koenig, and singles by Ruth and Lazzeri, left-hander Walter Stewart replaced Vangilder with none out. Stewart retired the Yankees without further scoring.

In a lackluster game, the Yankees added one run in the fifth on a walk to Lazzeri, a single by Gazella, and Collins's sacrifice fly. The Yanks scored again in the seventh on a walk to Meusel and a triple by Gazella making the score 7 to 3. In the Yankee eighth, Combs singled off Stewart. After Koenig made out, Ruth came up to bat.

The Babe smacked a home run off Stewart far into the Stadium's right-field bleachers up toward the scoreboard. As Combs and Ruth touched the plate, the Yankees led 9 to 3. The Browns scored a run in the ninth before Shocker retired the side.

Final score: Yankees 9, Browns 4.

Yankee Notebook for Thursday, July 28, 1927: Ruth had three hits; two singles, and a home run—number thirty-four—and went ahead of Gehrig by one . . . Gazella had a perfect day at bat with two singles, a triple, and a sacrifice . . . Collins also tripled . . . On the hill, Shocker (11-5) pitched a complete game, giving up twelve hits, walking none, and striking out one . . . O'Rourke and Miller touched Shocker for three hits each . . . Browns' pitchers Vangilder and Stewart gave up ten hits and walked a total of nine . . . It was the Browns' fifteenth straight loss to the Yankees . . . St. Louis was scheduled to return to New York for the last time in September.

In Washington, D.C., Senators' hurler Walter Johnson held the White Sox to six hits as his teammates pounded out sixteen against Ted Blankenship and Bert Cole and won the final game of the series, 12 to 2, at Griffith Stadium. At Shibe Park, Sam Gibson with help from Ken Holloway led the Tigers to a victory over the Athletics in the fifth and final game of the series, 5 to 2. In Boston, the Red Sox made it eleven out of sixteen games over the Indians that season with a sweep of a doubleheader by scores of 3 to 0 and 4 to 3.

Veteran hurler Bill Doak pitched well at Forbes Field in Pittsburgh and led the Robins to a victory over the Pirates, 7 to 5. Overcome by heat in the eighth, Doak fainted inside the dugout. Jesse Petty replaced him and held the lead. With 15,000 fans at Wrigley Field, Rogers Hornsby hit his seventeenth home run as the Giants defeated the Cubs, 6 to 5. At Sportsman's Park, the Cardinals staged a six run rally in the eighth inning and won the second game of the series from the Phillies, 10 to 8. Philadelphia's Cy Williams hit two home runs, bringing his total to twenty-two. In Cincinnati, Eppa Rixey held the Braves to nine hits as the Reds defeated the Braves, 11 to 6, at Redland Field.

Major League Baseball Standings
July 28, 1927
American League

	Won	Lost	P.C.
New York	71	26	.732
Washington	56	39	.589
Detroit	52	41	.559
Philadelphia	50	46	.521
Chicago	49	50	.495
Cleveland	40	57	.412
St. Louis	38	56	.404
Boston	27	68	.284

National League

	Won	Lost	P.C.
Pittsburgh	56	37	.602
Chicago	55	38	.591
St. Louis	54	40	.574
New York	52	46	.531
Cincinnati	43	53	.448
Brooklyn	42	52	.447
Philadelphia	37	53	.411
Boston	35	55	.389

PART 3

Clinching the Pennant

Chapter 26

Tony Lazzeri

Day after day at Salt Lake City, Utah in 1925, Bill Essick, a scout for the New York Yankees, watched a young infielder named Tony Lazzeri. Essick reported to Ed Barrow that Lazzeri was hitting the ball exceptionally well, batting .355 and hitting 60 home runs.

"But the air is thin out there," Barrow told Essick.

"The air may be thin but this player is solid," Essick responded.

Scouts from all the major leagues were watching Lazzeri. Most also felt that the altitude in Salt Lake City helped Lazzeri's batting average. They were wary of signing him, knowing other recent players with impressive numbers playing in that altitude had not succeeded. There was another reason the scouts shied away: Lazzeri was an epileptic.

South Market Street in San Francisco's Cow Hollow District was a rough neighborhood at the turn of the century. Living there at the time was an Italian born boilermaker named Augustine Lazzeri. On December 6, 1903, his wife Julia (Cheasa), also from Italy, gave birth to a son—Anthony (Tony) Michael Lazzeri.

Growing up in Cow Hollow, Tony Lazzeri often got into fights.

"I guess I was a pretty tough kid," recalled Lazzeri. "The neighborhood wasn't one in which a boy was likely to grow up a sissy, for it was always fight or get licked, and I never got licked."

Having no interest in his schoolwork at Daniel Webster Grammar School, Lazzeri spent most of the time boxing (he dreamed of becoming a prizefighter) and playing baseball on the Jackson Playground at the bottom of the hill at 17th and Kansas Streets.

In 1918, Tony Lazzeri was expelled from school at the age of 15. Glad to be finished, Lazzeri told his father that he wanted to go to work. Told to pack a lunch for the next morning, Lazzeri accompanied his father to the Maine Iron Works, where the elder Lazzeri worked as a boilermaker. Tony Lazzeri started as a helper, heating rivets and tossing them to the riveters. The job gave him extraordinary strength in his shoulders and forearms. With black hair and brown eyes, the young man developed into a lean, hard, 5 foot, 11 inch, 160 pounder. Lazzeri was soon earning $4.50 a day at the iron works and became a member of Local Union No.6.

Lazzeri also made a little money playing shortstop for a semi-professional baseball team. Later, while he was training as a boxer, Lazzeri became the shortstop of the Golden Gate Native Police Department, a good semi-pro team. He continued working at the iron works and playing for the Golden Gate Natives until 1922. At that time, as he was just about to become a full-fledged boilermaker, a friend of his named Tim Harrington convinced Duffy Lewis, manager of the Salt Lake City Bees baseball club of the Pacific Coast League (PCL), to give Lazzeri a tryout.

In 1922, 18-year-old Tony Lazzeri joined Salt Lake City as a utility infielder, playing third and first. He was paid $250 a month. However, Lazzeri had difficulty hitting a curve ball and started his professional career poorly, hitting only .192 in 45 games. In 1923 Lazzeri was sent to Peoria, Illinois of the Three-I League for more experience. Before reporting, he married Maye Janes, who he had met some six months earlier through her brother-in-law, Paul Pettingill, a teammate of Lazzeri's on the Golden Gate Natives.

Accompanied by his new wife, Lazzeri reported to Peoria. He had a good first month but was then benched while the manager tried out two other players at second. Lazzeri sat on the bench for three weeks until he was called on to pinch hit in the ninth inning of a game against Terre Haute. With two men on the bases and two runs behind, Lazzeri hit a home run that won the game. After that big hit, he became the regular second baseman on the club, playing in 135 games, hitting 14 home runs, and batting .248. Lazzeri rejoined Salt Lake City that fall.

Lazzeri reported to Salt Lake City again in the spring of 1924, starting at shortstop. Although playing well and hitting around .285 with 16 home runs, Lazzeri was asked by Duffy Lewis, the club's manager, to give Clark Pittinger, who had played for the Boston Red Sox, a chance at shortstop for a couple of days. Pittinger played very well. A few weeks later Lazzeri was farmed out to Lincoln, Nebraska in the Western League, where he played in 82 games, hitting 28 home runs and batting .329.

Returning to Salt Lake City in 1925, Lazzeri got his first real chance under the team's new manager, Oscar Vitt. Lazzeri had a sensational season playing in 192 games (in those days the PCL played a 197-game schedule). He batted .355 with 252 hits, 52 doubles, 14 triples, 222 RBIs, and 60 home runs, the most ever hit in professional baseball. Lazzeri also scored 202 runs and stole 39 bases.

The New York Yankees took an interest in the young slugger.

At that time the Salt Lake City club had a working arrangement with the Chicago Cubs. Knowing that Lazzeri had epileptic episodes off the field, the Cubs were afraid to buy him. The Cincinnati Reds also passed him up, and Garry Hermann, owner of the Reds, wrote to Yankee owner Jacob Ruppert and told him why his club had not bought Lazzeri.

Ed Barrow sent scout Ed Holly to Salt Lake City to look at Lazzeri. Holly reported he was sensational. He also confirmed reports about Lazzeri's medical disorder. Wanting to know more, Holly went on to San Francisco and looked into Lazzeri's family history. Barrow, meanwhile, sent head scout Paul Kritchell to Salt Lake City to watch Lazzeri. He also asked Bob Connery, president of the St. Paul Baseball Club of the American Association to see Lazzeri play.

Barrow received good reports. Holly found that no other members of his family were affected and that Lazzeri's insurance company was willing to increase his policy. Connery reported that Lazzeri was great. Krichell also told Barrow that the stories about Lazzeri's episodes, or fits as they were known, occurred only off the field.

"As long as he doesn't take fits between three and six in the afternoon, that's good enough for me," said Barrow.

As it turned out, Lazzeri's epilepsy never affected him on the playing field. The public never knew he had the disorder.

Ed Barrow purchased Lazzeri's contract from Salt Lake City in the fall of 1925 for five players and $50,000, a considerable amount of money at that time. Lazzeri signed a contract for $5,000 and reported to Spring Training at St. Petersburg, Florida in 1926.

Although Lazzeri played shortstop at Salt Lake City, Miller Huggins wanted him at second base. Huggins worked with him on switching positions and taught him to make the double play. Huggins, meanwhile, played another rookie Mark Koenig at shortstop. With two rookies in the infield, the sportswriters felt that the Yankees could not contend for the pennant in 1926 and predicted that the team would finish the season in the second division for the second straight year.

But Koenig and Lazzeri played well together in the field and helped the Yankees win the pennant that season. Lazzeri played in all 155 games in 1926, hitting .275, with 162 hits, 28 doubles, 14 triples, 18 home runs, and 114 runs batted in. Lazzeri's home run total (18) was third in the league behind Babe Ruth (47) and Al Simmons of the Athletics (19). Lazzeri's runs-batted-in mark (114) tied George Burns of the Indians for second place behind Ruth (146). As a rookie, he also stole 16 bases, sixth best in the league.

The 1926 World Series saw the Yankees play the St. Louis Cardinals. With the series tied at two games apiece, Pennock and Sherdel found themselves in a mound duel in St. Louis. With the score tied at two in the tenth, Lazzeri's sacrifice fly gave the Yankees a 3 to 2 lead, which Pennock held in the bottom of the tenth. The victory gave the Yankees a 3 to 2 lead in the series. After returning to New York for Game Six, Grover Cleveland Alexander won his second game and tied the series at three games apiece, setting the stage for the seventh and final game.

With the Cardinals leading 3 to 2 in the seventh inning, the Yankees filled the bases with two outs. Lazzeri was the next batter. To the surprise of everyone at Yankee Stadium that day, Rogers Hornsby, the Cardinals' player-manager, called Grover Cleveland Alexander into the game to stop the Yankee threat. In one of baseball's most dramatic moments,

Alexander struck out Lazzeri for the final out of that inning Alexander went on to retire the Yankees in the eighth and ninth, giving the Cardinals the world championship in 1926.

Lazzeri was a twenty-two year old rookie that season. Despite going on to have an outstanding career with the Yankees, that strikeout against Alexander was never to be forgotten.

Baseball fans talked about it for years. Lazzeri was always reminded of it. While Lazzeri was still an active ball player, Grover Cleveland Alexander went into the Baseball Hall of Fame in 1938, his plaque read:

> "He won the 1926 world championship for the Cardinals by striking out Lazzeri with the bases full in the final crisis."

In 1945, a year before his death, Lazzeri gave a poignant interview to Bob Considine, the syndicated sports columnist, in the tavern that the former Yankee owned and operated in San Francisco.

"Funny thing, but nobody seems to remember much about my ball playing, except that strikeout," Lazzeri told Considine. "There isn't a night goes by but what some guy leans across the bar, or comes up behind me at a table in this joint, and brings up the old question. Never a night."

After Lazzeri's death, sports columnist Red Smith wrote, "it was Lazzeri's misfortune that although he was as great a ball player as ever lived the most vivid memory he left in most minds concerned the day he failed."

A quite, modest man, Lazzeri would rarely talk about himself. The sportswriters found him to be difficult to interview.

"Interviewing that guy," one reporter complained, "is like mining coal with a nail file."

Popular with his teammates and respected by his opponents, Lazzeri was a leader, cool under pressure, and considered by many as one of the smartest men in the game. Even Miller Huggins acknowledged him to be the brains of the Yankee infield. Lazzeri took charge when events called for steady nerves.

Lazzeri was an excellent fielder, and for a smaller man compared to the likes of Ruth, Gehrig, and Meusel, he could hit the ball exceptionally far. He also had the knack of hitting with men on base, becoming one of the best "clutch" hitters in baseball.

As the first great ballplayer of Italian heritage to play in New York, the Italian-American fans in New York and elsewhere took great pride in Lazzeri. Because of him, thousands of people of Italian descent were introduced to baseball for the first time, and they came back again and again. At Yankee Stadium, their rallying cry was "Poosh-'Em Up Tony," imploring him to hit the ball, preferably out of the ballpark.

According to Lazzeri, the nickname, which remained with him always, was given to him while he was playing at Salt Lake City. A fan of Italian descent, who wanted him to get a hit and could not express himself properly, shouted "Poosh-"Em Up, Tony".

Beloved by the Italian community, *The New York Times* even compared him to Christopher Columbus at a time when Lazzeri was playing shortstop. "He didn't discover America,' wrote the *Times*, "but Columbus never went behind third for an overthrow to cut-off the tying run in the ninth inning."

Chapter 27

Gehrig Leads Race

On Friday, July 29, 1927, the Cleveland Indians opened a series against the Yankees at the Stadium. Last in New York City from June 11-14, the Indians lost two of three games with one rained out. Going into the game that afternoon, the Yankees had a fourteen game lead over the second place Washington Senators. Miller Huggins started George Pipgras, a right-hander, who had won six games in a row. Willis Hudlin, a right-hander, opened the series for Cleveland.

The Line-Ups

Indians	Yankees
Charlie Jameison lf	Earle Combs cf
Lew Fonseca 2b	Mark Koenig ss
Homer Summa rf	Babe Ruth rf
George Burns 1b	Lou Gehrig 1b
Joe Sewell ss	Bob Meusel lf
Luke Sewell c	Tony Lazzeri 2b
Ike Eichrodt cf	Mike Gazella 3b
Rube Lutzke 3b	John Grabowski c
Willis Hudlin p	George Pipgras p

The Indians scored three runs in the second on a single by J. Sewell, an error by Koenig on L. Sewell's ground ball, Lutzke's triple, and Lazzeri's wild throw of a relay. The Yankees picked up a run in the bottom half of that inning and two in the third, tying the game at three. Cleveland broke the tie in the fifth: Jamieson walked, went to third on

Fonseca's double and scored on a sacrifice fly. Then with two outs, J. Sewell walked and L.Sewell drove Fonseca home with a single. The Indians led 5 to 3.

In the sixth, Hudlin intentionally walked Ruth, loading the bases. When Gehrig beat out a hit to Burns, Combs scored; however, with the bases filled again, Meusel hit into a double play ending the inning. After Eichrodt opened the eighth with a triple off Pipgras, Huggins brought in right-hander Bob Shawkey, who gave up a hit. When Eichrodt came home, the Indians led 6 to 4.

In the Yankees' half of the eighth, a single by Combs, a double by Ruth, and an intentional walk to Gehrig loaded the bases with two outs. Meusel then forced Gehrig at second to end the inning. After Cedric Durst batted for Shawkey in the eighth, Myles Thomas, a right-hander, pitched the ninth. Huggins sent Ben Paschal up to bat for Thomas in the ninth, but he was retired.

Final score: Indians 6, Yankees 4.

Yankee Notebook for Friday, July 29, 1927: Although the Indians won that day, the Yankees out hit them fourteen to eleven . . . Combs had four singles, and Ruth doubled twice, singled, and walked twice . . . Gehrig had a base hit, was hit by a pitched ball in the first, and intentionally walked in the eighth with runners on second and third . . . Meusel and Lazzeri each stole a base.

Pipgras (6-1) went seven, giving up nine hits, walking three and striking out three . . . Shawkey and Thomas each pitched one inning and each gave up a hit . . . The Yanks had their share of injuries: Luke Sewell's foul ball split Grabowski's hand, and he was forced out of the game . . . Sewell then hit a ball that took a bad hop smashing Lazzeri in the jaw.

At Griffith Stadium in the nation's capital, the Senators bunched three hits and a walk for two runs in the eleventh and edged the Tigers, 5 to 4. Tom Zachary, pitching in his second game for Washington, held Detroit to six hits but was taken out in the eleventh when the first man up tripled. In Philadelphia, the White Sox behind Tommy Thomas defeated the Athletics, 6 to 4, at Shibe Park. Thomas walked four men in the first but settled down and scattered seven hits. At Boston's Fenway

Park, Charley Ruffing led the Red Sox to their first win that season against the Browns, 8 to 2. Ruffing gave up only six hits.

In Pittsburgh, Glenn Wright singled home the winning run after Pie Traynor tripled to tie the score as the Pirates scored three runs in the ninth and defeated the Robins, 4 to 3, at Forbes Field. With 32,000 fans at Wrigley Field on Ladies' Day, a record 14,381 women and girls saw the Cubs score two runs in the tenth and beat the Giants, 5 to 4.

At Sportsman's Park, Jesse Haines scattered four hits as the Cardinals swept the Phillies, 6 to 3. The victory was Haines's fifteenth. In Cincinnati, the game between the Reds and Braves was called because of rain in the last of the fourth inning. The Reds were leading 2 to 0 at the time.

With 40,000 spectators at Yankee Stadium in New York on Saturday, July 30, 1927, the Yankees and Cleveland Indians resumed their series with a doubleheader. Left-hander Dutch Ruether and Waite Hoyt, a right-hander opposed righty George Uhle and southpaw Joe Shaute.

Recovered from neuritis, Miller Huggins started catcher Benny Bengough. At 5' 7.5" and 168 pounds, the 28-year-old Bengough threw and batted right-handed. With the club since 1923, Bengough batted .381 in 36 games in 1926.

After being hit in the leg by Uhle in the first, Combs came out of the game. Cedric Durst filled in for him in centerfield. With the Indians leading 3 to 2, the Yankees came up to bat in the fifth. Right-hander Walter "Jumbo" Brown, who had replaced Uhle in the second, walked Ruth. Gehrig came to the plate and hit the ball high up against the sun seats in the right field bleachers. The Yankees led 4 to 3.

In the seventh, Ruether surprised everyone when he hit a home run into the right field stands with Lazzeri on base. His blast gave the Yanks a 6 to 3 lead. In the next inning, Gehrig came up again and hit his second home run off Brown that barely got into the left field seats. The home run was Gehrig's thirty-fifth, passing the Babe for the home run lead.

The game ended on a spectacular play.

Gehrig dove to his right and dug out Jamieson's hard hit drive out of the dirt with one hand. He then raced to the bag, beating the runner.

Final score: Yankees 7, Indians 1

In the second game, Hoyt and Shaute hooked up in a pitching duel over the first five and one-half innings. The Yankees took a 2 to 0 lead in the sixth, the big blow a home run by Meusel. In the eighth, singles by Hodapp and Shaute and an error by Paschal loaded the bases with one out. Hoyt got out of the jam when he forced Burns to pop to Gazella and struck out Summa. In the bottom of the eighth, the Yankees scored three more runs. Hoyt retired the Indians in the ninth.

Final score: Yankees 5, Indians 0.

Yankee Notebook for Saturday, July 30, 1927: In the first game, Ruether (12-2) gave up eight hits, walking three and striking out one. He also hit a batter—J. Sewell . . . The Yankees had eleven hits . . . Meusel had three singles . . . Gehrig hit two home runs, numbers thirty-four and thirty-five . . . Ruether also homered . . . Gazella and Bengough doubled . . . The club stole four bases . . . In the field, Koenig made an error . . . When Jamieson tried to score from second base, Ruth threw a perfect strike from the embankment to cut the runner down at the plate.

In the second game, Hoyt (13-4) gave up six hits, striking out three and walking none . . . At the plate, the Yankees had ten hits . . . Meusel hit a home run, Hoyt tripled, and Koenig and Gazella doubled . . . Since replacing the injured Dugan, Gazella had hit close to .400 and had not made an error.

In Washington, D.C., Bump Hadley scattered six hits as the Senators defeated the Tigers for the second time in a row, 10 to 1, at Griffith Stadium. Tris Speaker was forced to leave the game early for Washington when he sprained his wrist in a collision at first base. With the victory, the Senators had won twenty-nine of their last thirty-nine.

Philadelphia's Lefty Grove fanned seven and broke a tie game with a home run as the Athletics evened the series with the White Sox winning, 5 to 3. Ty Cobb also hit a home run with Zach Wheat on base. At Fenway Park, the Red Sox and Browns split a doubleheader with Boston winning the opener, 5 to 4, and St. Louis the finale, 9 to 2.

Despite losing to the Braves 3 to 2 in the tenth at Forbes Field on singles by Davy Bancroft and Andy High, and Jimmy Welsh's double, the Pirates held on to first place as the Cubs lost to the Phillies, 5 to 3, at Wrigley Field. In St. Louis, Rogers Hornsby drove in five runs on a double and two singles as the Giants defeated the Cardinals in the series opener, 13 to 2. Freddie Fitzsimmons yielded seven hits. Rain postponed the game between the Robins and Reds at Cincinnati.

The Yankees were rained out in New York on the afternoon of Sunday, July 31, 1927. With Gehrig taking the lead from Ruth, there was keen competition for the home run crown. Ruth wanted to keep that mantle and Gehrig would have liked to take it. On the surface there appeared to be a friendly, collegial relationship between the two men.

"One of the finest fellows in the game and a great hitter," Ruth said of Gehrig.

"The only real home run hitter that ever lived. I'm just fortunate to be even close to him." Gehrig said of Ruth.

Both men even joined up as partners on a bridge team in the clubhouse and on the train as the club traveled from city to city. Yet, some wondered how much of that public camaraderie was sincere or just for show?

The only other scheduled game that day in the American League saw Horace Lisenbee limit the Tigers to five hits as the Senators won their third straight from the visitors, 7 to 2, at Griffith Stadium.

In the National League, 30,000 fans crammed Wrigley Field. The Cubs gained one-half game on the idle Pirates as they hammered the Phillies, 12 to 5. Charlie Root won his eighteenth and Hack Wilson hit his nineteenth home run. With 25,000 fans at Sportsman's Park, George Harper's bases loaded home run in the eighth paced the Giants to a victory over the Cardinals 7 to 4. It was New York's second straight win over St. Louis. At Redland Field, 25,000 spectators watched the Reds and Robins split a doubleheader as Cincinnati won the first game, 6 to 2, and Brooklyn took the second in ten innings, 3 to 2.

On Monday, August 1, 1927 the Yankees played a doubleheader with the Cleveland Indians at Yankee Stadium. With 10,000 fans on-hand, Miller Huggins started left-hander Herb Pennock in the first game, and the Indians opened with southpaw Walter Miller. Pennock and Miller pitched well in the early innings.

By the third inning, it began to drizzle and darkness descended on the ballpark. With no score, the Yankees came up to bat in the fourth. Koenig opened the Yankees' half with a single to center. When Ruth laid down a perfect sacrifice bunt, Koenig moved to second. Gehrig's long sacrifice fly to center sent Koenig to third. Meusel then doubled to left field, scoring Koenig. The Yankees led 1 to 0.

Pennock retired the Indians in the fifth. In the sixth it began to rain. Jamieson opened with a single to left and went to second on Spurgeon's infield out. Summa then singled to right, scoring Jamieson with the tying run. When Ruth's throw to the plate took a bad hop away from Bengough, Summa went to third. Fonseca then singled to center, scoring Summa. The Indians led 2 to 1.

The Yankees did not score in the bottom of the sixth. With the Indians at bat in the seventh with two outs, the storm broke and players and fans scattered for shelter. With heavy rains flooding the field, the game was called.

Final score: Indians 2, Yankees 1.

Yankee Notebook for Monday, August 1, 1927: Pennock (11-6) went six and two-thirds; however, because the game reverted to the score at the end of the last complete inning, he was credited with working six frames . . . Although the left-hander struck out Eichrodt and Hodapp in the seventh, those strikeouts would not count in the records . . . Officially, Pennock walked one, struck out one, and gave up seven hits.

Miller yielded six hits for Cleveland . . . Meusel had the only extra base hit; a double . . . Ruth made an error . . . The second game of the doubleheader was postponed and would be played when the Indians returned to New York in September.

The game between the Browns and Red Sox at Fenway Park was called in the second inning because of rain. Wet weather also postponed the game between the White Sox and Athletics at Philadelphia.

At Wrigley Field in Chicago, the Cubs took over first place after defeating the Phillies, 6 to 5, on Earl Webb's game winning single that scored Sparky Adams in the ninth. In Pittsburgh, Vic Aldridge weakened in the eleventh as the Braves defeated the Pirates, 4 to 1. It was the second consecutive extra-inning game that Boston won from Pittsburgh. At Sportsman's Park, two home runs by Bill Terry and one by George Harper led the Giants to their third straight win over the Cardinals, 6 to 3. In Cincinnati, Dazzy Vance pitched the Robins to a 2 to 1 victory.

Major League Standings
August 1, 1927
American League

	Won	Lost	P.C.
New York	73	28	.723
Washington	59	39	.602
Detroit	52	44	.542
Philadelphia	51	47	.520
Chicago	50	51	.495
Cleveland	42	59	.416
St. Louis	39	58	.402
Boston	29	69	.296

National League

	Won	Lost	P.C.
Chicago	58	39	.598
Pittsburgh	57	39	.594
St. Louis	55	43	.561
New York	55	47	.539
Brooklyn	44	54	.449
Cincinnati	44	55	.444
Philadelphia	38	56	.404
Boston	37	55	.402

ii

The Yankees were not scheduled on Tuesday, August 2, 1927. The next day the Detroit Tigers were at Yankee Stadium to begin a series. However that afternoon, the Tigers were in Washington, D.C. playing the

Senators. Before the game at Griffith Stadium, Walter Johnson Day was commemorated. Twenty years earlier on August 2, 1907, Johnson, nicknamed "Barney" and the "Big Train," debuted for Washington.

With bands blaring and the crowd cheering, Johnson was honored on the field. Clark Griffith, President of the Washington Club, escorted Secretary of State Frank Kellogg, who presented Johnson with an award, a Distinguished Service Cross from the American League. The first award of its kind, the cross was studded with twenty diamonds, one for each year Johnson played with the Senators, honoring his brilliant career.

General Anton Stephan, Chairman of the Citizen's Committee, read a letter from President Calvin Coolidge, who was at the Summer White House at Rapid City, South Dakota. In remembering Johnson's anniversary, the President wrote: "I am sure that I speak for all when I say he has been a wholesome influence in clean living and clean sport."

At the climax of the ceremonies, the crowd of 20,000 cried out for a speech from Johnson.

"There's lots I'd like to say, but I can't." Johnson told the fans. "It's been a wonderful day and I want you all to know that I appreciate it."

Johnson pitched into the ninth that afternoon, but the Tigers rallied off Garland Braxton and Firpo Marberry and won, 7 to 6.

In other American League action, the White Sox and Athletics divided a twin bill as Chicago won the first game, 7 to 4, and Philadelphia the second, 6 to 5 in the twelfth inning at Shibe Park. In the first contest, Chicago's Bibb Falk had a perfect day at the plate with four hits and figured in all the scoring. In the finale, Mickey Cochrane's home run in the twelfth was the decisive blow.

At Boston, the Browns and Red Sox split a doubleheader as St. Louis's Lefty Stewart out pitched Danny MacFayden, 3 to 2, in the first game. Boston's Hal Wiltse limited the Browns to two hits, 3 to 0, in the second.

In Chicago, the Cubs increased their lead over the Pirates to a game and one-half by routing the Phillies, 6 to 2, at Wrigley Field. The Cubs scored four runs in the second against Alex Ferguson. In Pittsburgh, the Braves swept the three game series with the Pirates with a victory, 5 to 2. Boston's Kent Greenfield scattered nine hits. Pirate hurler

Carmen Hill was forced to leave the game in the seventh when he was injured after dropping Joe Harris's throw at first base.

At Sportsman's Park, the Cardinals rallied for six runs in the eighth and won the final game of the series from the Giants, 6 to 2. In Cincinnati, the Reds took both games of a doubleheader at Redland Field from the Robins, 3 to 1 and 5 to 4.

The Yankees played the Detroit Tigers in a doubleheader at the Stadium on Wednesday, August 3, 1927. Miller Huggins started right-handers Urban Shocker and George Pipgras, and Tigers' manager George Moriarty went with right-handers Lil Stoner and Sam Gibson.

First Game
The Line-Ups

Tigers	Yankees
Jack Warner 3b	Earle Combs cf
Charlie Gehringer 2b	Mark Koenig ss
Heinie Manush cf	Babe Ruth rf
Bob Fothergill lf	Lou Gehrig 1b
Harry Heilmann rf	Bob Meusel lf
Johnny Neun 1b	Tony Lazzeri 2b
Bernie DeViveiros ss	Mike Gazella 3b
Larry Woodall c	Pat Collins c
Lil Stoner p	Dutch Ruether p

With the Yankees trailing 2 to 0, in the second, Gehrig hit his thirty-sixth home run off Stoner into the right field bleachers. The Yanks went on to score four more runs after Meusel singled, Lazzeri doubled, Gazella walked, and Collins and Shocker singled. Leading 5 to 2, the Yankees had another chance to score but failed when Gazella tripled in the fourth but was out at the plate on a squeeze play.

The Tigers came up in the fifth trailing by three.

An error, two singles, and a home run with a man on base by Harry Heilmann into the left field bleachers gave Detroit a 6 to 5 lead. With one out, Huggins brought in Wilcy Moore, a right-hander, who retired the side. Stoner, meanwhile, settled down and worked out of trouble when needed.

In the sixth, Lazzeri tripled with none out, but Stoner retired the next three batters. Meusel opened the eight with a single, his third hit, but he never reached second. In a last ditch effort, Morehart opened the ninth and got as far as second before Stoner retired the side.

Final score: Tigers 6, Yankees 5 (First game).

In the second game, Pipgras pitched very well. In the first six innings he gave up only three singles. In the seventh, two hits, an error and a walk led to two runs. The Yankees, meanwhile, hit Gibson well, capped by a four-run rally in the seventh and a home run by Gehrig.

Going into the ninth, the Yankee led 8 to 2. Pipgras was still on the mound when he walked Manush and Fothergill singled. Huggins decided not to take any chances on the Tigers rallying again and brought in Moore, who walked Heilmann. Neun singled. McManus forced Neun and Bassler singled. The Tigers had four runs across the plate. Moore, however, retired Blue and fanned Warner to end the game.

Final score: Yankees 8, Tigers 6 (Second game)

Yankee Notebook for Wednesday, August 3, 1927: Gehrig's home run was his thirty-sixth . . . The Yankees had a total of eleven hits off Stoner . . . Meusel had three singles . . . Lazzeri doubled and tripled . . . Gazella singled and tripled . . . In the first game, Shocker (12-6) took the loss. He went 4 1/3 innings giving up eight hits, walking none, and striking out none . . . Moore finished, pitching the last 4 2/3. He gave up only three hits, walking one, and striking out two . . . In the field, Koenig and Gazella made errors. For Gazella, it was his first of the season.

Moore (11-5) made his second appearance of the doubleheader when he replaced Pipgras in the second game . . . Pipgras went eight innings, giving up only six hits. He walked five and struck out five . . . With two runners on in the ninth, Moore gave up two hits, but he retired the side, striking out one . . . Heilmann did not have a hit in the game ending his seventeen-consecutive-game streak.

The Yankees had thirteen hits off Gibson and George Smith, who pitched the eighth . . . Gehrig's second home run of the doubleheader was his thirty-seventh, and he led Ruth by three . . . Gazella had two doubles and Meusel and Ruth one each . . . The Yankees had four sacrifices; one each by Gehrig, Lazzeri, and Gazella . . . Meusel, Combs and Ruth made errors.

In addition to threatening Ruth's home run record of 59 in 1921, Gehrig was also challenging the Babe's record of 171 runs driven in, also set that season. With his second home run, Gehrig had 132 runs driven in with fifty-one more games to play.

At Shibe Park in Philadelphia, the Athletics won both games of a doubleheader from the Indians, 9 to 2, and 7 to 4. In the first game, Philadelphia hit Joe Shaute hard, and Ed Rommel held Cleveland to seven hits. In the second game, the Athletics scored three runs in the fifth to put the game beyond reach. In Boston, Charley Ruffing outpitched Tommy Thomas as the Red Sox defeated the White Sox, 2 to 1. Boston's victory was the club's seventh in its last ten games. Rain postponed the game between the Browns and Senators at Washington, D.C.

That day the Cubs easily won the opening game of the series with the Braves, 12 to 1, at Wrigley Field. It was Hal Carlson's eighth victory in ten starts since coming to the Cubs from the Phillies. At Forbes Field, Paul Waner's home run with two on capped a five-run rally in the sixth as the Pirates defeated the Phillies, 9 to 6. In St. Louis, Jesse Haines shutout the Robins 4 to 0. Rain postponed the game between the Giants and Reds at Cincinnati.

Ban Johnson's Boys' Day was celebrated at Yankee Stadium on Thursday, August 4, 1927. Ten thousand boys were packed into the left field bleachers as guests of Colonel Ruppert. On the field before the game, the Babe managed a team from the Boys' Club of New York against Tigers' manager George Moriarty's group from the Cyprus Team of Brooklyn. The fans enjoyed watching the Babe give advice to the boys. The game was called at the end of five innings with the score 3 to 3.

Miller Huggins sent Dutch Ruether, a left-hander, to the mound. Moriarty countered with right-hander Ownie Carroll, the former college star of Holy Cross. Opening the game, Ruether retired Warner and Gehringer; however, Manush, Fothergill, and Heilmann singled. When Lazzeri's bad throw to catch Heilmann off first allowed Fothergill to come home from third base, the Tigers led 2 to 0. The Yankees scored one in the bottom of that inning after Combs and Koenig singled, and Ruth hit into a double play.

The Tigers added one run in the third and one in the fourth. Trailing 4 to 1, the Yankees picked up a run in the fourth on a walk to Ruth, a single by Gehrig, and Meusel's infield out.

With one out in the ninth, Gehringer singled and stole second. Manush then singled and went all the way to third as Meusel's throw to the plate got past Collins. Fothergill, a right-handed batter, was due up next. Huggins brought in Bob Shawkey, a right-hander. Fothergill greeted Shawkey with a single, scoring Manush. The Yankees came up in the ninth trailing, 6 to 2. Both Ruth and Gehrig batted in the inning but could do nothing.

Final score: Tigers 6, Yankees 2.

Yankee Notebook for Thursday, August 4, 1927: Carroll pitched very well, giving up only five hits . . . Gehrig had a single and double . . . Collins tripled in the fifth with one out but was stranded at third . . . On the base paths, the Yankees did not have a runner reach first after Gehrig's double in the sixth with two outs . . . Ruether (12-3) took the loss for New York. He went 8 1/3 and gave up eleven hits, walking four, and striking out three . . . Shawkey pitched 2/3 of an inning and gave up one hit . . . For Detroit, Heilmann had two singles, a double, and triple . . . Gehringer had three singles . . . Defensively, Meusel and Lazzeri each made an error.

In Washington, D.C., Tom Zachary and Sloppy Thurston both pitched well as the Senators took a twin bill from the Browns, 5 to 1 and 11 to 2. Zachary gave up only four hits to his former team in the opener. Thurston scattered nine hits in the finale. At Shibe Park, Garland Buckeye blanked the Athletics as the Indians won, 3 to 0. In Boston, the Red Sox won their second in a row over the White Sox, 2 to 1. It was Boston's third consecutive victory.

At Wrigley Field, Cliff Heathcote's triple in the eighth scored two runs as the Cubs defeated the Braves, 5 to 4. Meanwhile, the Pirates drew one-half game closer to the Cubs after taking both games of a doubleheader from the Phillies, 8 to 5 and 7 to 3 at Forbes Field. In

Cincinnati, the Giants made it six of eight in the West with a victory over the Reds, 4 to 1. Larry Benton limited Cincinnati to six hits. At Sportsman's Park, Robins' hurler Bill Clark, with help from Jumbo Jim Elliott, stopped the Cardinals, 4 to 2.

Although the Washington Senators won twice the day before, the Yankees went into the final game of the series with the Detroit Tigers with an eleven and one-half game lead. Miller Huggins was a little concerned, however, with the club's play. The Yankees had not lost a series all season; however, they recently split the series with the Indians and needed a victory that day, Friday, August 5, 1927, to break even with the Tigers.

Yankees' catcher Pat Collins was in the line-up that day for his bat although he had started the day before. It was the first time that season one of the club's catchers played in two games in succession. Huggins sent Waite Hoyt against right-hander Ken Holloway. Both were right-handers.

Trailing 2 to 0, the Yankees came to bat in the bottom of the first. With one out, Koenig singled but was forced by Ruth. Gehrig then walked. When Meusel singled, Ruth scored, and Gehrig raced to third. After Lazzeri singled, Gehrig and Meusel scored. The Yankees led 3 to 2. In the third, Ruth's double against the center field bleacher, and Gehrig's triple added one more run. With the Yankees leading 4 to 2, Moriarty brought in right-hander George Smith, who retired the side.

It began to rain in the fifth.

As soon as the tarpaulin was spread on the infield it stopped raining. The game went on. Ruth came up to bat against Smith in the eighth. The Babe hit a long drive that dropped over the wire screen and into the right field bleachers for his thirty-fifth home run. Hoyt only gave up six hits after the first inning.

Final score: Yankees 5, Tigers 2.

Yankee Notebook for Friday, August 5, 1927: With the home run, Ruth trailed Gehrig by two in what some in the press have called the Great American Home Run Handicap . . . Ruth also doubled . . . Gehrig tripled, Lazzeri singled and doubled . . . Hoyt (15-4) gave up nine hits, walked none, and struck out two . . . The Chicago White Sox were in town next for a three-game series.

At Griffith Stadium in Washington, D.C., the Senators scored ten runs in the fourth and went on to defeat the Browns, 17 to 8. Washington's Goose Goslin hit his ninth home run. In Boston, Ira Flagstead's two triples led the Red Sox over the White Sox, 4 to 1, at Fenway Park. The victory gave Boston a sweep of the series and its fourth straight win. Rain postponed the game between the Indians and Athletics at Philadelphia.

On Ladies' Day at Wrigley Field, the Cubs increased their lead over the Pirates with a victory over the Braves, 5 to 2. Percy Jones held the visitors to five hits. He also had four hits in four times at the plate. In Cincinnati, Adolfo Luque held the Giants to five hits as the Reds won 3 to 0. Only one Giants' runner reached second base in the last eight innings.

At Forbes Field, Cy Williams had a perfect day at bat with a home run, triple, double, single, and walk and led the Phillies over the Pirates, 9 to 7. Williams's home run was his twenty-third and led the National League. A record 14,643 women on Ladies' Day at Sportsman's Park saw the Robins defeat the Cardinals on fifteen hits, 5 to 2, winning two out of three in the series.

Major League Standings
August 5, 1927
American League

	Won	Lost	P.C.
New York	75	30	.714
Washington	62	40	.608
Detroit	55	46	.542
Philadelphia	54	49	.524
Chicago	51	55	.481
Cleveland	43	61	.413
St. Louis	40	62	.392
Boston	33	70	.320

National League

	Won	Lost	P.C.
Chicago	62	39	.614
Pittsburgh	60	41	.594
St. Louis	57	45	.559
New York	56	49	.533
Cincinnati	47	56	.456
Brooklyn	46	57	.447
Boston	38	58	.396
Philadelphia	39	60	.394

Chapter 28

On the Road

Before leaving on the club's last road trip west, the Yankees hosted the Chicago White Sox in New York. For the start of a three game series on Saturday, August 6, 1927, Herb Pennock, a left-hander, faced the White Sox's ace right-hander, Ted Lyons.

The Line-Ups

White Sox	Yankees
Alex Metzler cf	Earle Combs cf
Willie Kamm 3b	Mark Koenig ss
Bill Barrett rf	Babe Ruth rf
Earl Sheely 1b	Lou Gehrig 1b
Bibb Falk lf	Bob Meusel lf
Aaron Ward 2b	Tony Lazzeri 2b
Roger Peckinpaugh ss	Joe Dugan 3b
Moe Berg c	Benny Bengough c
Ted Lyons p	Herb Pennock p

Pennock opened the game by giving up three hits and a walk. The Yankees trailed 2 to 0 coming to bat in the first. On Lyon's third pitch, Combs hit a home run into the right field bleachers. The Yanks took a 3 to 2 lead in the second after Pennock drove in two runs with a single to right.

Both Pennock and Lyons sailed along. Pennock gave up a hit in the third, fourth, and fifth. Lyons was equally as tough giving up only a base hit in the fourth and the fifth. Bengough, the Yankees' catcher, made a gutsy play at the plate in the fifth. Barrett hit a long triple and was heading home when Ruth's throw went over the catcher's head. When Barrett arrived home he found Bengough completely covering the plate. Barrett barreled into the catcher who dumped him over his head. Bengough then took Gehrig's throw from the backstop and tagged the runner out.

Going to the sixth, the Yankees still led 3 to 2. Suddenly, Pennock gave up three successive hits; the third a bunt that was pushed past him. With no one out, Huggins called in Wilcy Moore, a right-hander, who gave up two more hits and three runs. After Ray Morehart pinch-hit for Moore in the seventh, right-hander Bob Shawkey finished, surrendering a run in the ninth.

Final score: White Sox 6, Yankees 3.

Yankee Notebook for Saturday, August 6, 1927: That day's loss made five defeats in the last nine games for the Yanks . . . Ruth and Gehrig went hitless . . . The Babe struck out his first two times at bat, fouled to the third baseman, tapped a ball in front of the catcher and was thrown out . . . Gehrig did not fare any better. He grounded to second twice, bounced to the box, and struck out in his last trip to the plate . . . The Yankees had only eight hits off Lyons: Lazzeri and Dugan each had two . . . Pennock (11-7) went five innings, giving up nine hits, walking one, and striking out two . . . Moore and Shawkey pitched two a piece; each walked one and struck out one.

At Shibe Park in Philadelphia, the Athletics and Browns divided a doubleheader with Philadelphia winning the first game on Jimmy Dykes's single, 5 to 4, in the thirteenth inning, and St. Louis won the second, 2 to 0, behind the two-hit shutout of General Crowder. In Washington, D.C. Walter Miller scattered six hits as the Indians defeated the Senators in the first game of that series, 3 to 1, at Griffith Stadium. The Red Sox won their fifth game in a row with a victory over the Tigers in the first game, 4 to 2, at Fenway Park. Hal Wiltse outpitched Earl Whitehill.

In Chicago, the Cubs took a three game lead with a 6 to 2 victory over the Robins at Wrigley Field. Sheriff Blake held Brooklyn to six hits. Hack Wilson hit his twentieth home run. At Forbes Field, the Giants crushed the Pirates, 9 to 2. Carmen Hill was knocked out of the box in the fourth. Freddie Fitzsimmons stopped Pittsburgh on nine hits. New York's manager John McGraw sent southpaw Don Songer to Toronto for left-hander Jim Faulkner, who was scheduled to join the Giants in the middle of September.

At St. Louis, Grover Cleveland Alexander scattered seven hits as the Cardinals defeated the Braves in the first game of that series, 4 to 1. St Louis' Frankie Frisch and Les Bell homered.

With a crowd of 35,000 at Yankee Stadium in the Bronx on a gray and overcast day, the Yankees and Chicago White Sox met again on Sunday, August 7, 1927. Right-handers Urban Shocker and Ted Blankenship pitched that afternoon.

The Yankees came up in the fourth trailing 1 to 0 on Ward's home run to left. Gehrig opened that inning with a single to center. When Metzler misplayed the ball in center field, Gehrig ended up at third base. After Meusel grounded to Blankenship, Lazzeri walked. Dugan then singled, loading the bases. Bengough then tripled, scoring the runners. When Shocker bunted safely, Bengough scampered home. The Yankees led 4 to 1.

The White Sox did not quit.

The visitors scored two more runs in the fifth on a single by Metzler, a triple by Kamm, and a base hit by Barrett. With the score 4 to 3, Falk opened the sixth with a single. At that point, Huggins brought Wilcy Moore into the game. He retired the side.

As the game went into the seventh, eighth, and ninth, Moore pitched very well; his sinker baffled the White Sox. Working the last four innings, Moore gave up only one hit. No batter got as far as second base.

Final score: Yankees 4, White Sox 3.

Yankee Notebook for Sunday, August 7, 1927: Ruth went hitless but hit two balls that barely missed being home runs . . . One was hit straightaway that Metzler caught on the running track. The other just landed foul in the right field bleachers . . . Gehrig's only hit was the single that began the rally in the fourth . . . The Yanks managed only seven hits off Blankenship . . . Combs singled twice and Bengough tripled.

Shocker (13-6) yielded ten hits, walking one, and striking out two . . . In relief, Moore walked one and struck out three . . . Behind the plate, Bengough threw out two runners in the first; however, he was charged with an error later in the game.

The only other game played in the American League was in Washington, D.C. where Bump Hadley held the Indians to seven hits as the Senators won 12 to 3. Washington's third baseman Bobby Reeves had fourteen chances and played flawlessly.

In the National League, 35,000 fans at Wrigley Field saw the Cubs edge the Robins, 6 to 5 in eleven innings. Hack Wilson's single with two runners on the bases decided the game. The win was Chicago's eighth in a row and gave them a three and one-half lead. After an early shower at Sportsman's Park, the Cardinals defeated the Braves, 6 to 4. The big blow was Wattie Holm's home run in the eighth with one on. With a crowd of 20,000 at Redland Field, the Reds took both games of a doubleheader from the Phillies, 6 to 1 and 2 to 1. Jakie May struck out eleven Phillies in the first game. Red Lucas outpitched Les Sweetland in the second.

Rain cancelled the game between the Yankees and Chicago White Sox in New York on Monday, August 8, 1927. Although the Yankees had a twelve game lead, Miller Huggins was concerned about the team's performance. The club had split their last three series. Huggins felt the team needed to play better. Looking ahead, the Yankees played in Philadelphia the next day and then traveled to Washington for a four game series.

Huggins knew the Senators would have to sweep the Yankees to make a dent in their lead. Mathematically, the club had forty-seven more games to play. Even if the Yankees played .500 baseball, the Senators would have to win thirty-seven of their remaining forty-nine games just to tie. Chances were the Yankees would play better and the Senators worse.

The Yanks, however, took nothing for granted. It was announced that day the Yanks had purchased Gene Robertson, a former third baseman for the Browns, from the St. Paul Club of the American Association.

In Washington, D.C., the Indians knocked Walter Johnson from the mound in the sixth and defeated the Senators, 6 to 1. Joe Shaute held Washington to seven hits. That night the Senators announced that the club picked up outfielder Bill Lamar on waivers from the Athletics. At Boston's Fenway Park, the Red Sox won their sixth straight game defeating the Tigers, 3 to 2. Buddy Meyer scored the winning run in the third with two outs. Rain postponed the game between the Browns and Athletics at Philadelphia.

The games between the Giants and Pirates, Robins and Cubs (2 innings), and Braves and Cardinals were also postponed because of rain.

Major League Standings
August 8, 1927
American League

	Won	Lost	P.C.
New York	76	31	.710
Washington	63	42	.600
Detroit	55	48	.534
Philadelphia	55	50	.524
Chicago	52	56	.481
Cleveland	45	62	.421
St. Louis	41	63	.394
Boston	35	70	.333

National League

	Won	Lost	P.C.
Chicago	64	39	.621
Pittsburgh	60	42	.588
St. Louis	59	45	.567
New York	57	49	.538
Cincinnati	49	56	.467
Brooklyn	46	59	.438
Boston	38	60	.388
Philadelphia	39	62	.386

ii

On Tuesday, August 9, 1927, the Yankees played the Philadelphia Athletics for one game at Shibe Park. That afternoon Dutch Ruether and Rube Walberg, both left-handers, faced each other. Joe Bush, who was recently released by the Pirates and Giants, pitched batting practice for the Athletics. Bush began his career with Connie Mack in 1912.

Before the game, Herb Pennock brought a youngster to the park, and he began throwing to Benny Bengough. His name was Mathewson, a real good name for a pitcher some thought. Huggins, Gehrig, Hoyt, Combs, Koenig, Collins, and Pennock watched as Mathewson pitched. The opinion was that he had a chance to make the major leagues.

The Line-Ups

Yankees	Athletics
Earle Combs cf	Max Bishop 2b
Mark Koenig ss	Sammy Hale 3b
Babe Ruth lf	Walt French rf
Lou Gehrig 1b	Ty Cobb cf
Bob Meusel rf	Mickey Cochrane c
Tony Lazzeri 2b	Jimmy Dykes 1b
Joe Dugan 3b	Zach Wheat lf
Pat Collins c	Chick Galloway ss
Dutch Ruether p	Rube Walberg p

The Athletics scored in the second on doubles by Cobb and Dykes and added another in the third on Koenig's error and a double by French. Already leading 2 to 0, the Athletics scored three more runs in the sixth as Cochrane opened with a double and moved to third on Dykes's sacrifice. Wheat's single scored Cochrane. Bishop then singled to right, scoring Wheat. When Meusel's throw from right field to third base sailed to the stands, Galloway crossed the plate. Huggins then brought George Pipgras, a right-hander, into the game.

The Athletics added one more run in the seventh and two more in the eighth, which made the score 8 to 0. Meanwhile, Walberg allowed only five hits over eight innings. On the bright side, Gehrig came to bat in the ninth and hit his thirty-eighth home run over the right field wall for the Yankees' only run of the day.

Final score: Athletics 8, Yankees 1.

Yankee Notebook for Tuesday, August 9, 1927. The loss was the Yankees' sixth of the last eleven games. The team was not pitching or batting well and the defense was poor . . . With the exception of Gehrig's double and home run, the team managed only four other singles off Walberg . . . Ruth went through his third successive game without a hit . . . Ruether (12-4) and Pipgras gave up thirteen hits . . . Philadelphia's Cobb and French had three hits each . . . In the field, Combs, Meusel, and Koenig made errors.

The only other action in the American League was in Washington, D.C. Sloppy Thurston scattered nine hits as the Senators won over the Indians, 4 to 2, and split their four-game series. Rain postponed the game between the Tigers and Red Sox at Boston.

With a mid-week record crowd of 40,000 at Wrigley Field, the Robins and Cubs split a doubleheader as Chicago won the first game 2 to 0 and Brooklyn won the second, 5 to 4. The loss broke Chicago's nine game winning streak and reduced their lead to three games over the Pirates. In Pittsburgh, Paul Waner doubled home his brother Lloyd with two outs in the ninth breaking a tie score. Waner's timely hit gave the Pirates a 7 to 6 victory over the Giants in the second game of the series.

In the club house at Griffith Stadium in Washington, D.C. on Wednesday, August 10, 1927, Yankees' skipper Miller Huggins told reporters he thought the club was in a slump. Huggins felt the club needed to win three out of four in the series with the second-place Washington Senators or see the team's lead diminish. That afternoon Waite Hoyt, a right-hander, opposed left-hander Tom Zachary.

The Line-Ups

Yankees	Senators
Earle Combs cf	Sam Rice rf
Mark Koenig ss	Bucky Harris 2b

Babe Ruth rf	Tris Speaker cf
Lou Gehrig 1b	Joe Judge 1b
Bob Meusel lf	Goose Goslin lf
Tony Lazzeri 2b	Muddy Ruel c
Joe Dugan 3b	Ossie Bluege 3b
Pat Collins c	Bobby Reeves ss
Waite Hoyt p	Tom Zachary p

The Yankees got off to a good start. Combs hit a drive off Zachary to centerfield. Speaker first came in on the ball and then reversed himself. The ball landed over his head, and Combs raced on to third base with a triple. Ruth then singled, scoring Combs. Gehrig followed with a single, but the inning ended when Meusel hit into a double play. The Senators tied the game in the second on three successive singles by Judge, Goslin, and Ruel.

In the third, Combs and Koenig both singled, and then the Babe clouted a home run into the left center field bleachers. With Gehrig congratulating Ruth at home plate, the Yankees went ahead 4 to 1. Two innings later, Hoyt walked Ruel and Bluege singled. Hoyt then retired Reeves and Bennie Tate, who batted for Zachary. With two outs, Rice doubled, scoring Ruel and Bluege. Huggins then took Hoyt out and brought in Wilcy Moore, who struck out Stewart. The inning ended with the score in favor of the Yanks, 4 to 3. In the final three innings, Firpo Marberry and Moore battled each other, but neither team scored again.

Final score: Yankees 4, Senators 3.

Clarence Rowland, the home plate umpire, needed a police escort leaving the park. The fans were upset when he called out Reeves on a third strike and disallowed Bluege's claim that a pitch nicked his shirt. Manager Bucky Harris and third base coach Jack Onslow argued vociferously. After the game a crowd gathered at the clubhouse door and waited for Rowland. Police disbursed the angry fans, but they reassembled, and Rowland had to be escorted back to his hotel.

Yankee Notebook for August 10, 1927: Ruth went three-for-four with a home run and two singles, driving in all four runs that afternoon . . . The Babe's thirty-six home run put him two behind

Gehrig's major lead league mark of thirty-eight . . . Combs also had three hits; a triple and two singles . . . The Yankees had nine hits off Zachary and Marberry.

Hoyt (16-4) went 5 2/3 innings and gave up three runs and seven hits. He walked one and struck out four . . . Moore was outstanding . . . The Yankee right-hander finished the game, pitching 3 1/3, striking out the first three batters he faced, and a total of four in his stint . . . Moore allowed one hit and was never threatened.

In Philadelphia, the Athletics behind Lefty Grove stopped the Red Sox, 12 to 2, at Shibe Park. Grove struck out nine and gave up only four singles. Ty Cobb had a triple, double, and single. Attorneys for the Athletics announced that the decision of the Pennsylvania State Supreme Court banning professional Sunday baseball would be appealed to the United States Supreme Court. At Navin Field, three double plays helped Ownie Carroll outpitch Milt Gaston as the Tigers defeated the Browns in the opening game of the series, 2 to 1.

At Forbes Field, the Giants rallied for six runs in the eighth and beat the Pirates, 8 to 3. With the victory the Giants ended their visit in the West having won eight and lost four. In Boston, the Phillies and Braves split a doubleheader with Philadelphia at Braves Field taking the first game, 6 to 0, behind Shucks Pruett. Boston won the second, 5 to 1, as Bob Smith yielded only six hits.

The Yankees and Washington Senators were back in action at Griffith Stadium on the afternoon of Thursday August 11, 1927. Opposing each other were right-handers George Pipgras and Horace Lisenbee, who in his rookie season had pitched exceptionally well, particularly against the Yankees. The Yanks anticipated another tough game. Jack Onslow, the Senators' third base coach was indefinitely suspended as a result of the incident with umpire Clarence Rowland the day before, but manager Bucky Harris was back in the line-up.

Lisenbee and Pipgras were in total control over the first five innings.

With no score in the sixth, Combs singled for his third successive hit. Koenig then smacked a double to left. When Goslin threw wild to third base, Combs sped home with the first run of the game. The Senators answered with two runs in the bottom half of the sixth as

Lisenbee tripled and scored on Rice's single. Harris sacrificed, but Rice was thrown out at third. McNeely then singled, stole second, and scored on a single to center by Judge.

The Yankees tied the game in the seventh. Gehrig tripled to left, scoring on Dugan's two out single. Pipgras and Lisenbee dueled through the eighth, ninth, and tenth innings. The Yankees had only two base runners in those innings; Combs beat out a bunt in the eighth and Pipgras singled to right in the tenth.

The Senators' Joe Judge came to bat in the eleventh with one out and tripled off Pipgras to right. Ruth picked up the ball and relayed it to Koenig, who threw wildly to third in an effort to nab the runner. With the ball bouncing toward the seats behind third base, Judge raced home with the winning run.

Final score: Senators 3, Yankees 2 (Eleven innings)

Yankee Notebook for Thursday August 11, 1927: Pipgras (7-2) went the distance, giving up seven hits. He walked two and struck out three . . . The Yanks had only eight hits off Lisenbee with Combs having four of them . . . With Bengough behind the plate, Rice, Bluege, and McNeely each stole a base . . . Ruth also had a stolen base for the Yankees . . . The Yanks were scheduled to play an exhibition game with the Baltimore Orioles the next day in Maryland. The series with the Senators would resume on Saturday in Washington, D.C.

At Shibe Park, the Athletics and Red Sox split a doubleheader as Howard Ehmke threw Philadelphia's first shutout in the first game, 4 to 0. Boston's Slim Harriss blanked the Athletics in the second contest, 2 to 0. In Detroit, Marty McManus's three hits led the Tigers to a victory over the Browns, 6 to 2. Sam Gibson went the distance. At Cleveland's Dunn Field in the opening game of the series, the Indians defeated the White Sox, 2 to 1, in ten innings on Rube Lutzke's double and Lew Fonseca's single. Tommy Thomas and Jake Miller pitched the entire game.

At Wrigley Field, Charlie Root outpitched Adolfo Luque to win his twenty-first victory as the Cubs defeated the Reds, 2 to 0. In St. Louis, Grover Cleveland Alexander allowed only four hits as the Cardinals gained ground on the second-place Pirates with a 2 to 1 win. Jim Bottomley's home run after Frankie Frisch's double in the seventh was the deciding blow.

In New York, Bill Terry's sacrifice fly in the ninth scored Freddy Lindstrom with the winning run as the Giants edged the Robins, 3 to 2. Three walks and a single off Claude Willoughby in the sixth gave the Braves the deciding run over the Phillies, 5 to 4, at Braves Field.

On Friday, August 12, 1927, the Babe was back in his childhood city of Baltimore, where he thoroughly enjoyed himself in an exhibition game with the Orioles. With 7,000 fans at the ballpark, Ruth hit a home run and surprised the crowd when he took the mound in the ninth with the Yankees leading 7 to 4. The Babe last hurled for that same Orioles franchise in 1913. However, Ruth could not recapture the pitching skills of his youth. He gave up four runs, losing the game, 8 to 7. Guy Cantrell pitched the entire game for the Orioles. Cantrell struck out eleven, including Gehrig twice and Ruth once.

With 10,000 Boys' Days guests at Shibe Park, Ty Cobb and Zach Wheat each had four hits off Hal Wiltse as the Athletics handed the Red Sox a 7 to 1 defeat. Eddie Rommel, who showed some of his old form, pitched a complete game for Connie Mack. Rallying for four runs in the eighth off Elam Vangilder and Win Ballou at Navin Field, the Tigers came from behind and defeated the Browns 7 to 3 for the third successive time. In other news, former Boston Red Sox and New York Yankee infielder Everett "Deacon" Scott signed a contract with the Toledo Mud Hens.

At Sportsman's Park, the Cardinals went into a second-place tie with the Pirates after Jesse Haines bested Carmen Hill in a mound duel, 2 to 1, in eleven innings. Jim Bottomley's home run decided the game. After staging rallies in the eighth and ninth innings, the Giants went on to defeat the Robins, 7 to 6, in ten innings, at the Polo Grounds. Rogers Hornsby homered into the upper right field stands with the bases loaded in the eighth.

In Boston, the Braves won their fourth of the series from the Phillies, 12 to 6. Doc Gautreau, replaced Boston manager Davy Bancroft in the line-up. Gautreau had four hits and played brilliantly.

Back from the one-day trip to Baltimore, the Yankees and Washington Senators played again in the nation's capital on Saturday, August 13,

1927. Before the game, a number of the Yankee players visited ill and injured war veterans at Walter Reed Hospital. The visit visibly affected many of them emotionally. Benny Bengough, the Yankees' catcher, shook his head sympathetically and murmured, "We've got a lot of nerve to howl when we don't get our base hits."

There was a good crowd at Griffith Stadium. Although the bleachers were not filled, the grandstands overflowed. Right-handers Wilcy Moore and Bump Hadley pitched. Moore retired the first two batters in the first. McNeely then doubled down the left field line. Goslin hit a home run to the flagpole in center field.

It was the first home run ever hit off Moore in the majors.

The Yankees came right back and tied the game in the second. With one out, Hadley walked Gehrig, Lazzeri, and Dugan to load the bases. When Bengough singled to right, Gehrig and Lazzeri crossed the plate.

Going to the eighth the score was tied at two. After Hadley fanned Ruth, he walked Gehrig, gave up a single to Meusel, and walked Lazzeri. With the bases filled, Dugan bounced to the box, forcing Gehrig at home for the second out. Believing his chances for scoring were better with a left-handed batter, Huggins sent Dutch Ruether up to bat for Bengough with the bases loaded.

Hadley, who had been wild, threw three successive balls that were not even close. Harris decided to bring his best reliever, right-hander Firpo Marberry, into the game. His first pitch was a strike, but his next pitch was wide and low for ball four. Ruether walked, forcing home Meusel. The Yanks led 3 to 2.

The Yankees picked up three more runs in the ninth. The Senators got one back in their final at bat on a single by Bluege and a double by Bennie Tate, who batted for Marberry.

Final score: Yankees 6, Senators 3.

Yankee Notebook for Saturday, August 13, 1927: The Yankees had only seven hits off Hadley and Marberry, but they walked ten batters . . . Ruth and Gehrig each managed one hit, a single . . . Combs was not feeling well, and after a ball hit by Rice got past him, Huggins replaced him in the fifth with Cedric Durst . . . On the hill, Moore (12-5) gave up eight hits and three runs, striking out one and walking three . . .

One of Moore's walks was an intentional pass to Reeves to load the bases in the fourth to get to Hadley.

In Philadelphia, the Athletics reached Charlie Ruffing for three runs on a walk and three singles in the second and went on to defeat the Red Sox, 6 to 2, at Shibe Park. The victory made it four out of five for the Athletics in the series. Following singles by Harry Heilmann and Heinie Manush, Al Wingo doubled against the left-field fence with two out in the ninth at Navin Field and the Tigers won their fourth straight over the Browns, 8 to 7. In Cleveland, Willis Hudlin allowed only four hits as the Indians shutout the White Sox, 1 to 0.

At Wrigley Field, a pitching duel between Jakie May and Sheriff Blake at Wrigley Field ended in the tenth when Clyde Beck singled with the bases loaded as the Cubs defeated the Reds, 2 to 1. In St. Louis, the Pirates broke a second-place tie with the Cardinals with a 6 to 2 victory. Home runs in New York by Freddy Lindstrom, Rogers Hornsby, and Travis Jackson led the Giants to a victory over the Robins, 5 to 1. At Braves Field, the Braves and Phillies divided a twin bill as Philadelphia's Dutch Ulrich blanked the Braves on only five hits, 5 to 0, and Boston came back to take the second contest, 4 to 3.

It rained heavily through the night and was still drizzling the morning of Sunday, August 14, 1927. The fans and players did not think the game between the Yankees and Washington Senators at Griffith Stadium would be played. However, despite a threatening cloudburst and the infield and outfield drenched in water, the game went on with 20,000 fans at the ball park.

The word in the Yankees' clubhouse was that Clark Griffith did not want to lose the revenue that day since the team was not returning to Washington. On that dreary and wet day, Waite Hoyt, a right-hander, and Tom Zachary, a left-hander, pitched. The Yankees took a 3 to 0 lead in the first when Paschal, playing centerfield for Combs, singled. Koenig also had a base hit. When Ruth forced Koenig at second, Paschal scored. Zachary then walked Gehrig. After Meusel flied to Goslin, Lazzeri doubled sending Ruth and Gehrig home. The Senators scored one run in its half of the first.

The Yankees answered with three more runs in the fourth after Collins walked and Hoyt reached first on Harris's error. When Paschal doubled, Collins scored. Paschal and Hoyt then came around on Ruth's single. The last run of the day was scored by the Senators in the home half of the fourth.

Final score: Yankees 6, Senators 2.

Yankee Notebook for Sunday, August 14, 1927: The outfield was muddy and the playing conditions were bad . . . That afternoon Hoyt (17-4) gave up only five hits; two were doubles by Speaker. The right-hander struck out five and walked none . . . Washington's Garland Braxton and Bobby Burke followed Zachary and they gave up eight hits . . . Paschal had a single and double. Gehrig, Meusel, and Lazzeri doubled . . . The game was played in 1:39.

At Navin Field in Detroit, three errors by second baseman Ski Melillo set up scoring chances for the Tigers as they defeated the Browns for the fifth successive game, 6 to 5. In Cleveland, the White Sox ended their losing streak with a victory over the Indians, 7 to 3. Ted Blankenship went the distance for Chicago.

In Chicago, the Cubs finished a long-home stay with a sweep of the Reds behind the pitching of Percy Jones, 7 to 2. Chicago had won 13 out of 17 games at home with that day's victory. On a damp and overcast day at Sportsman's Park, the Pirates won the final game of that series, 5 to 1, behind the strong pitching of Ray Kremer. The victory left the Cardinals two games behind the Pirates and only one ahead of the Giants, who defeated the Phillies, 3 to 1, at the Polo Grounds. The second game was postponed because of rain. Behind Kent Greenfield at Ebbets Field, the Robins defeated the Braves, 4 to 0. The second contest was rained out.

On the way to Chicago, the Yanks played an exhibition game in Indiana with Indianapolis of the American Association on Monday, August 15, 1927. The Babe gave the overflow crowd of 9,000 a thrill with a soaring home run over the right field fence, but the Yankees lost the game, 8 to 5. Former Senator and Athletic outfielder Wid Mathews had a big day for Indianapolis with two hits, two walks, a stolen base, and four runs scored.

There were no games scheduled in the American League. Only one contest was played in the National League. At Philadelphia's Baker Bowl, the Braves defeated the Phillies in a slugfest, 12 to 11 in ten innings. There were thirty-two hits in the game.

Major League Standings
August 15, 1927
American League

	Won	Lost	P.C.
New York	79	33	.705
Washington	65	45	.591
Detroit	60	48	.556
Philadelphia	60	51	.541
Chicago	53	58	.477
Cleveland	47	64	.423
St. Louis	41	68	.376
Boston	36	74	.327

National League

	Won	Lost	P.C.
Chicago	68	40	.630
Pittsburgh	63	45	.583
St. Louis	61	47	.565
New York	62	50	.554
Cincinnati	49	59	.454
Brooklyn	47	64	.423
Boston	44	62	.415
Philadelphia	41	68	.376

Chapter 29

Herb Pennock

Herb Pennock was tall and fragile-looking for a pitcher. He looked easy to hit, but he was crafty and smart. His best pitches were a fastball, curve, and screwball. Bucky Harris, an admirer of Herb Pennock, managed the Washington Senators when the Yankee southpaw was at his peak.

"Nicest fellow in the world," Harris would say of Pennock. "Off the field that is. On the field, he just stands out there and looks at you . . . and tugs on the bill of his cap . . . and winds up and lets go. The ball is never where you think it's going to be. It was-just a split second before. But when you swing at it, the best you get is a piece of it. You fuss and fume and sweat and holler and he stands out there and looks at you . . . and tugs on the bill of his cap, and—aw, what's the use?"

With its trees and hills and horses and dogs, Marlborough Farm, two miles from Kennett Square, Pennsylvania made for a very pleasant home. Into this tranquil and picturesque setting, Herbert Jeffries Pennock, one of three children of Louisa (Sharp) and Theodore Pennock, was born on February 10, 1894.

The Pennock family was Pennsylvania Quakers of Scotch-Irish origin. Grandfather Pennock had invented road-building equipment, and his son Theodore later sold it. Theodore Pennock was also a great horseman and loved chasing the hounds; young Herb had a pony, which he learned to ride almost before he could walk.

As Herb grew older, the Pennock family began preparing him to eventually attend the University of Pennsylvania. When of age, he was sent to the Friends' School, a Quaker institution in West Town, Pennsylvania. Playing baseball at the age of six, Herb loved the game, but the school did not have an active sports program. Pennock switched to Cedar Craft School, a fashionable prep school in suburban Philadelphia, and he played first base for the school team.

One day in the spring of 1910, Pennock, who was sixteen, was told to pitch the ninth inning of a practice game. Pennock, a left-hander, threw a ball that curved. He struck out the side. The coach was impressed and decided to use him as a pitcher. In his first start, Herb struck out nineteen batters.

Connie Mack of the Philadelphia Athletics soon became interested in the youngster and he sent a scout to watch him. When Mack received a favorable report, he made arrangements for Pennock to play summer ball with a team called the Atlantic City Collegians in the Seashore League. Since the family expected Herb to go to the University of Pennsylvania, the elder Pennock was not happy about the prospect of his son becoming a professional ballplayer. He agreed to allow Herb to play with the Collegians, only if it would not affect his amateur status. It was so arranged, and Pennock went to Atlantic City for $100 a month and board.

When the Seashore League disbanded after a month, the Collegians continued to compete against semi-pro independent clubs. One Sunday three teams, two well-known Negro teams and the Collegians, were scheduled to play in Atlantic City. The Colored Giants and the St. Louis Stars played the first game. The Stars won and played the Collegians in the afternoon. Seventeen year-old Herb Pennock pitched and Earl Mack, son of Connie Mack, caught.

After the Collegians' lead off man singled, stole second, and scored on a base hit in the first inning, Pennock did not surrender a hit. The Collegians won 1 to 0. Afterwards, Earl Mack told Pennock: "You'll get all kinds of offers to pitch when news of this gets out. Do me a favor and don't promise anything until you've talked with Pa. I know he wants you."

In the fall of 1911, Herb Pennock transferred to Wenonah Military Academy in New Jersey. Before leaving for Wenonah, Herb Pennock and Connie Mack made an oral agreement that the young man would sign with the Athletics after school ended.

On May 11, 1912, Pennock signed with the Philadelphia Athletics. Mack invited him to Shibe Park to work out with the club and to watch and learn. Mack told him he would not use him for several weeks. Three days later on May 14, 1912, Pennock was at the far end of the bench at Shibe Park watching the Chicago White Sox pummel the Athletics' starter, John Wesley Coombs. All of a sudden, Mack called out to Pennock to warm up.

Pennock walked to the bullpen in disbelief.

With the White Sox leading 5 to 0 after five innings, Herb Pennock was called into the game.

"Bennock now pitching for Philadelphia," the field announcer incorrectly informed the small crowd through the megaphone. The skinny and frightened eighteen-year old walked in from the bullpen.

"Pitch to the hitter, watch me closely, don't worry," said Jack Lapp, the Athletics' catcher,

Behind Pennock was the Athletics' famous "$100,000" infield of Frank "Home Run" Baker, Jack Barry, Eddie Collins, and Stuffy McInnis. Collins and Barry came over and told him to pitch just as he had in school and not to worry. Pennock pitched well over the final four innings, giving up one hit, two walks, and one run.

Used mainly in relief in 1912 by Connie Mack, Pennock's first major league win was over Walter Johnson and the Washington Senators on June 28, 1912. Pennock pitched the last two innings and was credited with the victory after Johnson gave up a run in the tenth to lose 5 to 4.

Less than a month later, on July 20, 1912, Pennock started his first major league game against Jean Dubuc and the Detroit Tigers but lost 6 to 5. Overall in 1912, He won 1 and lost 2, posted 2 saves, and had a 4.50 era in 17 games. Pennock was wild, in 50 innings he walked 38.

Seeing less action in 1913 due to illness, Pennock appeared in only 14 games in the last few weeks of the season, again mainly in relief. He won 2 and lost 1, with a 5.18 era. Given his opportunity in 1914, Pennock showed good control, speed, and a good curve. He won 11 and lost 4, posted 3 saves, and had a 2.78 era.

The Philadelphia Athletics won their fourth pennant in five years that season, 1914. The club played George Stalling's "Miracle Braves" in the World Series. The Boston Braves had moved from last place to first between July 18, 1914 and August 25, 1914. The Braves ended the season in first by 10 ½ games.

With the Athletics down 3 games to 0 in the World Series, Bob Shawkey started for Philadelphia. A walk and an error led to a Braves' run in the fourth and two more in the fifth. With the Athletics down 3 to 1 after five innings, Connie Mack brought Pennock into the game. Pennock pitched three innings of shutout ball, but Dick Rudolph, the Braves' starter, held the Athletics hitless the rest of the game and Boston won the '14 World Series.

On Opening Day 1915, Connie Mack started Herb Pennock against the Boston Red Sox. It was a memorable game. Pennock had a no-hitter with two outs in the ninth and the Athletics leading 3 to 0. The Red Sox's last batter Harry Hooper hit a slow ground ball to Nap Lajoie, the Athletics' second baseman. Lajoie charged in, bare handed the ball and threw to first base, but Hooper beat the throw. Pennock ended the game with a one-hitter.

Partly due to an inflammation in his arm, he pitched poorly after that. In eleven games, Pennock won 3 and lost 6, with 1 save, and a 5.32 era. Subsequently, Pennock was waived by the Athletics. The story was that Mack was angry with Pennock when the young pitcher did not listen to his instructions in a game pitch situation against the Tigers. He also felt the youngster lacked ambition. Mack was to admit in later years that releasing Pennock was his biggest mistake in baseball.

The Boston Red Sox picked Pennock up on waivers for $2,500, but he had little chance to pitch. In 1915, the Red Sox had a championship team and an excellent pitching staff, which included Ernie Shore, Dutch Leonard, Joe Wood, and Babe Ruth. Pennock was farmed out to Providence, Rhode Island, where he won 6 and lost 4. He appeared in five games late in the season with the Red Sox and had no record.

The 1916 season was no different. Red Sox manager Bill Carrigan did not use him, and Pennock spent most of the season at Buffalo, New York, where he won 7 and lost 6. Pennock appeared in nine games for the Red Sox that season, winning 0, losing 2, 1 save, and a 3.00 era. In 1917, Pennock played in 24 games, mostly in relief, and won 5 and lost 5, with 1 save, and a 3.30 era.

With America at War, Herb Pennock enlisted in the Navy on January 2, 1918, and he and teammate Mike McNally, a Red Sox infielder, shipped out of the Boston Navy Yard. McNally was bound for Queenstown, Ireland, and Pennock for Gibraltar for destroyer duty. After nineteen days at sea, the ship arrived at Queenstown on June 19, 1918. About that time, plans were being made for a big Fourth of July celebration in London. One major event was a baseball game between the Army and Navy. The King and Queen of England attended and both services wanted to win badly.

Someone alerted the naval authorities in London that Herb Pennock, who had pitched for the Athletics and Red Sox, was in Queenstown. Messages flew between London and Queenstown. Soon Pennock was ordered to report to London to prepare for the game. When Pennock told them McNally was also in Queenstown, he was also told to report.

The Stadium at Stamford Bridge was decorated with bunting. With the flags flying and music blaring, the King and Queen of England and a crowd of 60,000 watched Herb Pennock of the Navy oppose Ed Lafitte of the Army. With the Navy leading 2 to 0, Pennock went into the ninth with a no-hit game. With two outs, the Army scored a run on a double and a single, but Pennock and the Navy won, 2 to 1. Afterwards, Pennock stayed in London and served in the Communications Department. He was discharged on December 22, 1918.

Pennock returned to the Boston Red Sox in 1919. The Red Sox's new manager was Ed Barrow, who had succeeded Jack Barry a year earlier. Pennock started a game against the New York Yankees in Boston's second series of the season but was knocked out in five innings.

Weeks went by before Barrow used Pennock again.

On the return from a road trip in the west, Pennock gave notice to the Red Sox that he was through with baseball and would leave the team when it reached Philadelphia for the Memorial Day series. Barrow told him he would get a chance in one of the holiday games, which he did. Pennock pitched a ten-inning game, but lost 2 to 1. After the game, Barrow persuaded Pennock to return to Boston with the team. In his next game, Pennock shutout the White Sox and then beat the Tigers, 2 to 1. Pennock played regularly after that.

Herb Pennock was determined to make himself into a pitcher. He learned to control and pace himself. He also learned to relax during the most critical ball game. Pennock watched the best pitchers from the other teams and remembered the strengths and weaknesses of the batters. His work paid off. He finished the 1919 season with 16 wins and 8 losses and a 2.71 era. Pennock started regularly for the Red Sox from 1920 through 1922, and he won 16, 12, and 10 games, respectively.

In the winter of 1922 Pennock and his family took a trip to Japan. On January 31, 1923, he returned to the United States and opened a newspaper to the sports page. Pennock read that he had been traded from Boston to the New York Yankees for Camp Skinner, Norman McMillan, George Murray, and cash.

In February 1923, Pennock reported to the Yankees for spring training camp. He came into his own with the Yanks that season; Pennock won 19 and lost 6, with 3 saves and a 3.14 era. His .760 winning percentage was the best in the American League. The Yankees faced the New York Giants in the '23 World Series.

After losing Game One at Yankee Stadium 5 to 4 in the ninth on an inside the park home run by the Giants' Casey Stengel, Pennock started Game Two. He defeated the Giants, 4 to 2, to even the series. Babe Ruth hit a pair of home runs.

In Game Three, Casey Stengel's solo home run gave the Giants a 1 to 0 win. With the Giants leading the series 2 to 1, Bob Shawkey started Game Four for the Yanks. Pennock relieved Shawkey in the eighth, and the Yankees won, 8 to 4. With the series tied at 2 to 2, Joe Bush pitched a three-hitter against the Giants in Game Five and the Yankees won, 8 to 1.

With the Yankees leading the series 3 to 2, Pennock pitched Game Six at the Polo Grounds. The Yankee southpaw gave up four runs in seven innings. With the Yankees trailing 4 to 1 in the eighth, Art Nehf, the Giants' starter, lost his control. Two singles and two walks forced in a run. Rosy Ryan replaced Nehf. After Ruth struck out, Bob Meusel singled. A wild throw from center cleared the bases. The Yankees led 6 to 4. Sad Sam Jones pitched the eighth and ninth and held the Giants scoreless. Pennock was the winning pitcher, his second victory of the series, and the Yankees won their first World Series championship in franchise's history.

Pennock had his best year in 1924. He won 21 and lost 9, with 3 saves, a 2.83 era, and 4 shutouts. However, the Washington Senators won the American League pennant that season by two games over the Yankees. The Yankees had a disastrous season in 1925. Pennock won 16 and lost 17, with 2 saves, and a 2.96 era. Washington won the pennant again. The Yankees finished seventh.

The 1926 season was a different story.

The Yankees won the American League pennant, and Pennock won 23 and lost 11 with 2 saves, and a 3.62 era. He pitched 266 innings, walking only 43, or 1.45 batters a game, the fewest per game in the American League.

Pennock opened the 1926 World Series in New York against the St. Louis Cardinals and Bill Sherdel. Pennock pitched a three-hitter and the Yankees won, 2 to 1. With the series tied at two games apiece, Pennock started Game Five in St. Louis. Sherdel was his opponent again. In another pitching duel, Pennock won in eleven innings, 3 to 2.

After Grover Cleveland Alexander and the Cardinals won game six, the seventh and final game was played at Yankee Stadium. Jesse Haines and Waite Hoyt faced each other. The Cardinals scored three runs in the fourth and led 3 to 2 after six innings. Pennock was brought in and pitched the seventh. With the bases loaded in the Yankees' seventh, Alexander relieved Haines and struck out Lazzeri to end the inning. Pennock and Alexander finished. Neither team scored as the Cardinals won the game and the '26 World Series.

Chapter 30

Final Tour West

On Tuesday, August 16, 1927, the Yankees visited Comiskey Park in Chicago, Illinois for the final time that season. On a dreary afternoon, 20,000 fans watched Herb Pennock, a left-hander, oppose right-hander Tommy Thomas.

The Line-Ups

Yankees	White Sox
Earle Combs cf	Ray Flaskamper ss
Mark Koenig ss	Willie Kamm 3b
Babe Ruth lf	Alex Metzler cf
Lou Gehrig 1b	Bill Barrett rf
Bob Meusel rf	Bibb Falk lf
Tony Lazzeri 2b	Aaron Ward 2b
Joe Dugan 3b	Bud Clancy 1b
John Grabowski c	Moe Berg c
Herb Pennock p	Tommy Thomas p

Combs opened the game with a triple to center. When Koenig grounded to short, Flaskamper tried to get Combs at the plate, but he beat the throw. With Koenig on first, Ruth walked and Gehrig popped to short. Meusel then doubled, sending Koenig home.

The Yankee went ahead 4 to 0 in the third after another walk to Ruth, Gehrig's double, and sacrifice flies by Meusel and Lazzeri. With none on in the fifth, the Babe drove one of Thomas's fast balls high and long over the roof of the double-decked right field stands. That ball was one of the hardest ever hit by Ruth in any park. It was later announced that it was the first time a ball had ever been driven out of Comiskey Park.

Meanwhile, the White Sox could not reach Pennock, who gave up only five hits, one in each of the first five innings. In the seventh, Ward's double and singles by Clancy and Neis, who replaced Falk, led to one run. The Yankees, however, scored three more runs in the eighth off Bert Cole, a left-hander, who had replaced Thomas in the sixth. That rally started with Collins's single and ended with Ruth's double.

Final score: Yankees 8, White Sox 1.

Yankee Notebook for Tuesday, August 16, 1927: Ruth's tremendous home run was his thirty-seventh . . . The Babe trailed Gehrig by one . . . The club had thirteen hits off Thomas and Cole . . . Meusel had a perfect day at the plate with four hits in four plate appearances . . . Combs, Ruth, and Collins each had two hits . . . The team made four sacrifices—Pennock (2), Meusel, and Lazzeri.

Pennock (12-7) gave up nine hits; Ward had three hits and Berg two, both doubles . . . The Yankee left-hander walked one and struck out two . . . Meusel stole a base . . . The Yanks played errorless ball in the field . . . Ruth made a perfect threw from deep left field in the first when he doubled Flaskamper at the plate.

At Navin Field in Detroit, the Tigers overcame a five run Red Sox lead to defeat the visitors, 10 to 7. Successive home runs by Harry Heilmann and Charlie Gehringer in the fifth put the Tigers back in the game. Boston catcher Fred Hofmann was carried from the field unconscious in the sixth after he was knocked down in a collision at the plate with Johnny Neun. Hofmann had a broken nose.

The Athletics opened their Western trip by taking two games from the Indians, 6 to 3 and 8 to 0 at Dunn Field. Sammy Hale's triple with the bases filled was the big blow in the first game. Poor defense hurt the Indians in the second contest. Rain postponed the game between the Senators and Browns at St. Louis.

In Brooklyn, Charlie Root won his 22nd game of the year as he shutout the Robins, 3 to 0, at Ebbets Field. It was the Cubs' 4th straight victory and the 14th win out of 16 games played that year against Brooklyn. At the Polo Grounds, Rogers Hornsby hit a home run into the upper right-field boxes with two on the bases that gave the Giants an 8 to 4 win over the Pirates.

In the series opener at Boston's Braves Field, the Cardinals broke a 3 to 3 tie in the eleventh and defeated the Braves, 5 to 3. Cardinals' manager and catcher Bob O'Farrell had five hits in six plate appearances. Frankie Frisch played brilliantly in the field. At Baker Bowl, the Phillies took the opener of a four game series with the Reds, 5 to 3.

At Comiskey Park, the Yankees and Chicago White Sox played the second game of the series on Wednesday, August 17, 1927. Right-handers George Pipgras and Sarge Connally were on the mound for the Yankees and White Sox.

The Yanks found themselves down 2 to 0 in the first after a walk to Hunnefield, a single by Kamm, Metzler's sacrifice, and a single by Falk. As the game went on Connally pitched very well. His assortment of slow balls, curves, and fast balls frustrated the visitors. However, in the fifth Gehrig doubled and scored on a foul sacrifice fly by Meusel and a fair sacrifice fly by Lazzeri.

Trailing 2 to 1, the Yankees came up in the eighth. Connally walked Lazzeri and Huggins sent Cedric Durst, a left-handed batter, to bat for Dugan. Durst popped out to Clancy. Huggins then had Dutch Ruether, another left-handed batter, hit for Bengough. Ruether singled to left, and Julie Wera ran for him.

Ray Morehart batted for Pipgras and he forced Lazzeri at third. Down to the team's last out, Combs singled, scoring Wera with the tying run. Koenig then walked, and Ruth came up with bases loaded. On a three and two count, Connally struck Ruth out on a change of pace to end the inning.

Wilcy Moore replaced Pipgras in the eighth. Moore and Connally pitched well. The game went into extra innings tied at two. With Connally on the mound in the eleventh, Ruth came up again. The Babe swung at one of Connally's curves and clouted the ball into the left field stands. Trotting around the bases, he was greeted by a smiling Gehrig at home plate. The Yankees led 3 to 2. Moore retired the White Sox in the bottom of the eleventh.

Final score: Yankees 3, White Sox 2 (Eleven innings).

Yankee Notebook for Wednesday, August 17, 1927: Ruth's game wining home run was his thirty-eighth . . . The Babe and Gehrig were tied for the major league lead. Cy Williams, of the National League's Philadelphia Phillies, was third with twenty-three.

Connally allowed only five hits in eleven innings and only three in the regulation nine . . . Moore (13-5) was spectacular for New York. In four innings of relief work, he gave up only two hits, walking none, and striking out one . . . Pipgras also pitched well, giving up four hits and two runs, while walking two and striking out two . . . The Yanks were flawless again in the field.

That day the Senators and Browns split a doubleheader at Sportsman's Park as Horace Lisenbee scattered four hits as Washington took the opener 4 to 1. St. Louis came back to win the finale 3 to 2 on Frank O'Rourke's single in the ninth. At Navin Field, Josh Billings, a former Brown University star, made his major league debut for the Tigers and defeated the Red Sox, 6 to 2. Billings allowed only four hits.

In Cleveland, Lefty Grove scattered eight hits and outpitched Willis Hudlin as the Athletics beat the Indians for their third successive win, 4 to 1. Ty Cobb tripled and singled, and Zach Wheat had a pair of doubles for the Athletics.

At the Polo Grounds in New York, Carmen Hill stopped the Giants on fives hits as the Pirates won, 4 to 1. The victory ended the Giants' six game winning streak. The Cubs lost ground to the Pirates when the Robins defeated them with a come-from-behind victory in the ninth, 6 to 5. In Boston, the Cardinals pounded Charlie Robertson in the seventh and went on to beat the Braves, 7 to 3. At Baker Bowl, Adolfo Luque held the Phillies to four hits as he outdueled Dutch Ulrich and the Reds edged the Phillies, 2 to 1. The game was played in 1:29.

With four victories in a row, Yankee manager Miller Huggins thought the club had regained some of the form it exhibited earlier in the season. Every aspect of the game, pitching, hitting and fielding, had improved. On that bright note, the Yanks took the field on a chilly afternoon at Comiskey Park in Chicago on Thursday, August 18, 1927.

Right-hander Urban Shocker pitched for the Yanks. Ted Lyons, a right-hander, took the hill for the White Sox.

Trailing 4 to 1, the Yankees batted in the fourth and picked up one run on a double by Lazzeri and a single by Dugan. In the fifth, the Yanks scored two runs more on singles by Combs, Gehrig, and Meusel.

In the eighth, the Yankees tied the score at four on Gehrig's double and Meusel's single to center. After Huggins sent Ben Paschal up to bat for Shocker in the ninth, Wilcy Moore pitched the last of that inning, retiring the White Sox.

Neither team scored in the tenth and eleventh.

In the twelfth, Koenig opened with a single, and Ruth sacrificed him to second. Lyons purposely walked Gehrig. Meusel fanned. Lazzeri then beat out a swinging bunt to third, loading the bases. Mike Gazella, who had replaced Dugan at third an inning earlier, came up to face Lyons. Gazella watched two strikes and three balls go by. When ball four was called, Gazella trotted to first and Koenig came home with the go ahead run. Moore set the White Sox down in the bottom half of the twelfth, and the Yankees won.

Final score: Yankees 5, White Sox 4 (Twelve innings)

Yankee Notebook for Thursday, August 18, 1927: For the second day in a row Moore (14-5) came in and pitched four innings in relief. He gave up only two hits, walked one, and struck out none . . . Shocker, who started for the Yanks, went eight and yielded nine hits and four runs . . . The Yankees had fourteen hits off Lyons, who went the distance . . . Lazzeri had four hits in six at bats; Dugan three and Ruth and Gehrig two each . . . Lazzeri, Gehrig, Ruth, and Dugan also doubled . . . The Yankees played for the final time in Chicago the next day and then traveled to Detroit and St. Louis.

At Sportsman's Park in St. Louis, the Browns made it two out of three from the Senators as they beat the visitors in the twelfth 6 to 5, when George Sisler scored on Ski Mellilo's sacrifice fly. In Cleveland, the Indians broke their four-game losing streak with a victory over the Athletics, 2 to 1. Cleveland's Joe Shaute scattered eight hits. Rain postponed the game between the Red Sox and Tigers at Detroit.

Bad weather canceled the National League games that day in New York, Boston, and Philadelphia.

The final game of the season for the Yankees at Comiskey Park in Chicago took place on a cold and wind swept afternoon on Ladies' Day, Friday, August 19, 1927. The Yanks went into the game with a fifteen game lead in the American League. Right-handers Waite Hoyt, who went into the game with seven straight victories, and Ted Blankenship faced each other.

The White Sox reached Hoyt for single runs in the first, third, and fourth innings. Meanwhile, Blankenship held the Yankees to only three hits in the first five. The Yanks came up in the sixth down 3 to 0, but cut the deficit to two runs on singles by Koenig and Ruth and a double by Gehrig.

Going to the ninth trailing 3 to 1, Gehrig opened the inning with a home run, and the Yankees pulled within one. After Durst, who played right field in place of Meusel, fanned, Lazzeri doubled to left. However, Dugan forced Lazzeri at third, and Collins was retired to end the game.

Final score: White Sox 3, Yankees 2.

Yankee Notebook for Friday, August 19, 1927: Blankenship held the Yanks to eight hits . . . Gehrig's double and home run were the big hits . . . The Yankee first baseman's thirty-ninth home run gave him one more than Ruth . . . Koenig and Lazzeri each had two hits . . . Ruth managed only a single off Blankenship . . . Hoyt (17-5) took the loss, giving up eight hits and three runs, walking three, and striking out four . . . Behind the plate, Collins made an error . . . Hunnefield and Metzler stole bases . . . The Yankees boarded a train to Cleveland after the game.

In St. Louis, the Browns won their third straight game from the Senators, 6 to 1, at Sportsman's Park. Ernie Wingard scattered six hits and hit a home run in the sixth with a man on base. At Navin Field, the Tigers took both games of a doubleheader from the Red Sox, 5 to 2 and 14 to 7, and extended their winning streak to nine games. In Cleveland, Rube Walberg's single in the eighth scored two runs and he won his own game as the Athletics defeated the Indians, 5 to 3.

At Ebbets Field, the Cubs and Robins split a doubleheader with Chicago winning the first game 3 to 0 and Brooklyn the second, 6 to 1. In New York, the Pirates and Giants divided a twin bill as Pittsburgh took the opener 9 to 3 and New York the finale, 5 to 2. In another doubleheader, the Braves took the first contest 6 to 1 and the Cardinals the second by the same score, 6 to 1, at Braves Field. In Philadelphia, the Reds won twice from the Phillies by scores of 5 to 3 in ten innings and 1 to 0.

On Saturday, August 20, 1927, the Yankees were at Dunn Field in Cleveland for the last series of the season with the Indians. The Yanks split a series there in May and took three of four games in July. Left-handers Dutch Ruether and Walter Miller pitched. Neither was effective that day.

Early in the game, the Yankees led 4 to 1. Ruth's home run over the right field wall was the big blow. After Miller was batted for in the second, George Grant, a right-hander, replaced him in the third. When the Indians tied the game in the home half of the third, Huggins brought in right-hander Bob Shawkey. The Yankees added a run in the fourth and led 5 to 4. In the sixth, however, the Indians erupted for four runs.

Myles Thomas, a right-hander, pitched the next two innings and the Indians scored six runs off of him. Left-hander Joe Giard pitched the eighth. The Yankees reached Grant for three runs in the ninth, but fell way short.

Final score: Indians 14, Yankees 8.

Yankee Notebook for Saturday, August 20, 1927: Ruth's thirty-ninth home run tied him with Gehrig. Yankee hurlers Ruether, Shawkey, Thomas, and Giard gave up nineteen hits and fourteen runs, both highs for the season. Shawkey (1-3) took the loss . . . For the Indians, Burns and L. Sewell had four hits apiece, and Fonseca, Summa, J. Sewell each had three.

The Tigers went into second place after Earl Whitehill blanked the Senators, 5 to 0, at Navin Field. In the second game, the teams battled fifteen innings to a 6—6 tie, which ended in darkness. At Comiskey Park, the Athletics rallied for four runs in the ninth and beat the White Sox, 5 to 2. Lefty Grove relieved Samuel Gray in the ninth with two runners on and saved the game for Philadelphia. In St. Louis, the Browns won their fourth of the last five with a victory over the Red Sox, 8 to 4.

At Braves Field, the first-place Cubs lost two games to the Braves by scores of 6 to 5 and 2 to 1. The Braves won the first contest by scoring four runs in the ninth off three pitchers. Hugh McQuillan outpitched Charlie Root in the second game. In Brooklyn, the Pirates cut the Cubs' lead to three and one-half games by defeating the Robins 10 to 7, at Ebbets Field. Pittsburgh won by scoring three runs in the eighth and ninth after the Robins rallied for five runs in the seventh and evened the score at 7 to 7. In Philadelphia, Grover Cleveland Alexander won his 17th of the season as the Cardinals defeated the Phillies, 8 to 2. With 20,000 fans at the Polo Grounds, the Giants behind Virgil Barnes routed the Reds, 6 to 2.

On a sunny afternoon, the Yankees and Cleveland Indians played at Dunn Field on Sunday, August 21, 1927. With 19,000 fans at the ballpark, George Pipgras, a right-hander and southpaw Garland Buckeye opposed each other.

The Indians jumped out to a four run lead with a pair of hits and a pair of walks in the first inning and two singles and Buckeye's double in the second. Buckeye pitched well: only two Yankees reached first base in the first three innings. However, in the fourth, the Yankees tied the game. Buckeye was then taken out, and Willis Hudlin, a right-hander, came in and retired the side. Meanwhile, Pipgras settled down after the second and was on the mound in the seventh with the game tied.

In the home half of the seventh, the Indians pushed two runs across the plate when Hudlin singled off Dugan's shins, Jamieson sacrificed, Fonseca bounced a single off Pipgras's glove, Summa singled, and Burns sacrificed. One more run off Pipgras in the eighth ended the scoring.

Final score: Indians 7, Yankees 4.

Yankee Notebook for Sunday, August 21, 1927: The Yanks played poorly and lost their third in a row . . . Pipgras (7-3) gave up eleven hits and seven runs, walked three, and struck out five. He also uncorked a wild pitch . . . The Yankees had only six hits off Buckeye and managed only two after Hudlin came in . . . Hudlin went six innings and was credited with the victory . . . After Ruth singled in the first, Huggins decided to rest him and Cedric Durst played right field.

At Navin Field in Detroit, Josh Billings won his second major league start with help from Harry Heilmann's three hits, as the Tigers defeated the Senators, 11 to 4, tightening their hold on second-place. In Chicago, the Athletics pounded four White Sox pitchers and won 8 to 6. The visitors jumped off to an early lead when Mickey Cochrane hit a home run off Elmer Jacobs with two men on in the first inning. At Sportsman's Park, the Browns ran their streak of victories to six as they defeated the Red Sox twice, 5 to 0 and 4 to 3.

With 40,000 excited fans at the Polo Grounds, the Giants took both ends of a doubleheader from the Reds, 9 to 8 and 6 to 1. Straw hats were thrown onto the field in celebration after the first game. The victories moved the Giants to within five and one-half games of the National League leading Cubs. At Ebbets Field, Carmen Hill and Bill Doak hooked up in a pitching duel as a crowd of 20,000 watched the Pirates sweep the two game series from the Robins, 2 to 1. Glenn Wright's hit scored Kiki Cuyler with the winning run in the ninth after the Robins tied the contest in the eighth.

The Yankees played for the last time that season at Dunn Field in Cleveland on Monday, August 22, 1927. Miller Huggins started right-hander Wilcy Moore against Indians' lefty Joe Shaute. After having lost the first two games of the series, the Yankees were on the verge of being swept for the first time. Huggins wanted to avoid that situation and was prepared to use his first-string pitchers to stop the Indians.

Cleveland scored two runs in the first off Moore on two singles and a double. A double by Dugan and a single by Collins in the third gave the Yankees one run. In the bottom half of that inning, Combs dropped a fly ball by Summa, who later scored on Burns's single. Burns was thrown out at the plate on J. Sewell's double, who himself was thrown out at the plate when his brother Luke grounded to Lazzeri. L. Sewell, however, scored when Eichrodt singled. Two doubles and a single gave the Indians another run in the fifth and a 5 to 1 lead.

Ruth came up and batted against Shaute in the seventh. The Babe hit a drive over the high right-field fence for a home run—his fortieth. Urban Shocker, a right-hander, pitched the eighth after Huggins lifted

Moore for a pinch-hitter in the seventh. When the first two batters got on base off Shocker, Huggins brought in Pennock, a left-hander.

With runners on first and third, Lazzeri made an error on L. Sewell's grounder. With the bases loaded, Lutzke singled, scoring one runner. Shaute drove in two more with a single, and Jamieson one with a sacrifice fly. Down 9 to 2, the Yanks scored two in the ninth before the game ended.

Final score: Indians 9, Yankees 4.

Yankee Notebook for Monday, August 22, 1927: The loss was the Yankees' fourth straight, and the first series they lost all season . . . Huggins felt the team's hitting, pitching, and fielding were unacceptable . . . The Yankees had only eight hits off Shaute: Dugan had two doubles and Meusel two singles . . . Gehrig went hitless . . . Ruth had one hit, his fortieth home run that gave him one more than Gehrig . . . Moore (14-6) gave up twelve hits in six innings, while Shocker gave up two and Pennock five . . . Combs made an error in center . . . The Yankees were scheduled to end their Western Tour with three games in Detroit and St. Louis.

At Navin Field in Detroit, the Tigers won their 13th in a row as they defeated the Senators twice, 4 to 2 and 7 to 3. Sam Gibson won the opener on five hits. Home runs by Heilmann and McManus off Walter Johnson in the fourth inning of the finale put the Tigers ahead. In Chicago, Ted Lyons won his 19th as the White Sox took the final game of the series, 6 to 3. Ty Cobb had two doubles, a single, and a walk in four times up.

In Boston, the Cubs lost their third straight game to the Braves, 5 to 3. Two unearned runs decided the game for the Braves as Clyde Beck, Woody English, and Earl Webb made errors and Doc Farrell, Earl Clark, and Charlie Robertson followed with hits. Braves outfielder Ed Brown set a new National League record when he played in his 534th consecutive game. Fred Luderus of Philadelphia held the previous record. In Philadelphia, Jesse Haines won his 20th as he outpitched Dutch Ulrich and the Cardinals blanked the Phillies, 1 to 0.

In the midst of a rainstorm, the Yankees arrived in Detroit, Michigan late in the afternoon on Tuesday, August 23, 1927. The club was scheduled to play the Tigers the next day. Despite playing poorly in

Cleveland, the Yankees arrived with a lead of twelve and one-half games. The Tigers, meanwhile, had won thirteen games in a row and were in second place. According to the Detroit newspapers, the Tigers' players were convinced the pennant race was not over and looked to the upcoming three games as a "crucial series." The game at Navin Field that day between the Tigers and Senators was postponed because of rain.

In the National League, the Cardinals hit four home runs and trounced the Phillies, 13 to 3, at Baker Bowl. Rain postponed the game between the Cubs and Braves at Boston.

Major League Standings
August 23, 1927
American League

	Won	Lost	P.C.
New York	83	37	.692
Detroit	68	48	.586
Washington	66	52	.559
Philadelphia	66	53	.555
Chicago	55	63	.466
Cleveland	51	68	.429
St. Louis	47	69	.405
Boston	36	81	.308

National League

	Won	Lost	P.C.
Chicago	70	45	.609
Pittsburgh	67	47	.588
St. Louis	67	43	.583
New York	67	52	.563
Cincinnati	52	63	.452
Boston	48	65	.423
Brooklyn	49	68	.419
Philadelphia	42	74	.362

Chapter 31

On the Way Home

A crowd of 20,000 watched the Yankees and Tigers at Navin Field on Wednesday, August 24, 1927 in the opening game of the final series at Detroit. That afternoon, right-handers Waite Hoyt and Ownie Carroll took the mound for New York and Detroit.

The Line-Ups

Yankees	Tigers
Earle Combs cf	Jack Warner 3b
Mark Koenig ss	Lu Blue 1b
Babe Ruth lf	Charlie Gehringer 2b
Lou Gehrig 1b	Harry Heilmann rf
Bob Meusel rf	Heinie Manush cf
Tony Lazzeri 2b	Bob Fothergill lf
Joe Dugan 3b	Marty McManus ss
Pat Collins c	Merv Shea c
Waite Hoyt p	Ownie Carroll p

With the Tigers leading 5 to 2, the Yankees came up in the seventh and tied the game as Collins beat out a single to short, Cedric Durst, batting for Hoyt, flied out, and Combs singled to center. Koenig then smacked a drive to right off Carroll that went past Heilmann, scoring Collins and Combs. Koenig ended up on third, scoring on Ruth's infield out.

Huggins brought Wilcy Moore, a right-hander, into the game to pitch the bottom half of the seventh with the game tied at five. Neither team scored in the seventh or the eighth.

In the Yankees' half of the ninth, Carroll walked Combs. Koenig then sacrificed Combs to second base, and he moved to third base on Ruth's long fly to center. With two outs and Combs on third, Carroll walked Gehrig and Meusel. With the bases loaded, Lazzeri came to the plate and hit a blast over the left field wall for a grandslam home run. Moore retired the Tigers in the last half of the ninth to end the game.

Final score: Yankees 9, Tigers 5.

Yankee Notebook for Wednesday, August 24, 1927: After four successive losses, the Yankees won . . . Lazzeri's home run ended Detroit's longest winning streak in their history—thirteen games. The Yankee second baseman's four-bagger was his sixteenth home run, placing him third in the American League behind Ruth (40) and Gehrig (39) . . . On the hill, Moore (15-6) was credited with the victory in relief. He pitched the final three and gave up only four hits, walking two and striking out one . . . Hoyt went six and allowed seven hits and five runs. The Yankee right-hander walked two and struck out three.

For Detroit, Carroll gave up twelve hits; Lazzeri had three and Koenig, Gehrig, and Collins two each . . . Ruth went hitless, but was walked the first two times and sacrificed . . . Combs and Koenig made errors . . . Lazzeri stole a base.

In St. Louis, the Athletics behind Rube Walberg halted the Browns' six game winning streak, 4 to 3, at Sportsman's Park. Walberg scattered five hits and hit a home run in the sixth for the deciding run. The victory moved the Athletics into third place in the American League. At Dunn Field, the Indians won their fourth straight game pummeling the Senators 7 to 1. Walter Miller held the visitors to four hits. Senators' manager and second baseman Bucky Harris went hitless, making 28 straight times without a hit. In Chicago, the White Sox bunched hits in the second and fifth innings and edged the Red Sox, 4 to 3.

At Baker Bowl in Philadelphia, Hack Wilson's three home runs in the doubleheader helped the Cubs split the twin bill with the Phillies as Philadelphia took the first game, 7 to 6, and Chicago took the second, 13 to 1. With Pittsburgh idle, the Cubs maintained a two and one-half game lead in the National League. Rain postponed the game between the Pirates and Braves at Boston.

With more than 20,000 fans at Navin Field in Detroit on Thursday, August 25, 1927, the Yankees and Tigers played the second of the three game series. Left-handers Herb Pennock and Earl Whitehill went for New York and Detroit, respectively.

In the second inning, Gehrig faced Whitehill and hit a home run against the right-field fence that dropped behind the wire screen. The Yankees broke opened the game in the fifth when they scored four runs on three singles, three walks, and a sacrifice fly. Leading 5 to 0, the Tigers came up in the home half of the fifth and picked up two runs on McManus's home run with Fothergill on base.

Don Hankins, a right-hander, pitched for the Tigers in the sixth. The Yankees scored again when Pennock doubled, Koenig singled, Ruth walked, and Gehrig drove in two runs with a single to center. When Rip Collins, a right-hander, gave up a single to Meusel, a double to Lazzeri, and an infield out in the ninth, the Yankees scored one more run.

Final score: Yankees 8, Tigers 2.

Yankee Notebook for Thursday, August 25, 1927: Gehrig's home run tied Ruth with forty . . . Gehrig drove in four runs that afternoon, giving him 147. With thirty-three games left, he was twenty-three short of Ruth's' record mark of 170 in 1921 . . . Pennock (13-7) limited Detroit to seven hits. In the first four innings, he allowed one hit. Over the final four, the left-hander gave up only three more. The southpaw went the distance, walking three and striking out one . . . Dugan, Lazzeri, and Pennock each doubled . . . That evening Lazzeri was the guest of honor at a dinner given him by the Italian community in Detroit . . . The victory that afternoon gave the Yankees a lead of fourteen and one-half games over the Tigers.

At Sportsman's Park in St. Louis, Ty Cobb had five singles in five at bats and drove in three runs to lead the Athletics over the Browns, 6 to 1. Eddie Rommel held the Browns to five hits. In Chicago, pitcher Danny MacFayden's single in the ninth scored the winning run as the Red Sox beat the White Sox, 6 to 4. At Dunn Field in Cleveland, the Indians won for the fifth straight time defeating the Senators, 7 to 5. Garland Buckeye, who relieved Willis Hudlin, registered his first victory over the Senators in the three years he had been with Cleveland. He had lost nine times to the Indians.

In Philadelphia, Charlie Root won his 23rd for the Cubs as he hurled a three-hit shutout over the Phillies, 8 to 0, at Baker Bowl. The Cubs picked up half a game in the National League standings after Kent Greenfield beat the Pirates for the fifth time as the Braves won the first game of a doubleheader at Braves Field, 5 to 1, but lost the second, 8 to 1. At Ebbets Field, Dazzy Vance led the Robins to a 2 to 1 victory over the Reds in the opener of a six game series.

On Friday, August 26, 1927, the Yankees and Detroit Tigers played their last game of the season at Navin Field. Right-handers George Pipgras and Lil Stoner were mound opponents. Pipgras pitched well over the first five innings, allowing only four hits and fanning four. However, in the sixth, with the score tied at two, Pipgras gave up two runs on a walk, three singles, and an error.

With the bases loaded and no one out, Huggins brought Joe Giard, a left-hander, into the game. On the first pitch, Bassler hit into a double play and a run scored. On the second pitch, Fothergill was caught stealing and the inning ended.

With the Tigers leading 5 to 2, Giard singled in the seventh. Stoner then walked Combs and Koenig singled. With the bases loaded, Ruth came up and he emptied the bases with a triple to deep center. With the game tied at five, Gehrig doubled, sending Ruth across the plate. The Babe's run gave the Yankees a 6 to 5 lead.

The Tigers pushed a run across the plate in the last half of the seventh and tied the game at six. Huggins then brought Wilcy Moore into the game, and he retired the Tigers. In the top of the eighth, Moore batted and faced right-hander Sam Gibson, who had replaced Stoner. Moore swung and hit a ball that rolled slowly down the third base line. Warner, Bassler, and Gibson gathered around it to see if it went foul. The ball stopped on the line. Moore was safe at first base.

When Blue booted Comb's grounder, Moore reached second. Koenig then singled and Moore raced home with the go ahead run. Earl Whitehill, a left-hander, then replaced Gibson and walked Ruth.

When Gehrig singled, Combs scored and the Yankees led 8 to 6. Moore held the Tigers in the eighth and ninth.

Final score: Yankees 8, Tigers 6.

Yankee Notebook for Friday, August 26, 1927. Behind the plate, Grabowski was badly spiked and Bengough replaced him. After talking with the doctor, Huggins sent Grabowski home. He was expected to be out for two or three weeks . . . That afternoon, Pipgras yielded seven hits in five innings before relieved by Moore (16-6), who won again in relief, giving up only two hits in three innings. Moore walked three . . . At the plate, the Yanks had a total of sixteen hits . . . Koenig had four hits in five plate appearances . . . Combs and Ruth each doubled and tripled . . . Gehrig and Meusel also doubled . . . Combs stole a base.

During spring training, Ruth saw Moore taking batting practice and thought he was the worst hitter he ever saw. Ruth bet Moore $300 to $100 that the pitcher would not get three hits all season. Moore's hit that day was his third. Interviewed after the game by reporters about his hitting and the fact that all of his three hits came at Navin Field, Moore said: "This is just an easy park to hit in."

Moore took the $300 and after the season he went back to his Oklahoma farm. He wrote Ruth and told him he bought two mules with the money. He named one Babe and the other Ruth. The Babe had a good laugh over that.

In St. Louis, Sam Gray held the Browns to five hits as the Athletics won, 7 to 0, at Sportsman's Park. At Dunn Field, the Indians won their sixth consecutive game defeating the Senators, 8 to 7. Indian hurler George Uhle saved the game in the ninth. The loss was the Senators tenth in a row. In Chicago, Tommy Thomas won his 15th allowing only three hits as the White Sox defeated the Red Sox, 9 to 1.

At Braves' Field, Jack Fournier's double off Johnny Miljus in the eighth started a two-run rally that broke a tie as the Braves defeated the Pirates, 6 to 4. The loss moved the idle Cardinals into second place in the National League, two percentage points in front of the Pirates. In Brooklyn, the Robins' Buzz McWeeny held on to defeat the Reds, 4 to 3, after Red Lucas drove in two runs for the visitors in the ninth. Rain postponed the games between the Cardinals and Giants at New York and the Cubs at Phillies at Philadelphia.

On Saturday, August 27, 1927, the Yankees visited the Browns at Sportsman's Park in St. Louis for the last series of the Western Tour. With only a small crowd of 3,000 fans at the opener, right-handers Waite Hoyt and Sad Sam Jones faced each other.

The Line-Ups

Yankees	Browns
Earle Combs cf	Frank O'Rourke 2b
Mark Koenig ss	Harry Rice rf
Babe Ruth lf	George Sisler 1b
Lou Gehrig 1b	Ken Williams lf
Bob Meusel rf	Bing Miller cf
Tony Lazzeri 2b	Ski Melillo 3b
Joe Dugan 3b	Leo Dixon c
Pat Collins c	Wally Gerber ss
Waite Hoyt p	Sam Jones p

The Browns took an early 1 to 0 lead in the first when they bunched three hits off Hoyt. However, the Yankees came back and scored three runs in the third on home runs by Ruth, Combs, and Meusel. Adding two more runs in the fourth, the Yanks took a 5 to 1 lead. Ernie Nevers, a right-hander, came on for Jones in the fifth.

The Yankees added nine more runs over the next four innings off Nevers, Win Ballou, and Walter Stewart. Four hits off Hoyt in the Browns' half of the eighth gave them three runs.

Final score: Yankees 14, Browns 4.

Yankee Notebook for Saturday, August 27, 1927: Ruth's home run sailed far over the roof of the right field stand. It was the Babe's forty-first of the year, giving him one more than Gehrig . . . Only three players in the game have ever hit more than forty home runs. Ruth had done it five times; the other two were Rogers Hornsby and Cy Williams . . . Gehrig had forty and was expected to join that exclusive club.

Hoyt (18-5) was in command, except when the Browns reached him in the first and the eighth. Overall, Hoyt gave up ten hits and four runs, walking four and striking out one. He also hit O'Rourke . . . The Yanks pounded out fifteen hits . . . Combs had four, including a double and home run . . . Koenig and Gehrig also doubled . . . Ruth tripled and sacrificed . . . Meusel homered . . . Gehrig stole a base . . . The victory was the club's sixteenth in a row over the Browns.

At Navin Field in Detroit, the Athletics rallied in the ninth for three runs and came from behind to beat the Tigers, 8 to 7. The victory moved the Athletics into second place and dropped the Tigers to third. The loss was Detroit's fourth straight. With four runs in the seventh, the Indians went on to defeat the Red Sox, 9 to 2, at Dunn Field. It was Cleveland's seventh consecutive win. In Chicago, Ted Lyons scattered four hits as the White Sox took the first game of the series from the Senators, 6 to 1. The loss marked the tenth straight defeat for the Senators.

At Baker Bowl, the Cubs held on to a three and one-half game lead in the pennant race over the Cardinals after splitting a doubleheader with the Phillies as Philadelphia won the first game, 2 to 1, and Chicago the second, 10 to 6 in ten innings. Dutch Ulrich limited the Cubs to seven hits in the opener. Chicago rallied for five runs in extra innings in the finale as Charlie Root was credited with his 24th victory in relief. Rain postponed the games at New York and Boston.

A pair of left-handers, Dutch Ruether and Ernie Wingard, pitched for the Yankees and Browns at Sportsman's Park in St. Louis on Sunday, August 28, 1927. Wingard retired Combs to open the game but then walked Koenig. Ruth came to the plate and hit a home run over the roof of the right field pavilion. As Gehrig congratulated Ruth at home, the Yankees led 2 to 0.

The Babe was cheered by the fans in the bleachers when he took his place in left field.

The Yanks scored two in the second and after scoring one more in the third, Wingard was taken out and Elam Vangilder, a right-hander, came in. The Yankees led 5 to 0 when the Browns got to Ruether for four runs, the big blow a home run by Ken Williams. With the score 5 to 4, Koenig homered off Vangilder. The Browns, however, came back to make the score 6 to 5 in the fourth on an error and a couple of infield hits. Huggins then decided to bring Urban Shocker, a right-hander, into the game. Shocker retired the side.

In the fifth, Combs drove in two more runs with a double. The Browns scored one run in their half of the fifth, making the score 8 to 6. Shocker and Vangilder settled down, and neither team scored in the sixth, seventh, and eighth.

The Yankees scored two in a wild ninth. An error put Gehrig on first and he went to second on a passed ball. Lazzeri then doubled, sending Gehrig home. Dugan then singled. Bengough smacked a double, scoring Lazzeri, but Dugan was out at the plate and Bengough was doubled going to third. Shocker retired the Browns in their last at bat.

Final score: Yankees 10, Browns 6.

Yankee Notebook for Sunday, August 28, 1927: Ruth's home run was his forty-second. The Babe was two up on Gehrig . . . After relieving Ruether, Shocker (16-6) went 5 1/3 and gave up only three hits, walking none, and striking out four . . . The Browns had eight hits off Ruether before he left . . . Wingard and Vangilder gave up eleven hits as Koenig, Gehrig, Lazzeri, Dugan, and Bengough had two hits apiece . . . Bengough doubled and tripled . . . Ruth and Gehrig made errors.

In the American League, the Athletics strengthened their hold on second place when they defeated the Tigers, 9 to 5, at Navin Field. Rube Walberg replaced Lefty Grove in the eighth and held the lead. The loss was the Tigers' fifth in a row. With a crowd of 20,000 at Comiskey Park, Ted Blankenship shut out the Senators, 4 to 0. Walter Johnson, Tom Zachary, and Bobby Burke pitched for the Senators. The loss was Washington's twelfth straight.

At Cleveland's Dunn Field, the Indians ended their seven game winning streak as the Red Sox edged them, 6 to 5, in eleven innings. Charlie Ruffing, who pitched the final three and two-thirds innings, won in relief of Danny MacFayden.

Rain postponed the games between the Cardinals and Giants at New York and the Reds and Robins at Brooklyn in the National League.

Miller Huggins was notified that his aunt was seriously ill and left for Tennessee to be with her. He planned to rejoin the club on Friday in

Philadelphia. Huggins turned over the team to Charlie O'Leary, the Yankees' first base coach. O'Leary played with the Detroit Tigers from 1904 through1912, primarily as a shortstop. He joined the St. Louis Cardinals in 1913 when Huggins managed the club and played second, short, and coached. In 1921, O'Leary came to the Yankees as a coach for Huggins.

With O'Leary at the helm, the Yankees and Browns played for the last time that season at Sportsman's Park in St. Louis on Monday, August 29, 1927. It was Ladies' Day and 8,000 women were in the stands. Herb Pennock, a left-hander, went against right-hander General Crowder.

The Yankees came up to bat in the third with no score. Dugan started things off with a double. After Bengough flied out, Pennock doubled, sending Dugan home. Combs singled, but Koenig forced him at second as Pennock scored. Ruth walked. With two runners on, Gehrig hit his forty-first home run over the roof of the right field bleachers. When Meusel singled, Browns' skipper Dan Howley brought in Milt Gaston, a right-hander, who retired the side.

The Yankees scored again in the sixth and the eighth while the Browns reached Pennock for one run in the fourth and two in the ninth.

Final score: Yankees 8, Browns 3.

Yankee Notebook for Monday, August 29, 1927: Gehrig's forty-first home run put him one behind the Babe . . . Ruth played a spectacular left field, making no less than six sensational catches . . . The Yanks had eleven hits off Crowder and Gaston, with Combs smacking two singles and a triple . . . Dugan, Pennock, Bengough, and Koenig doubled . . . Combs and Pennock sacrificed . . . Koenig and Lazzeri made errors.

Pennock (14-7) gave up eleven hits and three runs, walking two and striking out two. None of the hits were for extra bases . . . For the Browns, Rice had three singles and O'Rourke and Mellilo two each . . . The victory was the eighteenth straight over the Browns . . . After the game, O'Leary and the players took the train home to New York.

At Navin Field in Detroit, the Tigers suffered their sixth successive defeat as the Athletics' Jack Quinn blanked them on three hits, 5 to 0.

Sammy Hale, Joe Boley, and Zach Wheat led the Philadelphia attack. It was only the third time for the season that Detroit was shutout. In Cleveland, Slim Harriss gave up only two hits as the Red Sox made it two of three over the Indians, 10 to 2. The game between the Senators and White Sox at Chicago was called in the second because of rain.

With a crowd of 30,000 at the Polo Grounds, the Cubs lost a doubleheader to the Giants, 8 to 7 and 4 to 1, as rain canceled the second game after six. With those losses, the Pirates and Cardinals closed within two and one-half games of Chicago. The Giants trailed by three and one-half. Meanwhile, the Robins and Cardinals split a doubleheader by identical scores of 2 to 1. Jesse Petty bested Grover Cleveland Alexander in the opener.

At Baker Bowl, the first game of a doubleheader between the Pirates and Phillies ended in the sixth in a 2 to 2 tie after a heavy rain ended the game. In Boston, the Reds took both games of a doubleheader from the Braves, 4 to 2 and 6 to 5.

While Miller Huggins was in Tennessee on family business, the Yankees were back in New York on Tuesday, August 30, 1927. It was an off day. The Red Sox were next in town for two games and then there were brief trips to Philadelphia and Boston.

The club had only twenty-nine more games to play. Mathematically, the Yankees needed to win only thirteen to clinch the American League pennant. The New York newspapers thought the club had a chance to break the record of most victories ever recorded in the American League—105 by the Boston Red Sox in 1912. With eighty-eight wins, the Yankees would need eighteen victories in the final twenty-nine games to eclipse that mark.

There were no games scheduled in the American League. Ty Cobb, meanwhile, celebrated the completion of his twenty-second year in baseball while the Athletics traveled from Detroit to Washington. With a mark of .352, Cobb was fifth in the league in batting.

Burleigh Grimes led the Giants past the Cubs, 7 to 3, at the Polo Grounds for their seventh straight win and pulled within two and one-half games of the leaders in the National League. Twenty-five thousand fans were at the game. In Brooklyn, Dazzy Vance yielded only six hits and drove in the winning run as the Robins beat the Cardinals, 5 to 3. At Baker Bowl, the Phillies and Pirates divided a twin bill as Philadelphia won the first game in ten innings, 3 to 2, and Pittsburgh the second, 12 to 6. In Boston, Hugh McQuillan beat Pete Donohue as the Braves defeated the Reds, 2 to 1 in eleven innings.

Major League Standings
August 30, 1927
American League

	Won	Lost	P.C.
New York	88	37	.704
Philadelphia	72	53	.576
Detroit	66	54	.557
Washington	66	57	.537
Chicago	59	64	.480
Cleveland	55	70	.440
St. Louis	47	75	.385
Boston	39	84	.317

National League

	Won	Lost	P.C.
Chicago	73	50	.593
Pittsburgh	69	50	.580
St. Louis	68	50	.576
New York	70	52	.574
Cincinnati	54	66	.450
Brooklyn	53	69	.434
Boston	51	68	.429
Philadelphia	45	78	.366

Chapter 32

Earle Combs

James Combs, a mountain farmer, and his family lived in Owsley County in Eastern Kentucky at the turn of the century. Most of the soil was used to cultivate crops; however, there was some grazing land that Combs used for a small flock of sheep. When shearing time came, Mrs. Combs used the wool strands to knit socks for the seven Combs children, who wore them through the winter while attending the one-room schoolhouse at Pleasant Grove.

The youngest son, Earle always looked forward to that time. His father would unravel the wool from his old worn-through socks and wound it tightly into a ball. Then he would cut off the tops of his wife's high-top shoes, trim the leather, and sew it around the ball of yarn for a ball. Earle would cut a piece of poplar wood and make a bat, and he and his brothers and friends would play a game he loved—baseball.

Earle Bryan Combs was born May 14, 1899 to Nannie (Brandenburg) and James J. Combs at Pebworth, Kentucky. Earle planned on becoming a teacher and attended Eastern Kentucky State Teachers College in Richmond, Kentucky in 1918. While studying that first year at college, he watched the baseball team practice from the room in his dormitory. Absorbed with his studies and lacking confidence that he could make the team, Combs did not try out.

After completing six months of schooling, Combs went to Ida May, Kentucky, a small coal-mining community three miles from Pebworth, and taught eight different grades in a one-room school in 1919. At that time, a person could teach at age 18 after passing an examination. He was paid $37 a month and walked four miles each way from home to school and back. Combs enjoyed teaching and decided to make it his career, returning to school in the fall.

That summer Combs was invited to play in a pick-up game of baseball between faculty and students. The dean of men and a former professional pitcher, Dr. Charles Keith, was on the mound. Combs who had never used a polished bat before, drove a ball over the centerfielder's head. As the outfielder retrieved the ball, Combs raced around the bases and scored. Later in the game, Combs hit another drive and before the stunned outfielders could pick up the ball and throw it in, he rounded the bases for another home run.

Dr. Keith scolded Combs for not having tried out for the college team. With more confidence in his ability, Combs played on the Eastern Kentucky team and showed outstanding ability, playing shortstop and the outfield. Competing against teams from Kentucky Wesleyan and Lincoln Memorial, Combs batted .596 that first season, hitting one or more home runs in almost every game. Combs also played basketball and ran track.

To pay for college, Combs soon discovered he could earn more than twice as much playing semi-pro baseball than teaching. In the summer of 1920, he was paid $13 for playing shortstop in a game for the Winchester, Kentucky team with a promise of $10 a game the rest of the season. In 1921, he hooked up with the High Splint Coal Co., in High Splint, Kentucky, to play ball for the company's mining team. He was offered $140 a month. However, a regular job had to be found for Combs at the mine. When he was asked what he knew about carpentering, Combs replied, "I can drive nails."

"Then, we will place you on the payroll as a carpenter," said the manager, who also played third base and was the mine's bookkeeper.

In the summer of 1921, Combs played semi-professional ball with an independent team in Harlan, Kentucky. At that time, Cap Neal, the business manager of the Louisville American Association Club scouted Combs, who hit .444 for Harlan. Upon graduation from Eastern Kentucky in 1921, Combs received a certificate to teach school; however, he decided to play professional baseball.

On March 12, 1922, Combs signed a contract with the Louisville Colonels for $300 a month. Combs had never seen an American

Association game, but knew it was one level below the major leagues. Combs went to Pensacola, Florida with Louisville in the spring of 1922.

The first exhibition game of the season was with the Brooklyn Robins and the Colonels lost 3 to 0. The next game was also with Brooklyn. Al Mamaux, an outstanding National League pitcher at that time, was on the mound. The Colonels were losing again, when Joe McCarthy, the manager, needed a pinch-hitter for pitcher Tommy Long. McCarthy looked up and down the bench. He looked at his newest recruit. Unable at the moment to remember Earle's name, McCarthy said: "Hey, boy, go on up there and hit for Long and for Heaven's sake, get on base."

Combs unloaded on Mamaux's pitch and drove it over the left center field fence for his first hit in his first at bat in professional baseball.

Combs was a starter for the Louisville Colonels in 1922. He batted .344 and led the league in triples. That year, he married Ruth McCollum of Levi, Kentucky. The next year 1923, he was sensational, batting .380, with 14 home runs, 145 runs batted in, and 241 hits. His batting average was the second highest in a league in which Al Simmons and Bill Terry also played.

During a game that season his friends from Richmond and Louisville presented him with gifts; a shotgun and loving cup. Combs, who seemed to have a flair for showing his appreciation at such times, blasted a home run to the remotest section of center field off Eddie Schaack of Milwaukee.

Combs attracted a great deal of attention in 1923, but some major league scouts turned him down because they considered his throwing arm weak. Joe McCarthy, the Louisville manager, however, persuaded the New York Yankees of his worth, and Ed Barrow bought Combs's contract from Louisville for $50,000, a considerable amount of money at that time.

Earle Combs reported to the Yankees' Spring Training camp in New Orleans in 1924 and opened the season with the club. He was a switch hitter and threw right-handed. Combs came with a considerable reputation, particularly as a speedster on the bases. After he reported to the club, Miller Huggins asked him about his base running.

"Down in Louisville, "Combs said a little embarrassed, "they called me the Mail Carrier."

"Up here," Huggins said, stifling a grin, "we'll call you the Waiter. Whenever you get on base, you just wait there for Babe Ruth or Lou Gehrig or one of the other big fellows to send you the rest of the way around."

Confident that he could play in the majors, Combs wanted the opportunity to prove it. He got that chance when he replaced the club's centerfielder Whitey Witt. Flanked on his left by Bob Meusel and on his right by Babe Ruth, Combs took over center and played well, batting .400 in his first 24 games; however, he broke his ankle sliding into home plate at Cleveland on June 15, 1924 and was sidelined for the rest of the year.

Some thought Combs's career was finished, but he came back fully recovered in 1925, hitting .342, with 203 hits in his first full season with Yankees. Combs played well again in 1926 and helped the Yankees win the pennant. He had 181 hits, with 31 doubles, 12 triples, 8 home runs, and batted .299. Combs led the regulars in the '26 World Series with a .357 mark

A handsome man with prematurely gray hair, Combs was 6 feet tall and weighed 185 pounds. He did not smoke, drink, gamble, or use profanity. He was a religious man with a warm personality and an infectious smile. He was nicknamed "The Kentucky Colonel" and "The Grey Eagle" by the press.

As a lead off man, he had few equals. With a peculiar crouch style batting, he had a keen eye and was exceptionally fast on the bases. Pitchers feared him. He seldom swung at a bad ball and he forced opposing infielders to hurry every ball to get him at first. Often they did not know where to play him, knowing that he was just as likely to slash the ball down the left field line as to center or right. He hit the ball on a line and the outfielder had to catch a ball that was described as a twisting sinker. In centerfield, he made sensational catches regularly.

In 1949, when Casey Stengel took over as manager of the New York Yankees, he and Bill Dickey, who joined the club in 1928, talked about the Yanks of the twenties.

"Wuz they gentlemen?" asked the Ol' Perfesser.

"No," said Dickey, "but they all could hit .350. Wait a minute. We had at least one gentleman, Earle Combs."

Chapter 33

Ruth Clouts Five in Two Days

The Yankees were back at Yankee Stadium in New York to meet the Boston Red Sox on Wednesday, August 31, 1927. Charlie O'Leary managed the club in Miller Huggins absence. Right-handers George Pipgras and Charlie Ruffing pitched that afternoon.

The Line-Ups

Red Sox	Yankees
Jack Rothrock ss	Earle Combs cf
Buddy Myer 3b	Mark Koenig ss
Ira Flagstead cf	Babe Ruth rf
Bill Regan 2b	Lou Gehrig 1b
Jack Tobin rf	Bob Meusel lf
Wally Shaner lf	Tony Lazzeri 2b
Phil Todt 1b	Joe Dugan 3b
Fred Hofmann c	Benny Bengough c
Charlie Ruffing p	George Pipgras p

The Red Sox scored one run off Pipgras in the second. Despite two hits in the first and two more in the second, the Yankees did not score off Ruffing. However, in the third, the Yanks erupted for five runs off the Red Sox starter; the big blow a home run into the left field bleachers by Lazzeri with two men on. In the next inning, the Yankees took a 9 to 0 lead after Lazzeri hit another home run that landed in the right field bleachers.

Pipgras pitched well as did Tony Welzer, a right-hander, who replaced Ruffing in the fifth. In the bottom half of the eighth with the Yankees leading 9 to 1, Ruth came up and blasted a home run high into the right field seats off Welzer. The day's scoring ended when Rothrock hit an inside-the-park home run to right with a runner on base.

Final score: Yankees 10, Red Sox 3.

Yankee Notebook for Wednesday, August 31, 1927: Ruth's forty-third home run gave him two more than Gehrig . . . Lazzeri's pair was his seventeenth and eighteenth, which was the third best mark in the American League . . . For the Red Sox, Ruffing and Welzer gave up thirteen hits with Combs and Lazzeri having three each . . . Gehrig had one hit, a triple . . . Koenig and Ruth each swiped a base . . . Gehrig and Meusel sacrificed.

Pipgras (7-3) pitched a complete game, giving up nine hits, walking three, and striking out four . . . Koenig and Lazzeri played very well in the field . . . Bengough made an error . . . The victory, with the Athletics loss to the Senators, gave the Yankees a 17 game lead . . . New York needed only 11 more wins to clinch the American League pennant.

In Washington, D.C., Bump Hadley ended the Senators twelve-game losing streak with a 5 to 3 win over the Athletics at Griffith Stadium. Hadley walked ten batters. Goose Goslin led Washington's attack with his eleventh home run and a triple. Meanwhile, timely hitting by Ken Williams and Harry Rice helped the Browns sweep a doubleheader from the Tigers at Sportsman's Park, 3 to 1 and 4 to 3.

At Philadelphia's Baker Bowl, the Pirates gained a full game on the Cubs with a double win over the Phillies, 3 to 2 in thirteen innings and 7 to 2. The two victories slashed the Cubs lead to one game. The Cardinals played their final game of the season at Ebbets Field with Flint Rhem yielding only four hits as the visitors defeated the Robins, 3 to 1. Five thousand fans were at the game. In Boston, Reds' pitcher Adolfo Luque allowed only six hits and shutout the Braves, 1 to 0, at Braves Field. Charlie Robertson gave up the one run.

Rain postponed the game between the Yankees and Boston Red Sox in New York on Thursday, September 1, 1927. The game was the visitor's last of the season at Yankee Stadium. As the Yanks were scheduled to play the next day at Philadelphia and could not make up the game with the Red Sox, it was expected the game would be played when the Yankees were in Boston the following Monday.

Bad weather also postponed the game at Philadelphia between the Athletics and Senators. At Sportsman's Park, meanwhile, the Tigers ended their eight game losing streak when they scored four runs in the tenth inning and beat the Browns, 8 to 4. Each team used four pitchers. In the first game of the series at Comiskey Park, the Indians bunched hits off Tommy Thomas and Elmer Jacobs and defeated the White Sox, 8 to 5. Willis Hudlin gave up thirteen hits to the White Sox but received good support at the plate and in the field.

At Forbes Field, the Pirates took over first place by defeating the Cubs, 4 to 3. Lee Meadows bested Hal Carlson on the mound with help from Joe Harris, whose home run, double, and sacrifice figured in the Pirates' scoring. Sparkling throws by the Waner brothers also supported Meadows. Art Nehf, veteran southpaw, who was unconditionally released by Cincinnati a few days before, signed with the Cubs. Rain postponed the game between the Robins and Braves at Boston.

On Friday, September 2, 1927, 15,000 fans were at Shibe Park in Philadelphia on a warm and sunny afternoon. Connie Mack's team had a successful trip west, where they won twelve of fourteen. The Yankees, however, came into the game with an eighteen game lead in the American League.

Back from attending to family business, Miller Huggins started Waite Hoyt, a right-hander. Mack went with left-hander Rube Walberg.

The Line-Ups

Yankees	Athletics
Earle Combs cf	Max Bishop 2b
Mark Koenig ss	Sammy Hale 3b
Babe Ruth lf	Walt French rf
Lou Gehrig 1b	Ty Cobb cf

Bob Meusel rf	Mickey Cochrane c
Tony Lazzeri 2b	Jimmy Dykes 1b
Joe Dugan 3b	Zach Wheat lf
Pat Collins c	Joe Boley ss
Waite Hoyt p	Rube Walberg p

With two outs in the first inning, Ruth came up and clouted Walberg's pitch over the right field wall toward the score board in center. On the very next pitch, Gehrig drove the ball out on a line onto the housetops across the street for a home run. The Yankees scored five more runs in the second after an error, singles by Collins and Combs, a double by Koenig, a sacrifice by Ruth, and Gehrig's second home run. At that point, Sam Gray, a right-hander, replaced Walberg.

Three more runs off Gray in the third made the score 10 to 0. Hoyt, meanwhile, was pitching well. The Yankees scored again in the eight and ninth and led 12 to 0. Going to the bottom of the ninth, Hoyt had given up only five scattered hits. However, an error by Koenig and a single by Perkins put runners on second and third. Both scored on a pair of sacrifices.

Final score: Yankees 12, Athletics 2.

Yankee Notebook for Friday, September 2, 1927: On the hill, Hoyt (19-5) pitched a complete game. He gave up only six hits, walking four and striking out one . . . For the Athletics, Walberg and Gray yielded twenty hits as Combs, Koenig, and Gehrig had four hits apiece and Lazzeri three . . . Ruth's home run was his forty-fourth . . . Gehrig's pair gave him a total of forty-three . . . The Yankees needed ten more victories to win the pennant.

At Sportsman's Park in St. Louis, Milt Gaston allowed six hits and drove in the winning run in the ninth as the Browns defeated the Tigers, 3 to 2. In Chicago, a White Sox rally in the ninth fell short by one run as the Indians won, 7 to 6. After returning from illness, Chicago's star Johnny Mostil appeared in his first game of the season as a pinch runner and was applauded by the fans.

The Pirates extended their lead to one full game as they turned back the Cardinals, 5 to 3, at Pittsburgh, while the Cubs lost to the

Reds at Cincinnati. Pittsburgh's Ray Kremer bested St. Louis's Grover Cleveland Alexander that day. The Waner brothers, Paul and Lloyd, collected a total of seven hits for Pittsburgh. Former Boston Braves' star Rabbit Maranville, who was purchased by St. Louis from Rochester, was at shortstop for the Cardinals. At Redland Field, Jakie May scattered three hits and struck out seven as the Reds blanked the Cubs, 5 to 0. In Boston, Eddie Farrell scored one run and drove in two more as the Braves edged the Robins, 3 to 2.

A crowd of 25,000 came out to Shibe Park in Philadelphia on Saturday, September 3, 1927 to see Lefty Grove and the Athletics play the Yankees for the last time that season. Miller Huggins gave the mound assignment to right-hander Wilcy Moore.

Wearing the home white uniform of the Athletics, Grove opened the game by retiring Combs and Koenig. Ruth lined a sharp single to left, but Gehrig flied to Wheat in left for the third out. With the crowd roaring in the second, Grove struck out Meusel, Lazzeri, and Dugan on ten pitched balls. In the Athletics' fourth, Cochrane doubled to right off Moore and scored on Dykes's single.

From the second to the eighth Grove was tough, retiring the Yanks in order each inning. With the Athletics leading 1 to 0, the Yankees threatened in the eighth after Dugan doubled with two outs. Grove pitched carefully to Collins and walked him. Huggins then sent up Ben Paschal, a right-handed batsman, to hit for Moore. Paschal, however, flied out to French in right. Herb Pennock pitched the eighth and retired the Athletics.

The crowd was silent in the ninth.

With a 1 to 0 lead, Grove took the mound. Combs opened the inning with a drive to Grove that he caught. Koenig then flied to Cobb in center field. With two outs, Ruth hit his second single of the day to left center. As Gehrig come up to bat, there was uneasiness among the fans. However, the game ended when Gehrig took a third strike.

Final score: Athletics 1, Yankees 0.

Yankee Notebook for Saturday, September 3, 1927: Grove gave up only four hits and struck out nine . . . The Philadelphia southpaw was the first pitcher that season to toss a shutout against the Yankees . . . For New York, Moore (15-7) pitched very well, giving up one run on five hits in seven innings . . . Pennock gave up a single to Hale in the one inning he worked . . . At the plate, Ruth had two singles and Lazzeri one . . . Dugan doubled . . . Both teams played flawlessly in the field. Gehrig made two fine plays digging hard hit grounders out of the dirt for force plays at second. Koenig returned one of those for a double play.

Successive singles by Muddy Ruel, Garland Braxton, and Sam Rice in the twelfth gave the Senators a victory over the Red Sox, 4 to 3, at Griffith Stadium. At Sportsman's Park, Bing Miller's single in the ninth scored the winning run as the Browns triumphed over the Tigers, 11 to 10. Ken Williams hit his fifteenth home run for the Browns. In Chicago, Red Faber held the Indians to five scattered hits as the White Sox won, 4 to 1.

The Pirates' Carmen Hill won his twentieth as he scattered five hits and the Pirates crushed the Cardinals, 14 to 0, at Forbes Field. However, Pittsburgh lost a half game in the standings when the Giants won two games from the Phillies at the Polo Grounds, 6 to 5 and 7 to 4. Rogers Hornsby hit his twenty-third home run in the second contest.

The Cubs lost ground in the race as the Reds defeated them for the second straight time, 2 to 1, at Redland Field. Red Lucas yielded only five hits and won his own game with a single. In Boston, the Braves and Robins split a doubleheader. Boston won the first game, 4 to 3 in eleven, and Brooklyn took the second contest, 6 to 4.

Convinced that their straw hats had something to do with their first shutout, the Yankee players smashed them on the train back to New York from Philadelphia. A dozen of the players walked through Pennsylvania Station bareheaded. The Babe was unaffected. He wore a cap year round.

The Yankees played an exhibition game with Jersey City of the International League on Sunday, September 4, 1927. Although Miller Huggins had the regulars in the line-up, the Yankees managed only five hits against a recent graduate from the University of Florida named Jim Chaplin and lost 1 to 0.

With that second straight shutout, the Yankees found a few more straw hats and smashed them too.

In Washington, D.C., Phil Todt's second home run of the day at Griffith Stadium gave the Red Sox a 5 to 3 victory in the eleventh over the Senators. At Comiskey Park, George Uhle held off the White Sox in the final two innings as the Indians defeated the White Sox, 6 to 3. In St. Louis, the Browns came from behind in the eighth and went on to beat the Tigers, 4 to 3, at Sportsman's Park. The victory was the Browns' fifth in six games.

At Redland Field, the Pirates pounded Adolfo Luque over six innings and routed the Reds, 8 to 4, holding on to a two game lead in the National League. With 35,000 fans at the Polo Grounds, the Giants turned backed the Phillies, 6 to 0, on Burleigh Grimes's shutout. The victory was the Giants' tenth straight. Bill Terry homered.

A crowd of 38,000 jammed into Wrigley Field but were disappointed as they watched the Cubs lose to the Cardinals, 2 to 1. The fans saw a great pitching duel between Charlie Root and Willie Sherdel. At Ebbets Field, 18,000 fans saw the Robins and Braves split a twin bill as Boston won the opener, 3 to 2, and Brooklyn the finale in thirteen innings by the same score, 3 to 2.

On Labor Day, Monday, September 5, 1927, the Yankees visited the Red Sox for the last series of the season in Boston. Interest in the home run battle between Ruth and Gehrig brought more than 36,000 fans, the largest crowd at Fenway Park in twelve years, to attend the holiday doubleheader.

With the fans swarming all over the field as game time drew near, a score of patrolmen and mounted police cleared the field. The police roped off the overflow of people around the outfield. Outside more than 15,000 people were turned away after the gates had been ordered closed. Right-handers George Pipgras and Charlie Ruffing pitched the first game. Urban Shocker, a right-hander, opposed left-hander Hal Wiltse in the second.

First Game
The Line-Ups

Yankees	Red Sox
Earle Combs cf	Jack Rothrock ss
Mark Koenig ss	Buddy Meyer 3b
Babe Ruth lf	Ira Flagstead cf
Lou Gehrig 1b	Bill Regan 2b
Bob Meusel rf	Jack Tobin lf
Tony Lazzeri 2b	Wally Shaner rf
Joe Dugan 3b	Phil Todt 1b
Ben Bengough c	Bill Moore c
George Pipgras p	Charlie Ruffing p

With the Red Sox leading 4 to 0 in the first game, the Yankees came up in the third and scored four runs to tie the game. The big blow was a home run into the right field bleachers by Gehrig with Koenig on base. Pipgras was knocked out of the game in the fourth with the Red Sox leading, 7 to 6. Joe Giard, a left-hander, pitched the next three and Bob Shawkey followed.

Coming to bat in the top of the ninth, the Yankees trailed 8 to 6. Huggins sent Ray Morehart up to bat for Dugan, and he walked with one down. Ben Paschal batted for Shawkey, and he doubled, sending Morehart to third. Combs then singled over third base, scoring both Morehart and Paschal. The game was tied at eight. Huggins brought Wilcy Moore in to pitch the bottom of the ninth. The Red Sox did not score. Ruffing and Moore battled in extra innings.

Inning after inning went by.

Ruffing finally left the game in the fifteenth for a pinch hitter, and Hal Wiltse, a left-hander, came in. In the seventeenth, the Yankees jumped on Wiltse for three runs on a walk, a sacrifice, a single by Combs, a double by Koenig, a walk to Ruth, an error, and Gehrig's fourth hit. The Yankees were ahead 11 to 8 as the Red Sox came up in the seventeenth.

With Moore on the mound, Regan doubled and Tobin singled. At that point, Huggins took Moore out and called in Waite Hoyt, a right-hander. When Shaner and Moore lofted balls into the crowd for ground rule doubles, the score was tied at eleven.

Wiltse held the Yankees scoreless in the top of the eighteenth. Then in the bottom of the eighteenth, Meyer hit a double into the crowd in center. Flagstead then dropped a double into right field, scoring Meyer and the Red Sox won the game.

Final score: Red Sox 12, Yankees 11 (First game in eighteen innings)

After pitching three innings in the first game, Hal Wiltse opened the second contest against Urban Shocker. The Yankees scored two in the third inning and three in the fourth. When darkness fell at Fenway Park, the game was called after five.

Final score: Yankees 5, Red Sox 0 (Second game called for darkness)

Yankee Notebook for Monday, September 5, 1927: The first game went eighteen innings and took 4 hours and 20 minutes . . . The Red Sox's Ruffing pitched fifteen innings and Wiltse three . . . Ruffing struck out twelve . . . For the Yankees, Pipgras pitched three; Giard three; Shawkey two; Moore eight and Hoyt one and one-third . . . Hoyt (19-6) took the loss . . . Yankee pitchers gave up twenty hits . . . Red Sox hurlers surrendered twenty-three: Combs had five hits; Gehrig four, and Koenig three . . . Ruth, Meusel and Gehrig each stole a base . . . The Yankees left twenty-three men on the bases . . . Gehrig's home run was his forty-fourth, tying Ruth once again for the major league lead.

Because of the late start of the first game and the length of the contest, the second game was called after five innings when darkness engulfed Fenway Park . . . Shocker (15-6) was credited with the victory . . . Combs had two doubles and Dugan a stolen base before it ended.

On Labor Day, the Athletics took two games from the Senators, 2 to 1 and 3 to 0, at Shibe Park and strengthened their hold on second place. The Athletics made a triple play in the seventh of the second contest. Meanwhile, the Indians and Browns split a doubleheader with Cleveland winning the opener, 7 to 6, and St. Louis the finale, 3 to 2. In Detroit, the Tigers and White Sox divided morning and afternoon games as Chicago won the first game 5 to 0 and Detroit the second, 10 to 6.

In Pittsburgh, the Reds took both ends of a morning and afternoon doubleheader from the Pirates, 8 to 6 and 4 to 3, and tightened up the pennant race. With the largest crowd of all time at the Polo Grounds, 58,000 fans watched the Giants lose the opening game of a doubleheader to the Braves, 6 to 1, and win the second in the ninth, 9 to 8, on Jack Cummings double with two out. The victory coupled with Pittsburgh's two losses put the Giants only one game behind the leaders.

An overflow crowd of 40,000 at Wrigley Field watched the Cubs win the first of two games, 6 to 1 and lose the second as Jesse Haines and the Cardinals won, 2 to 0. At Ebbets Field, 15,000 spectators saw the Phillies take two games from the Robins, 6 to 1 and 7 to 1. Philadelphia's Cy Williams hit two home runs.

On Tuesday, September 6, 1927, the Yankees and Boston Red Sox played their second doubleheader in two days. With 20,000 fans at Fenway Park, Herb Pennock, a left-hander, opposed right-hander Tony Welzer in the opener. Left-hander Dutch Ruether and Jack Russell, a right-hander, pitched in the second game.

Already leading 4 to 2 after four innings, the Yankees came to bat in the fifth. Welzer was pitching when Gehrig came to the plate. The Yankees' first baseman drove Welzer's pitch on a line into the right field bleachers. As the crowd cheered, Gehrig circled the bases and was congratulated by Meusel at home. The home run was Gehrig's forty-fifth.

With Welzer still on the mound and two runners on in the sixth, Ruth hit a tremendous drive over the barrier in dead center. The people who kept the records at Fenway declared it to be the longest ever hit. Ruth came up again in the seventh with one on and blasted a second home run that dropped just inside the right field bleachers.

Pennock breezed along and except for giving up two runs in the third he was in total command. Bob Cremins, left-hander, pitched the final two innings for the Red Sox. Pennock retired the home team in the bottom of the ninth.

Final score: Yankees 14, Red Sox 2. (First game)

In the second game, Russell was tough. Over the first eight innings, the Yankees were held to only three hits, while the Red Sox bunched six hits off Ruether in the fourth and fifth for four runs. One more run in the sixth on two hits gave the Red Sox a lead of 5 to 0. In the ninth, the Yankees scored two runs off Russell. The big blast was Ruth's third home run of the day that sailed into the right field bleachers.

Final score: Red Sox 5, Yankees 2. (Second game)

Yankee Notebook for Tuesday, September 6, 1927: Ruth's three home runs that day at Fenway Park were his forty-fifth, forty-sixth, and forty-seventh and tied his total mark in 1926 . . . The Babe was still twelve away from his record of fifty-nine established in 1921. On the same day that year, Ruth already had fifty-four . . . Gehrig's home run that day was his forty-fifth.

In the first game, Pennock (15-7) gave up seven hits, walking one and striking two . . . The Yankees had twenty hits off Welzer and Cremins . . . Gehrig and Meusel had four hits and Lazzeri three . . . Meusel had two doubles and Lazzeri, Koenig, Gehrig, and Combs one each . . . Lazzeri stole two bases . . . Koenig made an error . . . In the second game, Ruether (12-5) took the loss . . . Boston's Russell scattered six hits . . . Gehrig singled and tripled . . . Meusel singled and doubled.

That day the Senators made their last appearance at Shibe Park and split a doubleheader with the Athletics winning the first game, 14 to 9, and losing the second, 4 to 0. Washington's attack in the opener featured six triples. Goose Goslin and Ossie Bluege hit home runs for the Senators. Ed Rommel scattered only four hits in the second contest. At Navin Field, Bill Barrett's home run with the bases loaded in the seventh was the deciding hit as the White Sox took the closing game from the Tigers, 9 to 6. Behind the pitching of Milt Gaston, the Browns ended their last series at Dunn Field with a 7 to 2 win over the Indians.

At Forbes Field, Ray Kremer scattered three hits and faced only twenty-eight Reds as the Pirates won, 5 to 0. With the victory, the Pirates retained a one game lead over the Giants. Behind the pitching of Larry Benton and Burleigh Grimes, the Giants kept pace by beating the Braves, 9 to 6, at the Polo Grounds. With Grover Cleveland Alexander on the mound, the Cardinals took over third place by defeating the Cubs, 13 to 1, at Sportsman's Park. The second game of that day's doubleheader was rained out.

The Yankees played their final road game of that season against the Boston Red Sox at Fenway Park on Wednesday, September 7, 1927. Myles Thomas and Danny MacFayden, both right-handers, pitched that afternoon.

Ruth came to the plate in the first inning with two out. Facing MacFayden, the Babe homered over the left field barrier. The home run was his forty-eighth. The game stayed 1 to 0 until the Red Sox fourth when Boston exploded for eight runs. Huggins brought in Joe Giard, a left-hander.

Down 8 to 1, the Yanks rallied in the sixth. After MacFayden walked two in a row, Ruth doubled and scored both runners. Gehrig's double brought the Babe home. When MacFayden walked another batter, Red Sox manager Bill Carrigan brought in right-hander Slim Harriss. Harriss walked a batter, loading the bases. An error by Hofmann, the catcher, allowed another run, and Bengough's single drove two more home. The Yankees were only down by one run 8 to 7.

The Yankees took a 10 to 8 lead in the seventh on another double by Gehrig and a single by Meusel. When Giard ran into trouble in the seventh, Huggins brought in right-hander Bob Shawkey, who held the Red Sox to one run.

In the eighth, Ruth was up with one man on base and Harriss on the mound. Ruth clouted his second home run of the game and fifth in three successive days. The ball landed in the far corner of the center field bleachers. The Red Sox scored their final run in the eighth.

Final score: Yankees 12, Red Sox 10.

With his forty-eighth and forty-ninth home runs, there was serious talk around baseball that Ruth had a real possibility to break his record of 59 home runs set in 1921. Ruth had twenty games left to hit eleven to establish a new mark. By comparison in 1921, Ruth hit twelve homers in the last twenty contests.

Ruth's five home runs in three successive games tied the major league record according to the statisticians; Ruth did it once before in 1921, Ken Williams of St. Louis Browns in 1922, Michael Muldoon of

Cleveland in 1882, and Mike Kelly of Chicago in the National League in 1885. Ruth's two home runs that day gave him four more than Gehrig.

Yankee Notebook for Wednesday, September 7, 1927: Shawkey (2-3) was the winning pitcher. The veteran right-hander went three innings and gave up three hits, walked none, and struck out one . . . Thomas and Giard both had to be relieved . . . Ruth had four hits and drove in five runs, and Gehrig had two hits, both doubles . . . Meusel and Gazella each stole a base . . . The Yanks played errorless ball in the field . . . After the game, the Yankees took the train back to New York to open the club's last home stand against the West at Yankee Stadium . . . The first visitors were the St. Louis Browns.

There were no games scheduled in the American League.

In the National League, the Pirates lost to the Reds, 6 to 5, at Forbes Field. Reds' Charlie Dressen led the attack with a triple and two doubles. Errors hurt the Pirates. With the second place Giants idle, the loss cut the Pirates' lead on first place to one-half game. The third place Cardinals and fourth place Cubs divided a doubleheader as St. Louis won the first game, 6 to 2, and Chicago the second, 8 to 4, at Sportsman's Park. At Baker Bowl, the Robins and Phillies split a twin bill as Philadelphia won the opener, 3 to 2 and Brooklyn the finale, 9 to 1.

Major League Standings
September 7, 1927
American League

	Won	Lost	P.C.
New York	93	40	.699
Philadelphia	76	56	.576
Detroit	70	61	.534
Washington	69	61	.531
Chicago	62	68	.477
Cleveland	59	73	.447
St. Louis	54	77	.412
Boston	42	89	.321

National League

	Won	Lost	P.C.
Pittsburgh	76	53	.589
New York	75	53	.586
St. Louis	73	54	.576
Chicago	75	57	.568
Cincinnati	60	68	.469
Boston	55	73	.430
Brooklyn	56	76	.424
Philadelphia	48	84	.364

Chapter 34

Winning the Pennant

Tony Lazzeri Day was celebrated at Yankee Stadium in New York on Thursday, September 8, 1927. Before the game with the St. Louis Browns, the Yankees and the Italian-American community paid tribute to the Yankee second baseman. In the absence of New York City Mayor Jimmy Walker who was in Europe, Acting Mayor Joseph V. McKee presented Lazzeri with a floral horseshoe. Also paying tribute to Lazzeri was Humbert Fugazy, sports promoter and honorary chairman of the committee that arranged the event. That day's crowd of 20,000 saw right-handers Waite Hoyt and Sad Sam Jones pitch for the Yanks and Browns.

Line-Ups

Browns	Yankees
Frank O'Rourke 2b	Earle Combs cf
Harry Rice rf	Mark Koenig ss
George Sisler 1b	Babe Ruth rf
Ken Williams lf	Lou Gehrig 1b
Bing Miller cf	Bob Meusel lf
Steve O'Neill c	Tony Lazzeri 2b
Ski Mellilo 3b	Mike Gazella 3b
Wally Gerber ss	Pat Collins c
Sam Jones p	Waite Hoyt p

Anxious to please the crowd, Lazzeri came up in the first with two outs and Ruth, Gehrig, and Meusel on the bases. The crowd roared

"Push 'em up, Tony." However, Lazzeri went down swinging. In the second, the Yanks reached Jones for one run after Gazella and Hoyt walked and Sisler threw wild past second on a roller by Combs and Gazella scored. Actually, Sisler made a good play, but Gerber came up on the wrong side of the bag and the ball went into left field. Hoyt, meanwhile, was pitching masterfully and the Browns were unable to mount an attack.

In the fifth, Jones walked Ruth. When Meusel doubled, the Babe raced to third base. Lazzeri then came up. He had fanned again in the third and was determined to show his appreciation to the crowd. This time Lazzeri hit a fly to Rice in right, and Ruth tagged up and raced home safely on a beautiful slide at the plate. The Browns averted a shutout in the seventh when Ken Williams clouted a home run over Ruth's head into the right field bleachers.

Final score: Yankees 2, Browns 1.

Yankee Notebook for Thursday, September 8, 1927: Both Jones and Hoyt pitched well . . . Jones gave up four hits and Hoyt (20-6) only three, walking none, and striking out six . . . With his 20th victory, Hoyt earned a $2,500 bonus . . . Ruth did not have much of a chance to add to his home run total; he was walked three times and in his only chance to hit, he lofted a foul ball to Sisler . . . The game was played in 1:58 . . . The loss was the Browns nineteenth in a row to the Yankees.

That evening Ruth, Gehrig, Colonel Jacob Ruppert, Ed Barrow, and Miller Huggins joined a thousand people at the Hotel Commodore as Lazzeri's Italian-American friends gave him a dinner. A chest of silver valued at $1,000 was presented to him.

At Shibe Park in Philadelphia, Lefty Grove won his 19th as the Athletics pummeled the Tigers, 9 to 1, in the opening game of the series. Grove struck out eight and helped with a home run, a single, and a sacrifice for three runs. In Washington, D.C., Carl Reynolds's home run to right center with Alex Metzler on base gave the White Sox a 4 to 3 victory over the Senators. Goose Goslin hit his thirteenth home run for Washington. At Fenway Park, the Red Sox came from behind and scored seven runs in the sixth and seventh innings to defeat the Indians, 10 to 8.

In St. Louis, the Cubs took the final game of the series from the Cardinals, 11 to 7, at Sportsman's Park and moved into third place by one percentage point. Charley Root won his 25th.

On Friday, September 9, 1927, the Yankees played the St. Louis Browns again at Yankee Stadium. That afternoon right-handers Urban Shocker and Elam Vangilder were on the mound. The Yankees jumped away to a 1 to 0 lead on a triple by Combs and a single by Ruth. In the fourth, Shocker ran into trouble walking batters and the Browns tallied three runs.

Trailing 4 to 1, the Yankees came up in the fifth. Shocker started things off with a walk. Combs singled. Koenig sacrificed the runners to third. Then the Babe singled for the second time to right, scoring Shocker and Combs. Vangilder walked Gehrig but Meusel singled, scoring Ruth. Gehrig moved to third. Lazzeri then popped up to Gerber at short and Gehrig tagged and came home. The scoring continued when Meusel stole second base and went to third after Dixon, the catcher, threw the ball into center. Meusel scored when Miller's throw sailed into the Yankee dugout.

The Yankees led 6 to 3.

In the sixth, the Yankees knocked Vangilder out of the box. Ernie Nevers, a right-hander, came in and the Yanks picked up three more runs. Shocker had no trouble with the Browns after the fourth.

Final score: Yankees 9, Browns 3.

Yankee Notebook for Friday, September 9, 1927: Shocker (16-6) allowed the Browns only three hits and duplicated Hoyt's performance the day before. The right-hander walked four and struck out three . . . The Yankees had eight hits off Vangilder and Nevers: Combs, Ruth and Meusel had two apiece . . . Combs and Meusel had the only extra base hits in the game, a triple and double, respectively . . . Meusel stole two bases . . . Gehrig, who went hitless in three plate appearances, made an error . . . The victory was the Yankees twentieth in a row over the Browns.

At Shibe Park in Philadelphia, the Tigers evened the series by taking the second game from the Athletics, 5 to 2, behind Earl Whitehill's strong pitching. Whitehill held the Athletics to four hits.

Teammate Bob Fothergill had two doubles and a triple. In the nation's capital, Ted Lyons blanked the Senators on three singles as the White Sox won, 8 to 0.

In Boston, the Red Sox took their second straight from the Indians, 6 to 1, as Slim Harriss gave up only five hits. Wesley Ferrell, from Oak Ridge Academy, Guilford, N.C., made his debut for Cleveland in the eighth.

At Forbes Field in Pittsburgh, the Pirates edged the Phillies, 3 to 2, in the opening game of the series and held on to first place by half a game over the Giants. With 35,000 fans at Wrigley Field, the Giants, behind the pitching of Burleigh Grimes, defeated the Cubs, 7 to 2. At Sportsman's Park, Les Bell's home run with two on and two out in the tenth gave the Cardinals a victory, 8 to 6. In the first game of the series at Redland Field, the Reds bunched hits in the fourth and eighth off the three Braves' pitchers and went on to win, 8 to 1.

With 25,000 fans at Yankee Stadium in New York on Saturday, September 10, 1927, the St. Louis Browns and Yankees continued their series. The newspapers were making much of a record that the Yankees were close to establishing. Victories over the Browns that day and the next would give the Yankees the distinction of being the first major league club to sweep an entire season's series of twenty-two games from another club.

Miller Huggins started Wilcy Moore. Brown's manager Dan Howley sent Walter Stewart to the mound. The game turned into a tense-pitching duel as neither team could do anything against the opposing pitcher over the first seven and one-half innings. In the home half of the eighth, Meusel doubled to left off Stewart to open the inning. Meusel then took third base on Lazzeri's sacrifice and came home on Gazella's long sac fly to center.

Final score: Yankees 1, Browns 0.

Yankee Notebook for Saturday, September 10, 1927: Moore (17-7) went the distance, walking none, and striking out three . . . The Browns reached Moore for seven scattered hits; the only extra base hit was Gerber's double . . . Moore has been very valuable; without him the Yanks would no doubt have been in a closer pennant race. The right-hander had played in forty-five games, mostly in relief, and hurled 177 innings . . . At the plate that day, the Yankees had only seven hits off Stewart; Lazzeri had two . . . Combs's single off Stewart in the fifth was his 200th hit of the season, becoming the first American League player to reach that mark in 1927.

In Philadelphia, Jimmy Foxx drove in the tying run in the sixth with a double and Sammy Hale's single in the seventh scored the winning run as the Athletics defeated the Tigers, 6 to 4, at Shibe Park. At Griffith Stadium, the Senators and White Sox divided two games as Chicago won the opener, 6 to 5, and Washington took the second, 11 to 1. Bump Hadley held the visitors to four hits in the finale. In Boston, George Uhle scattered eight hits at the Indians took the third game of the series from the Red Sox, 3 to 1.

Pittsburgh's Ray Kremer scattered eight hits as he shutout the Phillies, 4 to 0, at Forbes Field. Sensational fielding by George Grantham, Pie Traynor, and Paul Waner helped Kremer. In Chicago, the Cubs defeated the Giants, 2 to 1, as a crowd of 25,000 watched Guy Bush give up only six hits. The loss dropped the Giants one and one-half games behind the Pirates.

The Cardinals picked up a game on the Giants as Grover Cleveland Alexander won his 19th, 5 to 2, over the Robins at Sportsman's Park. Rain postponed the game between the Braves and Reds at Cincinnati.

The St. Louis Browns made their last appearance of the season at Yankee Stadium on Sunday, September 11, 1927. Having lost twenty-one games in a row to the Yankees, the Browns were looking to salvage the final game and avert being the first club ever to lose twenty-two games to a rival.

Before the game, the White Plains Lodge of Elks, No. 535 presented Yankees' third baseman Joe Dugan, a brother Elk, with a gift. Knowing that Tony Lazzeri was given a floral horseshoe and did not get a hit, the Elks did not want to jinx Dugan by giving him the same gift. Instead, the Elks gave him a diamond-studded card case. New York Supreme Court Justice Humphrey J. Lynch made the presentation.

In front of a crowd of 35,000, southpaw Herb Pennock faced Milt Gaston, a right-hander. With the score tied at one, the Browns came up in the fourth and scored four runs off Pennock, the big blow a triple by Sisler that drove home two runs. With two outs, Huggins brought in Bob Shawkey, a right-hander, who retired the Browns.

Behind 5 to 1, the Yankees came up in the home half of the fourth. With the White Plains Elks' band playing and the fans making noise, Ruth walked to the plate to lead off. With a count of three and one, the Babe caught hold of a fast ball and drove it into the far right field bleachers.

It was home run number fifty.

As Ruth trotted around the bases, the fans in the upper tiers threw straw hats onto the field. The celebration lasted for three minutes. Coaches and players had to join the stadium workers in helping to remove the hats from the field.

The Browns scored one more run in the ninth off George Pipgras, who had come in for Shawkey. Gehrig opened the ninth with a single over second, but was forced by Meusel. The game ended when Lazzeri hit into a double play.

Final score: Browns 6, Yankees 2.

Yankee Notebook for Sunday, September 11, 1927: Ruth's fiftieth home run put him nine behind his record of fifty-nine in 1921. At the same point in time in the '21 season, the Babe already had had fifty-four . . . Pennock (15-8) took the loss. He went 3 2/3 and was hit badly . . . Shawkey and Pipgras were also ineffective . . . The Yankees managed only five hits off Gaston . . . Dugan singled twice . . . The victory was the Browns' first over the Yankees. The statisticians found that the last time a club took twenty-one of twenty-two games from another was when the Cubs did it to the Braves in 1909.

The only other action in the American League took place in Washington, D.C., where the Senators defeated the White Sox, 6 to 5 in twelve, on Ossie Bluege's double followed by Jackie Hayes's single.

On a beautiful afternoon at Wrigley Field, a crowd of 38,000 watched the Cubs score six runs in the sixth and topple the Giants, 7 to 5. The loss dropped the Giants two games behind the Pirates, who were idle, in the National League. Meanwhile, the Cardinals moved into a second place tie with the Giants as they beat the Robins, 5 to 0.

St. Louis won behind a four-hit shutout of rookie Fred Frankenhouse, who was called up from the Texas League.

In Cincinnati, the Reds took a doubleheader from the Braves, 8 to 4, and 16 to 5. Braves' coach Dick Rudolph, a member of the famous Boston team of 1914, pitched the closing inning of the second game. The Reds scored one run off of Rudolph.

The Yankees were off on Monday, September 12, 1927 and waited for the Cleveland Indians to open the last series between the teams with a doubleheader the next day. The Yanks needed two victories to clinch the pennant, and Ruth, who was in pursuit of his home run record, needed ten home runs. The Yankees had seventeen games left.

There was not much talk anymore about Gehrig challenging Ruth. The Yankee first baseman had forty-five and had last hit one on September 6 in Boston. In fact, Gehrig was not hitting at all. What the press and public did not know was that his mother was seriously ill in the hospital. Fearing she might not live, Gehrig was concerned and distracted.

Philadelphia was the site of the only game scheduled in the American League that day. Baby Doll Jacobson's single and a sacrifice fly scored the winning run in the eighth as the Athletics defeated the Tigers, 5 to 4. Jacobson had been recently picked up from the Indians.

In the National League, Carmen Hill won his 21st with the help of home runs by Glenn Wright and Earl Smith as the Pirates beat the Phillies, 3 to 2, at Forbes Field. In Chicago, Rogers Hornsby's twenty-fourth home run led the Giants to a 7 to 5 victory over the Cubs at Wrigley Field. The Cub's Hack Wilson hit his twenty-seventh, which led the league. Unhappy with a call by umpire Charley Pfirman in the ninth, the Chicago fans hurled bottles at him. At Redland Field, Adolfo Lucas and Red Lucas led the Reds to two victories over the Braves, 6 to 4, and 3 to 0.

On Tuesday, September 13, 1927, the Yankees played the Cleveland Indians in a doubleheader in New York. Two victories that day would give the Yankees and the City of New York the American League pennant. Yankee manager Miller Huggins started right-handers George

Pipgras and Waite Hoyt. The Indians sent Willis Hudlin, a right-hander, and lefty Joe Shaute to the mound.

First Game
The Line-Ups

Indians	Yankees
Johnny Gill lf	Earle Combs cf
Lew Fonseca 2b	Mark Koenig ss
Homer Summa rf	Babe Ruth rf
George Burns 1b	Lou Gehrig 1b
Joe Sewell ss	Bob Meusel lf
Luke Sewell c	Tony Lazzeri 2b
Sam Langford cf	Joe Dugan 3b
Rube Lutzke 3b	Ben Bengough c
Willis Hudlin p	George Pipgras p

The Yankees trailed 3 to 1 in the first game until the seventh. Koenig singled and Ruth came up to bat. The Babe faced Hudlin and homered into the right field stands. It was home run number fifty-one. After Gehrig rolled out to Fonseca, Meusel singled and Lazzeri doubled. Huggins then sent Cedric Durst up to bat for Dugan. Durst lifted one to Gill. J. Sewell intercepted the throw in and trapped Lazzeri at third. Meusel reached the plate before Lazzeri was called out so the run counted and the Yankees led 4 to 3. The Yanks added one run in the eighth. Pipgras retired the Indians in the ninth.

Final score: Yankees 5, Indians 3. (First game)

The Yankees were behind again in the second game. Coming to bat in the fourth trailing 2 to 1, Ruth led off the inning with his second home run of the day, number fifty-two, off Shaute. Gehrig then singled sharply to left center. Lazzeri singled to left. With Gehrig on third, Dugan doubled, scoring the lead runner. Lazzeri then scored on Collins's Texas leaguer, and when J.Sewell fumbled Hoyt's grounder, Dugan came home making the score 5 to 2. The Indians added a run in the fifth. Hoyt retired the Indians in the ninth, and the Yankees clinched the American League pennant.

Final score: Yankees 5, Indians 3. (Second game)

There was no celebration by the fans or the players. Everyone had taken for granted for weeks that the club would win and knew the only real celebration would be the one after the Yankees won the world championship—the prize that eluded them the year before. Yet, there was much to be proud of. The Yankees had won their second straight pennant and fifth in the last seven years. After being in first place the entire season, the team won the flag with an eighteen-game lead and was clearly the strongest club in the league. As the manager of the Yankees, Huggins had won five pennants equaling the American League record held by Connie Mack of the Athletics.

Yankee Notebook for Tuesday, September 13, 1927: In capturing the flag that afternoon, the Yankees got good pitching from Pipgras (8-3) and Hoyt (21-6) . . . In total, the Indians scored six runs that afternoon and had ten hits in each game . . . Ruth's fifty-first and fifty-second home runs put him seven behind his record and eight away from a new mark. The Yankees had fifteen games left to play . . . After the game, Miller Huggins's told the reporters that his job was to keep the team focused and to see that they went about their work with determination and confidence.

At Philadelphia's Shibe Park, Ty Cobb and Joe Boley led an attack that saw the Athletics pound the White Sox, 15 to 5. Cobb hit two doubles and a pair of singles. Boley had a single, double, and triple. Lefty Grove was credited with the victory. In Washington, D.C, the Senators took two from the Tigers by scores of 3 to 2 and 5 to 3. At Fenway Park, the Red Sox won both ends of a doubleheader from the Browns, 5 to 4 in thirteen innings and 3 to 2.

In Pittsburgh, the Pirates won a doubleheader from the Braves at Forbes Field as Lee Meadows won his 18th by a score of 6 to 1 and Vic Aldridge got the decision in the second, 5 to 4. By the end of the day, the Pirates held a three-game lead in the National League. At Sportsman's Park, the Giants and Cardinals split a doubleheader as 30,000 fans watched the hometown team win the opener, 5 to 2 behind Bill Sherdel and lose the finale, 12 to 6. The crowd was very upset after Larry Benton beaned Frankie Frisch.

The pennant hopes of the Cubs faded as the Robins won 6 to 5 at Wrigley Field. The loss dropped Chicago five full games behind Pittsburgh. In Cincinnati, Ray Kolp relieved Eppa Rixey in the ninth and stopped a Phillies' rally as the Reds won, 5 to 3.

Colonel Jacob Ruppert received the following telegram from Joseph V. McKee on Wednesday, September 14, 1927:

"As Acting Mayor I extend to you, Manager Huggins and the players of the New York Yankees' baseball team the congratulations of myself and of the City of New York upon your success in the American League race. We all know that you will bring another world's championship banner to the Yankee Stadium this Fall."

That afternoon Miller Huggins started left-hander Dutch Ruether and Walter Miller, a left-hander, opened for the Indians. The Yankees opened the scoring in the third. Bengough tripled down the left field line and the ball caromed off the wall. After Ruether struck out, Combs singled past Fonseca scoring Bengough.

In the fourth, the Yanks went ahead 4 to 0 when Combs scored after Koenig and Gehrig singled. Lazzeri had a base hit to right and raced to third on Bengough's single. Lazzeri scored on an attempted double play by the Indians. With Ruether safe at first, Combs and Koenig then singled, scoring the runner.

After Miller was batted for in the sixth, right-handers George Grant and Willie Underhill pitched. Ruether, meanwhile, blanked the Indians until the ninth when they scored one run on two singles and a pair of sacrifices. Up to that time, Ruether had not allowed an Indian to reach third base and only three batters had gotten as far as second.

Final score: Yankees 4, Indians 1.

Yankee Notebook for Wednesday, September 14, 1927: Ruth had a disappointing day. The Babe managed a single, a pop up to the catcher, a strike out, and a base on balls . . . The Yankees had nine hits off Miller, Grant, and Underhill; Combs, Koenig and Bengough had two hits apiece . . . On the mound, Ruether (13-5) gave up seven hits, walking one, and striking out two . . . The victory was the club's ninety-ninth.

In Philadelphia, Jimmy Foxx's single scored Walt French with the winning run as the Athletics rallied in the ninth against the White Sox and beat them in the eleventh by a score of 5 to 4, at Shibe Park. At Griffith Stadium, three runs in the third were enough for the Senators to defeat the Tigers, 3 to 2. In Boston, the Red Sox made it three in a row from the Browns as they won, 9 to 6.

At Forbes Field, the Pirates won for the seventh straight time as they took a doubleheader from the Braves, 6 to 2 and 3 to 0. Ray Kremer won the first game and Johnny Miljus the second. Both pitchers gave up only six hits. With the doubleheader sweep, the Pirates took a four game lead in the National League.

With 30,000 fans at Sportsman's Park, the Cardinals and Giants split a doubleheader as St. Louis won the first game on Chick Hafey's home run in the tenth, 6 to 3, and New York took the second, 9 to 3. Meanwhile, Dazzy Vance's pitching and Max Carey's bases loaded home run helped defeat the Cubs, 10 to 6, at Wrigley Field. The loss dropped the Cubs six and one-half games behind the Pirates.

At Redland Field, the Reds stretched their winning streak to seven consecutive games as they beat the Phillies, 7 to 6. Rube Bressler's triple in the ninth with the bases filled gave Cincinnati the victory.

The Yankees and Cleveland Indians faced each other for the final time that season at Yankee Stadium in New York on Thursday, September 15, 1927. Looking to win their 100th game, Miller Huggins sent Myles Thomas, a right-hander, out to the mound to face the Indians. Opposing the Yankees was the club's old nemesis, right-hander George Uhle.

With the game tied at one, the Indians came up in the sixth. J. Sewell opened with a single. Langford then hit a fast ball off Thomas that landed in the bleachers for a home run. The Indians led 3 to 1.

Joe Giard, a left-hander, replaced Thomas in the eighth. In the bottom of that inning, Ruth doubled off the screen in deep right and scored on Gehrig's single to right. Meusel reached first when his drive was deflected off Uhle's glove toward Fonseca. Gehrig stopped at second. The rally ended when Lazzeri flied to left center and Wera struck out.

Final score: Indians 3, Yankees 2.

Yankee Notebook for Thursday, September 15, 1927: It was a disappointing day. The Yankees failed to win their 100th game and managed only seven hits off Uhle . . . Meusel had two hits, a single and double . . . The Babe had one hit, a single. Summa took one of his drives off the right field screen as he leaped and made a one-handed catch. Another drive struck the top of the screen in deep right for a double.

Thomas (7-4) gave up eleven hits in seven innings. He walked none and struck out five . . . Giard surrendered one hit in two innings . . . Ruth had an error in right field . . . Combs stole a base . . . The Yankees won twelve of the twenty-two games played with the Indians.

In Philadelphia, a double steal by Walt French and Ty Cobb at Shibe Park led to the winning run as the Athletics swept the three game series from the White Sox, 5 to 4. Athletics' first baseman Jimmy Foxx hit a home run with two on in the third. After losing three in a row, the Tigers won the finale from the Senators, 6 to 5, at Griffith Stadium. At Fenway Park, the Browns took the final game of its season series with the Red Sox, 2 to 1. The winning run came on a home run in the sixth by Harry Rice into the right-field bleachers.

On another sweltering hot afternoon in St. Louis, 30,000 fans saw the Giants and Cardinals split a doubleheader. New York won the first game on Bill Terry's two home runs, 11 to 3, and St. Louis took the second, 8 to 5, when the game was halted at the end of the eighth because of darkness. The Giants and Cardinals both lost ground to the Pirates, dropping four and one-half games behind. Rain postponed the game between the Robins and Cubs at Chicago.

Major League Standings
September 15, 1927
American League

	Won	Lost	P.C.
New York	99	42	.702
Philadelphia	82	57	.590
Washington	74	65	.532
Detroit	72	67	.518
Chicago	65	73	.471
Cleveland	61	78	.439
St. Louis	56	83	.403
Boston	47	91	.341

National League

	Won	Lost	P.C.
Pittsburgh	84	53	.613
New York	80	58	.580
St. Louis	80	58	.580
Chicago	78	61	.561
Cincinnati	67	68	.496
Brooklyn	58	80	.420
Boston	55	83	.399
Philadelphia	48	89	.350

Chapter 35

Hoyt Wins 22nd

The Yankees' front office was issued instructions from Commissioner Kenesaw M. Landis on how the public would obtain tickets for the World Series. Tickets could be purchased by mail for reserved and box seats in sets of three for games 3, 4 and 5 to be played at Yankee Stadium. If game 5 was not played, the money received for those tickets would be refunded.

For those that did not want to purchase tickets ahead of time, 15,000 general admission tickets to the upper grand stand and 20,000 bleacher tickets would be placed on sale at the Stadium at 10 o'clock on the day of the game. The prices of tickets would be $6.60 for box seats, $5.50 for reserved seats, $3.30 for general admission, and $1.10 for the bleachers.

That afternoon, Friday September 16, 1927, the Chicago White Sox visited Yankee Stadium to open their final series with the Yankees. Wilcy Moore and Ted Blankenship, both right-handers, were mound opponents.

The Line-Ups

White Sox	Yankees
Roy Flaskamper ss	Earle Combs cf
Willie Kamm 3b	Mark Koenig ss
Alex Metzler cf	Babe Ruth rf
Bill Barrett rf	Lou Gehrig 1b
Bibb Falk lf	Bob Meusel lf
Bud Clancy 1b	Tony Lazzeri 2b

Moe Berg 2b	Joe Dugan 3b
Buck Crouse c	Benny Bengough c
Ted Blankenship p	Wilcy Moore p

The Yankees opened the scoring in the first. Combs singled to right off Blankenship, but Ruth forced him at second base. Blankenship then walked Gehrig. Meusel doubled to left and as the ball caromed off the wall, Ruth and Gehrig scored. In the third, the Babe came up again and smashed a home run into the right field stands. With the crowd cheering, Ruth circled the bases. Gehrig was at home plate waiting to congratulate him.

The White Sox picked up a run in the fourth making the score 3 to 1. In the Yankees' half of the fourth, the most unexpected event happened. Moore, who had singled in the second for his first hit ever at Yankee Stadium, socked a home run off Blankenship into the right field seats. The players on the bench jumped all over Moore when he came back to the dug out.

The Yankees added a run in the fifth on Meusel's inside-the-park home run to deep center field. The White Sox scored another run in the seventh on Crouse's double, and the Yankees added two more in the eighth off Bert Cole, a left-hander, who had replaced Blankenship in the seventh.

Final score: Yankees 7, White Sox 2.

Yankee Notebook for Friday September 16, 1927: The victory was the club's 100th . . . Ruth's home run was his fifty-third . . . The Babe needed six to tie his record and seven to break it. The Yankees had twelve games left to play. The newspapers were quick to point out that at this stage of the season in 1921 Ruth had fifty-six . . . Moore (18-7) pitched very well. He gave up two runs and seven hits, walking two and striking out six . . . The Yankees had a total of thirteen hits off Blankenship and Cole . . . Meusel had three hits and Combs, Koenig, and Moore two each . . . Meusel and Moore homered.

That day the Athletics won their sixth game in a row by defeating the Browns, 6 to 3, at Shibe Park. Ty Cobb had three singles, and thirteen hits in his last eighteen at bats. Jing Johnson went the distance for Philadelphia. At Fenway Park, Harry Heilmann's home run with

Charlie Gehringer on base helped the Tigers win the first game of the series over the Red Sox, 4 to 3.

At Forbes Field, the Pirates won their ninth in a row with a 4 to 3 victory over the Braves and swept the six game series. Lee Meadows held Boston to eight hits. The loss was the Braves' thirteenth successive defeat. The Pirates led the National League race by four and one-half games. After splitting three straight doubleheaders at Sportsman's Park, the Giants beat the Cardinals, 6 to 3, on a very hot afternoon. Home runs by Freddie Lindstrom and George Harper led the Giants' attack. In Chicago, the Robins swept the three game series from the Cubs with a 4 to 3 victory. Buzz McWeeny and Jumbo Jim Elliott pitched for Brooklyn.

With Babe Ruth chasing his home run record and the Yankees looking to establish a new mark for most victories in a season, 35,000 fans came out to the Stadium and watched the Yankees and Chicago White Sox play a doubleheader on Saturday, September 17, 1927.

The first game saw right-handers Urban Shocker and Red Faber oppose each other. Left-hander Herb Pennock and George Connally, a right-hander, pitched the second game.

In the opener, Metzler led off the third with an inside-the-park home run off Shocker to deep center field. Combs tried to make a shoestring catch and missed. Faber pitched well, and the White Sox's one run lead held until the seventh when the Yankees went ahead 2 to 1. Lazzeri singled past Berg at second and went all the way home when Kamm at third base threw Dugan's grounder over Clancy's head at first. Dugan raced to third on the wild throw and scored on Collins's hit.

Amid boos from the fans, Faber walked Ruth in the eighth for the third time in the game. After Gehrig and Meusel flied out, Ruth moved to second on Lazzeri's hit and came home on Dugan's single to left. The Yankees led 3 to 1.

When Roger Peckinpaugh, a former captain of the Yankees, came up in the ninth to pinch-hit for Faber, the fans at the Stadium gave him a warm reception. Peckinpaugh reached first on an error by Koenig. He went to second on Metzler's single. Flaskamper then flied to Meusel.

When Barrett singled sharply to left field, Peckinpaugh raced home. Falk fouled to Collins. The game ended when Kamm lofted an easy fly to Gehrig.

Final score: Yankees 3, White Sox, 2 (First game).

Between games Combs was called to home plate. He was presented with a watch and chain from the fans in the right field bleachers. The gift was in appreciation of his play in center field. The collection of monies was taken up during the season. Combs thanked his admirers with a home run and two singles in the second contest as the Yanks had fifteen hits off Connally and the club scored eight runs.

The White Sox's only run off Pennock in the second game came in the fifth—it was unearned. With one out, Connally and Metzler singled. When Metzler's ball bounded away from Combs, Connally scored. Koenig then made a brilliant stop on Peck's hard grounder and Ruth made a great running catch to end the inning.

Final score: Yankees 8, White Sox 1 (Second game)

Yankee Notebook for Saturday, September 17, 1927. The two victories gave the Yankees 102 wins, and they were three away from the record for games won over a 154 game schedule . . . For the afternoon, Ruth had no home runs, but did connect for four singles . . . The Babe was walked four times, including an intentional pass in the fifth inning of the second game that threw the fans into a frenzy. Ray Schalk, the White Sox's manager, was the target of boos and catcalls for the remainder of the game.

In the opener, Shocker (17-6) held the White Sox to six hits, walked none, and struck out two . . . In the finale, Pennock (16-8) surrendered nine hits. The left hander walked one and struck out two . . . In the doubleheader, the Yankees had a total of twenty-three hits off Faber and Connally: Combs and Lazzeri had four and Ruth three . . . The Babe also stole a base.

In Philadelphia, Ty Cobb had four hits in seven at bats as the Athletics and Browns split a doubleheader at Shibe Park. St. Louis, behind Elam Vangilder, won the first game, 6 to 0, and the home team took the second on Ed Rommel's four hit shutout, 13 to 0. At Griffith Stadium, Horace Lisenbee allowed only eight hits as the Senators defeated the Indians, 3 to 0. At Fenway Park, the Tigers won both ends of a doubleheader from the Red Sox by scores of 8 to 4 and 11 to 5.

Behind the solid pitching of Ray Kremer and Vic Aldridge at Forbes Field, the Pirates took both games of a doubleheader from the Robins, 2 to 1 and 6 to 0. The victories ran the Pirates' winning streak to eleven straight. Lloyd Waner had three hits in the second game, running his hit total to 201, a record for a rookie.

With 15,000 fans watching on a sweltering day at Redland Field, the Giants won both games of a doubleheader from the Reds, 5 to 1 and 8 to 7. Meanwhile, on a muddy field at Sportsman's Park, the Cardinals pounded out eighteen hits as Art Reinhart blanked the Phillies, 11 to 0. In Chicago, the Braves' losing streak was extended to fifteen games as the Cubs won both games of a doubleheader, 3 to 2 and 5 to 3.

On Sunday, September 18, 1927, a crowd of 45,000 came out to Yankee Stadium to cheer Babe Ruth as he neared his record mark of fifty-nine home runs. The Yankees and Chicago White Sox played a doubleheader and closed the final series of the season between the clubs. Right-handers George Pipgras and Tommy Thomas pitched the first game. Ted Lyons and Waite Hoyt, also right-handers, opposed each other in the second.

With the score tied at one in the first game, the Yankees came up in the sixth. Gehrig tripled to center. The ball hit the grass near the flagpole and only fast fielding by Metzler kept Gehrig on third base. Thomas walked Meusel. Then Lazzeri hit a sacrifice fly to center, Gehrig tagged and came home. After giving up two hits in the second when the White Sox scored their one run, Pipgras gave up only two more singles over the next seven innings.

Final score: Yankees 2, White Sox 1 (First game)

In the second game, the Yankees jumped out to an early 3 to 0 lead in the third off Lyons on a single by Hoyt, Combs's double, and singles by Koenig, Ruth and Gehrig. With the score 3 to 1 in the fifth, Ruth came up to bat again. With Koenig on first base, the Babe ripped into one of Lyon's curve balls and hit it into the right field bleacher section.

As Ruth circled the bases, the crowd cheered loudly and threw a few straw hats onto the field. Koenig and Gehrig congratulated him at home plate.

It was Ruth's fifty-fourth and equaled his second best season, 1920.

When the Babe went to right field at the end of the inning, a youngster of about 10-years-old rushed onto the field from his seat in the bleachers. He went up to Ruth with the home run ball and a pen. Ruth signed the ball. The fans in the bleachers cheered. Hoyt, meanwhile, breezed along. Left-hander Bert Cole pitched the seventh and eighth for the White Sox. Hoyt retired the visitors in the ninth.

Final score: Yankees 5, White Sox 1 (Second game)

Yankee Notebook for Sunday, September 18, 1927: Ruth had only eight games left to hit five homers and equal his record of fifty-nine . . . The Yanks registered their 103 and 104 victories and were only one game behind the American League record of 105 set by the Boston Red Sox in 1912 . . . The statisticians also figured out that the Yankees had a chance to be the first American League team to finish with a percentage over the .700 mark.

For the Yankees, Pipgras (9-3) and Hoyt (22-6) both pitched exceptionally well. Pipgras gave up one run on four hits, and Hoyt yielded one run on eight hits . . . White Sox hurlers Thomas and Lyons gave up a total of twenty hits; Combs had five and Koenig four in the twin bill . . . In the field, Koenig made an error in the second game, but he was involved in three double plays with Gehrig and Lazzeri.

The only other game played that afternoon in the American League was in Washington, D.C. George Burns's double scored two runs in the tenth inning as the Indians defeated the Senators, 6 to 4. In the National League, the Pirates were idle. The Giants, however, failed to gain ground on the league leader as they split a doubleheader with the Reds at Redland Field. Cincinnati's Red Lucas blanked them on three hits, 7 to 0, and New York came back to take the finale, 4 to 2. In St. Louis, the Cardinals picked up a game on the Pirates and Giants as they swept a twin bill from the Phillies, 7 to 3 and 8 to 3, at Sportsman's Park.

At Wrigley Field, the Braves snapped their fifteen game losing streak by defeating the Cubs, 11 to 7. When the Braves retired the

Cubs in the ninth, the players hoisted pitcher Bob Smith to their shoulders and carried him off the field cheering. It was their first victory since Labor Day.

The Yankees were off on Monday, September 19, 1927. Looking at the schedule, the club was off again the next day, then opened a four game series with Detroit, played a single contest with Philadelphia, and finished the season with three against Washington. All the games were at Yankee Stadium.

Miller Huggins told reporters he was out to win every game that remained without taking any unnecessary chances on injuries. Huggins was glad that the club was finishing the season against the stronger clubs in the league because it would keep the players on their toes and hold on to their fighting edge.

At Griffith Stadium in Washington, D.C., the Indians made five errors and lost to the Senators, 4 to1, in the final game of the season between the clubs. The game was called in the sixth because of rain. Rain also postponed the games between the Tigers and Red Sox at Boston and the Browns and Athletics at Philadelphia.

In Pittsburgh, the Robins' Dazzy Vance and Babe Herman combined to defeat the league leading Pirates, 3 to 0, at Forbes Field. Vance outpitched Carmen Hill that afternoon. Herman's double and Jake Flower's single in the sixth scored all of Brooklyn's runs. In Cincinnati, Bill Terry led a fourteen hit attack against the Reds with a home run, triple, and two singles as the Giants beat the Reds, 10 to 6.

At Sportsman's Park, the Cardinals won their fourth in a row from the Phillies, 12 to 5. The victory was pitcher Frank Frankenhouse's fourth straight since being called up from the minors. In his first start for the Cubs, Art Nehf shutout the Braves, 3 to 0, at Wrigley Field.

The Yankees were scheduled to resume play on Wednesday, September 21, 1927. Their opponents were the Detroit Tigers. The teams had played each other eighteen times that season; the Yankees won twelve and the Tigers six. With excitement building around Ruth's home run chase, a close look at the Tigers' pitching staff showed that six of the Babe's fifty-four home runs were off the Tigers; Earl Whitehill yielded two, Ken Holloway two, Rip Collins one, and George Smith one.

In Philadelphia on Tuesday, September 20, the Athletics and Browns finished the season series with the host team taking both games of a doubleheader from St. Louis by scores of 4 to 1 and 7 to 3. General Crowder held the Athletics from scoring until the ninth when the home team rallied to win. The big blow was a home run by Al Simmons with Mickey Cochrane and Jimmy Foxx on. At Fenway Park, the Tigers and Red Sox closed the season series as Detroit took a twin bill from Boston, 4 to 3 and 5 to 3.

The Robins won their second straight from the Pirates, 3 to 0, at Forbes Field. Brooklyn's Bill Doak allowed the home team only two hits. Since the Worlds Series tickets went on sale the day before in Pittsburgh, the Pirates have been shutout twice and have lost one and one-half games of their lead over the Giants.

In St. Louis, home runs by Frankie Frisch and Chick Hafey helped the Cardinals win their fifth in a row from the Phillies, 5 to 4, at Sportsman's Park. The victory put St. Louis into a second place tie with New York. In Chicago, the Cubs made it four out of five with a victory over the Braves, 8 to 5, at Wrigley Field.

Major League Standings
September 20, 1927
American League

	Won	Lost	P.C.
New York	104	42	.712
Philadelphia	86	58	.597
Washington	76	66	.535
Detroit	77	67	.535
Chicago	65	78	.455
Cleveland	62	80	.437
St. Louis	57	87	.396
Boston	47	96	.329

National League

	Won	Lost	P.C.
Pittsburgh	87	55	.613
New York	85	59	.590
St. Louis	85	59	.590
Chicago	82	63	.566
Cincinnati	68	72	.486
Brooklyn	61	82	.427
Boston	56	88	.389
Philadelphia	48	94	.338

Chapter 36

Jumpin' Joe Dugan

As Joe Dugan, his seven brothers, two sisters, mother, and father sat down to dinner one night in New Haven, Connecticut in 1915, the doorbell rang. Mrs. Dugan answered the door and told Joseph that there was man to see him. The 17-old high school junior got up from the table and almost fainted. The man at the door was Connie Mack, the manager of the Philadelphia Athletics.

Sitting down with the family, Mack told Mr. Dugan, a poor working man, that he had heard Joseph was a pretty good ball player. Mack reached into his pocket and put five $100 bills on the table in front of Mr. Dugan.

"I want you to promise me," said Mack, "when Joseph comes of age and decides to go into organized baseball you'll let him come to the Philadelphia Athletics."

Looking at the money, and then glancing at Joseph's seven brother and two sisters, the elder Dugan told Mack:

"For $500 you can take the whole family."

Joseph Anthony Dugan was born to poor Irish parents on May 12, 1897 in Mahanoy, Pennsylvania. At the age of fifteen months, Joseph's family moved to Winstead, Connecticut, where the youngster grew up and played baseball. Batting and throwing right-handed, Dugan played for Gilbert High School for two years, before his family moved to New Haven, Connecticut.

While in high school, scouts for the Philadelphia Athletics saw Dugan and reported to Connie Mack that the youngster had potential. The summer after the Dugan family promised Connie Mack that Joe would sign with the Athletics, the youngster played on a semi-professional team called the Colonials in New Haven.

After graduating from New Haven High School in 1917, Dugan attended Holy Cross College at Worcester, Massachusetts. As an infielder, he attracted much attention in a game against the University of Pennsylvania at Franklin Field in Philadelphia. With several big league scouts at the game, Dugan played very well in the field and had four hits in four times at bat. Four professional teams soon offered Dugan a contract.

Keeping his promise to Connie Mack, Joe Dugan signed with the Philadelphia Athletics. At twenty-years of age, Dugan went directly from Holy Cross College to the major leagues and played in his first major league game on July 5, 1917 at Fenway Park in Boston.

Dugan did not have an auspicious debut.

When Whitey Witt sprained his ankle, Dugan was in the line-up for the Athletics, and faced the Red Sox's Carl Mays and Ernie Shore in a doubleheader.

"They'd knock you down and then throw that big curve ball. I went 0-for-8." Dugan remembered. "The next day it was Dutch Leonard and that curve ball coming in from Kenmore Square. I was 0-for-4. The last day it was Ruth, and I was 0-for-16."

Dugan asked Connie Mack if they were all like this?

"Don't worry, son, they'll get easier as you go along," Mack answered.

"So we went to Chicago and I hit against that spitballer, Red Faber," Dugan later recalled. "He turned my cap around with a pitch, and I said, 'What was that for?' He answered. 'Respect, kid. Respect.' The next day I looked at Eddie Cicotte. They were too tough for me. I should have been sent out, but it was the War, and I stayed."

In his rookie season, Dugan played shortstop and second base and appeared in 43 games. In 134 plate appearances, he batted only .194. While he was struggling, Dugan received a great deal of verbal abuse from the Athletics' fans, which saw him as untalented and raw.

Dugan did not like the fans' boos or the city of Philadelphia, and he decided to jump the club and return home to New Haven and his family and friends. A few days later, Dugan rejoined the club and Connie Mack took him back. After this happened a few times, the Athletics' fans dubbed him "Run-Home Dugan" and "Disappearing Joe." Philadelphia Inquirer sportswriter Tony Maxwell nicknamed him "Jumping Joe Dugan."

The Athletics finished the 1917 season in last place. The 1918 season was no better for Dugan or the Athletics: playing in 121 games, he came to the plate 411 times and batted a very poor .195. The Philadelphia fans, meanwhile, continued to hurl terrible verbal abuse at him.

"I'd walk onto the field and waves of sound would pound down from the stands, The howls . . . beat my ears back," Dugan recalled.

Dugan pleaded with Mack to trade him, but the Athletics' manager would reassure him, like a father to son, that things would get better. The heckling toward Dugan continued and, to make matters worse, the 1918 team finished in last place again.

By 1919, Dugan improved at the plate, finishing the year with a respectable .271 batting average. Playing shortstop, second, and occasionally third base, Dugan was becoming a very able infielder. It all came together in 1920, when he had the best year of his career. Playing in 123 games, Dugan came to the plate 491 times, and batted .322. Despite his wonderful season, the Athletics again finished last.

In those days, Mack was undecided if Dugan would eventually replace Jack Barry at third base or Eddie Collins at second. He kept moving him from third to second and back again. But in 1921, Mack decided Dugan was more suited for third and moved him there permanently. Dugan found third easier than shortstop or second base, and he became an outstanding third baseman.

While the Philadelphia Athletics finished in last place for the fifth straight year, Dugan ended that season with a .295 batting average and led all third basemen in the league in fielding, with a .953 percentage.

A brilliant fielding third baseman, Dugan was outstanding at anticipating a batter. He had extraordinary ability to come in on a slowly hit ball and throw out the runner. Whether leaping in the air to spear a line drive or picking up a hard hit ground ball one-handed,

Dugan made all the plays at third base. Some considered him the best third baseman of that era.

Finally, in 1922 Dugan escaped the fans and the city he hated. In a big three-way deal involving Philadelphia, Boston, and Washington, the 25-year-old Dugan was traded to the Red Sox. The trade occurred after Washington sent Bing Miller, an outfielder; Jose Acosta, a young Cuban pitcher, and $50,000 to Philadelphia for Dugan. Washington then traded Dugan and Frank O'Rourke, an infielder, to Boston for Roger Peckinpaugh, an infielder and former Captain of the New York Yankees. (Clark Griffith, President and part owner of the Washington Club wanted Peckinpaugh as his manager.)

Prior to the deal, the Chicago White Sox, Cleveland Indians, and the Yankees made offers for Dugan. Several times Yankee co-owners Jacob Ruppert and Cap Huston talked trade with Connie Mack and would have paid $50,000 for Dugan, but Mack had declined.

After four years of the worst verbal abuse any ball player had to bear, Dugan was ecstatic to leave Philadelphia. Coming over to Boston, he played well over the first three months, batting around .285. However, on July 23, 1922 the baseball establishment and fans everywhere were shocked to learn that Joe Dugan had been traded by Boston Red Sox owner Harry Frazee to the New York Yankees, who were in a close pennant race with the St. Louis Browns.

To obtain Dugan from the Red Sox, the Yankees gave up utility players Johnny Mitchell, Chick Fewster, Elmer Miller, an excellent defensive outfielder, and a player to be named later—which was pitcher Frank "Lefty" O'Doul. Red Sox owner Harry Frazee also received a considerable amount of cash.

The Boston Herald had this to say about the trade:

"Another disgusting trade between the Red Sox and the Yankees was made yesterday . . . Frazee has tightened his hold on the title of "Champion Wrecker of the Baseball Age."

Replacing an aged Frank "Home Run" Baker at third base, Dugan solidified the Yankee infield, joining Deacon Scott (shortstop), Aaron Ward (second base) and Wally Pipp (first base). With the Yankees and Browns embroiled in a very tight pennant race, St. Louis fans were outraged. As it turned out, the Yankees opened a four game series with the Browns in St. Louis right after the trade. The Browns' fans booed Dugan as soon as he got off the train.

Dugan played in 60 games for the Yankees that season, batting .286 with three home runs and twenty-five runs driven in. The Yankees finished in first place, one-game ahead of the St. Louis Browns. In the 1922 World Series, Dugan batted .250, with one double. As the regular third baseman from the Yankees the next four seasons, Dugan batted .283 (1923), .302 (1924), .292 (1925) and .288 (1926). He also hit well in the 1923 and 1928 World Series at .280 and .333, respectively.

Dugan suffered with a "trick knee," that began to give him trouble soon after joining the Yankees. The knee would lock and interfere with his play. In 1925, he had a very delicate operation and was in bed for six weeks. The surgery helped, but Dugan never played without the knee acting up on occasion.

Joe Dugan always made light of his hitting on the great Yankee powerhouses. He told one anecdote to highlight the power of those teams and what he felt was his more modest contribution: in one inning the first five or six Yankee batters all hit safely—doubles, triples, and a home run. According to Dugan, when he came to bat and hit a single, Miller Huggins fined him for breaking up a rally.

Chapter 37

Ruth Draws Closer

With a small crowd at Yankee Stadium in the Bronx on Wednesday, September 21, 1927, the Yankees and Detroit Tigers opened the last series of the season between them. After being idle for two days, the Yankees wanted to get back into competition. That afternoon their skipper Miller Huggins started Dutch Ruether, a left-hander. Tigers' manager George Moriarty went with right-hander Sam Gibson.

The Line-Ups

Tigers	Yankees
Lu Blue 1b	Earle Combs cf
Charlie Gehringer 2b	Mark Koenig ss
Heinie Manush cf	Babe Ruth rf
Harry Heilmann rf	Lou Gehrig 1b
Bob Fothergill lf	Bob Meusel lf
Mary McManus 3b	Tony Lazzeri 2b
Jackie Tavener ss	Joe Dugan 3b
Larry Woodall c	Pat Collins c
Sam Gibson p	Dutch Ruether p

The Yankees played very poorly. The club made six errors and failed to hit at critical times with men on. The Tigers scored a run in the first on a walk, an error by Koenig, and a single by Heilmann. The visitors added three more in the third on three singles, two sacrifices, and errors by Koenig and Combs. The Yanks, meanwhile, could do nothing with Gibson, who threw his curveball effectively.

The Tigers picked up one more in the sixth, one in the seventh, and one in the ninth. Trailing 6 to 0, the Yankees came up in the ninth. Ruth caught one of Gibson's pitches on the outside and lifted it into the bleachers in deep right field. The Babe's home run was his fifty-fifth. Gibson then retired the side and the game ended.

Final score: Tigers, 6, Yankees 1.

Yankee Notebook for Wednesday, September 21, 1927: Losing that day, Ruether (13-6) pitched a complete game, giving up eleven hits. He walked five and struck out one . . . The left-hander received no help in the field as Koenig made three errors and Combs, Gehrig, and Lazzeri one each . . . At the plate, the club had seven hits and left fourteen men on the bases . . . Gehrig singled and doubled . . . Ruth had two singles and a home run . . . The Babe had seven games left to hit four home runs to tie his record and five to break it.

At Shibe Park in Philadelphia, the Indians won the opening game of the series with the Athletics in the ninth, 6 to 5. Ty Cobb played his last game of the season and left to go on a hunting trip in Wyoming. Cobb said he was undecided about playing the next year. In Washington, D.C., Senators' pitcher Horace Lisenbee shutout the Browns on five hits and won 10 to 0. Rookie outfielder Foster Ganzel had a perfect day at the plate with four hits for the Senators. At Fenway Park, Red Rollings's pinch hit double in the ninth sent Buddy Meyer home with the winning run as the Red Sox edged the White Sox, 3 to 2.

At Forbes Field, the Pirates defeated the Robins, 4 to 2, and picked up half a game. The Pirates led the National League by three and one-half games over the Giants.

On the afternoon of Thursday, September 22, 1927 the Yankees and Detroit Tigers hooked up again at Yankee Stadium in New York. Right-handers Wilcy Moore and Ownie Carroll pitched.

The game was a see-saw battle.

Going to the top of the ninth, the Yankees led 6 to 4. After McManus and Tavener reached base off Moore, Johnny Neun batted for Carroll and tripled to center, scoring both runners. With the game tied, Huggins brought in southpaw Herb Pennock. When Bluege sacrificed to right, Neun scored and the Tigers led 7 to 6. Ken Holloway, a right-hander, was on the mound when the Yankees came up to bat in the bottom of the ninth.

Koenig opened the ninth with a clean single. As the crowd cheered wildly, Ruth came up to bat. On Holloway's third pitch, the Babe hit his fifty-sixth home run into the right field bleachers. The homer drove in Koenig, and the Yankees won the game.

Before Ruth rounded first base, a youngster in knickerbockers raced onto the field and cut across the field, catching up with the Babe as he rounded third. The boy slapped Ruth on the back with both hands. As the Yankee slugger crossed home plate, the youngster held on to the bat that Ruth carried. As the crowd spilled on to the field, Ruth raced to the dugout with the boy dragging behind.

Final score: Yankees 8, Tigers 7.

Yankee Notebook for Thursday, September 22, 1927: It was a day of achievements . . . The victory was the Yankees' 105th and tied the American League record set by the Red Sox in 1912 . . . Gehrig drove in two runs that brought his total to 172, breaking Ruth's record of 170 set in 1921 . . . Ruth was three home runs from tying his record of 59 and four from setting a new mark with 60 . . . The Yankees had six games left.

On the mound, Pennock (17-8) won the game after pitching 2/3 of an inning . . . Moore went the first 8 1/3 and gave up six runs and nine hits, walking four and striking out none . . . The Yanks had twelve hits off Carroll and Holloway . . . Leading the Yankees in hits was Combs with three triples . . . Gehrig singled and doubled . . . Koenig had two singles and made another error in the field.

That day the Athletics took both games of a doubleheader from the Indians at Shibe Park by scores of 4 to 3 in thirteen innings and 5 to 2. Rookie outfielder Charley Bates, recalled from Pittsfield of the Eastern League, had six hits in the twin bill, including a triple and two doubles.

At Griffith Stadium, the Senators defeated the Browns, 10 to 7. Walter Johnson hit a home run before being knocked out of the box in the fourth. The Senators went on to score nine runs. In Boston, the White Sox lost their twelfth successive game as they were beaten by the Red Sox in thirteen innings, 2 to 1.

With 40,000 fans at Forbes Field, the Pirates and Giants clashed in a doubleheader as New York won the opener 7 to 1 and Pittsburgh took the finale 5 to 2. The loss dropped the Giants to third. In St. Louis, the Cardinals moved into second place after beating the Braves, 6 to 5, at Sportsman's Park. The Pirates finished the day with a three game lead.

At Wrigley Field, Hack Wilson's twenty-eighth home run helped Charley Root defeat the Phillies, 8 to 4. The victory was Root's twenty-sixth. In Cincinnati, the Reds won both games of a doubleheader from the Robins by scores of 2 to 1 in twelve innings and 4 to 3.

The Yankees were not scheduled on Friday, September 23, 1927. The final two games of the series with the Tigers would resume on Saturday and Sunday. Meanwhile, Commissioner Kenesaw Mountain Landis announced that the World Series would open on October 5, 1927 in the home park of the National League pennant winner.

Landis also announced that two umpires from each league would be chosen to officiate the games. In the event a game was called when it was tied, the teams would continue with the series. If the game was needed to decide the championship, the game would return to the city where it had been called after the rest of the games had been finished.

At Fenway Park in Boston, the White Sox snapped their twelve game losing streak with a victory over the Red Sox, 2 to 1 in eleven innings. The game between the Athletics and Indians was postponed by mutual agreement because of a broken water pipe at Shibe Park. The game would be played the next day as a doubleheader.

A crowd of 18,000 at Forbes Field was stunned that day as the Giants overcame a five run Pirates' lead and won, 6 to 5. Coupled with the Cardinals' loss to the Braves by a score of 3 to 2, the Giants climbed back to second place in the National League, two and one-half games behind the leaders.

In Chicago, Hal Carlson shutout the Phillies on seven hits as the Cubs won, 10 to 0, at Wrigley Field. At Redland Field, the Reds and Robins split two games as Cincinnati won the first, 6 to 3 and Brooklyn the second, 4 to 3.

Fifteen thousand fans, one of the smallest crowds of the season, were at Yankee Stadium to see the Yankees and Detroit Tigers on Saturday, September 24, 1927. The club was looking to win its 106th victory and establish a new record for games won in a season. The Babe, meanwhile, was hoping to add to his home run total. Right-handers George Pipgras and Lil Stoner pitched.

In the second inning, Ruble, the left fielder, dropped Meusel's liner. Meusel then stole second and went to third when he beat Tavener's throw to McManus on Dugan's grounder. Pipgras singled, sending Meusel across the plate. Additional runs in the third and sixth gave the Yankees a 3 to 0 lead.

Pipgras was outstanding as he struck out six of the first nine men he faced, and only sixteen batters faced him in the first five innings. The first hit off the Yankee right-hander came in the sixth by Stoner.

In the eighth, the Yanks added three more runs off George Smith, a right-hander, who had replaced Stoner. Going to the ninth, the Tigers trailed by six runs and had only one hit. Gehringer opened with a single. After Manush flied out, Heilmann singled but was forced at second by Ruble. McManus ended the game with a high foul to Bengough.

Final score: Yankees 6, Tigers 0.

Yankee Notebook for Saturday, September 24, 1927: The victory was the Yankees' 106th and set a new record for victories in a single season in the American League . . . Ruth did not homer that day; he had to settle for two singles, while walking one and fanning twice. Once he swung so viciously that he wrenched his left shoulder . . . On the mound, Pipgras (10-3) was superb, allowing only three hits, walking three and striking out seven . . . At the plate, the Yankees had a total of eleven hits . . . Lazzeri and Combs doubled . . . Meusel and Ruth had stolen bases . . . Meusel, Dugan and Bengough sacrificed.

In Philadelphia, the Athletics and Indians split a doubleheader as the home team won the first game, 4 to 3, when Joe Boley drove home the winning run in the eighth. Cleveland came back and took the second, 4 to 3. At Griffith Stadium, the Browns dropped their third straight to the Senators, 5 to 2, as Bump Hadley allowed only five hits. Ending the season's series at Fenway Park, the Red Sox behind Jack Russell defeated the Indians, 3 to 0.

With 40,000 disappointed fans at Forbes Field, the Giants beat the Pirates 3 to 1 by scoring the tying run in the eighth and tallying two in the ninth. The game was decided on Rogers Hornsby single, Bill Terry's triple, and Travis Jackson's sacrifice. The loss cut the Pirates' lead to one and one-half games.

Pitcher Fred Frankenhouse won for the fifth straight time as the Cardinals edged the Braves, 4 to 3, at Sportsman's Park. The victory moved St. Louis to within one-half game of New York and two games of Pittsburgh. At Wrigley Field, the Cubs swept the five game series from the Phillies with a 10 to 2 victory. Hack Wilson and Cy Williams each homered for their teams. Both were tied for the home run lead in the National League with twenty-nine.

In Cincinnati, the Robins and Reds split two games at Redland Field as Cincinnati won the opener in the tenth, 1 to 0. Brooklyn took the finale, 5 to 3, with a three run rally in the ninth.

On a day filled with sunshine, a crowd of 25,000 came out to Yankee Stadium to watch the Yankees and Detroit Tigers faced each other for the last time that season on Sunday, September 25, 1927. With five games left in the schedule, the fans were hopeful that the Babe would hit a home run or two that day, adding to his total of fifty-six. Waite Hoyt, a right-hander, and southpaw Earl Whitehill closed out the series.

The Tigers scored one run in the first; two in the second and two in the sixth. Trailing 5 to 0, Miller Huggins sent Julie Wera up to bat for Hoyt in the sixth, but the Yankees did not score. Right-hander Urban Shocker pitched the seventh and eighth.

Whitehill walked Lazzeri in the eighth. After Gazella popped out, Huggins sent Ben Paschal up to bat for Shocker, but he also popped out. Combs then singled, his third hit of the afternoon, scoring Lazzeri. Left-hander Joe Giard pitched the ninth and he gave up one run. Whitehill retired the Yankees in the bottom of that inning.

Final score: Tigers 6, Yankees 1.

Yankee Notebook for Sunday, September 25, 1927: The Yankees played a listless game . . . The club's hitting and pitching were poor . . . Ruth went to bat five times; he struck out the first time, grounded to the box, singled, and walked twice . . . With fifty-six home runs, the Babe had only four games left to equal or surpass his record of fifty-nine in 1921.

On the mound, Whitehill gave up six hits; three by Combs . . . Hoyt (22-7) gave up eight hits in six innings, including home runs by Blue and Tavener. The Yankee right-hander walked two and struck out one . . . Shocker pitched two and Giard one . . . In the field, Koenig and Meusel had errors . . . Lazzeri stole a base.

In Washington, D.C., Tom Zachary scattered seven hits to his former teammates as the Senators won their fourth straight over the Browns, 10 to 0, at Griffith Stadium. At Dunn Field, Willis Hudlin gave up only four hits as the Indians defeated the White Sox, 10 to 1.

At Wrigley Field, the Pirates took a twin bill from the Cubs behind the superb pitching of Vic Aldridge and Ray Kremer, 2 to 1 and 6 to 1. The victories gave Pittsburgh a two game lead over the second place Cardinals, who took a doubleheader from Boston at Braves Field, 4 to 1 and 6 to 5.

Before a record crowd of 32,000 at Ebbets Field on a very hot day, the Giants and Robins played to a 0 to 0 tie that was called in the seventh because of darkness. The tie game dropped the Giants to third place, two and one-half games behind the Pirates. At Redland Field, the Phillies hammered Jimmy Beckman and beat the Reds, 8 to 3. The start was Beckman's first in the major leagues.

On Monday, September 26, 1927, the Yankees were not scheduled. After the poor game the team played on Sunday, Miller Huggins told the players in no uncertain terms that they needed to take the remaining games seriously and play with determination. He told them that letting down with the series coming up could lead to a disaster. They needed to fight hard and not just go through the motions.

At Fenway Park in Boston, the Senators took a doubleheader from the Red Sox, 4 to 2 and 11 to 1, Horace Lisenbee won the first game, holding the home team to six hits. Boston made ten errors in the second game behind John Wilson, who had been called up from Waterbury of the Eastern League. In Cleveland, Josh Billings scattered three hits as the Tigers edged the Indians, 2 to 1. Cleveland's Walter Miller pitched well.

In Chicago, the Pirates defeated the Cubs, 1 to 0, at Wrigley Field behind the fine pitching of Johnny Miljus. The game was halted at the end of the sixth by rain. At Redland Field, the Cardinals beat the Reds, 3 to 1 in thirteen innings. Meanwhile, the pennant hopes of the Giants were dimmed at Baker Bowl as the Phillies beat them, 9 to 2.

Major League Standings
September 26, 1927
American League

	Won	Lost	P.C.
New York	106	44	.707
Philadelphia	89	60	.597
Washington	82	66	.554
Detroit	80	69	.537
Chicago	66	82	.446
Cleveland	65	84	.436
St. Louis	57	91	.385
Boston	50	99	.336

National League

	Won	Lost	P.C.
Pittsburgh	92	58	.613
St. Louis	90	60	.600
New York	88	61	.591
Chicago	85	66	.563
Cincinnati	72	76	.486
Brooklyn	63	87	.420
Boston	57	92	.383
Philadelphia	50	97	.340

Chapter 38

60th Home Run

The Philadelphia Athletics were in New York for one game on Tuesday, September 27, 1927. That day Commissioner Kenesaw Mountain Landis approved the official list of twenty-seven eligible Yankee players that would participate in the World Series.

Miller Huggins had decided to go with nine pitchers: Ruether, Giard, Hoyt, Moore, Pennock, Pipgras, Shawkey, Shocker, and Thomas. The outfielders, infielders and catchers were Ruth, Combs, Meusel, Durst, Paschal, Gehrig, Lazzeri, Dugan, Koenig, Gazella, Morehart, Wera, Bengough, Collins, and Grabowski. Rounding out the twenty-seven were coaches O'Leary and Fletcher and manager Huggins.

With 15,000 fans at Yankee Stadium, left-handers Herb Pennock and Rube Walberg started that afternoon.

The Line-Ups

Athletics	Yankees
Max Bishop 2b	Earle Combs cf
Jimmy Dykes 3b	Mark Koenig ss
Charlie Bates rf	Babe Ruth rf
Al Simmons cf	Lou Gehrig 1b
Mickey Cochrane c	Bob Meusel lf
Jimmy Foxx 1b	Tony Lazzeri 2b
Walt French lf	Joe Dugan 3b
Joe Boley ss	John Grabowski c
Rube Walberg p	Herb Pennock p

With the Athletics leading 1 to 0, the Yankees batted in the fourth. Facing right-hander Jack Quinn, Gehrig hit his first pitch into the right field bleachers. Sam Gray, a right-hander, finished the inning.

Lefty Grove pitched the fifth. The Yankees picked up a run on a walk, a steal, and Meusel's double and led 2 to 1. In the sixth, Grove was back on the mound. A single by Dugan and walks to Grabowski and Combs loaded the bases. Ruth came to the plate. With the crowd cheering loudly, the Babe hit Grove's pitch high up in the right field bleachers for his fifty-seventh home run. The fans roared as Dugan, Grabowski, Combs, and Ruth circled the bases. Gehrig met Ruth at home plate and congratulated him.

The Yankees picked up one more run in the seventh off Ike Powers, a right-hander. Wilcy Moore pitched the last four innings. With lack of support in the field, Moore gave up runs in the seventh, eighth, and ninth.

Final score: Yankees 7, Athletics 4.

Yankee Notebook for Tuesday, September 27, 1927: Ruth's home run with the bases filled was only the sixth grand-slam in his career and third with the Yankees . . . The Babe had fifty-seven home runs with three games left, all against the Senators at the Stadium . . . Gehrig's homer was his forty-sixth and first since September 6 at Fenway Park . . . The Yankees set another record. By scoring seven runs they had run their total for the season to 952, a new American League record. The major league record at that time was 1,221 set by the Boston Braves of the National League in 1894.

That afternoon Pennock (18-8) was the winning pitcher. He went five innings, giving up four hits. The left-hander walked none and struck out three . . . The Yanks had ten hits off Walberg, Quinn, Gray, Grove, and Powers . . . Lazzeri and Dugan had three hits each and Ruth two . . . Dugan and Meusel doubled . . . The infield played poorly—Koenig made two errors and Gehrig and Lazzeri one each.

Rain postponed the game between the Senators and Red Sox at Boston in the American League.

In the National League at Wrigley Field, the Pirates retained a two-game lead over the Cardinals as they completed a four-game sweep of the Cubs, 2 to 1. George Grantham's home run with Pie Traynor aboard decided the game. Lee Meadows, Carmen Hill, and Ray Kremer pitched for Pittsburgh.

In Cincinnati, Grover Cleveland Alexander allowed only three hits—two singles and a triple—as the Cardinals defeated the Reds, 4 to 1. Looking to pass the Cardinals and finish second, the Giants pounded the Phillies for eighteen hits, 5 to 2, at Baker Bowl.

The Yankees were idle on Wednesday, September 28, 1927 and waited for the Washington Senators to come into New York and finish the season with a three-game series. The talk in New York and across the country was whether Ruth with fifty-seven home runs could break his record with three games left in the season.

John Drebinger's account in the *New York Times* that day captured what the record meant to Ruth. Drebinger wrote:

"There is no denying that the Babe has his heart set on a new record and wants it badly. Back in 1921, after the Babe had carved his mark of fifty-nine, experts were free in predicting that the record, unless surpassed at once in the year or two to follow by Ruth himself, doubtless would stand for many years. As season after season rolled by with Babe, as well as all others, failing to approach the mark the critics were convinced that the high-water in home run hitting had been reached."

"But today, six years later, finds the Babe standing on the threshold of topping that great record. It has been an arduous campaign and Ruth himself realizes quite fully that the breaks of the game may never afford him another opportunity of getting that close to the mark again."

At Griffith Stadium in Washington, D.C., the Senators and Red Sox ended their season series as the home team won, 2 to 1 and 6 to 4. Clark Griffith, President of the Senators, announced that pitcher Sam Jones was obtained from the Browns and would join the club in Spring Training next season. The game between the Tigers and White Sox was postponed because of wet grounds at Chicago. Rain cancelled the contest between the Indians and Browns at St. Louis.

In Philadelphia, the Giants edged the Phillies, 5 to 4, at Baker Bowl. Cy Williams hit his league leading thirtieth home run for the host team. Rain postponed the game between the Cardinals and Reds at Cincinnati.

On Thursday, September 29, 1927, the Yankees and Washington Senators opened the last series of the season at Yankee Stadium in New York. There was a small crowd of about 7,500 at the ballpark. Rookie right-hander Horace Lisenbee, who had won eighteen games with four shutouts, opened for manager Bucky Harris. Looking for his eighteenth victory was the Yankees' Urban Shocker.

The Line-Ups

Senators	Yankees
Sam Rice rf	Earle Combs cf
Bucky Harris 2b	Mark Koenig ss
Foster Ganzel cf	Babe Ruth rf
Goose Goslin lf	Lou Gehrig 1b
Joe Judge 1b	Bob Meusel lf
Bennie Tate c	Tony Lazzeri 2b
Ossie Bluege 3b	Joe Dugan 3b
Bobby Reeves ss	Pat Collins c
Horace Lisenbee p	Urban Shocker p

With two outs and no one on, the Babe came up in the first. Lisenbee threw two quick strikes over the plate. He then tried to throw a curve for the third strike. However, Ruth swung and drove the ball a few rows up in the right field bleachers for his fifty-eighth home run.

The Yankees knocked Lisenbee out of the box in the second, scoring seven runs. During the scoring spree, Ruth hit a long ball that struck the left wing of the bleacher barrier for a triple. Marberry replaced Lisenbee and pitched two and a third innings.

The Yankees were ahead 11 to 4 when the club faced Paul Hopkins, a right-hander, who had picked up his first major league victory when he debuted two days earlier. Ruth came up with the bases loaded and walloped a pitch that landed half way up the right bleachers. It was home run number fifty-nine.

Ruth had equaled his mark of 1921!

The crowd roared and cheered as the Babe trotted around the bases. Ruth doffed his cap and shook hands with Gehrig at the plate.

After Shocker went four innings, Huggins brought in left-hander Dutch Ruether for three innings of work and right-hander Bob Shawkey for two.

Final score: Yankees 15, Senators 4.

Yankee Notebook for September 29, 1927: The Babe had two games left to set a new home run record of 60 . . . That day the Yankees reached Lisenbee, Marberry, and Hopkins for nineteen hits: Koenig, Ruth, Meusel and Lazzeri had three hits each . . . Meusel had two doubles and a triple . . . Collins also doubled . . . Lazzeri stole a base . . . Koenig made another error at shortstop . . . Shocker (18-6) was credited with the victory, giving up two runs on three hits, walking one, and striking out none . . . Ruether and Shawkey finished the game.

In the American League at Shibe Park in Philadelphia, rookie pitcher Jack Bradley held the Athletics to five hits as the Red Sox won, 6 to 1. Rain postponed the games between the White Sox and Tigers at Detroit and Indians and Browns at St. Louis.

The Pirates were idle and by the end of the day needed only one win in the upcoming series at Cincinnati to clinch the National League pennant. With only 340 fans at Redland Field, the Reds just about ended the Cardinals' pennant hopes by edging the visitors on a rain soaked field, 3 to 2. The best the Cardinals could do was tie for the pennant if they won both their remaining games and the Pirates lost their final three. At Braves Field, rookie Russ Miller scattered eleven hits as the Phillies defeated the Braves, 7 to 1.

Ten thousand fans came to Yankee Stadium on Friday, September 30, 1927 for one reason only, to see Babe Ruth set a new home run record. That afternoon left-hander Tom Zachary pitched for the Senators. George Pipgras, a right-hander, hurled for the Yankees.

For three innings there was no score. The Senators broke through for two runs in the fourth, and the Yankees came back with one run in the bottom half of the inning. The Yanks tied the game in the sixth after Ruth singled to right, moved to second on Gehrig's single, and scored on a single to center by Meusel.

After Pipgras went six innings, Huggins replaced him with Herb Pennock. With the score still tied in the eighth, Koenig tripled with one man out.

Ruth came up to the plate and faced Zachary.

The southpaw's first pitch to Ruth was a fast ball that was called a strike by umpire Bill Dineen. The next pitch was high. On the third pitch—a fast ball, low and on the inside of the plate—the Babe pulled away from the plate then stepped into the ball and connected. As the crowd stood and roared loudly, everyone in the stadium watched the ball travel on a line, landing a foot inside fair territory about half way up the right field bleachers.

It was home run number sixty!

As the fans and players cheered, Ruth jogged around the bases slowly, almost majestically, touching each bag firmly and carefully. Hats and torn up paper were thrown onto the field in celebration. Zachary watched the ball land in the bleachers. Knowing that he would go into the record books as the one who gave up the historic home run, he tossed his glove to the ground and turned to his teammates, almost for consolation.

Koenig scored and headed to the dugout. Ruth tipped his cap to the crowd and was congratulated by Gehrig at home plate. Ruth strolled backed to the dugout with Eddie Bennett, the club's mascot along side holding the Babe's bat.

The players and Huggins were standing in the dugout applauding.

As Ruth strolled to his position in right field in the ninth, the bleacherites waved handkerchiefs, and the Babe returned the fans' greetings with a succession of snappy military salutes. The game ended after Pennock retired the Senators in the ninth.

Final score: Yankees 4, Senators 2.

Yankee Notebook for Friday, September 30, 1927: The fan that had caught Ruth's historic home run rushed to the dressing room after the game to let the Babe know he had the ball. His name was Joe Forner, about forty years of age, who lived on First Avenue in Manhattan . . .

That afternoon, Pennock (19-8) was the winning pitcher. The left-hander went the final three innings and gave up only one hit, walking one and striking out none . . . Pipgras had worked the first six and left with the game tied . . . For the Senators, Zachary gave up nine hits . . . Ruth had three hits, the home run and two singles, driving in all four runs that day.

In Chicago, the White Sox won two games from the Tigers, 5 to 4 in thirteen and 4 to 1. Bibb Falk's run scoring single in the first contest gave Tommy Thomas his eighteenth victory. In St. Louis, the Browns and Indians split a twin bill as Cleveland won the opener, 5 to 4, and St. Louis took the finale, 9 to 4. By agreement, the Red Sox and Athletics called off the game for unspecified reasons and decided to play a doubleheader the next day, winding up the baseball season in Philadelphia.

At Redland Field, the Pirates failed to clinch the National League pennant as the Reds, behind the brilliant pitching of Red Lucas and sensational fielding by second baseman Hughie Critz, beat the league leaders, 2 to 1. The loss cut Pittsburgh's lead to two games over the Cardinals, who were idle. The Giants were eliminated from the race after losing to the Robins and Dazzy Vance, 10 to 5, at Ebbets Field. At Braves Field, the Braves pounded Lefty Tabor and Jack Scott for eighteen hits and beat the Phillies, 12 to 2.

On the next to last day of the major league baseball season, the Yankees played their last scheduled game on Saturday, October 1, 1927. Closing out the series with the Washington Senators was Wilcy Moore. Pitching for Manager Bucky Harris was left-hander Bobby Burke. The crowd of 20,000 hoped to see the Babe add to his historic home run total of sixty.

In the first inning, the Yankees scored four runs off Burke before he retired a batter. The Yanks scored after Combs bounced a hit off the pitcher and came home on Koenig's triple that bounced off the barrier in front of the left field stands. Ruth was walked amid boos from the crowd. Gehrig then came to the plate and homered into the right field bleachers.

The Senators fought back.

They got one of the runs back off Moore in the second on Goslin's double and Tate's single. Hits by Barnes and Reeves gave them another in the third and they scored another in the fifth. With the score 4 to 3 in the sixth, Huggins brought in Waite Hoyt. After giving up a leadoff double to Tate, Hoyt finished the game and did not allow another base runner.

Final score: Yankees 4, Senators 3.

Yankee Notebook for Saturday, October 1, 1927: The Babe struggled against Burke and Braxton . . . Burke walked Ruth the first time up, held him to a high pop fly to right in the third inning, and an infield out in the fifth. In his last at bat of the season in the eighth, Braxton struck him out . . . Gehrig's home run was his forty-seventh of the season, second most in the majors . . . The victory was the Yankees' 110th of the season, a new American League record . . . The four runs they scored gave the club a total of 975, which set another league record.

Moore (19-7) was credited with the victory. He went five innings and gave up six hits, walking one and striking out two . . . Moore also ended up with thirteen saves, tied with Braxton for most in the major leagues . . . Hoyt gave up one hit in five innings, walking none, and striking out one . . . At the plate, Combs and Meusel each had two of the eight hits Burke and Braxton yielded . . . Koenig had an error.

The Athletics ended their season at Shibe Park by taking a doubleheader from the Red Sox by scores of 10 to 2 and 3 to 2. In the twin bill, Al Simmons had five hits in seven times at bat. In the finale, Eddie Collins came to the plate four times and had four hits. Jimmy Dykes pitched the final inning of the second game and retired the Red Sox without a hit.

At Comiskey Park, the White Sox took a doubleheader from the Browns, 8 to 5, and 5 to 3. The second game was called after five because of darkness. Rain postponed the game between the Indians and Tigers at Detroit.

The Pirates clinched the National League pennant by defeating the Reds, 9 to 6, at Redland Field. The game was decided on Pie Traynor's single with the bases loaded with two outs in the sixth. The pennant was the Pirates' second in three years and their sixth in franchise history.

At Ebbets Field, the Giants ended the season rivalry with the Robins with a victory, 6 to 1. In Boston, the Braves took a doubleheader from the Phillies that day, 14 to 9, and 8 to 6. Rain postponed the game between the Cubs and Cardinals at St. Louis.

On Sunday, October 2, 1927, the major league baseball season ended. Having finished the season the day before, the Yankees were off and packed for the trip that evening to Pittsburgh by train. The World Series was to open on Wednesday.

On the final day of the season in the American League, the Senators closed with a victory over the Athletics, 9 to 5, at Griffith Stadium. With the loss, the Athletics finished in second place, nineteen games behind the Yankees. At Navin Field, the Tigers completed their schedule with two victories over the Indians, 11 to 5 and 5 to 4. The Browns defeated the White Sox, 8 to 3, at Comiskey Park.

The National League schedule ended with the Pirates losing to the Reds, 1 to 0, at Redland Field. The only regular in the Pittsburgh lineup was Lloyd Waner. The Cardinals finished in second place as they beat the Cubs, 6 to 4, at Sportsman's Park in a game called in the eighth because of rain. The Giants ended the season defeating the Phillies, 5 to 4, in ten innings at the Polo Grounds. At Ebbets Field, the Robins finished with a victory over the Braves, 5 to 3.

Major League Final Standings
October 2, 1927
American League

	Won	Lost	P.C.
New York	110	44	.714
Philadelphia	91	63	.591
Washington	85	69	.552
Detroit	82	71	.536
Chicago	70	83	.458
Cleveland	66	87	.431
St. Louis	59	94	.386
Boston	51	103	.331

National League

	Won	Lost	P.C.
Pittsburgh	94	60	.610
St. Louis	92	61	.601
New York	92	62	.597
Chicago	85	68	.556
Cincinnati	75	78	.490
Brooklyn	65	88	.425
Boston	60	94	.390
Philadelphia	51	103	.331

Epilogue

On Sunday evening October 2, 1927, more than a thousand people were jammed around the gate that led down the stairway to the train platform at Pennsylvania Station in New York City. The *Yankee Special* was waiting to take the New York Yankees to Pittsburgh for the opening of the World Series. As the players, manager, coaches, and executives arrived, a special contingent of policemen cleared a path. Amidst the people and noise, red caps were scurrying with the Yankees' baggage.

The crowd kept an eager look out for the Babe Ruth. When he showed up the people cheered and almost knocked him off his feet as they wanted to shake his hand. There were numerous youngsters in the crowd. Ruth shook hands with many of them, telling them that he felt that he was going to crash a few home runs in the World Series. As Ruth descended the stairs, the crowd cheered loudly.

On the platform, Yankees' official Mark Roth distributed train tickets and assigned berths. Everyone on the team was expected on the train with the exception of Herb Pennock, who would be picked up at the train's first stop at the North Philadelphia Station.

Waite Hoyt showed up about two minutes before the train was scheduled to leave. As the *Yankee Special* was ready to pull out with its doors closing, Bob Meusel and Tony Lazzeri boarded. As a score of people waved and cheered on the platform, the train left at 10:30 p.m. As the *Yankee Special* pulled out of the station, Ruth and his teammates waved back.

On the train heading West, Miller Huggins met with reporters and talked about the Pittsburgh Pirates. The biggest threat at the plate was outfielder Paul Waner, who had batted .380 and won the batting crown, with 237 hits. Waner had driven in 131 runs, another league high. His brother Lloyd, an outfielder, could also hit, batting .355 in his rookie year. Third baseman Pie Traynor had a fine year batting .342 and hard-hitting first baseman Joe Harris hit .326. The Pirates batted a league high .305 but hit only fifty-four home runs as a team.

On the mound, the Pirates had right-handers Ray Kremer (19-8, 2.47 era); Lee Meadows (19-10 3.40 era), Carmen Hill (22-11, 3.24 era), and Vic Aldridge (15-10, 4.26 era).

Some later said the series was decided the day before it began. That was the day the Yankees practiced at Forbes Field. The Pirates had worked out first on Monday, October 3, 1927, showered, changed, and left the clubhouse. Before heading back to their homes, however, many of them sat in the stands and watched the Yankees take batting practice. Most had never seen the team and wanted a look.

Miller Huggins wanted to show the Pirates what they were in store for and gave instructions to the batting practice pitcher to lay them in for the batters.

The Yankees really put on a show.

Babe Ruth and Lou Gehrig walloped one ball after another into the right field stands. Then the Babe knocked one out of Forbes Field in right center. After Ruth and Gehrig batted, Bob Meusel and Tony Lazzeri hammered one ball after another into the left field stands. One by one, the Pirates got up and left the park. Many people, including Ruth, thought that the Yankees' awesome batting exhibition that day affected the Pirates' confidence.

Before the World Series began, Huggins met with the players in the clubhouse and reminded them of the importance of attitude.

"Feel that you want to play this series," said Huggins. "Realize just what a great team you are. Play the games as fun, have a good time when out in your positions. Forget your mistakes and errors. Above all, hustle all the time."

The 1927 World Series opened under sunny skies and balmy weather at Forbes Field in Pittsburgh, Pennsylvania on Wednesday, October 5. The crowd of 41,467 saw right-handers Waite Hoyt (22-6, 2.64 era) and Ray Kremer (19-8, 2.47 era) oppose each other in Game One.

Kremer was the Pirates' ace, known for a blazing fast ball, a good curve, and an effective change of pace.

The Governor of Pennsylvania, John S. Fisher was at Forbes Field, as well as New York City Mayor Jimmy Walker. Commissioner

Kenesaw Mountain Landis was seated near the Yankees' dug out. National League President John A. Heydler was in another field box.

Adding to the festivities was a brass band in red coats that paraded around the field before the game. The photographers took pictures of Pirates' Manager Donie Bush and Miller Huggins shaking hands. The Babe was photographed with Huggins, Bush, Mayor Walker, Lou Gehrig, and the Waners.

Sitting with the Yankee party in Colonel Jacob Ruppert's field box was Bob Connery, the President of the St. Paul Club and former chief scout of the Yankees. Waite Hoyt went over to Ruppert before the game.

"Don't be nervous, Colonel," Hoyt said.

"Don't you be nervous," retorted Ruppert. "Never mind me. I don't have to pitch."

The Line-Ups

Yankees	Pirates
Earle Combs cf	Lloyd Waner cf
Mark Koenig ss	Clyde Barnhart lf
Babe Ruth rf	Paul Waner rf
Lou Gehrig 1b	Glenn Wright ss
Bob Meusel lf	Pie Traynor 3b
Tony Lazzeri 2b	George Grantham 2b
Joe Dugan 3b	Joe Harris 1b
Pat Collins c	Earl Smith c
Waite Hoyt p	Ray Kremer p

Combs hit the first ball Kremer threw and drove it deep to left field, where Barnhart caught it. After Koenig struck out swinging, Ruth came up. He swung at the first ball and singled to right field for the first hit of the series. Then on a count of three and two, Gehrig hit a short fly to right field. P. Waner tried to make a shoestring catch, but the ball got through him for a triple and Ruth scored.

In the bottom of the first, the Pirates tied the game at one. L. Waner was hit by a pitch, moved to third on his brother's double, and tagged on Wright's sacrifice fly. With one out in the third, Grantham kicked Koenig's grounder behind first base for an error. Ruth again hit Kremer's first pitch and smashed a single to right, sending Koenig to third. Gehrig walked.

With the bases loaded, Kremer walked Meusel, forcing home Koenig. Lazzeri then grounded to Wright, who got the ball to second in time to force Meusel, but Grantham could not get rid of it in time to complete a double play. Ruth scored. With Gehrig on third and Lazzeri on first, a double steal was attempted. Smith made a bluff throw to second and then threw to Traynor at third, catching Gehrig halfway between the bases, but Smith let Traynor's return to the plate get past him for an error. Gehrig scored. The Yankees led 4 to 1.

The Pirates picked up one run in the bottom of the third on Kremer's double and P. Waner's single, making the score 4 to 2. After Hoyt developed a blister on a finger of his pitching hand in the fourth, Huggins watched him carefully. Koenig doubled to center in the fifth and went to third when Ruth grounded out to Grantham. Gehrig's sacrifice fly to P. Waner scored Koenig.

The Pirates came back with one run in the bottom of the inning on L. Waner's double and Barnhart's single to left. After Lazzeri doubled in the sixth, Pirates' Manager Donie Bush lifted Kremer and brought in right-hander Johnny Miljus, who retired the side.

Pittsburgh came up in the eighth trailing 5 to 3. Wright lined a single over Lazzeri's head. Then Traynor lined a single to center. Wright stopped at second. Huggins decided that Hoyt had enough and called for Wilcy Moore.

Grantham grounded to Gehrig who threw to Koenig in time to force Traynor at second. On the play, Koenig was bowled over and had the air knocked out of him. Wright went to third on the play and scored on Harris's single to center, making the score 5 to 4. On a daring run and long slide, Grantham beat Combs's throw to third. Smith then grounded to Gehrig, who stepped on first to end the inning. Moore retired the Pirates in order in the ninth. The Yankees won Game One of the World Series, 5 to 4.

With a crowd of 41,634 at Forbes Field, the Yankees and Pittsburgh Pirates played Game Two of the World Series on Thursday, October 6,

1927. Under sunny skies with warm temperatures, right-handers George Pipgras (10-3, 4.12 era) and Vic Aldridge (15-10, 4.26 era) pitched for the Yankees and Pirates, respectively.

The Pirates opened the scoring in the bottom of the first after L. Waner tripled down the left field foul line. Then Barnhart drove Ruth up against the concrete wall in right to catch his sacrifice fly. Waner scored.

Down 1 to 0, the Yanks came up in the third. Combs singled between Harris and Grantham. When Koenig lined a single over second, Combs raced to third. Then L. Waner fumbled the ball, Combs scored, and Koenig reached third. Ruth then lifted a high sacrifice fly to L. Waner and Koenig scored. Gehrig doubled to the exit gate in right center. Wright then made an acrobatic stop of Meusel's drive toward left but could not regain his balance to throw Meusel out. Gehrig reached third base. When Lazzeri hit a sacrifice fly to P. Waner, Gehrig scored. The Yankees led 3 to 1.

Pipgras pitched beautifully. His fast ball was blazing and his curve broke well. Over the first seven innings, he scattered only six hits. With the score 3 to 1 in the eighth, Meusel singled over second. On a hit-and-run play, Lazzeri singled to right field. Meusel raced to third. When Aldridge threw a wild pitch almost knocking Dugan down, Meusel scored and Lazzeri went to second. Dugan attempted a sacrifice, but Gooch pounced on the ball and threw to third base to get Lazzeri, who was called out as he slid over the bag.

Aldridge then walked Bengough and Pipgras. With the bases loaded, Bush took out Aldridge and replaced him with Mike Cvengros, a left-hander, who hit Combs forcing in Dugan. When Koenig singled, Bengough scored making the score 6 to 1.

In the home half of the eighth the Pirates scored a run on a walk, a single, and a sacrifice fly. Pirates' right-hander Joe Dawson pitched the ninth. Pipgras retired the Pirates in the bottom of the ninth. The Yankees won, 6 to 2, and led the series two games to none. Game Three was scheduled for New York the next day.

On Friday, October 7, 1927, the third game of the World Series was played at Yankee Stadium in New York. With 60,695 fans at the ballpark, left-hander Herb Pennock (19-8, 2 saves, 3.00 era) pitched for the Yankees, and Lee Meadows (19-10, 3.40 era), a right-hander, started for the Pirates. Before the game Babe Ruth and Lou Gehrig were presented with a floral horseshoe and floral bats.

The Line-Ups

Pirates	Yankees
Lloyd Waner cf	Earle Combs cf
Hal Rhyne 2b	Mark Koenig ss
Paul Waner rf	Babe Ruth rf
Glenn Wright ss	Lou Gehrig 1b
Pie Traynor 3b	Bob Meusel lf
Clyde Barnhart lf	Tony Lazzeri 2b
Joe Harris 1b	Joe Dugan 3b
Johnny Gooch c	Johnny Grabowski c
Lee Meadows p	Herb Pennock p

Pennock opened the game by retiring L. Waner on an easy roller to Koenig. Rhyne, who replaced an injured Grantham, and P. Waner then hit fly balls to Meusel in left. With the Yankees up in the first, on a count of two and two Combs slapped a single over second. Koenig got an infield hit on a ground ball that bounced off Meadow's glove and was kicked about by Rhyne. Combs reached second. After Ruth popped to Wright behind second, Gehrig got hold off a fast ball and drove it to the running track in left center field. Combs and Koenig scored, but Gehrig was thrown out at the plate. The Yankees led 2 to 0.

Pennock was in total control. He retired the Pirates in order with out a hit over the first seven innings. Lazzeri opened the home half of the seventh with a single into short center, only the Yankees' fifth hit of the game. Dugan sacrificed Lazzeri to second, and when Meadows tried to beat the runner to the bag, Dugan was safe at first.

Huggins sent up Cedric Durst to bat for Grabowski. When he grounded out, Lazzeri went to third and Dugan to second. Rhyne fielded Pennock's slow grounder but threw to the plate too late to get Lazzeri.

Dugan landed up on third and Pennock on first. Koenig then doubled to the right-field bleachers scoring Pennock and putting Combs on third.

Left-hander Mike Cvengos replaced Meadows. Ruth then walloped a home run high into the right-field bleachers. The crowd cheered wildly as he trotted around the bases behind Combs and Koenig. The inning finally ended when Cvengos struck out Gehrig and Meusel. The Yankees led 8 to 0.

In the eighth, Benny Bengough replaced Grabowski behind the plate. Pennock had not given up a hit. The southpaw got Wright to ground out to Koenig, but the perfect game ended when Traynor singled to left. Barnhart then doubled to right center scoring Traynor. That made the score 8 to 1.

In the ninth, Heinie Groh, hitting for Cvengos, popped up to Pennock. L.Waner then singled down the third base line. Rhyne flied to Combs for the second out. After L.Waner stole second uncontested, his brother Paul popped up to Lazzeri for the final out of the game. Behind Pennock's three-hit masterpiece, the Yankees won Game Three of the World Series, 8 to 1.

The players were jubilant. Pennock was masterful. Ruth and Gehrig hit well and Dugan, Lazzeri, Koenig, and Combs glittered in the field.

"Pennock pitched a wonderful ball game. He had everything except for weak moments and for a time I thought he was going to have not only a shutout but a no-hit game to his credit," Huggins told reporters.

Looking to become the first American League club to sweep a World Series in four straight games, Miller Huggins sent right-hander Wilcy Moore (19-7, 13 saves, 2.28 era) to the mound against the Pirates on Saturday, October 8, 1927. Right-hander Carmen Hill (22-11, 3 saves, 3.24 era) pitched for the Pirates.

L. Waner opened the game with a drive off Moore's glove that the Pirates' outfielder beat out for a hit. Koenig threw out Barnhart as Waner advanced to second. Wright singled to right and Waner scored. The Yankees tied the game at one in the bottom of the first. Combs singled to right, moved to second on Koenig's hit to right, and scored on Ruth's single to right.

The Yankees came up in the sixth. Combs singled to short center field. After Koenig missed a third strike, Ruth came up and hit his second home run of the series into the center field series. The crowd cheered wildly. Ruth circled the bases and was greeted at home plate by Gehrig. The Yankees led 3 to 1.

In the seventh, Smith grounded to Gehrig and was beaten by a toss to Moore, who came to cover first base; however, Moored dropped the ball for an error. Emil Yde ran for Smith. Fred Brickell batted for Hill.

Lazzeri in his haste to make a double play on Brickell's grounder, misplayed the ball. Yde reached second, and Brickell was safe at first. Then L. Waner dropped a sacrifice bunt, moving Yde to third and Brickell to second. Barnhart singled over second base, scoring Yde and sending Brickell to third. The Pirates tied the game at three when P. Waner lifted a sacrifice fly to Combs, scoring Brickell.

There was a new battery for the Pirates in the seventh: right-hander Johnny Miljus and catcher Johnny Gooch. The score remained tied through the seventh, eighth and top of the ninth. The Yankees came up in the ninth with a chance to win the game and the series.

Miljus opened the ninth with a walk to Combs. Koenig then dropped a bunt down the third base line for a single. With Ruth batting, Miljus suddenly let loose a wild pitch. Combs took third and Koenig went to second. Bush ordered Miljus to walk Ruth.

The bases were loaded. Gehrig came up and missed a third strike. Meusel then came up with one out, and Miljus struck him out on a called third strike for the second out. Lazzeri was the next batter. With Combs, Koenig, and Ruth on the bases, Lazzeri swung and hit a long foul ball into the left field bleachers for strike one.

On the next pitch, Miljus uncorked another wild pitch, and Combs raced home with the winning run.

The Yankees won the 1927 World Series.

With the series over, the Yankees went to the clubhouse and celebrated. The players were singing, dancing, and laughing. Commissioner Landis was among the first visitors, congratulating the players and Miller Huggins. Wally Pipp, the former Yankees' first baseman, and former scout Bob Connery were also there.

The reporters assembled around Huggins and asked for a statement.

"I want you boys to say something nice about the Pittsburgh team," Huggins told them. "They have had a lot of tough luck in this series. They had their greatest piece of tough luck just a few minutes ago out there on the field. I am glad we won. I'm happy beyond words that we took the series in four games. I've known all along that we had a great ball club. Now I guess everybody will admit we have. But that Pittsburgh team is a better team than it has been in this series. I know it's tough to lose, just as I knew all along we were their masters. But they deserve a break. Give it to them."

Then Jacob Ruppert came into the clubhouse, so happy he could hardly talk.

"Well, Jake," the Babe yelled at Ruppert, "I guess this makes you feel better after the way we blew the 1926 series on you."

"You're right, 'Root,' replied Ruppert. "I never was so happy in my life. The team was wonderful and you were great."

Amid the yelling and laughing of the players, Miller Huggins listened to the good-natured banter and smiled.

The End

Afterword

For those with an interest in what happened to the principals on the Yankees after the 1927 season, a brief summation of their life on and off the baseball diamond is offered.

Edward Grant Barrow . . . Recommended Joe McCarthy as manager for the 1931 season after Bob Shawkey managed the club to a third place finish in 1930 . . . Rebuked by Yankees' owner Jacob Ruppert in 1930 for assaulting Bill Slocum, a veteran New York sportswriter, within the stadium grounds . . . Acquired Joe DiMaggio from the San Francisco Seals in November 1934 for $25,000 and players . . . Built a farm system with his assistant George Weiss.

Named president of the Yankees in 1939 after the death of Jacob Ruppert . . . Retained his duties as business manager . . . Resigned as president in January 1945 after a syndicate headed by Larry MacPhail, Dan Topping, and Del Webb purchased the Yankees for $2,800,000 . . . Served as Chairman of the Board of Directors . . . Disposed of his stock for $300,000 and retired after the 1946 season . . . Won 14 pennants and 10 world championships . . . Finished with a managerial record of 311 wins and 321 losses . . . Honored on May 13, 1950 at Yankee Stadium.

Elected to the Hall-of-Fame in September 1953 . . . Died from cancer at United Hospital in Port Chester, New York on December 15, 1953 at the age of 85 . . . Honored on April 15, 1954 with a plaque dedicated to his memory on the centerfield wall in Yankee Stadium . . . Buried in Kenisco Cemetery in Valhalla, New York.

Miller Huggins . . . Won his sixth pennant as manager of the Yankees in 1928 . . . Defeated the St. Louis Cardinals in the '28 World Series, 4 games to 0 . . . Began losing weight and feeling ill in September 1929 . . . Developed a large, ugly pimple on his cheek . . . Hospitalized at St. Vincent's in New York City on September 20, 1929 . . . Turned the team over to Art Fletcher with eleven games left . . . Died on

September 25, 1929 at the age of 50 from erysipelas—a form of blood poisoning . . . The team learned of his death at Fenway Park in Boston . . . Players and coaches wept openly on the bench.

Funeral services were held in New York City on September 27, 1929 . . . Ten thousand people stood outside the church in tribute . . . All American Leagues games were cancelled on the day of the funeral . . . Arthur Fletcher, Charles O'Leary, Babe Ruth, Herb Pennock, Bob Shawkey, Tony Lazzeri, Lou Gehrig, and Earle Combs served as pallbearers.

Honored on May 30, 1932 with a monument in center field at Yankee Stadium . . . Overall record as major league manager: 1,413 wins and 1,134 losses . . . As manager of the Yankees: 1,067 wins and 719 losses . . . Won six pennants and three world championships . . . Elected to the Hall-of-Fame in 1964 . . . Buried at Woodlawn Cemetery in Cincinnati, Ohio.

George Herman Ruth . . . Played with the Yankees through the 1934 season . . . Wanted the Yankee managerial position but was turned down by Ruppert and Barrow . . . Given his unconditional release and signed with the Boston Braves in 1935 as player, coach, and vice president . . . Retired in June 1935 . . . Elected to the Hall of Fame in 1936 . . . Coached for the Brooklyn Dodgers for part of 1938 . . . Homered twice off Walter Johnson before 69,000 fans in a War Bonds exhibition game at Yankee Stadium on August 23, 1942 . . . Stricken with throat cancer in 1946.

Honored during ceremonies on "Babe Ruth Day" on April 27, 1947 . . . Made his last appearance at Yankee Stadium on June 13, 1948 at the Old Timers' Game . . . Established or equaled 54 major league records . . . Played in 2503 games, scored 2174 runs and had 2873 hits, including 714 home runs . . . Played in seven World Series . . . Died of throat cancer at the age of 53 on August 16, 1948 in New York City.

Laid in state for one and a half days at Yankee Stadium as more than 100,000 mourners paid their respects . . . Funeral services were held at St. Patrick's Cathedral . . . Pall bearers were Waite Hoyt, Joe

Dugan, Whitey Witt, Connie Mack, and sportswriter Fred Lieb . . . Buried in Mount Pleasant, New York.

Henry Louis Gehrig . . . Won the American League Most Valuable Player (MVP) Award in 1927 . . . Drove in a major league record 184 runs in 1931 . . . Hit four consecutive home runs on June 3, 1932 . . . In the 1932 World Series hit three home runs in four games, drove in eight and batted .529 . . . Won the Triple Crown in 1934 (.363, 49 homers, 165 RBIs) . . . Named MVP in 1936 . . . Played in 2130 consecutive games from June 1, 1925 through April 30, 1939.

Diagnosed in 1939 with a fatal disease—amyotrophic lateral sclerosis—and was forced to retire . . . In 17 seasons had 2721 hits, 493 home runs, and batted .340 . . . Honored on July 4, 1939 at Yankee Stadium on "Lou Gehrig Appreciation Day". With almost 62,000 fans at the ballpark, Gehrig gave an emotional speech and said, in part. "Today I consider myself the luckiest man on the face of the earth."

Elected to the Hall of Fame in 1939 . . . Appointed a special assistant by New York City Mayor Fiorello LaGuardia to work with young juveniles in 1940 . . . Died on June 2, 1941, just before his 38th birthday, in Riverdale, New York . . . A monument was dedicated in his memory at Yankee Stadium on July 4, 1941 . . . Cremated and buried in Westchester, New York.

Robert William Meusel . . . Played for the Yankees only two more seasons—1928 and 1929 . . . Batted .261 with 10 home runs and 57 runs batted in 1929 with the Yankees . . . Sold to the Cincinnati Reds on October 16, 1929 . . . Batted .289 with the Reds in 1930, with 10 home runs and 62 runs batted in . . . Played with Minneapolis of the American Association in 1931 and batted .283 . . . Finished his baseball career in 1932 with Hollywood of the Pacific Coast League, batting .329 . . . Acted in Joe E. Brown's movie "Alibi Ike" in 1935 . . . Spent 10 years in the major leagues and batted .309, with 1693 hits, 368 doubles, 95 triples, 156 home runs, and 1067 runs batted in . . . Played in six World Series and batted .225 . . . Worked for 15 years as a security guard with the U.S. Navy . . . Died November 28, 1977 at age 81 of heart failure at Kaiser Foundation Hospital, Bellflower, CA . . . Cremated on December 1, 1977 at Rose Hills Crematory.

Mark Anthony Koenig . . . Played for the Yankees until May 1930 . . . Traded to the Detroit Tigers with Waite Hoyt . . . Developed problems with his eye sight . . . Tried out as a pitcher by the Tigers . . . Signed with the San Francisco Missions Club in the Pacific Coast League in 1932, where he batted .335 . . . Purchased by the Chicago Cubs in August 1932 . . . Batted .353 and was credited with helping the Cubs win the pennant . . . Faced the Yankees in the '32 World Series. There were bad feelings between the Yankees and Cubs because Koenig was voted only half share of the Series money.

Traded to the Philadelphia Phillies in November 1933 and then sent to the Cincinnati Reds in a trade in December . . . Batted .272 in 151 games for the Reds in 1934 . . . Played for the New York Giants in 1935 and 1936 . . . Appeared in his fifth World Series in 1936 against the Yankees . . . Ended his career with the Missions Club in 1937 . . . Compiled a batting average of .279 in twelve seasons with 1190 hits, 195 doubles, 49 triples, 28 home runs, and 443 runs driven batted . . . Bought two gas stations in San Francisco after his playing days ended . . . Died April 24, 1993 at the age of 88 of cancer at a convalescent hospital in Willows, California.

Waite Charles Hoyt . . . Won 23 games in 1928 for the Yankees and saved 8 . . . Posted two victories (2-0, 1.50 era) in the '28 World Series . . . Traded to the Detroit Tigers on May 30, 1930 . . . After struggling in 1931 (3-8, 5.87 era) with Detroit, joined the Philadelphia Athletics (10-5, 4.22 era) in June . . . Started Game Five of the 1931 World Series for the Athletics and lost 5 to 1 . . . Pitched for the Brooklyn Dodgers and the New York Giants in 1932 . . . From 1933 until 1937, played for the Pittsburgh Pirates . . . Finished the 1937 season with Brooklyn and ended his career there in 1938.

Pitched on six Yankee pennant winning teams and won 157 games in ten years in New York . . . Overall, won 237 and lost 182 with a 3.59 era in twenty-one major league seasons . . . Appeared in twelve

World Series games (6-4, 1.83 era) . . . Retired from baseball and became a popular play-by-play radio broadcaster for the Cincinnati Reds for twenty-four years . . . Elected to the Hall of Fame in 1969 . . . Died at the age of 84 from a heart attack at Cincinnati Jewish Hospital in Cincinnati, Ohio on August 25, 1984.

Anthony Michael Lazzeri . . . Played second base for the Yankees through 1937 . . . Batted a career high .354 in 1929 . . . Hit two home runs in the 1932 World Series, one a grandslam . . . Set an American League single game record with eleven RBIs by hitting a triple and three home runs on May 24, 1936 in Shibe Park. Two of the home runs were with the bases filled . . . Played for the Chicago Cubs in 1938 and appeared in the fall classic against the Yankees . . . Finished his major league career with the Brooklyn Dodgers and New York Giants in 1939.

Managed Toronto of the International League during part of 1939 and 1940 . . . Played for San Francisco, California of the Pacific Coast League in 1941 . . . Played and managed Portsmouth, Virginia of the Piedmont League in 1942 . . . Ended his baseball career as player-manager of Wilkes-Barre, Pennsylvania of the Eastern League in 1943, batting .271 in 58 games.

Helped the Yankees capture six American League Pennants and five World Championships . . . During his twelve years with the Yankees batted .293 with 1784 hits, 327 doubles, 115 triples, 169 home runs and 1154 RBIs . . . Owned and operated a tavern in San Francisco after leaving baseball . . . Died alone at the age of 42 of a heart attack on August 6, 1948. Found slumped on the landing of his home in Millbrae, California . . . Buried at Sunset-Berkley Mausoleum in San Francisco . . . Elected to the Hall of Fame by the Veterans Committee in 1991.

Herb Pennock . . . Pitched for the Yankees six more seasons (1928-1933) . . . Released after the 1933 season . . . Signed with the Boston Red Sox . . . With the Red Sox in 1934 (2-0, 3.05 era) . . . Finished a 22-year career with 240 wins, 162 losses, 35 shutouts and 3.60 era . . .

Compiled 5-0 record in eight World Series appearances with a 1.79 era.

Named business manager of the Charlotte Hornets Club [Red Sox farm team] in 1935 . . . Coached and scouted for the Red Sox from 1936-39 . . . Joined the Red Sox front office as supervisor of the organization's farm clubs in 1940 . . . Named general manager of the Philadelphia Phillies of the National League in 1943 . . . Died January 30, 1948 at the age of 53 from a cerebral hemorrhage on the way to a National League meeting in the Waldorf Astoria Hotel in New York City . . . Elected to the Hall-of-Fame in February 1948 . . . Buried at Union Hill Cemetery in Kennett Square, Pennsylvania.

Earle Bryan Combs . . . Played eight more seasons . . . Finished his career with the Yankees in 1935 . . . From 1925 through 1932 scored at least 100 runs and averaged 195 hits a season . . . Led all American League outfielders in assists in 1927 (411) and 1928 (424) . . . Suffered a sprained wrist after crashing into the wall at Detroit on the next-to-last day of the 1928 season . . . A broken finger limited him to one appearance as a pinch-hitter in the '28 World Series, driving home a run on a sacrifice fly . . . Led the league in triples with 21 in 1928 and 22 in 1930 . . . Hit safely in 29 straight games, a Yankee record until broken by Joe DiMaggio's 56 game streak . . . Batted .350 in four World Series (1926-28 and 1932).

Crashed into an outfield wall at St. Louis on July 24,1934 and suffered a fractured skull and other serious injuries . . . Retired on July 28, 1935 . . . Coached the Yankees from 1935-1944 . . . Coached the Browns (1947), the Red Sox (1948-1952) and the Phillies (1954).

Appeared in 1455 games, scored 1186 runs, and had 1866 hits, including 309 doubles, 154 triples, 58 home runs and 633 runs driven in twelve seasons with the Yankees . . . Inducted into the Hall of Fame in 1970 . . . Died at the age of 77 in Richmond, Kentucky on July 21, 1976.

Joseph Anthony Dugan . . . Plagued with knee problems . . . Appeared in only 94 games with the Yankees in 1928 . . . Waived to the Boston Braves in 1929 . . . Batted .304 in 60 games at Boston . . . Retired after the 1929 season . . . Played eight games with the Detroit Tigers in 1931 . . . Owned "Joe Dugan's Restaurant, Bar and Grill," at 107th St. and Amsterdam Ave in Manhattan in the 1930s . . . Testified in the racketeering trial of Tammany district leader James J. Hines in 1938 . . . Struck by an automobile in Boston and suffered a concussion in 1944.

Managed the Newburgh Hummingbirds of the Class D North Atlantic League in 1945 . . . Scouted for the Boston Red Sox from 1955-1966 . . . Joined Red Sox public relations department in 1967 . . . Compiled a .286 batting average in his seven years with the Yankees . . . Played on five pennant winning clubs in New York . . . Died at the age of 85 after a stroke and pneumonia in Norwood, Massachusetts on July 7, 1982 . . . Buried at St. Joseph's Cemetery in Boston.

The Statistics

The '27 Yankees

Infielders and Outfielders

	G	AB	R	H	2B	3B	HR	RBI	AVG
Bengough, Ben	31	85	6	21	3	3	0	10	.247
Collins, Pat	92	251	38	69	9	3	7	36	.275
Combs, Earle	152	648	137	**231**	36	**23**	6	64	.356
Dugan, Joe	112	387	44	104	24	3	2	43	.269
Durst, Cedric	65	129	18	32	4	3	0	25	.248
Gazella, Mike	54	115	17	32	8	4	0	9	.278
Gehrig, Lou	155	584	149	218	**52**	18	47	**175**	.373
Grabowski, John	70	195	29	54	2	4	0	25	.277
Koenig, Mark	123	526	99	150	20	11	3	62	.285
Lazzeri, Tony	153	570	92	176	29	8	18	102	.309
Meusel, Bob	135	516	75	174	47	9	8	103	.337
Morehart, Ray	73	195	45	50	7	2	1	20	.256
Paschal, Ben	50	82	16	26	9	2	2	16	.317
Ruth, Babe	151	540	**158**	192	29	8	**60**	164	.356
Wera, Julie	38	42	7	10	3	0	1	8	.238

Pitchers

	W	L	PCT	G	SHO	SV	IP	BB	SO	ERA
Giard, Joe	0	0		16	0	0	27	19	10	8.00
Hoyt, Waite	**22**	7	**.759**	36	3	1	256	54	86	2.64
Moore, Wilcy	19	7	.731	50	1	**13**	213	59	75	**2.28**
Pennock, Herb	19	8	.704	34	1	2	210	48	51	3.00
Pipgras, George	10	3	.769	29	1	0	166	77	81	4.12
Ruether, Walter	13	6	.684	27	3	0	184	52	45	3.38
Shawkey, Bob	2	3	.400	19	0	4	44	16	23	2.86
Shocker, Urban	18	6	.750	31	2	0	200	41	35	2.84
Thomas, Myles	7	4	.636	21	0	0	89	43	25	4.85

Bolded figure represents league high

Notes

Prologue

1. Rhem on Alexander in the bullpen: See Charles C. Alexander, *Rogers Hornsby*, New York: Henry Holt and Company (1995): 119.
2. Hornsby and Alexander: See Ibid.
3. Lazzeri and Huggins: See Harry T. Brundidge, "Believe it or Not, Tony Lazzeri Got His Biggest Thrill When He Fanned with Bases Loaded in World's Series," *The Star Chronicle* (December 11, 1930): Hall of Fame (HOF) archives.
4. O'Farrell and Alexander on the mound: See Lawrence S. Ritter, *The Glory of Their Times*, New York: Vintage Books (1985): 253.
5. On Ruth's attempted steal to end the series: With the Yankees trailing by one run, Babe Ruth's attempted steal of second base in the ninth inning of the seventh game with two outs was highly controversial. Fans and players talked about it for years. Bob O'Farrell, who threw Ruth out, went barnstorming with the Babe a year or two later and asked him why he tried to steal second. Ruth told O'Farrell that he thought Alexander had forgotten about him. Ruth also thought that they way Alexander was pitching, the Yankees would never get two hits in a row off of him, and he would be in a better position to score on one. See Lawrence S. Ritter, *The Glory of Their Times*, New York: Vintage Books (1985): 253.

Chapter 1: Edward Grant Barrow

1. Barrow and Huggins's first meeting: See Edward Grant Barrow with James M. Kahn, "*My Fifty Years in Baseball*," New York: Coward-McCann, Inc. (1951): 126.
2. Barrow and Ruth confrontation: See Ibid: 105.

Chapter 2: Spring Training

1. Ruppert talking about Ruth's salary demands: See "Ruppert Believes Ruth Will Relent," *The New York Times* (February 28, 1927).
2. Ruppert and Ruth on a new contract: See "Ruth Gets $210,000 For 3 Years As Yank," *The New York Times* (March 3, 1927).
3. Huggins on his young pitchers: See "Veterans Will Bow to Yankee Youths," *The New York Times* (March 6, 1927).
4. Huggins on Moore: See "Moore May Laugh As Cynics Repent," *The New York Times* (March 4, 1927).
5. Huggins and Ruth talking to reporters: See James R. Harrison, "Babe's Mighty Arm Has Power of Old," *The New York Times* (March 8, 1927).
6. Ruppert on Pennock's Salary Demands: See James R. Harrison, "Bob Meusel Signs on the Dotted Line," *The New York Times* (March 17, 1927).
7. Ruppert Giving Pennock Ultimatum: See James R. Harrison, Ruppert to Demand Action by Pennock," *The New York Times* (March 19, 1927).
8. Huggins's Prediction: See "Huggins and McGraw Expect Open Races; Robinson Has Confidence in Robins," *The New York Times* (April 10, 1927).

Chapter 3: Opening Day

1. The descriptions and highlights of the games beginning with April 12, 1927 were painstakingly recreated from the newspaper accounts of the day. Often accounts from various New York newspapers as well as those from out-of-town were cross-checked to ensure that complete information was obtained. It should be noted that daily newspaper articles did not provide a full-range of baseball statistics, as we are accustomed to seeing today. As an example, pitchers' won-lost records were not given nor batters' runs batted in. Standings of the major league clubs were given daily, however, they were presented as games won and lost and per-

centage and did not show the number of games a team trailed behind the leader.

2. Huggins statement after the game (April 12, 1927): See Frederick G. Lieb, "Slugging Yankees Tackle Athletics For Two Straight," *The New York Evening Post*, (April 13, 1927).

Chapter 5: Miller Huggins

1. Ruth on meeting Huggins for the first time: See Babe Ruth as told to Bob Considine, *The Babe Ruth Story*, New York: Signet (1992): 75.
2. Huggins and Ruth confrontation: See Robert W. Creamer, *Babe: The Legend Comes to Life*, New York: Simon & Schuster (1974): 292-301.

Chapter 7: Griffith Stadium and Fenway Park

1. Ruth talking to reporters (April 25, 1927): See G.H. Fleming, "*Murderers' Row*,"New York: William Morrow (1985): 118.

Chapter 9: Babe Ruth

1. Ruth on his childhood: See Babe Ruth as told to Bob Considine, *The Babe Ruth Story*, New York: Signet Books (1992): 2. Originally published in 1948, this book was also written with the assistance of sportswriter Fred Lieb, who was actually a co-author, but whose name never appeared on the title page.
2. Hooper on Ruth: See Lawrence Ritter, *The Glory of Their Times*, New York: Vintage Books, 1985): 144-45.
3. Ruth on going to Spring Training in 1920: See *The Babe Ruth Story:* 77.
4. Bodie on rooming with Ruth: See Robert W. Creamer, *Babe: The Legend Comes to Life*, New York: Simon & Schuster (1984): 222.
5. Huston and Ruth on new salary contract: See *Babe: The Legend Comes to Life*, 254.

Chapter 11: Sportsman's Park and Navin Field

1. Huggins on the weather (May 15, 1927): See James R. Harrison, "Snow Keeps Yanks Idle Another Day," *The New York Times*, (May 16, 1927).

Chapter 13: Lou Gehrig

1. Krichell on Gehrig: See Edward Grant Barrow with James M. Kahn, *My Fifty Years in Baseball*, New York: Coward-McCann (1951): 148.
2. Gehrig on signing: See Fred Lieb, *Baseball As I Have Known It*, New York: Coward, McCann & Geoghegan (1977): 170.

Chapter 14: Griffith Stadium

1. Barrow on rescheduling rainouts (May 25, 1927): See James R. Harrison, "Yankees Deluged By Postponements," *The New York Times*, (May 26, 1927).
2. Lazzeri at West Point: See Rud Rennie, "Yankee Lead Cadets, 2-0, as Rain Descends," *The New York Herald Tribune*," (May 27, 1927).

Chapter 16: Bob Meusel

1. Huggins on Meusel Batting: See John J. Ward, "Bob Meusel, the Rookie Who Slugs Like Babe Ruth," *Baseball Magazine*, (September 1920): HOF archives.
2. Huggins on Meusel Playing Third: Ibid.
3. Stengel on Meusel: See John S. Radosta, "Meusel, Yankee Outfielder Dies: A Member of Murderers' Row," *The New York Times*, (November 30, 1977): HOF archives.

Chapter 19: Mark Koenig

1. Letter from Harry E. Strider to Garry Hermann: See letter dated November 28, 1924. HOF archives.

Chapter 20: Lindy! Lindy! Lindy!

1. Ruth on Lindbergh (June 16, 1927): See James R. Harrison, "*Lindbergh Misses Ruth's 22d Homer*," *The New York Times*, (June 17, 1927).
2. Heydler's suspension and fine of Earl Smith (June 24, 1927): See "Smith Suspended for 30 Days, fined $500 for Bancroft Attack," *The New York Herald Tribune*, (June 25, 1927).

Chapter 22: Waite Hoyt

1. O.B. Keeler on Hoyt: See O.B. Keeler, "Waite Hoyt Is About Ripe for Big League; Brooklyn Boy Pitching Sensation in South," *The New York American,* (May 20, 1917): HOF archives.
2. Hoyt on Wanting to be Traded: See Arthur Daley, "Elevation to Olympus," *The New York Times,* (February 7, 1969): HOF archives.
3. Hoyt Meeting Ruth: See "Waite Hoyt on Babe Ruth as told to Ritter Collet, Sports Editor of The Dayton Herald." Inserted by Hon. Charles W. Whalen, Jr. of Ohio in *The Congressional Record* (September 18, 1973): E5855.

Chapter 26: Tony Lazzeri

1. Essick's report to Barrow: See "Tony Lazzeri Truly Great in Murderers' Row Era," Column by Daniel. *The New York World Telegram* (August 8, 1946): HOF archives.
2. Lazzeri on growing up in Cow Hollow: See Harry T. Brundidge, "Believe it or Not, Tony Lazzeri Got His Biggest Thrill When He Fanned with Bases Loaded in World's Series," *The Star Chronicle* (December 11, 1930): HOF archives.
3. Lazzeri's interview with Considine: See Bob Considine *"On the Line With Considine,"* syndicated column, September 8, 1945.
4. Smith on Lazzeri: See Red Smith's column of August 4, 1946, "A Man Who Knew the Crowds" in *Red Smith on Baseball,* Chicago: Ivan R. Dee, Publisher, Chicago (2000):17.

5. Difficulty interviewing Lazzeri: Ibid.
6. Comparison to Columbus: See Mark Gallagher, "*The Yankee Encyclopedia,*" Volume 3, Illinois: Sycamore Publishing (1997): 123.

Chapter 27: Gehrig Leads Race

1. Ruth and Gehrig as teammates (July 31, 1927): See Richards Vidmer, "Yanks Are Stopped But Only By Rain," *The New York Times,* (August 1, 1927).
2. Walter Johnson Day (August 2, 1927): See "Johnson Is Honored, Then Detroit Wins," *The New York Times,* (August 3, 1927).

Chapter 28: On the Road

1. Bengough on visit to Walter Reed Hospital: See Richards Vidmer, "Yanks Go Walking And Trim Senators," *New York Times,* (August 14, 1927).

Chapter 29: Herb Pennock

1. Harris on Pennock: See Frank Graham, Graham's Corner, "He was a Great Pitcher," HOF archives.
2. Earl Mack telling Pennock to wait on offers: See Rud Rennie, "Pennock Found by Connie Mack While Pitching for School Team," HOF archives.
3. Pennock's first game: See J.G. Spink, "Looking Them Over," (June 8, 1939), HOF archives.

Chapter 32: Earle Combs

1. Combs playing semi-professional ball: See By Campaigner, Released to Sunday papers of February 3, 1929. HOF archives.
2. McCarthy and Pennock: See Bruce Dudley, "Colonel Combs, 'Dollar-A-Year Man' Of Big Show, Puts Comeback Ahead of All Other Considerations," *Louisville Courier Journal,* (1935), HOF archives.

3. Huggins and Pennock: See Tony Kornheiser, "Earle Combs of Yankees Dead After Long Illness," *The New York Times*, (July 22, 1976).
4. Stengel and Dickey: See Arthur Daley, "The Kid and the Colonel," *The New York Times*, (February 3, 1970).

Chapter 34: Winning the Pennant

1. Congratulatory message from McKee: See "Yankees Congratulated by City On Winning the Pennant Again," *The New York Times*, (September 15, 1927).

Chapter 36: Jumpin' Joe Dugan

1. Mack's visit to the Dugan home: See John F. Buckley, *The Evening Gazette*, Worcester, Massachusetts (February 12, 1970): 21.
2. Dugan's major league debut: See Yesterday Heroes with Jack McCarthy, *The Boston Herald* American, Boston, Massachusetts (February 6, 1977): 52.
3. Dugan on the verbal abuse: Burr Van Atta, "Jumpin' Joe Dugan, 85, Played with Phila. A's, Yankees in '20s," *The Philadelphia Inquirer*, Philadelphia, Pennsylvania (July 10, 1982). HOF archives.
4. Boston Herald on Dugan's trade to Yankees: Paul Kenney, "Jumping Joe Remembers the Babe," *The Hartford Courant Magazine*, Hartford, Connecticut. HOF Archives.

Chapter 38: 60th Home Run

1. John Drebinger on Ruth: See John Drebinger, "Ruth's Heart Set On New Homer Mark," *The New York Times*, (September 29, 1927).

Epilogue

1. Hoyt and Ruppert (October 5, 1927): See James R. Harrison, "Ruth Blasts Road To Yankee Victory Over Pirates, 5 to 4," *The New York Times*, (October 6, 1927).

2. Huggins on victory (October 7, 1927): See "Jubilant Yankees See Sweep Ahead," *The New York Times*, (October 8, 1927).
3. Huggins on World Series sweep: See "Yankees Overjoyed Over Sweep," *The New York Times*, (October 9, 1927).
4. Ruth and Ruppert: See Babe Ruth as told to Bob Considine, *The Babe Ruth Story*, New York: Signet Books (1992): 156.

Bibliography

Books

Alexander, Charles C. *Rogers Hornsby.* Henry Holt and Company: New York, 1995.

Barrow, Edward Grant with James M. Kahn. *My Fifty Years in Baseball.* Coward-McCann: New York, 1951.

Creamer, Robert. *Babe Ruth: The Legend Comes to Life.* New York: Simon and Schuster, 1977.

Fleming, G.H. *Murderers' Row: The 1927 New York Yankees.* New York: William Morrow and Company, Inc, 1985.

Gallagher, Mark. *The Yankee Encyclopedia.* Volume 3. Illinois: Sagamore Publishing, 1997.

Honig, Donald. *Baseball America: The Heroes of the Game and the Times of Their Glory.* New York: Macmillan Publishing Company, 1985.

Lieb, Fred. *Baseball As I Have Known It.* New York: Coward, McCann & Geoghegan, 1977,

Lowry, Philip J. *Green Cathedrals.* New York: Addison-Wesley Publishing Co., Inc., 1992.

Malone, Dumas, editor. *Dictionary of American Biography. Vol. 9.* John Kiernan, contributor. New York: Scribner and Sons, 1932.

Mosedale, John. *The Greatest of All-The 1927 New York Yankees.* New York: The Dial Press, 1974.

Okkonen, Marc. *Baseball Uniforms of the 20th Century.* New York: Sterling Publishing Co., Inc, 1993.

Robinson, Ray. *Iron Horse: Lou Gehrig in His Time.* New York: W.W. Norton & Company, 1990.

Robinson, Ray and Christopher Jennison. *Yankee Stadium.* New York: Penguin Studio, 1998.

Ruth, George Herman. *Babe Ruth's Own Book of Baseball.* Lincoln and London: University of Nebraska Press, 1992.

Ruth, Babe as told to Bob Considine. *The Babe Ruth Story*. New York: E.P. Dutton, 1948.

Thorn, John and Pete Palmer. *Total Baseball*. New York: Warner Books, 1989.

Archives

Baseball Hall of Fame, Cooperstown, New York

Wire Services

Associated Press

Newspapers

Boston Herald
New York Daily Mirror
New York Daily News
New York Evening Post
New York Herald Tribune
New York Times
Philadelphia Inquirer
Washington Post